THE INFERNO

Living in Latin America

Robert M. Levine
Series Editor

The Inferno: A Story of Terror and Survival in Chile
Luz Arce
Translated by Stacey Alba Skar

*Minor Omissions: Children in Latin American History
and Society*
Edited by Tobias Hecht

*We Alone Will Rule: Native Andean Politics
in the Age of Insurgency*
Sinclair Thomson

THE INFERNO

A Story of Terror and Survival in Chile

Luz Arce

Translated by
Stacey Alba D. Skar

THE UNIVERSITY OF WISCONSIN PRESS

The University of Wisconsin Press
1930 Monroe Street, 3rd Floor
Madison, Wisconsin 53711-2059
uwpress.wisc.edu

3 Henrietta Street, Covent Garden
London WC2E 8LU, United Kingdom
eurospanbookstore.com

Printed in the United States of America

Library of Congress Cataloging-in-Publication Data

Arce, Luz.
[Infierno. English]
The inferno: a story of terror and survivial in Chile / Luz Arce;
translated by Stacey Alba D. Skar.
p.   cm. — (Living in Latin America)
Includes index.
ISBN 0-299-19550-3 (cloth: alk. paper)
ISBN 0-299-19554-6 (pbk.: alk. paper)
1. Chile—Politics and government—1973–1988.
2. Chile. Central Nacional de Informaciones.   3. Political persecution—Chile.
4. Human rights—Chile.   5. Arce Luz.
I. Skar, Stacey Alba D., 1969–   II. Title.   III. Series.
F3100.A66713   2004
983.06´5—dc22
2003020532

ISBN 978-0-299-19554-0 (pbk.: alk. paper)
ISBN 978-0-299-19553-3 (e-book)

For Juan Manuel, my husband, who, with his love,

continues helping me search

beyond my own story.

For those who are no longer . . .

Contents

A Note on This Translation

Thirty years after the military coup in Chile on September 11, 1973, and ten years following the publication in Spanish of *El infierno* (Santiago, Chile: Planeta, 1993), Luz Arce's testimony continues to grow in importance as a testament to the crimes against humanity committed during the years of the military regime (1973–1990) led by Augusto Pinochet. This current publication makes Arce's story of torture, fear, collaboration, and survival available to English readers. However, I must acknowledge both the challenges I faced in this English translation as well as the invaluable support I received from others who made it possible.

One of my greatest challenges in translating this memoir was my desire to respect the integrity of Arce's style, which is often conversational, and her tone, which is confessional at times. I have tried to maintain a consistent voice in this translation while simultaneously seeking to clarify linguistic ambiguities from Arce's use of colloquial Chilean Spanish and the long, baroque sentences that frequently appear in the Spanish version. The editors at the University of Wisconsin Press offered indispensable assistance in this endeavor to maintain a balance between necessary clarifications and syntactical changes without sacrificing the author's original meaning and narrative style. I am greatly indebted to them for their assistance in editing my translation.

Besides translating Arce's memoir, I have also added a series of footnotes to provide the reader with additional information that I consider helpful for understanding the context of Arce's references. Much of this additional information about political and religious organizations, the Chilean military apparatus, and details regarding the detention and disappearance of people mentioned in Arce's memoir came from researching recent human rights publications in Chile, Chilean newspapers, and other international news sources. One book that was particularly helpful in providing information for many of the footnotes included in this translation was *La historia oculta del régimen militar: Memoria de una época, 1973–1988* by Ascanio Cavallo, Manuel Salazar, and Oscar Sepúlveda (Santiago, Chile: Grijalbo, 1997). While the vast majority of the notes that appear in the translation are my own, I have also translated the author's footnotes from the Spanish version, and I have clarified these as Arce's notes.

Another important aspect in translating this memoir was the need to have knowledge of colloquial Chilean Spanish from the 1970s in order to suggest appropriate equivalents in English. Furthermore, there are many references in the original text to specific places in Chile and organizations that existed during the Popular Unity government of President Salvador Allende (1970–1973). Many of these required in-depth research and support from someone who had firsthand experience as a citizen of Chile during those years. I found that assistance in my best friend and greatest intellectual partner, who is also my husband, Javier Campos. As a student who had recently graduated from the University of Concepción in Chile when the coup occurred, Javier was familiar with numerous cultural references and colloquialisms that would have been very difficult to identify through traditional forms of research.

I would also like to express my appreciation to Ksenija Bilbija for recommending me for this project at the University of Wisconsin Press. In addition, I am very grateful to Eugenio Ahumada for generously sharing his personal copy of the Spanish version of Arce's memoir when he heard that I couldn't find it in any bookstore in Chile. For their solidarity and generosity, I offer Javier, Ksenija, and Eugenio my most sincere gratitude and love.

Stacey Alba D. Skar
March 2004

Acknowledgments

In Germany and Austria:
For Jan Philipp Reemtsma
For Hamburguer Stiftung Zur Förderung Von Wissenschaft Und Kultur
For Erick and René
For Elke Mühlleitner and Johannes Reichmayr

In Chile:
For the Order of Preachers from the San Lorenzo Mártir Province
For Pedro Alejandro Matta Lemoine
For Lautaro Videla and his wife
For my son, Juan Manuel
For Mili Rodríguez and Carlos Orellana

I would especially like to thank Cristián Asmüssen C.o.p., José Luis de Miguel o.p., Félix Fernández R.o.p., and all those above, because they made it possible for this book to become a reality with their teaching, their support, and their affection.

Prologue

What is the price of truth? To what lengths must we go in our search for it? Does anyone have the right to patent the truth? Do we have the right to remain silent about horrific acts that, if they remain unknown, may one day be repeated? Who can measure the pain of so many people whose loved ones are still unaccounted for?

In the following pages, their author, Luz Arce, pours out what has been her truth, the truth of her infernal experience during the long, dark years of her life and of Chilean history, days that coincide, in large part, with the dictatorship of General Augusto Pinochet.

The book is written in a realistic, straightforward language that might also be called shocking, with its detailed, heartrending, chilling descriptions of torture, rape, and acts of cruelty, oppression, humiliation, and manipulation of every kind, acts the author experienced as victim or witness. At times the work achieves a level of great poetic lyricism, which reveals the noblest of sentiments and of the human soul.

Luz Arce writes in the first person. It is her story, an important part of her life. And she writes neither evasively nor fearfully, without hatred or a desire for revenge, but by telling the whole truth, her truth, without seeking personal gain.

The Inferno is a confession that also seeks conversion, catharsis, reconciliation, and the triumph of truth, the naked truth, even when the truth hurts or proves embarrassing or dangerous, not least to the one who lived it and writes it.

Doubtless, some will continue to consider this story, which is larger than its protagonists and that speaks to the nation as a whole, as science fiction, a politicized exaggeration, biased toward a political party, and so forth. These are the same ones who always refuse to believe that something like this could have happened under the military regime.

The author has endured countless hours of interrogation and confrontation in the courts, at times with some of the very people who figure in the book. That explains how she has been able to arrive at the "undressing" of herself. In her need to spill the whole truth, she reveals aspects of her intimate life, including those that are less than flattering.

Although polished in recent years, *The Inferno* was born in an earlier period when the author had a cathartic need to recount her experience during the dictatorship, to forgive others and herself—not in a general sense but in relation to her own life story, which is unique and inalienable. By that time, she had already had what she calls her "reencounter" with God, a decisive encounter for Luz's future, and I would even say for the development and publication of this work. As she would confirm, in the Lord, in her roots, she reencountered the meaning of life, as well as of her life; the meaning of redeeming pain: "pain," she says, "makes brothers out of the survivors," which is what it would mean to be truly free. The personal freedom, as well as the freedom of others, her life-long obsession was paradoxically taken away from Luz Arce for a long time.

But the pain, the cross, has, as Pedro Casaldáliga points out, two sides: that of the crucified and that of the crucifiers, that of the tortured, and that of the torturers. It is necessary to know how to read from both sides. Only the crucified, the tortured, can make the cross redemptive and liberating. They, better than anyone else, understand the cross. For the crucifiers and torturers, the cross is iniquitous, damned. The cross does not free the soldiers from responsibility, but it is above all the Herods and the Pilates of the day that it judges.

Freedom, for its part, has a price, a high price. "To be free," says Luz, and she says it with the whole force of her life, "has costs, but also the happiness of knowing that only a being who is free can love, or at least try."

During these years of searching and of inner struggle, Luz Arce managed to discover, not without surprises, that what her heart most desired was to be free, free to love and to give meaning to her own existence. Long silences—sometimes imposed, violent, and bitter, the silences of an animal crouching before persecution and danger, other times sought in rich solitude and in the peacefulness of communion with God—offered her soul the right conditions for forgiveness: complete, selfless, Christian forgiveness for her victimizers. And the petition for forgiveness for those she, in turn, caused pain.

She needed more. She needed to set a new precedent that emerged from her own infernal experience, so that this dark story would never again repeat itself, so that memory, even if painful, is conserved. The memory of oppression and death that shattered peaceful coexistence and national values. The idea was not only to show the way but also to walk it—the real and "painful stations" that lead from disharmony to reconciliation and peace. In this way, victory will be on the side of the truth, the foundation for a more dignified future for mankind: "I cannot avoid feeling that we owe future generations at least a coherent and truthful explanation of what happened."

José Luis de Miguel, o.p.
Santiago, January 1, 1993

Preliminary Thoughts

Happiness, I found your hair scandalous
Pablo Neruda

My name is Luz Arce. It has been very difficult for me to recover that name. There is a kind of black legend about me, a vague story created out of a horrific, humiliating, and violent reality.

Not everything people have said about me is true. The main reason for this is that I haven't been here in Chile, and that I've been silent until now.

In the past, I didn't even think that one day I would take this step. Now I know that it's not enough for me to tell my truth. The testimonies of others should be added to it so that the facts can be established accurately in the future. But I didn't return to Chile to defend myself, and I will not change my stance. I feel it is part of the price that I long ago understood I would have to pay, for my own actions and for those of others, in order to live in my homeland.

I am not talking about justice or injustice, or even about forgiveness. I have said that I ask for forgiveness, but I don't expect it. I do believe that in the deepest part of every human being, beyond personal issues, there is a place where the truth can be found. I believe everybody should confront his or her own story. This is what I am trying to do, but these other stories that are entangled with my own mean that doubts remain about Luz Arce's story. I hope that some day they can merge into one, not to validate my word, since that isn't what is most important, but to be able to reconstruct a painful part of our memory with dignity.

For years I have had to overcome many fears in order to be able to write these pages. There is a truth that hurts here, and I am trying my best not to turn it into a knife. This narrative is neither beautiful nor entertaining. Without holding back what I know, I have tried to protect others who are implicated, even members of the DINA/CNI who did not play a repressive role.[1] These decisions are based on a distinction between those who want to make defending people's rights an important objective in their lives and those who do not. There is nothing easy about making this case in daily life. Sometimes it is difficult enough just to make sense of one's own life.

If there is one important thing I have learned, because I've lived it myself, it is that you cannot fight for the rights of some by disregarding the rights of others. However, these pages do include references to some people's private lives because otherwise it would be impossible to relate this story.

I try to be honest. That is why, although it hurts, I must say that I was not deprived of my rights by the DINA alone. It took me years to be able to come to terms with a few things. I collaborated with the DINA, under pressure. I was a member of that organization, and I resigned in 1979. My personal travail brought me before the National Truth and Reconciliation Commission in 1990.[2] Then, in January of 1991, I traveled to Europe. While there, I decided to return to appear before the courts again. I arrived in Chile on January 16, 1992. Today, twenty years after the military coup, I offer this book. Unlike my actions in the past, these last decisions have been voluntary and part of a search for the path that could lead me away from the inferno.

Unfortunately, my contribution to the Truth and Reconciliation Commission's investigation was limited. It wasn't that I wanted it that way. I simply didn't have any more information. I don't know where the disappeared prisoners are. I wish I did . . .

I cannot be accused for not knowing more than I know. But I can, for having collaborated, for having been a DINA employee, and for needing so many years to decide to appear in court.

---

1. The DINA (Directorate of National Intelligence) was created in 1973 following Chile's military coup. It was responsible for the investigation, interrogation, and elimination of members of opposition groups. In 1977 the DINA was replaced by the CNI (National Information Center).

2. The National Truth and Reconciliation Commission was created during the democratic transition under President Patricio Aylwin in 1990. This Commission was responsible for investigating cases of human rights abuses during the military dictatorship (1973–90). The commission's findings were published in a document known as the *Informe Rettig* (Rettig Report).

Part 1

1

EARLY EXPERIENCES

Looking back is a source of great sadness for me, and I am not just referring to the period when I worked for the DINA. I had already encountered limitations, frustrated yearnings, and pain. What stands out most as I look back on my past is a feeling of loneliness. For as long as I can remember, I would have given anything for a smile, a friend, a caress, an "I love you."

The strange thing is that I could have experienced these things, especially through sports, but I was always afraid of people, even if they were my own age. For some reason I still don't understand, ever since I was a child I pretended I was all right and that I knew what I wanted and needed, even if I really didn't. I would have never admitted that I needed affection. I hid by distancing myself, and with time I disguised that distance as strength, as aggression.

I was a typical eldest daughter from a lower-middle-class family, shy, someone everyone expected to be everything her parents weren't. And I wanted to be something, anything. I wasn't exactly sure what that was, but I wanted to be as different as possible from the people around me.

Always feeling guilty created problems for me. I remember my hunger for affection. I don't know what happened, or exactly how it happened, but I grew up so remote from everything. Every day I noticed that even what for other children was simple and ordinary and natural, felt strange, unfamiliar, and hostile to me. I spent my childhood and my adolescence, my entire youth, filled with doubt and fear. I looked, listened, and tried to figure out what I didn't understand. As I grew older, I ended up accepting only my own answers. I achieved everything I set out to do. It never mattered what amount of effort I would have to invest to make it happen.

I wanted the years to go by quickly so that I could live on my own. I didn't realize back then that I was an unstable, insecure adolescent. I took those symptoms as a sign of difference: there was something strange in me, and I lived it like something awful.

When I got to university, sports were my passion. I devoted myself with the fanaticism that has characterized my entire life and that seemed even stronger when I was involved in sports. I met my first husband then, and we were married in 1967. We both worked, and when our son Rafael was born, we had just about finished building a house that was my pride and joy, even though it was small.

Looked at from a traditional perspective, we were a couple with our whole lives ahead of us. However, soon after my son was born, I began to feel that marriage had been a mistake. Now I know that back then I wasn't able to identify, much less express, what I was feeling. But I did sense I would never be able to take on as my own many of the ideas held by my son's father. I realized that I didn't know anything about myself. When I questioned some of my ex-husband's goals, I said to myself: What about me? Can I have goals? I had never imagined that I could ask myself: What about me, what do I want?

I was starting to develop my own thoughts and ideas. My misgivings were strong, and they were mine. I felt I had something of my own for the first time, and I liked the feeling. I realized I wanted a separation from my husband. I didn't see how we could make it as a couple. I think the separation was good for both of us. However, years had to go before I could appreciate having a family, a partner, and everything this entails.

My ex-husband agreed to the separation. In exchange, he asked only to be able to take all our belongings with him, and half the value of the house. Since the land it was on was the property adjacent to my parent's house, my father took out a loan and gave him the money. A few days later, my ex-husband arrived with my father-in-law, and they took everything. When they left, I was alone, and I walked through the house. It seemed a lot bigger when it was empty. My son's crib looked tiny in the empty bedroom. I took my little boy in my arms, and I remember that I held him tightly against me and said to him, "Don't worry, what can be bought once can be bought again."

I experienced that separation like a failure that hurt a lot. I gave up my job as a coach at the stadium so I would never have to see the father of my son again. And even though we tried to live together again, it didn't work. Now I know that, back then, I was totally incapable of facing any kind of adult relationship. The separation was hard, but I experienced it like my first real opportunity to be myself. Ever since then, I have felt a compulsive need to feel that I was, that I am free.

I tried to make a living painting. It was a dream. I wound up painting T-shirts with apples and butterflies for young people and Mickey Mouse and Goofy for kids, and I did watercolors that I sold door-to-door. I wasn't making enough money so I started looking for work.

IN THE GAP (GROUP OF PERSONAL FRIENDS OF THE PRESIDENT)[3]

As I remember it, Raúl was two years older than I was. His full name was Raúl Juvenal Navarrete Hancke, and in time I learned to call him "Martín." He lived with his mother a few blocks from my house, off a street called Los Nidos. He was a young man with liberal ideals, and he was a member of the GAP. I met him soon after my separation and told him I needed to find work. He told me to go the Moneda Palace the following day, and that he could find me a job as a secretary.[4]

I had an interview with Enrique Huerta. He was the Palace Administrator at that time, and he introduced me to "Carlos Alamos," which was Jaime Sotelo Ojeda's assumed name, and "Bruno," whose real name was Domingo Bartolomé Blanco Tarré. All three are still disappeared to this day. Enrique, Carlos, and Bruno were all members of the GAP's leadership.

I was hired after that interview. In the beginning, I started learning to work as an administrative assistant and a receptionist. I began meeting members of the GAP and others who worked at the Moneda. I gradually started to identify more and more with them. It was a beautiful time.

Carlos Alamos was my immediate superior. When he noticed my interest in studying, he started to lend and even give me books. Everything I learned was new for me. My whole being was shaken, and what had started out as just a job was becoming my reason for living. I would ask

3. Arce notes that the GAP was "a group of Salvador Allende's personal friends" and an "organization in charge of security for the president at his home and wherever he traveled."

4. The Moneda Presidential Palace is located in the center of Santiago. On many occasions in her testimony Arce refers to it simply as the "Moneda."

Carlos Alamos about things I read but didn't understand, and he would explain them to me. Little by little, I began assuming other duties that were taking me away from secretarial work and into security functions.

It was an unforgettable time. I discovered a lot of things. But everything was happening too fast, and the pace made it impossible to reflect on each step. On the occasions when I was at the president's home, on Tomás Moro Street, I was impressed by Salvador Allende's serenity. He was always polite and affectionate with each member of GAP, and he knew all of us by name. I must confess that I was completely ignorant in those days. I tried very hard to study, but there was so much I didn't know. Carlos Alamos took on the task of helping me. He corrected the summaries I made of my readings and he started making copies of them to hand out to my compañeros.[5]

A few days after I entered the GAP, Carlos asked me if I knew how to drive, and I told him that I did. Then he told me to get a driver's license, and I became his chauffeur.

I went to El Cañaveral, which was the residence of Mirya Contreras Bell, known as "Payita." She was the president's secretary and friend. I went with Carlos the first time, and he allowed me to attend as he met with members of the GAP assigned to El Cañaveral's Guard. At the end of their conversation, Carlos laughed and said, "The compañera's presence at this meeting made all of you act like gentlemen. I think that's good." And he looked at me and asked, "Compañera Hilda, would you like to be a member of El Cañaveral's Guard?" I happily agreed. Carlos explained to me that I was not going to receive any special treatment or exceptions from the daily routine just for being a woman. I would be just another "man" in the guard, and I would have to fulfill all the demands of the job.

I knew the daily regimen was tough, but I felt like I was in good physical shape. We talked it over with the compañeros, and they gave me a warm welcome. Carlos told me he had to meet with "Payita," and we said good-bye after he took me to the residence that housed the members of the guard who were in charge of security on the property. There was one bed available.

I awoke early and went down to the first floor. I found some compañeros by the woodstove. I had some coffee, and they told me Carlos had

5. "Compañero" is a term with special social and political connotations that Arce uses to refer to her fellow comrades and friends. Since it does not have an exact English translation, it will appear throughout this text in the original Spanish.

left his car so I could go home to get my things. That was the day I began living in that beautiful place by the river at the foot of the mountains.

I started attending classes at the GAP's Militant Training School and I was added to the guard's list. Our routine began each day with physical exercise, followed by a bath in the cold water of a mountain spring and breakfast. There were guard posts at the different entrances to the house and guards around the whole property on both sides of the river. We ate lunch together, and we had time to study in the afternoon. The group of teachers slept in a building down by the river. The classrooms were there too.

The president usually spent his weekends at El Cañaveral in search of peace and quiet, which was even better with the beautiful landscape. He made time for informal work meetings and to receive his associates and friends.

My health had deteriorated by the end of August, and Dr. Danilo Bartulín recommended I leave the Cañaveral Guard. When I left the GAP, my superiors suggested they could recommend me for work somewhere else. And since my family had been asking me to go work for the state-run railroad for a long time, and since my father could recommend me, I applied and got the job.

"Payita" gave me a presidential recommendation, and then I went to have an interview with the general director for the railroad, Alfredo Rojas, and his private secretary, Gustavo Saint Pierre, both militants in the Socialist Party.

The GAP has borne the brunt of criticism that obscures the important role it played as a political-paramilitary structure. During the dictatorship, the debate was transformed into a denigrating crusade, which was part of the politics of extermination that was applied to its members.

The GAP's origins can be traced back to the period before the presidential elections on September 4, 1970. Miguel Enríquez, the MIR's general secretary, put some of his most distinguished militants at the disposal of presidential candidate Salvador Allende Gossens.[6]

This group included Max Joel Marambio, Mario Ramiro Melo Pradenas, and, later, Humberto Sotomayor and Sergio Pérez Molina.

6. The Revolutionary Left Movement (MIR, Movimiento de Izquierda Revolucionaria) supported the use of force to effect political change in Chile. The MIR's connections to the Popular Unity coalition and President Salvador Allende gave it more influence than it otherwise may have had without the creation of such a coalition, given that it was a relatively new political party in Chile.

After the GAP came to be led by MIR militants, it became part of the Socialist Party structure. Toward the end of 1971, the GAP was divided into four divisions:

1) Escort. Members physically accompanied President Salvador Allende.

2) Guard. This division was in charge of guarding places or properties frequented by the president, such as his house on Tomás Moro, the Moneda Palace, the presidential residence in Viña del Mar, and El Cañaveral. Juan José Montiglio Murúa was in charge of this division.

3) Services and the Militant Training School. This division was under Domingo Bartolomé Blanco Tarré's command.

4) Operatives—Travel and intelligence: This division was led by "Mariano" (a survivor).

While I was there, this structure was reorganized as follows:

1) Presidential Escort, under the command of Carlos Alamos.

2) Planning Presidential Travel, under "Bruno's" command.

3) Security, or guarding places the president often visited, under Juan José Montiglio Murúa's command. He was known as "Aníbal."

4) Services, or Provisions and Information—Intelligence on possible assassination attempts, which was controlled by the GAP's elite: Carlos, Enrique, and Bruno.

SOCIALIST MILITANT

Early in 1973, when I was already working for the railroad, I joined a branch of the Socialist Party. This branch was made up of managers who were socialists, which, by the way, they all were. The office was located on the corner of Alameda Bernardo O'Higgins and Serrano. Due to its location, the branch was part of the Eighth District, whose headquarters was on 38 Londres Street.[7]

In addition to being a member, I started attending meetings at district headquarters, and I became a member of the Elmo Catalán Brigade (BEC) which in early 1973 worked on Carlos Altamirano's senate campaign.

I realized that militancy in that branch didn't require previous training or involve any party responsibilities. My goal was to dedicate all my

7. The city of Santiago is divided into various political districts. Arce is referring to the Eighth, the "Octava Comuna."

time to the party because I wanted to train myself politically, which is why I gave up my job at the railroad.

During the parliamentary election in March 1973, I participated as a party official at one of the district voting centers for women. I was young, ignorant, and full of energy that I didn't know how to channel. I tried to do the most and the best I could when I was assigned to the district. My biggest surprise was when, on one occasion, the political secretary asked me where I wanted to go with all that effort. What I considered an attitude of "political commitment," he had seen as some kind of ambition to climb the political ladder. I remember that my only response was to allude to what I had read about emulation in Che Guevara's writing. The compañero made some comment like I had been influenced by the training I received in the GAP. He was referring to my supposed paramilitary training, which, frankly, was pretty inadequate at that time. He told me there was a more appropriate job for me, and he scheduled a meeting for me with compañero Gaspar Gómez.

Gaspar belonged to the district's leadership. He often attended meetings on 38 Londres Street. He questioned me in detail regarding my time in the GAP and about why I had stopped working for the railroad. After that interview he told me to go to INESAL (the Latin American Social Studies Institute). This was a front for Arnoldo Camu's "Apparatus," which was the party's military structure. (According to the "official" version, Arnoldo Camu was killed in a military confrontation.)

INESAL was located at 12 Bustamante Street. It was demolished during the dictatorship, for reasons unknown to me. Gaspar was my superior, and he was in charge of the institute's public relations division. For me, this marked the beginning of a period dedicated to my training.

Gaspar had lost his right hand and an eye while handling explosives. I never found out how the accident occurred. I just listened to him since I assumed it wasn't my place to ask questions. He drove his car in spite of his physical limitations, but when I started working with him I became his chauffeur.

When I listened to my compañeros, my limited training become more apparent to me, and Gaspar gave me time off to study. On June 29, 1973, the day of the "Tancazo," Gaspar informed me that he had received a call from the Central Committee.[8]

---

8. The "Tancazo" was a failed attempt at a military coup that occurred on June 29, 1973, in front of the Presidential Palace.

We said good-bye to each other since we were now assigned to different divisions, which meant that we wouldn't be able to remain in contact. Gaspar told me that he had supported my new assignment.

GEA (SPECIAL SUPPORT GROUPS)

Wagner Erick Salinas, alias "Silvano," received me at Central Committee (CC) headquarters. I had met him in the GAP. He informed me that I would be one of the directors of the GEA. This was an organization controlled by the Socialist Party's National Committee.

The GEA had a public function and another compartmentalized one. The eight members of the GEA were Silvano, Felipe, Aníbal, Bernardo, Ignacio, David, Leonor, and myself. We had all been part of the GAP. The GEA's public function was to implement a militant training school. The project was put in place with the support of militants from the Eighth District and Downtown Santiago who were instructors. It remained in operation for a month and a few days. The GEA was also an operative unit for the Political Commission. That was what they told us. Silvano was the contact for the organization and he told us it was our unit's duty to go undercover. He said that as far as the party was concerned, we were in charge of the Militant Training School, but that our undercover mission was to transform ourselves into a special information-gathering unit for the Political Commission and to carry out some missions proposed by the party's leadership. Faced with this proposition, we were obviously disquieted, but we accepted the instructions, both out of a sense of duty and with the understanding that a party's Political Commission must have all available information at its disposal in order to make decisions.

The Popular Unity coalition was weakened by the wide spectrum of positions at its core. Violence began to take center stage. Right-wing groups frequently attacked the headquarters of the left's political parties. For this reason, in addition to working all day, we had to spend our nights guarding the party's headquarters and some public administration buildings near the Moneda Palace. We held off the attacks with stones that we threw from the terraces and the upper floors in the buildings.

Patria y Libertad had more resources than we did, and they had modern, imported equipment at their disposal, what is called "antiriot" gear today.[9]

9. "Patria y Libertad" (Fatherland and freedom) refers to a right-wing group that was involved in armed struggle against the Popular Unity government.

I remember one occasion when we stopped what we were doing to avoid killing a police officer. They had sent us police protection on that very day. It is true that I did participate in armed confrontations. I am not trying to defend this, but I do want to clarify that the GEA never tried to kill anyone.

The Socialist Party, with Carlos Altamirano—who was under great pressure from the rank and file—as general secretary, gravitated toward the most radical left positions of MAPU, the Christian Left, and the MIR.[10]

The continuous confrontations, the growing opposition activity, and everyone's belligerent discourse filled our daily routine with apprehension. It took me months to realize the real dimensions of our actions. I became aware of this once when I was undercover and had a conversation with Gustavo Ruz Zañartu, who was my superior then and a member of the Central Committee. I realized that he didn't know anything about these activities and that he didn't agree with them.

I remember today the naïveté of our dreams. The school that began to operate at Headquarters started with a group of workers who attended classes daily, juggling their studies with work. It was a life affirming experience. The majority were veterans of the worker's movement and had invaluable experience. Our "old timers," as we affectionately called them to show our admiration, were supposed to receive political and military training. We knew then that the opposition was going to launch a frontal attack. After the "Tancazo," the Popular Unity government came up with the idea to begin implementing a Santiago Defense Plan. It was called the "Star Plan" or the "Five Point Plan," which we knew about since we were part of the GEA and since our old timers would constitute its backbone, together with militants from the public administration. Each of the industrial sectors made up the star's other four points, or units. Together, we were all supposed to defend President Allende's government, with weapons if necessary, from any attempted coup.

Obviously, the plan hadn't been fully organized by the day of the coup. The "Star Plan," what I knew of it, wasn't created to assassinate

10. Arce is referring here to the United Popular Action Movement (MAPU, Movimiento de Acción Popular Unitaria), the Christian Left, and the Revolutionary Left Movement (MIR). These political groups attempted to pressure the Popular Unity coalition to adopt a more radical political platform. This caused greater fragmentation of the Popular Unity's structure and aided the growing opposition to the Allende government.

people or members of the armed forces. These were five units that were supposed to defend the constitutionally elected government for a nation that, at the ballot, had wanted Salvador Allende Gossens to be its president and to implement his political platform.

I had met Alejandro when I was an athlete at the Universidad Católica and he was at the Universidad Técnica. We saw each other every weekend at the National Stadium. I knew he held the record for the 400-meter dash, and he knew that I held the record for the 800-meter.

I didn't recognize him when I saw him again in the Socialist Party. "It took me ten years to find you again, and I'm not going to let you get away this time," he said. We developed a warm friendship. Alejandro was a militant in the Cathedral unit in downtown Santiago. I never knew the nature of his work for the party. He did find out about some of my activities since, as a member of the downtown unit, he was assigned to be an instructor at the Militant Training School that my division was in the process of implementing. We both knew that we had been assigned to different divisions in the party, at least for part of our duties.

I always got the impression that he knew more about my activities because he often talked to me about subjects that were useful to me. In May 1972, when I joined the GAP, I had started reading all the newspapers. During the time I was with INESAL, I started learning to process public information, but it was in the GEA that I was officially assigned to work in the Public Information Division.

Frequently, after finishing my work for the GEA and leaving the Central Committee Headquarters, I stopped by the downtown Santiago office, our neighbors on San Martín Street. Alejandro told me that he used to get together with several of his compañeros from the Socialist Party's Cathedral Unit at around nine o'clock at night to go over the daily news.

Alejandro and I often used to meet for lunch at "La Cabañita," a restaurant located next to Central Committee Headquarters. Before I knew it, Alejandro started taking up all my free time. It was obvious from the very beginning that there was a strong attraction between us, but it bothered me to feel like this attraction was turning into a need to see him. A few days later, Alejandro came to my office and said, "I need to talk to you, tomorrow at ten, at the post office."

He was referring to the post office on the corner of Morandé and Moneda Street. It seemed strange, and I assumed he wanted to talk

12

about something personal. I went the following day. We had already gone over the situation, at least a couple of times, especially since it seemed really difficult for me at that time to start a relationship and be involved in the party at the same time. I was afraid I wouldn't be able to reconcile such intense desires. Ever since I had seen Alejandro again, I had begun losing the freedom I had before, that complete enthusiasm for and concentration on party work. Alejandro was taking over everything, my thoughts, my feelings, everything.

Each day I was more and more aware of what time it was, if Alejandro was coming to see me or not, if he would manage to have lunch with me or not. Every time he didn't want to or couldn't come, I felt completely let down, even if we hadn't explicitly agreed on anything. All our encounters were supposed to look coincidental. Even my visits downtown were sort of happenstance. I felt like I was involved in two relationships, and I declared myself incapable of reconciling them.

That day, August 1, 1973, Alejandro was waiting for me at the entrance to the post office. He took my hand and dragged me to one of the little windows. He mailed a letter, and then he practically yanked me out of there. At the entrance of Morandé, surrounded by a bunch of people, he hugged me and kissed me. I tried to wriggle free, but I couldn't. I was absolutely incapable of saying anything. All my arguments seemed to have gotten lost somewhere. He took my hand again. Then he hailed a taxi and, without saying a word, we continued to kiss each other and went to a hotel.

During those hours, we decided to try and have a relationship. He told me that he was leaving for Cuba in thirteen days and that he would return on September 18, 1973. That was why it was so important for him to start a relationship with me before he left. He said that the separation would be a long one, that thirty-five days was a lot for a relationship that would only be thirteen days old, but that he knew he loved me and that he was sure about his feelings.

We didn't leave until the following morning, when I had to go to the GEA and he had to go somewhere else. I didn't know where, but it was where the group traveling to Cuba was meeting. He explained that the militants who were going to the island would be living together until then, but that he would find a way to come see me.

We spent a lot of nights together during those thirteen days. I think it was the first time I was so close to loving someone. We said goodbye on the morning of August 14, 1973. Alejandro had to arrive before

13

seven o'clock in the morning to be able to go with the group to the airport. He gave me "la negrita," which is what he called his CZ-635 pistol.[11]

He put it in my hands and said, "Other than you, this is what I love most."

I went down to Alameda. I was really sad. I went home. I didn't go to the GEA. I felt nervous. Logically, I knew that thirty-five days would fly by. I knew his code name, the one he was traveling under, and I impulsively felt like I needed to hear his voice so I called him at the airport. I didn't know it would be the last time I would be able to hear him. . . .[12]

11. The nickname "la negrita" refers to the color of the pistol, which is black. The use of the diminutive indicates both its compact size and the almost personified affection Alejandro had for his weapon, as "la negrita" could also refer to a woman.

12. In July 1993 Arce noted, "I have just discovered that Alejandro survived and that he remains in exile."

2

SEPTEMBER 11, 1973

I experienced September 11th like an invasion of what was then my world, like a destructive force that annihilated everything that was important in my life. It was a catastrophe that made everything incoherent and incomprehensible, filling my life with sorrow. God! If only that were all.

It was a numbing emptiness, not seeing, not knowing, nothing.

In this chapter, I am not going to respect a linear chronology of events. I can't. In this chapter, I simply cannot. . . .

On December 4, 1989, I stopped to buy the newspaper on my way home. And that day *Punto Final* was there, hanging from some clothespins.[13]

I stood there gazing at it, caressing the emotions I was finding inside myself. I bought the magazine, and when I arrived home, walked over to the window in my apartment.

Looking toward the hilltop in the center of Santiago, where the Virgin stands like a crown, I asked her to help guide me through those minefields of painful memories. Fearfully, I began to read. The magazine was number 201. They had resumed counting from the issue that had been interrupted by the coup. I asked myself: Will I be able to resume my life? I felt a sense of terror. It seemed as though I had been absent from my own being for more than a decade and a half and that the hour of truth was approaching. I stopped and closed my eyes, taking in with my thoughts that obscure parenthesis where what was alive and burning was consuming me like a fire. I felt, once again, the fear that paralyzed me for years.

13. *Punto Final* is one of the only remaining alternative news sources from the left in Chile. It was discontinued during the dictatorship but is currently published weekly.

I started reliving President Salvador Allende's last speech.

"The nation must defend itself, but not sacrifice itself. The nation must not allow itself to be subjugated or tormented, but it cannot be humiliated either.

"Workers of my nation: I have faith in Chile and her destiny. Other men will overcome this dark, bitter moment when treason tries to impose itself. Continue with the knowledge that much sooner than later the great avenues will again be opened where free men will travel to build a better society. Long live Chile! Long live her people! Long live the workers!

"These are my final words. I am certain that my sacrifice will not be in vain. I am certain that it will at least be a moral lesson that will punish felony, cowardice, and treason."

From each soul-rending wound flowed drops of sorrow, like petals blooming from old wilted flowers. I couldn't or I wouldn't stop myself. An image emerged, one of life like a continuous line between birth and death. Mine had been interrupted. I couldn't keep eluding that part, those years, painful as they were. I started opening myself up to the uninterrupted parade of the dead, the executed or disappeared, the exiled, and the tortured. I evoked those who had also survived that war, that carnival of power.

I knew that each time I had started down that path, I had closed it off again. But it was there as it had always been, locked tight within me, wanting to get out. Fear had always overpowered my strength and compelled me to don the merciful veils that allowed me to escape. But that time I couldn't, or wouldn't, I don't know. . . .

My memory took me back to September 11, 1973. Sitting in front of the old radio in a Mademsa office, with tears in our eyes, we kept looking at the floor so no one would see our pain. I couldn't believe it; I couldn't accept it; I couldn't understand it; I didn't want to. . . .[14]

Looking back from a distance, I remembered "Silvano." On September 10th, our friend received news that one of his children was ill. At least, that was what we were told at Headquarters the morning of September 11, 1973. "He went to his home in Talca, and some neighbor must have alerted the new authorities to the whereabouts of 'Silvano.' He was arrested, tortured, and assassinated." That version of "Sil-

<hr>

14. Mademsa was a factory in Santiago's manufacturing sector.

vano's" death had me thinking for years that he had died on the morning of the coup.

In October 1990, when I testified before the Truth and Reconciliation Commission, I discovered that "Silvano" had heard about the troop movements and had tried to return to Santiago. He was intercepted on the highway and executed days later, apparently on the 4th or 5th of October, 1973.

I thought of Yucatán, Ollagüe, Terranova, and other places in Chile.[15]

The regime made every effort for the country to seem clean, with tree trunks and paths marked with stones that had been painted white. I asked myself many times: Will they paint white the blood and the shit that keeps piling up? . . . I returned, immersed in my memory, to September 10, 1973. . . .

It was a normal work day, with worries that ranged from the most routine, like trying to find time to be with my young son, to duties that the fragile political situation in the country was generating; Chile was practically paralyzed by the opposition's fierce determination to destabilize it. When I finished my workday at the party's office at about nine o'clock at night, I went to headquarters in downtown Santiago for a meeting with the group that recruited supporters each day from within the party.

That night we were busy analyzing rumors that consistently pointed to the possibility of a coup. I imagine the party authorities possessed better information. We mistakenly concluded that there wouldn't be a coup. We trusted the Palace Guard. That afternoon, the police force had sworn their institutional loyalty to the government. We were aware of General Carlos Prats's constitutional positions and of the commanding ability he had demonstrated the day of the "Tancazo" on July 29th that same year. And even though General Prats had been replaced as the military commander, we dismissed reports that the Air Force had moved its Hawker Hunters to Talcahuano.[16]

We concluded that it was logical given their participation in Operation Unitas with the navy.

The meeting ended around two o'clock in the morning. I decided to walk home. The transportation strike had paralyzed everything, and

15. These were detention centers where prisoners were held and interrogated.
16. The Chilean Air Force purchased its Hawker Hunter aircraft from England in the 1960s and they arrived between 1970 and 1971, just in time to serve as an important weapon in the 1973 military coup with the bombing of the Presidential Palace in Santiago.

the only alternative would have been to stay at party headquarters without being able to take a shower or change clothes. It was a beautiful night. I thought of my son, my reason for living and my motivation. I wanted a new world for him and for all children, where justice would reign and where human beings would be valued just for existing. The new man, only emulating, not competing. El Che, Cuba . . . Alejandro was on the Island. . . . I felt a sudden nostalgia and sensed the taste of broken love, of loneliness.

It was the morning of September 11th. I walked home deep in thought. My son was still sleeping. I lay on the sofa in my parents' living room wide-awake, smoking, and thinking that when Alejandro returned, he would meet my son and we would go to a park or to see cartoons. . . . Everything suddenly disappeared when the telephone rang. It was Toño, from headquarters. He was on duty, "Compañera, Red Alert."

I showered and dressed quickly. A red alert was serious. The driver of a CCU (United Beer Company) truck agreed to give me a ride.

6:30 A.M.: "David," Ignacio," and I listed to the information that Toño sent us. The telex was working at full speed. Information was coming in about troop movements from every section and region in the country where militants were on night duty, and they were asking for instructions.

We asked Toño if he had warned all of the GEAs. He said that he had, except for "Silvano," because he hadn't been able to find him yet.

"Toño, are there any instructions for us?"

"There are no specific orders for anyone. I only activated the warning, since the information is serious. But I hope someone from the leadership will contact us at any moment. Don't worry. As soon as Ariel calls or comes in, I'll let you know."

7:00 A.M.: The first construction workers arrive.

During the following half hour, "Felipe," "Bernardo," and "El Gato" arrive after hearing the Red Alert code.

Shortly thereafter, "Ignacio" appeared, looking very pale. He told us, "'Silvano' is dead. They arrested him just after midnight at home. They tortured him right there, in front of his wife and kids. They are really shaken, at a neighbor's house."

Dismayed, we returned to Toño's office at around 7:30 to ask him for more information, "Toño, have you heard anything from higher up?"

"Altamirano is in the Cerrillos sector; Ariel Ulloa is en route to the Argentine Embassy, and the rest are nowhere to be found."

18

"Ariel, seeking asylum? Are you sure?"

"Yes, compañera, his secretary is coming to look for his personal things and some documents for him to take."

I felt an uncontrollable rage that clouded my thoughts: Bastard! I have remembered that moment on many occasions over the past twenty years. I don't know how the rest felt but I felt betrayed. . . . Much later, I was able to understand that this was how it was, and that we all have to face ourselves and everyone else and take responsibility for our own decisions.

That 11th of September, with my heart mourning "Silvano's" death, feeling like what was happening wasn't real and with twenty minutes left until 8:00 in the morning, I got through to the Moneda Palace.

"252, good morning."

"Compañero Carlos, please. Hilda speaking."

I remembered that Hilda had been my first political name. Carlos gave it to me in memory of a Cuban woman in the FAR (Revolutionary Armed Forces) who died in the Sierra Maestra. They used to say that she was Carlos's compañera while he was training in Cuba in Punto Cero.

Carlos was a man without much formal education, but he had the kind of wisdom that comes from a combination of a hard life and social sensitivity. He patiently introduced me into militant life, in spite of the many weaknesses that he called "Hilda and her bourgeois vices."

He had his as well. He told me several times: "At home I am a complete chauvinist. But you, Hilda, aren't my wife. You are my assistant. You aren't a woman; you're a militant. Agreed?" And what today, looking back through time and with the benefit of experience, seems ridiculous, at that moment was necessary support. I was twenty-two years old, recently separated, and Carlos helped me discover that there were things I could do. Being a woman didn't mean that I was a second-class citizen. Near him, with his guidance, I grew.

In just a few seconds, everything flashed through my mind. I remembered El Cañaveral, "Payita's" house in the foothills of the Arrayán, the place she managed to transform into a safe haven for the president to come and rest. It was a beautiful place near the river. The Militant Training School. . . .

I reacted when I heard Carlos's voice: "Compañera Hilda? Where are you?"

"At Headquarters. Carlos, we're heading over there. We had a meet-

19

ing. There are six of us left. 'Silvano' died this morning in Talca. There are nineteen construction workers. We have six AKs and six handguns with two cartridges each and some ammunition."

"Hilda, listen. There is no time. I must return to be with the president. And the leadership?"

"Seeking asylum or out of reach."

"Hilda, this is an order! In the absence of the Political Commission, I am taking control of the GEA. Burn the files. Set fire to the building, and don't leave anything. Tell the workers they're off duty. Send them home and you too, lay low. Good-bye. I'm returning to the president."

"No, Carlos. Don't hang up, listen. . . . I'll set the office on fire, and I'll tell the workers they're off duty, but I'm going with the volunteers. . . ."

He interrupted me by shouting, "Compañera, this is an order! Do you have any money? Divide it among yourselves, and go home. Set up contacts with the volunteers for one or two months from now. You must rebuild the party. If you show up here, compañera, I'll shoot you. Good-bye."

He hung up.

It was the last time I heard him, and he remains disappeared to this day.[17]

We obeyed part of the order. Ariel's secretary came and told us that he would take care of the files and the office. He would burn it. We divided up the money between those of us in the group, three thousand pesos each. We dismissed the compañeros who weren't part of the GEA leadership, and decided to go to the Cerillos Sector. We would put ourselves at Carlos Altamirano's disposal. We would resist.

I am moved by the memory that some of our compañeros wanted to go with us. We had to force them to leave. If we had had more weapons, perhaps, but as it was, it would have been very irresponsible to take them along. We took the weapons and three of the Fiat 125s that were assigned to the GEA and we went to Cerillos.

When we arrived, the compañeros told us the CUP (Popular Unity Committee) was in session. We were there awhile, and then we realized that they were involved in an ideological debate with the compañeros from the MIR. We realized that this was useless at this stage, so we left in time to listen to Salvador Allende's message.

17. Since the initial publication of the Spanish version of this text in 1993, Arce discovered that his remains had been found in 1991 in area 29 in the General Cemetery.

We were deeply moved. When we realized that they were bombing the Moneda Presidential Palace, El Cañaveral, Tomás Moro, and the radio stations aligned with the Popular Unity government, we began to understand the magnitude of what was happening. . . . Faces flashed through my mind, so many memories of compañeros in the GAP, "Carlos," "Bruno," "Juan," "El Manque," "Francisco," "Silvano," and so many others. . . .

We left in a hurry to get to the Mademsa factory warehouses. We met with some of the workers and briefly explained the situation to them. We told them they were free to go home. They told us they were making some bombs called Vietnamese cones. That made us think we might be able to organize a core of resistance. "Felipe" and "Ignacio" went to find out what materials we had, if there was a first-aid kit, food, or water, in other words, what we needed to put up a fight. Bernardo went to inspect the factory's entrances and fences to see if it would be feasible for us to barricade ourselves in. We went with "David" to see the cones.

The shop boss accompanied us. A helicopter started to fly over the area. When we arrived at the warehouse, the compañero told us proudly, "We make the cone's cover out of the plastic from the refrigerators. And look, compañeros, the shrapnel is over there. They are making it over in Cintac. They brought this a few moments ago, but don't worry, they're still working."

All lined up, the containers looked like a bunch of really strange beings. They were kind of cute. They looked like little Martians in formation, and they were a source of pride for the compañero who took great care in explaining to us how they had designed and built the mold. He said smiling, "What do you think?"

"Good, compañero, well done. Let's arm them. Bring the explosives, the detonators, fuses. Bring all you've got. Quick, man, move it."

The shop boss looked like he was stuck to the floor. He looked at us. . . .

"Compañera, I . . . I am only in charge of doing this. It is my duty, and I fulfilled it, compañera. I know about the shrapnel because the guy in charge of that over in Cintac is a friend of mine. But I don't know anything about who's in charge of what you're asking me to do. We each have our job to do, compañera."

He was moving backwards, and he seemed frightened looking at the little colored Martians—green, baby-blue, yellow, mustard, and orange—like the refrigerators. He kept repeating: "I fulfilled my duty,

I did my part. All of us here at Mademsa did our duty." Huge tears welled in his tired, incredulous eyes. He suddenly looked like he had the weight of the world on his shoulders. Looking older, worn out, he turned to me and repeated, "Compañera! You know, I did my duty. . . ."

He had understood before I had that his effort and everyone else's was all in vain, and he was crying unreservedly. I felt an immense sorrow, "Compañero, I know, and all of us here know you did your part, and you did it well. Don't worry. Get your workers together and go home. Are you married? Do you have children? Go quickly. They must be anxious. Go, and don't worry."

I watched him walk away. He was the very image of defeat.

It seems like a lie. It seems like a joke, but that's how it was. The six of us got together, and each of us reported what we found. The situation was similar in each case. We dismissed the rest of the personnel, assuring them that we would take full responsibility for their going home. We spoke with them briefly about rebuilding the left's political parties in the future and of the agreement to set up contacts one or two months later. Some of them started to leave.

After a brief conversation, we took ourselves off duty. Thinking of their wives and children, "Ignacio," "Felipe," and "Bernardo" decided to go home. They took two of the cars, and "David," "El Gato," and I went in the third. We tried to reach the Moneda. No one intercepted us on the way, despite the fact that we ran into various military units.

When we reached the center, everything was over. We watched the smoke rising from the Moneda in the distance. We didn't know yet that the president had died. In front of the main entrance, we could see compañero Bruno's white car in flames.

I only remember that in terms of those hours and those days, my mind seemed to have drawn a blank. We left the vehicle in an abandoned field. We wiped our fingerprints from it before we got out. After having gone to the homes of several militants who had garages, we left the AKs there. No one wanted to hide the vehicle, much less the weapons.

My next memory is of being at home, sitting and watching television with my son in my arms. Those hours don't exist for me. I was just there, sitting and watching. I haven't been able to decipher that period. Maybe I felt something. Maybe I thought, I don't know. I know I couldn't have seen the images of the Moneda, El Cañaveral, or Tomás Moro on television, when they were destroyed by the bombings and the repeated raids that followed, without feeling anything. We shared so many things:

sorrows, dreams, studies, meals, duties. I loved them and they loved me. They were my compañeros. Perhaps those feelings are imprinted on some part of me. I don't know.

I found out something many years later when I attended rallies celebrating the Concertation government's victory.[18]

In the midst of the crowd, I felt joy. I remembered them one by one, some by name and others by face, an event, or a detail. Today I know that many died. But over the years, I have been happily discovering that some are still alive, and not just in my memory and their families' memories. They are part of the new Concertation government.

18. The term "concertation" refers to the coalition of democratic parties that has held power since Chile's democratic transition in 1990. Since then, there have been three Concertation governments led by Patricio Aylwin, Eduardo Frei Ruiz-Tagle, and Ricardo Lagos, respectively. The first two were from the centrist Christian Democratic Party, and Ricardo Lagos is Chile's first Socialist president since Salvador Allende.

3

CLANDESTINE LIFE

Intensity versus time, it is the variable that dominates clandestine life. At least that is how I experienced it. Everything changes rhythm. Then there is the rational awareness of the risk you're taking. This is combined with information that transforms history into a statistic that says that the average length of survival underground is six months. These are both life-changing realities.

Sergio Muñoz, alias "Cochín," asked me, "Have you ever seen a fish out of water? With its lips instinctively opening and closing, trying to find a mouthful of water with the oxygen it needs to live in the midst of a world that is not its own?" This is how I began learning to live, day by day, away from what had been my world. We appreciated everything around us, confronted with the possibility of losing it. Life, the sun, a child's smile, dreams. In the midst of that urban landscape, during that summer that seemed to burn in the city's concrete, I discovered a flowerpot with geraniums on the balcony. It was as if they were trying to toss red and white smiles and green sparkles to those who were still looking up toward the rooftops of the buildings, trying to make out a sky that had crumbled for us.

Now the streets are either safe or unsafe. The best blocks are the short ones since they allow you to get to the corner quickly. Turn the corner and hurry. Check your back. You associate street names with the time it takes to get from one end to the other. They become three or four minute blocks at a normal pace. Local businesses, restaurants, and cafes with more than one entrance, each leading to a different street, and enormous shop windows are excellent. Remember the direction of the traffic, and walk in the opposite direction to avoid being followed by a car. Always keep some change on hand for the phone. Know the neighborhood. Maintain safe havens, and the more the better. It's the same with people. There are no longer people with a similar or different destination. A person may be a detective or from the DINA. Or they may be militants from another organization or another party about to make contact, and then the risk is doubled. Be attentive. Don't just look: observe and record everything in your mind. Don't look anyone in the eye. It is more difficult to recognize a face if you haven't seen an expression. Observe the attitudes of normal people and imitate them. Quickly learn techniques for memorization and association. Don't confuse passwords, secret signs for greetings or warnings, or meeting times and places. Don't write anything down. It's better to memorize. Walk naturally, and follow the manuals and the experience of other organizations, like the Tupamaros, Errepos, Montoneros, and others.[19]

It can mean the difference between prison and freedom, life and death.

One of the things that worked in our favor in the beginning was the repressive organizations' lack of experience. This was combined with the government's desire to sow terror in the general population and turn it against the opposition movement, which led them to publish any documents that they found in their raids. That is how we were able to count on the publication of manuals, reports, and other documents, especially ones about the MIR, which appeared in *El Mercurio* and other newspapers. Our daily duty was to stay alive and maintain an attitude of normalcy. And you had to distance yourself from members of your family to avoid endangering them.

Homeless and unemployed, most of us learned the hard way how hostile the world of marginal life could be. Without a doubt, we were marginalized. Our options were to assimilate ourselves to a way of life that the majority of our families considered "safe" and "reasonable" or to continue our militant resistance at home and abroad. The Socialist Party always looked after the safety of its militants. It was just that some of us denied ourselves that option.

A PERSONAL CHOICE

It took me several days to make a decision. The San Cristóbal Hill was a silent witness to my doubts, my sorrow, my hopes, my denial, and,

19. Arce is referring to other clandestine revolutionary groups operating in Uruguay (Tupamaros) and Argentina (Errepos—members of the ERP—and Montoneros).

finally, my decision. On the one hand, there was the tranquility of my parents and raising my five-year-old son, and on the other, the memory of compañeros who were dead or imprisoned. There were militants who were waiting for answers, instructions, and leadership. The party was fragmented, and corpses were appearing on bridges and on the banks of the Mapocho River.[20]

There was terror and increasing repression amid truncated hopes and lost ideals. The mission had been burnt into our memory, and it hurt. Salvador Allende's last words before he died, Carlos Alamos's words on September 11th just minutes before eight in the morning: "You must rebuild the party, compañera. . . ." The realization that what was occurring in my country was outrageous.

Everything in my soul was agitated like an ocean. Fear was growing by the day as we received information from the new repressive apparatus. It wasn't the Bureau of Investigations or the Air Force Academy (AGA). It was the Directorate of National Intelligence (DINA). We whispered that name without knowing much about it, and we trembled in fear. I felt as though the howl of the sirens and the noise of the helicopters over the houses had permeated my guts. I would turn off the light and watch, trying to guess what was happening, identify the location of the iron fist whose image was being shown on television and that seemed poised to strike.

Something I could never understand was the loss of a compañero. You had to wait in vain at a predetermined meeting place. You could only wait a couple of minutes. Three was too long. If he didn't arrive, had he been arrested? At first, you would refuse to accept it. You'd wait another minute. Then the questions would start: What does he know? How long will he resist? And then you would have to wait for the reconnection. Maybe he's running late, or he's sick, or something else. Some of them arrived surrounded by DINA personnel. But you had to show up. The compañero could have broken contact to protect himself, and we couldn't leave him in the lurch. Our life only had meaning if we remained united.

These intense moments are difficult to describe even today, so many years later: the anguish of walking naturally while your whole being is crying; daily heartbreak; your face adopting a new appearance that is composed and lacking expression; your mouth silent and dry; your

---

20. The Mapocho River runs through the center of Santiago.

gaze serene, your soul broken, your heart beating quickly; and the sweat rolling off your skin.

I didn't give up. How could I have told my son when he grew up, "I was afraid, and I accepted the unacceptable?" How could I have told him, "I wanted a different world for you, but I didn't do anything to build it?" How could I have looked at my compañeros and said to them, "I'm leaving"? How could I have looked myself in the mirror without disgust? That was when I decided to live like a fish out of water, without knowing that, in time, I would learn the hard way that this was impossible.

Several days after the coup, we met with Toño. Until the coup, he had been a party employee, one among many who were in charge of information services at Central Committee headquarters. That is why so many militants knew how to find him. When the curfew was lifted, we approached him to get information. Or when we simply found ourselves out of the loop, we told him of our desire to continue in the resistance.

During that conversation, Toño told me that he had also lost contact with the party leadership. He added that it was desirable to get an idea of each person's situation, and that those who could keep their jobs without running any risks should do so. He told us to try to keep in contact while we waited for the party leadership to get in touch with us.

Days went by, and a new kind of party structure was being created around Toño. Logic indicated that it was preferable for us to break into small militant base groups, or what we called "troikas," with compartmentalized functions.

Very soon it was obvious that we were going to need some minimal infrastructure, so we started communicating our needs to the compañeros. We wanted to determine whether we and our contacts could centralize some resources, in order to redistribute them according to the needs of the party. Since most of us didn't have any resources of our own, we needed paper, mimeographs, safe houses or meeting places, and the like.

Neither Toño nor I had any source of personal income. At the end of the day, we were tired and hungry. That is why we quickly broke the most essential rule of safety: we started meeting at his house. I met his mother and his brothers. His mother welcomed us warmly, and we had lunch almost every day with them while Toño was living at home with his family.

Our daily interaction grew into a beautiful friendship. I came to love him like a brother. I told him about Alejandro, and one day he told me to write him a note. He had apparently found a way to get the letter to Cuba through an embassy.

CONTACT ON ITALIA AVENUE

The party's leadership reconnected with Toño, although he never told me how. When he told me that we were to meet with Gustavo Ruz Zañartu, a member of the Central Committee, I cried tears of joy. That very afternoon, Gustavo picked us up on the corner of Irarrázaval and Italia. He came in his blue MG. It was a risk.

We gave Gustavo all the information we had gathered up to that day. I updated him in his car about the GEA's situation on the day of the coup and about each of the steps we had taken to date. I also told him about the infrastructure we had been able to salvage. With regard to the militants, I indicated that I had lost touch with the others and that I still had some meetings that were pending.

Gustavo explained that he intended to remain in the country, and that, given the absence of other leaders, he was assuming party leadership in Chile. I thought Gustavo was saying this to avoid handing over any more information about the leadership. He listed what he believed were the immediate tasks at hand and how he thought we should go about carrying them out. They included attempting to reconnect the militants, rebuilding clandestine party structures, supporting compañeros who were in trouble or who needed asylum, creating financial systems, reconnecting the party to the provinces, and contacting other parties and organizations.

I felt a sense of sadness as I listened to Gustavo. It wasn't that I had expected to find an organization that was spontaneously working and that had already adapted to the new situation, but everything was so volatile.

When Gustavo learned that I had belonged to a compartmentalized structure until September 11th, one that depended on the party's Organization, he asked if I could offer him security and infrastructure. I explained to him that we didn't have much at our disposal but that I could let him stay at my house for a few days if he really needed to. I only stipulated that it was right next to my parent's house and that if he decided to live there, my family couldn't be allowed to notice. I told him I could make sure that his presence would go unnoticed while I was at the house next door. I said that he could stay there for two or three days, until he found a safer place. He accepted.

He suggested I keep working with Toño for the time being and that we should also direct our efforts toward obtaining infrastructure for him. I started contacting people I knew who were against the current regime, even though they weren't militants. They, and their homes or offices, hadn't been so unlucky.

We learned as we went along how to deal with our losses and lovingly rise above our many personal limitations. We worked as a group, respecting each person's idiosyncrasies, fuelled by an energy I think was pure adrenaline.

I think there was a widely shared feeling of being responsible for the mistakes that we made as militants and as parties during the Popular Unity's 1,000 days. We thought we knew the risks of clandestine life. All I can say is that I never had any idea just what we would have to face in the very near future. I wasn't prepared for what was to come; nobody was.

PARTY WORK

I continued working with Toño. We soon learned that Gustavo had been successful in contacting Exequiel Ponce, Víctor Zerega, and Ricardo Lagos. The party was beginning to take shape. Day after day, more and more compañeros and some leaders joined our ranks. New contacts were also made with MAPU's sectors.

We were able to rebuild some infrastructure, and I suggested that Gustavo alter his appearance. He agreed. I gave him a perm and we provided him with clothing that was different from what he had always worn. He looked like a student with his curly hair, jeans, a short jacket, and tennis shoes. A few days later, looking really happy, he told me he had allowed himself the luxury of personally scheduling a meeting. He said that he had stood next to Víctor Zerega for several minutes without being recognized. That was really something since not only were they both members of the party leadership, they also had known each other for quite some time. Víctor was detained a few days later and murdered.

Sometimes I drove Gustavo's car to take him from one place to another. On other occasions he met with other leaders in the car. Little by little the number of Gustavo's contacts was growing, as were his resources. Therefore, once the sense of urgency had passed, I returned to my duties working with Toño. Gustavo Ruz informed me that he was going to get in touch with me soon so that I could start working with the Squatters Front in an area of Quinta Normal.

I had been lucky. While I was still living with my parents, some police officers came to the house saying that neighbors had reported that I had carried several boxes into the house before the coup. They searched the house. Fortunately, since my brother had gotten married in August, and the gifts he received were there and still wrapped, I was able to justify it that way. I had the house fairly "clean," and the search wasn't very thorough. On that occasion, they didn't find the weapons or the documents I was hiding.

My parents were afraid that the situation could be more difficult the next time. They told me I had to make a decision. I could stay there and live with them only if I stopped working for the party. My father was very clear. He took the phone and started to dial the Bureau of Investigations. I grabbed my purse, said good-bye to my son, and left quickly.

Toño helped me. I stayed at his house that night, and the following day I looked for a room to rent. Everything I owned was in a gym bag. Toño had received some money to use for communications, mobilization, and renting rooms in boardinghouses for compañeros who had nowhere else to go.

Toño and I kept building infrastructure, reconnecting militants, and saving weapons that others were throwing away out of fear. The room was not a good place since they frequently raided pensions and university houses in that sector. However, I was reassured by the fact that in my parents' neighborhood I was known only as someone from the left and that the repression at that time apparently wasn't that selective. I used a false name as a contact, but I lived under my real identity.

On one occasion, I dropped Gustavo off at the place where he was living and I took his car. I was supposed to pick him up the next day. It was a Saturday afternoon and since I didn't have anything to do for a few hours, I decided to go and see my son. When I was near the Santa Laura Stadium a police officer stopped me. He asked for the car's registration and my driver's license. I gave him the documents. He asked me who Gustavo Ruz Zañartu was, since the car was registered in his name. I told him that he was my husband, that I had just dropped him off at the stadium, and that I was going to pick up our son to take him to a birthday party. He looked in the car and when he saw some knitting that

I had put in the backseat as a precaution, he smiled at me and said: "Have a nice day, ma'am."

We were clearly taking risks. A few days later Gustavo offered to help me seek asylum, saying he knew from a reliable source that the Bureau of Investigations had a file on me because of my work with the GAP. That made me vulnerable and it put the party in jeopardy. Years later, as a DINA employee, I was able to see the information the Bureau had about me. I knew then that Gustavo had been right to worry about my safety.

I talked with Gustavo and asked him to allow me to have a different assignment. I told him I could do something else and not spend so much time out on the street as a contact. He agreed. I was supposed to continue working with Toño until he gave me my next assignment. I was happy and told him that I would try to assume another identity.

I slowed down my work, limiting it to accompanying Toño. He had also stopped spending time out in the open once the contacts had begun taking over those duties. Since I was living on España Avenue and Toño lived on Ricardo Cumming, and given our need to retreat from the city's center where we were already pretty well known, we began relocating our meetings from Alameda toward the south.

I felt tied down, limited. Something inside of me couldn't accept the situation in which we were living. Nevertheless, I realized that doors were being closed on a daily basis. People who even just suspected that you were still active in some political party from the left walked by you, with their heads down and looking the other way. I started to feel that they were right. My presence was dangerous for those I knew, above all for my family.

It was hard not to call on the phone, not to go home on a regular basis, but my son's safety was at stake, along with that of the rest of the family. Quite often, while resting after a meeting or killing time before another, I used to watch people who seemed to have freedom to live and something to do without hiding. Toño was my only source of company. I used to watch the pigeons and the sparrows, and I would have liked to be able to feel free like them. I knew that, somehow, I was free deep inside. I had made a choice. No one had asked me to stay, but the walls were gradually closing in on me. I often thought I would even forget how to talk. I really wanted to cry, but in those days I didn't let myself. There were too many problems already to go around complaining.

RICARDO RUZ ZAÑARTU

On one occasion, after I had just finished a meeting, I was walking down Toesca and Eighteenth Street when I ran into Ricardo. I had met him once setting up a meeting between him and my boss. Gustavo and Ricardo were brothers. That day, Ricardo approached me. We realized that we had chosen similar places and times for our meetings.

We went to a café where we talked. It was the first in a series of transgressions of party norms, since he was a member of the MIR's Central Committee. It was understood that we weren't supposed to have any meetings other than the ones required by the party. Even so, we started seeing each other.

I really enjoyed being with him. If we had met at a time other than the one we were living, I believe Ricardo wouldn't have been anything other than a great friend. However, although only for a short time, we started a wonderful relationship. There were thousands of things about him that mostly just made me laugh. What struck me most of all was how he constantly worried about whether I was eating and sleeping all right. I looked at him astounded, and I found it sweet that under the circumstances someone would worry about things like that.

It was wonderful getting to know him little by little. He seemed to enjoy life. Many times I thought about how different his way of life was from mine. I remember how once in a restaurant, one of the many we frequented on Matta Avenue, he reminded me of Alejandro as I listened to him telling funny anecdotes. I had laughed like that once with Alejandro. Ricardo realized that something had darkened my mood, and he thoughtfully changed the subject. He asked me about his brother, and he was happy he was doing well.

The truth is that I soon realized that seeing him was becoming really important, just as had happened with Alejandro. Ricardo fascinated me. He was sophisticated, intelligent, thoughtful, and a good conversationalist. He even liked chess! One day he asked me, "Do you know my name?"

"Yes. What should I call you?"

"I think it would be better if you called me Alexis. And you?"

"Gloria."

In one of our encounters he mentioned something about how I had changed his brother Gustavo's appearance, and he asked if I would do the same for some of his compañeros from the MIR. I agreed, and that is how I met "Tano" (Hugo Ramón Martínez González), "Tacho" (Luis Fuentes Riquelme), "Chico" Pérez (Sergio Pérez Molina), and Lumi Videla Moya. I kept in touch with the first two, especially "Tacho." We became good friends during the time when Ricardo and I began a romantic relationship, which lasted a little more than a couple of months. It was interrupted when I was detained in March 1974.

Ricardo and I decided to live together. We rented a room in an old mansion on Eighteenth Street. He assumed my ex-husband's identity. During that time he introduced me to "Momio" Castillo and asked him to make me a fake ID. "Momio" chose a name for me: Isabel del Carmen Romero Contreras. I was carrying that ID when they detained me in March 1974. On November 27, 1979, according to the press at the time, Ricardo Ruz Zañartu, still using my ex-husband's identity, died in a shootout with police.

Up until the day I decided to live with Ricardo I still hoped I would get some message from Alejandro. It hurt me not to hear anything about him. I assumed he had chosen another option, and I held onto the precious memory of those 13 days. But I couldn't help counting each day that separated me from him.

When I decided to stay in Chile, I gave up the idea of seeking asylum and searching for him. I was sure that being a militant was his priority. I hoped that this would be the case. I knew that if he returned to Chile, he would do it with a compartmentalized assignment and with some duty for the party. I finally concluded: "If he stays in Cuba, he has the option of living free of danger, of finding another partner." I tried to convince myself that the best thing for him would be for us not to see each other again. . . . I didn't know then how right I was.

For me, Ricardo became my joy in life, a beautiful parentheses that lasted a little bit longer than my days with Alejandro when everything was left unfinished and still to come. It was different with Ricardo. Everything flowed freely, and each moment felt as though it was enough in itself. Perhaps, since there was no option of seeing a future, it eliminated any kind of necessity for one. It never bothered me that he was married. I never felt hurt by it or jealous. It was enough for me to know that our time together was ours and beautiful. Just once I was left wondering, but only for a few moments. Ricardo had left and "Tacho" invited me to have a cup of coffee. During the conversation he said, "Ricardo is really lucky. With his wife he has a woman and children. With you, the ideal compañera and militant." I asked him, "Tacho, am I not a woman?" He gave me hundreds of explanations, but he didn't convince me. But in those days, for me, it was a real compliment to be considered above all a militant.

Ricardo and I started going to the pool in the morning with "Tano" and "Tacho." I taught all three of them how to swim. We chose the Monserrat pool near the San Cristóbal Hill. A couple of afternoons each week we went to the Chess Federation to play. My life changed radically. Ricardo took time to read out loud while I cooked, or vice versa because he cooked better than I did. He also explained analyses of the political situation to me, as well as the MIR's instruction manuals. Over the years I have come to the conclusion that the compañeros from the MIR at that time were all great cooks. Paradoxically, and with exceptions, of course, we women who had a militant past are terrible cooks and housewives. Not so long ago a friend said to me, "And this is something the military doesn't know. . . ."

"Of course," I answered. We were really serious about the idea that there are no predetermined roles. "And, since you cook so well, we give you the opportunity to practice your feminism. . . ."

When Ricardo wasn't around, he asked "Tacho" to accompany me. We spent many hours together. Ricardo and his friends are special to me. He, Lumi, and "Tano" were murdered by the dictatorship. "Chico" Pérez and "Tacho" are disappeared. But they live in my heart just like in those days, and I feel like I won't have peace until the circumstances surrounding their deaths are known.

4

AT THE YUCATÁN DETENTION CENTER

It was early March 1974. I was still living with Ricardo on Eighteenth Street, and he was using my ex-husband's name. We thought it was a good cover for him.

I was still in touch with Toño. One day Gustavo Ruz didn't show up at the scheduled meetings and he didn't send contacts. Toño and I started to get worried. I went to see Toño on the morning of March 17th. We called a compañero's home where Gustavo had been living. He set a meeting for four o'clock in the afternoon at a soda fountain called "La Ruca," which is on Nueva de Matte Street, near the intersection with Independencia Avenue.

Soon after we got there I realized we were going to be arrested. Through the windows in the door, I saw our compañero walking toward us between two men. All I managed to say to Toño was, "We're screwed! Remember, I'm carrying a fake ID and my name is Isabel del Carmen Romero Contreras."

Toño managed to repeat that name. Everything happened quickly. One of the agents came over to us. Threatening us with a revolver, he practically threw us against the wall, yelling at us to put the palms of our hands up against the wall and to spread our legs wide. I turned my head a bit and I could see that one agent was searching my purse while the other made a phone call. I was happy not to be carrying any arms. A police van arrived minutes later from the Fifth Precinct, which is where they drove us. In the van, they tied our hands and blindfolded us.

That is when I realized I wouldn't be able to keep the promise I had made to my son that morning, that I would be home early to make a cover for his schoolbook and sew his name in his shirt. The following day was going to be his first day of school.

At the police station, I gave them the information from the ID card that "Momio" had made for me. I knew they would soon realize that it was phony, but I decided I wasn't going to just tell them my name. They came to interrogate me several times about Toño and insult me. I decided to follow the version of the story that we had talked about once. I was cold. Given the stench, it seemed like we were in the precinct's cells. I tried to think about what I was going to say. Since it was Sunday, my guess was that they would verify my address the following day and that then they would know I wasn't Isabel. I would have time until then. I tried to imagine what Toño could be saying.

I had cut my hair, but I was wearing a wig that day. It helped me for a while so that the police wouldn't recognize me since the precinct was near my parent's house. I thought about my son a few blocks away, unaware of what was happening to me. I remembered the weapons I had in my bedroom closet, and I knew that I would have to endure at least three days before telling them my name so that my brother would realize that I had been detained and would get rid of everything. I couldn't run the risk of having them find the weapons at my parents' house.

Lost in thought, I remembered one by one the instructions from the different manuals that compiled information from parties with years of experience in clandestine life. I couldn't help thinking about all the blood, tears, and pain, all the shattered lives behind the pages in each one of those manuals.

I told myself over and over, I have to stay calm. Suddenly I heard voices, and shouting from someone who was getting closer. "Stand up, cunt!" They pulled me so hard by the sleeve of my blouse that it tore.

"Didn't I say 'stand up!' Full of shit communist," said the man hitting me on the shoulder. I felt pain and thought, "This is serious, I'm going to scream a lot" and I started to yell. I knew my blouse was torn and that my hands were tied behind my back. I felt a blow to my stomach and something escaping from within. It wasn't a real scream, more like air violently leaving my body. Someone kicked me from behind. Now there were two of them, although I hadn't heard anyone else enter. But it didn't hurt. I guessed they were wearing soft shoes, which made me think they were civilians. I heard they were going to take me somewhere else and I trembled. Was it the DINA? I started to panic. I started saying to myself: I have to erase Ricardo from my mind. I remembered that that night we were going to have Chinese food for dinner with my parents. I stood still. My wrists hurt as well as an elbow that I couldn't

36

avoid falling on because my hands were tied. I had also hit my forehead. I pretended to faint. I felt like smiling even under these conditions because my wig was firmly in place.

I remember them yelling at me to move forward. I refused. I don't know why, but I thought they would put me in something full of water and that I would die of suffocation. I knew I wasn't getting anywhere by resisting, but I couldn't avoid disobeying, even though they beat me.

The journey that began moments later would last many years. . . . I felt the truck entering a closed area. I heard a noise. I was surprised since it was the just like the screeching noise from the gate at 38 Londres Street that had housed the Socialist Party's Eighth District. In fact, the location that had once belonged to the Socialist Party was now serving as a detention center the DINA called Yucatán. Now the address is number 40 and it's the headquarters of the O'Higgins Institute. My blindfold had shifted with all their punching and pulling as they took us out of the truck. Some tears got the tape wet and I could see the black and white tiles beneath me. Then I was sure. It was 38 Londres Street. They pushed us, and I heard several young men's voices. One of them said "Sergeant! Two more have arrived!" I felt a slight brush against my left arm and I knew that Toño was standing beside me. That gesture felt to me like a "here I am."

"Search the asshole! What's "yer" name?"

"Samuel. . . ."

"Your full name, idiot! Name and surname!"

"Samuel Antonio Houston Dreckmann."

"Spell your last name." I heard Toño, softly, slightly hoarse, with the kind of voice that comes from a dry throat, start to say, "H . . . O . . . U . . . S . . ."

"Address. . . ."

While Toño was giving them his information I was trying to remember mine from the ID. . . . I remember "Momio" had told me, "One, two, skip the next two, five, and six." That was my address, Carmen 1256. I thought about Ricardo.

"Is little Samuel clean?" Someone asked.

"Yes, sir, only keys, some coins and. . . ."

"Now the woman. Hurry up lazy ass, get undressed. . . ." I was dumbfounded, disconcerted, and I heard another one say, "Didn't you hear him? Start taking off your clothes or I'll rip them off you." I only managed to say, "I'm tied up." They untied my hands.

37

"Are you gonna get undressed or not? Look, I don't like it when bitches get smart."

"But that's better so I can take it off you," said another guard.

They tore off my blouse, while another one pulled down my pants. I tried to avoid it but soon I was naked and I heard someone saying, "Search her. These bitches hide things in their cunts!"

They held me tight and one man tried to pry open my legs. I managed to bite the hand that had me by the neck, but then I got hit in the face and I fell to the ground while someone put his fingers in my vagina. I started screaming. They let me go, and they said they would get to me soon enough, that they had all night for that. I gave my false identification and they took me to a chair they put in the tiny basement. I tried to get into my pants and to cross my blouse, tying the two ends around my waist to cover myself before they tied me up again, this time to the chair.

I had just heard eleven bells ring from the Church of San Francisco when someone said slowly, "Get up. I'm taking you with me. My superior wants to talk to you." I let myself be led, feeling the insecurity of someone who has never walked without being able to see. The man indicated the way, the stairs, where to turn, etc. Once we got to the room I realized that there were more people there. Without saying anything at all they threw me on a mattress and they raped me. Several men. At first I tried to resist. I tried to keep them from taking off my clothes, and I kicked blindly. Later on the floor, and with the weight of those individuals on top of me, their putrid breath, I ached inside as if they had broken me, with a pain in my whole body. I am crying. I don't have any strength anymore. I only sense that I am something thrown down there that is being used; that if I resist it's like a stimulus, and that if I remain still, if I drift mentally to other places, it seems to be less of an incentive for them. I am a dismembered doll. Two men hold my legs while they touch me. My mouth is gagged with a dirty rag that keeps going down my throat, making me nauseous, first one, then another, then another. . . . I am a single, huge mass of growing nausea. I am overcome, and I vomit. I can't expel the vomit that hits the gag and comes back in. It drowns me, more vomit. I can't breathe. Something warm overwhelms and suffocates me.

I am just beginning to learn how to die. They continue on top of me, and I feel my body shaking spasmodically and someone says, "Sir, something's wrong with her." I don't remember anything else, just that before I lost consciousness someone said, "The bitch vomited."

I awoke with my pants on, without any underwear. My wig was still on my head. . . . I wasn't blindfolded or tied down. I remembered the previous hours, and I cried silently. I heard the familiar sound of the bells ringing from the Church of San Francisco again. I felt lost right in the middle of downtown Santiago. I drew in my legs and hugged them, hiding my face. I wanted to take up as little space as possible. I felt lost, more abandoned than ever. I thought about how it was March 18th and that that the sun was probably rising. Soon the city would begin to stir. My son was now the child of an absent mother. He would go to school that morning without me, and who knows how many more times. . . . That thought made me react. I was still alive, and I had been free until just hours before. I had a lot to live for. . . . "I am Isabel," I told myself while I tried to erase what had happened that night, meticulously going over my story with an almost obsessive determination.

I started hearing noises, and someone came for me. I don't know why, but I didn't look at the guy, perhaps with the hope that not seeing him would mean he didn't exist. He blindfolded me again, and he took me to the basement. I sensed more people arriving, and I tried to find out if Toño was there or not. I started to cough. I needed him to make a sound, something that would allow me to feel him close by. I heard orders to go search some place. Surely they were talking about our residences. Toño had given his mother's address. I started feeling cold, and I was scared.

I heard a frightening scream, the first of many that would forever invade my mind. It was Toño. They had him upstairs already. I barely finished hearing the dull scream that all tortured humans recognize, and that you never forget because there is nothing like it, when he screamed again. I felt his pain as though it were my own. I felt all the hair on my skin stand on end, and a pain tore through me that paralyzed my thoughts and froze my entire body. There were some really monstrous beasts there. I felt like I would go crazy. I clenched my fists so hard that I dug my fingernails into the palms of my hands. When I remembered Ricardo, I felt a new sense of strength. I was able to collect my thoughts by repeating: "Ricardo doesn't exist. None of my friends from the MIR exist. My superior doesn't exist, nothing, only these beasts." My body was curled up and shaking.

Soon they came for me. I realized it a few minutes before when I sensed that the men who had gone to search my phony address had arrived. They picked me up and took me to the bathroom with

39

aquamarine tiles, which is where they had Toño. They started beating me. They took my clothes off again, and they put me in a chair. I heard them applying the electric current to Toño's anus, and I felt my friend writhing in pain on the makeshift table where they would put us. The one who gave the order was the same one who then said:

"The dirty asshole shit on himself. Let him eat it."

They began to interrogate me. I said what we had agreed I would.

"Sir, I met him just a little while ago in the street. His name is Toño. It's true. He asked me to have a drink with him. That's where we were when all of you came and arrested us."

Toño insisted that I didn't have anything to do with anything, which they never believed because they already knew I had given them a phony address, and they guessed my name and my ID were fake too. They took Toño out and they applied electric shock to me. They filled my mouth with a rag and tied me up. They told me to lift a finger when I was ready to talk. This happened several times. I don't know how many. There were two questions: What is your name? and Where is Miguel? . . . They were referring to Miguel Enríquez Espinoza, the MIR's general secretary. In spite of the agony that made me writhe in pain over and over, I thought they were really stupid to ask me about Miguel. After all, they hadn't even asked us what party we belonged to. Later I told myself that maybe they just wanted to terrorize us.

They tortured me over and over. They took me up and down the stairs. They carried me around like a dead weight, and several times I thought that I would get lucky and break my back when the electric current arched my body. I hoped that the heart defects that interrupted my athletic career would reappear and that I would die. I didn't die. I regained consciousness over and over again. I assumed that I was still alive and I tried to be conscious of the days and the hours to know when to stop that torture and tell them my name.

One morning I was sure that sufficient time had passed. Just when they were about to take my fingerprints, I raised one of my fingers and said: "My name is Luz Arce."

They took me downstairs, and they tied me to a chair in the tiny basement. When the team arrived that had gone to search my parent's house, one of the agents put a blanket over my shoulders. Mom had sent it. I could smell her perfume on it. I heard them say that they hadn't found anything at the house. A few hours later they transferred me to another detention center, Tejas Verdes.

40

5

TEJAS VERDES

I could smell the ocean for a long time during the trip, and images of it filled my thoughts. I took a deep breath and wondered, "Are they going to throw us in the ocean?" I was cold in spite of the blanket, and I thought I was going to die. I realized that even when you want to die, being close to death makes your skin crawl. Would I drown? Would I die from a bullet wound?

The truck stopped, and someone helped us get out, that is if you can call it helping when they're yanking you. They lined us up against a wall. I stood there in pain, blindfolded, tied-up, dirty, and I could feel the cement wall behind me. I told myself they would fire, imagining a firing squad. . . . I started to call to mind the image and faces of my loved ones. I thought I would remember them for the last time. They called roll.

"Fifty-three."

"Present, sir!"

"It's Toño," I thought to myself.

"Fifty-four."

"Present." They were referring to me. I was DINA prisoner number fifty-four.

They continued until they were finished. I don't remember how many more of us there were. I didn't even see them, neither at 38 Londres Street, nor during the trip.

I didn't know where I was. All my senses registered was the smell of the ocean, and I was filled with a desire to die. I had the sensation of being empty. I imagined myself pale and disoriented, and dirty, very dirty.

Someone shoved me to one side and said, "Walk!"

I was getting used to walking without fear, even though, just for fun, the guards would often give us directions to make us fall down or crash. By now I had noticed that showing fear was like a stimulus for them to amuse themselves even more.

"Step up."

It was a stair.

"Open!"

It was a wooden door. I was shoved over to the other extreme of the enclosure,. I felt someone moving, trying to keep me from falling on top of her. Several hands tried to support me. They slid a bolt shut and I heard someone say, "Number fifty-four is ready and locked up."

The very soft voice of a woman said to me, "Take off your blindfold."

I heard the sound of water, but it wasn't the ocean. It seemed like a river that made the air feel wet and cold.

I took off my blindfold. Eight women looked like they were emerging out of some strange darkness. Disheveled and thin, they looked even more gaunt in the light of a tiny bit of candle. "We are sorry you're here, but if that's how it has to be, welcome."

"Hi," I said, sitting down. At the same time I recognized "Patricia." My eyes must have lit up because she made an almost imperceptible gesture asking me to keep quiet.

"What's your name?"

"I looked again at those faces, one by one. Sad faces, questioning faces, faces of silence."

"My name is Luz. Luz Arce."

"When were you detained?"

"On the 17th.

The candle was flickering, and air was coming in through the walls. It was cold. I tied my blouse together and wrapped myself up in the blanket. One of the women banged at the door.

"What's that matter, you pieces of shit! Shut up or you're going to wake the dead!" someone yelled outside.

"The new arrival needs to go to the infirmary."

I curled up in the exact place where I had fallen. Patricia came over to me. I knew her. She was married to "Quila," a member of the MIR's leadership.

She came closer and said slowly, "I don't know who everyone else is, so it's better if we don't know each other."

"Don't worry."

"Did they get anything out of you?"

42

"My name."

"Were you detained with a fake ID?"

"Yes."

"Don't say anything here. We only live from one day to the next, and I don't trust some of them."

I am trying to relive that moment. I can even see myself, but I think all I wanted to do was sleep, close my eyes, and stop existing.

The door opened and someone shouted, "The new one, out here!"

I didn't want to answer. I didn't want to stand up. I didn't want anything. I just stayed there, dazed, staring. I didn't feel sorrow or pain. . . . Nothing. Someone helped me stand. I walked but the exhaustion and the stress made me unsteady. I could barely hold myself up. The soldier took me to the infirmary, and they lay me down on a cot. A nurse was looking at me. She seemed really out of place there, like she was from another planet. She looked like one of those beautiful young women from a Hollywood film: blonde with big blue eyes, makeup, and an olive green uniform. She opened what was left of my blouse and helped me take off my pants. I felt dirtier than I had ever been in my life. The nurse sent a soldier to get some water. They brought in some buckets, and she started to wash me. My whole body burned. I had scrapes and burns on my skin, especially on my breasts, my stomach, my genitals, and in my pubic area. I was still bleeding. It was as if I had a really heavy period.

"Did they use electric shock on you?" the nurse asked.

I didn't answer. I thought it could be a trap. They gave me two injections and made me swallow a couple of pills. One was a sedative because I fell asleep afterwards. She put an enormous wad of cotton between my legs and said: "Wash your pants. If you hang them out in the wind they will be dry in the morning."

I tried to speak. I wanted to thank her, but all that came out was a strange moan. My eyelids were heavy. The nurse smiled and said, "Take it easy, sleep. They won't come for you tonight, I think!"

"Her mouth and tongue are broken!" said another nurse as they dressed my wounds.

I awoke in the cabin. Everyone was asleep, and I heard some snoring. "Patricia" sat down beside me. "Are you feeling better?"

"Yes, much better. Did someone take my clothes?"

"Yes, one of the girls washed them."

"Did they put some underwear on me?"

43

"Yes, the nurse gave them to you. You didn't have any underwear when you got here."

"They must be at 38 Londres Street."

"Where?"

Crouching, almost whispering in her ear, I told her that I had recognized the detention center since it had belonged to the Socialist Party's Eighth District before the coup. "Patricia" talked to me about her husband, and she said that she was worried about her sheets. They were brand new, and she had left them at home—"soaking in bleach," she added in a very serious tone. As I listened to her, I experienced an irreproducible feeling of tenderness. It seemed funny that she would be worrying about her sheets under those circumstances. I felt very close to her. The cold air and the first light of dawn were filtering in through the cracks in the cabin. Patricia told me to try to sleep.

I curled up more by her side trying to sleep. I thought it would be nice to be able to take a shower, but is there any kind of water capable of washing away such horrific memories?

I awoke to the sounds of the changing of the guard. A little while later, they opened the door. It was Tomasito, a tall soldier with a dark complexion, a square forehead, and big hands. He looked tough, but he was really sweet. "Okay, girls, here are eight jars and eight pieces of bread."

"Hey, Tomasito, there are nine of us! This is Luz."

He added another jar and another piece of bread. When he left, they told me he gave them cigarettes after breakfast. He seemed like a nice person.

"Oh, girls, the fact is that I don't know how to be tough on women," he would tell us. "It would be like hitting my mother. That must be awful! And I don't even have a mother, just you, my beautiful girls," and he laughed again. He looked at my face and said, "My, what an ugly bruise! Do you want some aspirin or would you rather have something to help you sleep?"

"No," I managed to say, until someone pinched my arm.

"Yes, Tomasito, bring her all you can. She didn't sleep at all."

They explained that they put all the pills together and that they took several at a time before the interrogation sessions. During breakfast they started telling me about the routine at that prison camp. At about ten in the morning, they started taking us to the bathrooms, which were actually just some outhouses with black holes in the ground that were dirty, smelly, and full of worms. But you ended up getting used to everything.

44

There were seven cabins at that time. Two were for women and five were for men. Walking made me feel better. When we returned, they took me out of line. The nurse dressed my wounds again, and she gave me more cotton since I was still bleeding. I told her I hadn't been able to sleep, and she handed me a whole bunch of pills. Our stash at the cabin would grow even larger.

I felt better after I returned. I knew they were going to interrogate me again sometime. I had to keep my spirits up. If I sat around waiting, not only would time crawl by slowly and monotonously, but I would be trapped in the anguish of someone who knows that torture is coming, which is worse than torture itself. Before the soldier closed the door, I asked him who was in charge of that place and to tell him I wanted to speak with him.

The soldier left saying that he would talk with the lieutenant. It surprised me that he didn't even ask me why. Maybe no one had ever asked him that, and maybe he hadn't realized that he could make a decision, I thought. He was just trained to take things one place or another and to follow orders.

The officer arrived a few minutes later. He had a dark complexion, stiff black hair, and olive-green eyes. I would see him again years later at DINA Headquarters, and he wouldn't recognize me. But I recognized him. His face was forever etched in my memory. Perhaps it was because he was the first DINA officer who spoke to me without hiding his face.

I asked him to let us clean the cabin, and I said that we wanted to exercise in the morning, just like the men. At the end of the conversation we asked if we could have mass on Sundays. The officer authorized the cleaning and the exercise. Regarding mass, he told us to go to hell.

After a while, a soldier came with a broom. We shook out the mattresses and blankets, we swept, and, without realizing it, someone started to sing. Pretty soon we were all singing the songs we remembered. Most of them were from the Spanish Civil War. When we finished, we looked at the result: the cabin was clean. But we had really only moved the dirt from one place to another. Now we had it in our hair, on our skin, in our eyelashes. We were all laughing. I looked in my purse where there was a tiny mirror. Some of the women looked in their things and found eyebrow pencils and mascara. We sat down in a corner and shared our makeup. We combed our hair and realized we could still laugh. We were still alive.

"And now what?" someone asked.

I asked, "Have you read *Historias de cronopios y de famas* by Julio Cortázar?" and then we entertained ourselves remembering.[21]

One day I got a page from a notebook and drew a map of the camp. Then I wrote: "Please pass this from cabin to cabin, it's for Toño." I folded it until it was transformed into a little ball. Two girls held hands so I could stand on them to reach the tiny hole in the wall and throw the note toward the cabin that was next to ours. I never knew if Toño received it.

They didn't interrogate me at Tejas Verdes. At noon on March 27th, before lunch, they told me I was leaving. I thought I was going to be interrogated so I took several sleeping pills and gave the rest to "Patricia." We said good-bye with a big hug. Upon leaving, they put tape over my eyes and tied my hands. As I was walking to the vehicle, I heard the girls in the cabin singing: *"Free, like the wind that blows. . . ."*

21. Julio Cortázar (1914–84), an Argentine, was one of the most famous twentieth-century Latin American writers. His book *Historias de cronopios y de famas* (1962) is a collection of short stories. It was translated into English by Paul Blackburn in 1969 as *Cronopios and Famas*.

6

MILITARY HOSPITAL (HOSMIL)

The truck set off toward Santiago. I remember little about that trip, only that I was nauseous. They gave me some coffee when we arrived at 38 Londres Street, and for several hours different people interrogated me about my personal life and urged me to tell the truth about my political participation.

I accepted their accusations in silence, but insisted that everything was a mistake, that I wasn't a militant, and that my only crime was that I had started dating a guy. They also asked me about the fake ID, about why I had it if it was phony, and about who had given it to me. I repeated the same thing over and over, but they kept insisting with their absurd questions: "What papers?" "Where did they give it?" "From whom?" Later another person came to ask how I could get involved in this mess when I had such a beautiful son and family. I kept denying everything.

All of a sudden I heard noises that sounded like two or more people fighting. There were shouts and insults, and then there was a metallic sound like a weapon falling to the floor and a bang. A split second later I felt something go through my foot. It didn't hurt, but the sensation was like a hot knife slicing through a stick of butter. I thought, "They shot me. That was a gun." And then I yelled but mostly from the shock. I curled myself up in a ball with my forehead against my knees. They laid me down on the cement floor in that tiny basement and left.

I don't think I ever lost consciousness. I remember that I could feel my foot swelling and that I was colder and in more pain as time went on. I tried to relax, and with a sad sense of relief I thought I was going to bleed to death. When several minutes went by and I was still alive, I realized that the bullet hadn't ruptured any arteries. I could feel my foot

47

was wet, but there was no hemorrhage. My veins had clotted after bleeding a while.

I was shocked. I thought the wound would get infected. A feeling arose from some remote place in my childhood memories that was neither resignation nor hope, just a very profound sorrow. I would have liked to know for certain that God existed. "If you exist, take me, please; free me from this madness, from this pain." I said this and then I immersed myself in memories of my son. I decided just to focus on him for as long as I stayed conscious. How I longed to see him and give him a kiss, a caress, or tell him "I love you."

I heard voices coming closer, and they asked me my name. Since I was blindfolded, it was easy to pretend I had fainted and not respond. I heard an argument, and someone who seemed like the officer on duty said he didn't want to be responsible for my dying there. They came and went several times. It sounded like they made some telephone calls. Then someone wrapped me in a blanket and they carried me. I let myself be carried like a dead weight. I thought they would throw me out of the truck somewhere, but when the truck stopped, I heard, "Take her blindfold off. She's going to know she's at the Hosmil anyway. . . . And you, missy, listen, I'm taking a risk myself by bringing you to the hospital, so you keep your snout shut. Don't say anything. Got it? Nothing. I'll take care of everything."

I just looked at him. What could I say?

"Take her out carefully. If she dies on us here it's going to be even worse."

"Sir, I told you we should just leave her somewhere. Now we're in a mess."

"Shut up. I'm in charge here."

And turning to me he added, "And, you, don't forget! Keep your mouth shut!"

I was really beaten up. I couldn't feel my face because it was so swollen. It was inflated like a balloon. My tongue still hurt. It felt like it didn't even fit in my mouth from all the electric shock. I felt a sharp pain in my right ear, but I was emotionally still in one piece. I didn't feel frightened. The more they beat me the stronger I felt. Filled with rage and determined to resist, I felt safe thinking that the only thing that could happen to me was that I could die.

Suddenly, without realizing it, I felt like everything was spinning, like everything was turning around me. I heard myself say, "Hit me, faggot! You sons of bitches, no woman could have ever given birth to shit like you." And I heard them say again, "Where is Miguel? Raise a finger when you want to talk!" And they stuck their fat, dirty, disgusting fingers into my mouth to remove the bloodied gag. And then another gag, and everything started all over. What they never knew was that I didn't have any way of knowing anything about Miguel Enríquez.[22]

Or maybe they did know and they were just "softening me up."

I woke up like I had violently plummeted to earth. My foot hurt. I had been having nightmares about the interrogation sessions from the previous days. A nurse came over and said, "What is your name? Tell me. . . . What is your name?"

Without answering, I opened my mouth so she could see my tongue.

"Her tongue is swollen, doctor."

The nurse added, "I don't think she can talk, doctor."

The doctor came over to me and started explaining what was happening with my foot. At one point he said, "You're Luz Arce, right? I am Doctor Dragicevic, Cecilia's brother. Do you remember her? She's an athlete at the Stade Français.

Yes, I remembered Cecilia. She was younger than me. The doctor made me feel I could trust him. I realized he didn't have a clue about political prisoners or the DINA, so I told him I wasn't allowed to talk.

"I understand. Just rest. I'm going to give you a tetanus shot. It's not going to hurt." I smiled. How was a little needle going to hurt me after so much pain? Months later I would feel the same way when I had to give Christian Mallol or "Tano" injections of antibiotics.

"Doctor, may I see my foot?"

He came over to me and helped me sit up. It looked like a flower had bloomed out of my right foot, a huge red camellia of skin, bones, and tendons. "Luz, I'm going to go scrub before going to surgery. I want you to rest, but remember, don't fall asleep. I need you to be conscious for the anesthesia. The trauma specialist is on his way."

The nurse started to wash my face and hands. She took off my clothes, and I felt embarrassed. I was so dirty! She put one of those long gowns

22. Following the coup in 1973, Miguel Enríquez Espinosa, the MIR's general secretary, led the party's clandestine operations. In the DINA's desire to annihilate the MIR, Miguel Enríquez became a key target, virtually an obsession. When the DINA finally discovered his location after arresting several important members of the organization, they shot him to death on Saturday, October 5, 1974.

on me, the ones that look like a priest's vestment and that tie on the side, and she took me to the operating room.

Doctor Dragicevic injected the anesthetic into the IV solution that they had put in my left hand. Then he put a mask over my mouth and said, "Luz, count backwards from one hundred."

"Ninety-nine, ninety-eight, ninety-seven. . . ."

I awoke in a pretty room. There were three people there. Instinctively, I closed my eyes trying not to show that I had regained consciousness. I was in a lot of pain. My whole leg ached. I tried to reconstruct mentally what I had been able to see: my foot up in the air in some kind of metal sling, probes and drainage tubes hanging from my foot where blood was dripping into some containers. My leg felt stiff. They had put a cast on me up to my knee. I found out later that it was a kind of cast with openings around the wounds.

I paid attention and tried to listen, but a much stronger inner feeling told me: "You are alone, alone in a corner, as always alone and in the shadows. . . ." It frightened me. Was I going crazy?

"I'm sorry, but she is a patient here, and she's not leaving until the attending physician discharges her."

"But, major, I have orders to take her back to the barracks right away."

"I'm sorry. She's not leaving this hospital until she has been discharged. Tell your superior to contact me."

"But, major, your patient, as you call her, is a criminal, and it is my responsibility to make sure she doesn't get away."

"Don't be stupid. The patient cannot even get out of bed, and there's an armed guard a few feet away. . . ."

I couldn't help but shudder at the thought of returning. . . . I had to try my best to stay there as long as possible. I heard approaching footsteps. Someone uncovered me a little and shook my shoulder. It was a young man, about 25 years old, thin, with a dark complexion and straight black hair. (Later, from November 1974 until 1975, I would see him again as an agent assigned to the DINA's special intelligence units: Purén, BIM, Terranova/Villa Grimaldi.)[23]

---

23. The DINA's structure was composed of several military units whose names generally referred to the locations and names of detention centers. The Metropolitan Intelligence Unit (BIM, Brigada de Inteligencia Metropolitana), was in charge of some of the DINA's most important clandestine centers, including Terranova, also known as Villa Grimaldi, in Santiago. Arce refers to this unit frequently in the following chapters since it was assigned to Villa Grimaldi, where she was held after her second arrest.

The young man asked me, "Do you know a 'Gloria'?"

I realized they had discovered my letter to Gustavo that was hidden in the cover of the book I was carrying when they arrested me. The note was mine. In it I was asking Gustavo Ruz when I would start my work in the shantytowns. I started to answer with a vagueness that seemed logical for someone who isn't a militant, "Yes, sir, I know several people with that name."

"Do they belong to the Socialist Party?"

"I don't know, sir, I haven't seen some of them for a long time."

"And where did you meet them?"

"Well, in high school I had a friend who. . . ."

I was abruptly interrupted, "Look, we're already onto you so you can stop with your stories. I want to know who 'Gloria' is in the Socialist Party."

"I don't know, sir. I've already told you that I don't belong to any party. I don't know anything about politics."

"Let's see, take this. . . ."

He gave me a pencil and a notepad and added, "Write your name."

I thought they would try to see if my handwriting was the same as in the note so I decided to alter it as much as I could. I tried to sit up. My head felt heavy and my hand hurt a lot. I hadn't realized that the IV was now connected to my right hand. That helped me alter my writing even more.

I laid my head in the pillow, and huge drops of sweat ran down my back. I closed my eyes, determined to avoid more questions. Right then an army health sergeant entered the room. A few days later I found out he was Sergeant Cabello, "Sorry, but I have orders from my major. The lady cannot have visitors. And the doctor is coming any minute." The man showed the sergeant something that to me looked like his credentials.

"I'm sorry, but these are my orders. You will have to leave. Go talk to the major." He came over to me. "How do you feel?"

"A little sore, especially my foot and this hand."

"Try to be patient. I'm going to wash you, and then the doctor will come."

I felt more comfortable. He began monitoring my vital signs just in time when the doctor arrived.

The doctor was a young man, a trauma specialist, Doctor Elgueta. He was very polite. I asked him to explain what was going on with my foot.

When they brought my breakfast I was really surprised: tea with milk, soda crackers, and cheese. It was quite an event!

The date was March 28, 1974. A young man dressed in civilian clothes came in that afternoon and told me that, from then on, I would have a guard on duty in my room, besides the guard outside in the hallway.

OTHER PRISONERS AT THE HOSMIL

I started learning the Military Hospital's routine. I was on the third floor. My neighbors were Osvaldo Puccio (senior) and Julio Palestro. They had been brought from the detention center at Dawson.

I decided to be patient and to respond to everything they asked. That way I would be able to obtain information and have a clearer understanding of my situation. Besides, I had to find a way to let someone know I was there. Everybody was asking me hundreds of questions: the guards from the DINA, the guards in the hallway who were conscripts from the Cavalry School at the Quillota Army Academy, the officers in charge of those guards who generally were army lieutenants, and nurses and other personnel from the Military Hospital. I had other worries, however. I was afraid that Osvaldo Puccio would recognize me, and that he would unwittingly let something slip about my time in the GAP. But Osvaldo always acted like he didn't know me. On one occasion, when we were able to talk alone in my room, we talked about that period, about him, and about his son. That day I took the opportunity to thank him for all the kindness that he, his wife, his sister, and Mr. Palestro had shown me.

Osvaldo Puccio and Mr. Palestro had visitors, and they started helping me as soon as they realized I was there. Mrs. Puccio brought me pajamas, underwear, two wool vests, and a beautiful green coat that accompanied me through all my future stays in detention centers. For my birthday they sent me a huge piece of meringue and cream cake with strawberries and a glass of grenadine.

Day after day I was learning the routine at the Hosmil. I knew every sound. That was how I could determine the exact time of day, the changing of the guards, the nurse's shifts, the doctor's visit, bath or medication times. I remember that any change in the routine made me feel uneasy. A new feeling of insecurity started taking root within me, a fear of the unknown.

The fact that this hall was the area reserved for political prisoners was

52

clear from the absence of female nurses and the presence of an enormous machine gun, a ".30 caliber" behind the screen separating us from the rest of the third floor. There was also a sizable military contingent on guard.

In the testimony I gave before the Truth and Reconciliation Commission I spoke of a young man who had been brutally tortured and whose fingernails had been ripped from his hands. I didn't know his name. Today I know who he is and a little bit more about his story. Of course it is as harsh and painful as the experiences of many others, but since I haven't asked for his permission to publish it, I'm just going to call him Nelson. I mentioned him to the Commission in an attempt to identify him because for years I was afraid he had died. Thank God he was able to survive, although he lost part of two of his fingers because of the torture.

They justified the show of military personnel and arms by alleging that those of us imprisoned there were dangerous. In spite of the macabre nature of the situation, that argument made me laugh. I can imagine what a sad spectacle Osvaldo Puccio, Mr. Palestro, and I would have presented if we had tried to escape. They were both recovering from myocardial infarction, and I had just had surgery and couldn't even get out of bed. The other prisoners who arrived later were Nelson, who was young, but whose hands had been impaired, Gonzalo Toro Garland, who to this day remains disappeared, and a Mr. Giacamán, whom I haven't been able to identify. They had both been shot. Gonzalo had been literally perforated by the five bullets in his stomach, his intestines, and his right collarbone. Perhaps the only one who would have tried to escape if he could, Vallavela from the MIR, was tied up, handcuffed, and immobilized. The guard said that he was constantly untying himself and that he had tried to strangle himself with the sheet around his neck by pulling on a sort of tourniquet with his own hands. This event caused quite a commotion among the hospital's paramedical and military personnel.

I was shocked when I heard about it. I frequently saw the image of a man killing himself that way in my dreams. It made me panic to think that he must have been suffocating and that he kept turning the tourniquet. It still makes my skin crawl today just to think about it. That fear felt cold and slimy.

I started feeling pain as if it were a material reality, like an appendage, like another part of my body. I saw Osvaldo get increasingly debilitated as he remained in custody after his heart attack, and Mr. Palestro often had weak vital signs. And Gonzalo was getting thinner right in front of my very eyes. He could only be given saline solution because his stomach had been perforated. I saw his hands, pieces of dead skin hanging over the ends of the cast and falling off in clumps. When I was able to get around more by hopping on my left foot, I went to his side and gently removed his dead skin with some cream. It was like a freak show. We were a collection of isolated beings who had been taken from our places in life. You could say that we were being destroyed day by day in the military hospital. Each second we were there was not like time passing by. Time was only pulling us toward a new encounter with the DINA, toward those other tunnels of horror that awaited us in their camps.

Unlike the others, I was the only one who also had a DINA guard in my room. It was hard for me to believe that they thought I was so dangerous. That's why I thought they were there for reasons other than to keep me from getting away. Perhaps it was to monitor my daily contact with the medical and paramedical personnel, so that no information got out that could put me in touch with the outside world. Even though the hospital personnel belonged to the military, I knew and the DINA also understood that the simple fact of my stay there implied leaving a trail that was difficult for them to control.

Personnel from the Cavalry School at the Quillota Army Academy stood guard in the wing where the prisoners were held in the Military Hospital. It was composed of conscripted soldiers under a second lieutenant's command. They remained on site for twenty-four hours, and the officers made rounds in order to verify whether or not their subordinates were carrying out their duties.

The conscripts from the class of '73 were nineteen or twenty years old and came from sectors around Quillota, Quilpué, Limache and elsewhere. They arrived with minimal academic preparation and conflicts they didn't know how to articulate. Being "the fatherland's soldiers" was not just a source of pride for them. It meant being able to put a roof over their heads and food on the table. From the very first day, I realized they were subjected to a constant onslaught of stories about criminals and marxist whores. They were convinced they had only one alternative: it was either going to be them, along with their families, or us.

With genuine naïveté, several of them came to ask me if it was true that my compañeros and I were going to kill them.

The unlimited trust they had in their superiors surprised me. They

54

saw them as somehow infallible. Often I thought that the soldiers had no choice. How could they question what they were doing? I wondered what would happen if they saw the extent of the contradiction.

For my part, and without falling into "proselytism," I tried to talk to them about what I defined as a humanist outlook on life. In exchange, I got plenty of anecdotes and other stories. These were practically legends in vogue at the Academy. The officers passed them down as humorous stories to their subordinate personnel, about their love affairs, and tales of how numerous ghosts wandered around the grounds of the Academy.

That is how, with a cup of coffee in my hand, I came to understand what kind of world they inhabited, and I saw them as entirely disconnected from daily life, from my life and that of so many others.

I realized that the DINA guards behaved differently. Some of them just came, started their shift, sat in a chair, read magazines, talked with the guard in the hallway, and ignored me. Others asked me questions all day long about my detention and about the statements I had made during the first days. I pretended to sleep and thought hard to try and reconstruct word for word what I had said in order to make my story seem consistent.

My foot bothered me more and more every day. Doctor Elgueta visited me daily to clean and dress the wound. He said the first operation was just for "cleaning," that he took out pieces of bone and muscle that were broken, and that he had put in drainage tubes. The rest was up to my own organism. That is why bony splinters appeared every day, which the doctor took out together with little pieces of skin and tissue that were dying. It hurt a lot even though he cut them very gently with special scissors.

I clenched my teeth and held on to the sides of the bed. Those cleanings were so painful that I started fearing them.

Osvaldo Puccio and Mr. Palestro sent a television over to my room. It was on from the beginning to the end of the daily programming of all the channels that existed at the time. Several of the guards followed the soap operas with interest, and they gave me a nickname from one of them that stayed with me for years, "Lucecita."

CONVERSATION WITH THE ASSISTANT DIRECTOR

On my second day in the Military Hospital, after lunch, I had fallen asleep thinking, but awoke startled. The man who had stopped the

DINA from taking me away right after the operation was at my bedside.

"How are you? I'm Major Silva, the Hospital's Assistant Director. I'm a dentist, and I work with the army. I don't know what you did, but I do want you to know that, while you are here, you are a patient and you will be treated and cared for as such. Do you need anything?"

I was silent. He wasn't going to be able to give me what I needed. He remained standing, quiet and looking at me as if he could hear what I was thinking. I was surprised. It looked like tears were welling in his eyes, but he quickly changed the subject, "What is your name? How old are you?"

"One of these days, Major, on March 31st, I'm going to be 26 years old. And my name is Luz. Luz Arce."

He went to get a chair, and I could only move my head. I thought to myself that he seemed human, but that set off an alarm. Watch out! It could be a trap. I was still a prisoner, and I had been lying.

During the days when I was being held at 38 Londres Street, I felt very violent inside. I transformed every memory and feeling into insults, curses, and attempts to strike back. Many had been kicked and bitten by me. I knew that I would fall apart if I allowed myself to feel anything else.

The major told me it was March 30th. I started remembering what had happened when I was arrested. I remembered my son and how I hadn't been there to take him to school. . . .

"Are you in a lot of pain? Have they given you sedatives?"

"Yes, Major."

"Are you thinking about your husband?"

"No, my son."

"I understand."

I realized that when they treated me well, sadness and memories automatically came to the surface. I had to learn how to control that too. . . .

Before he left the doctor asked, "Luz, would you like a priest to come?"

I wasn't sure. At the Tejas Verdes camp I had asked to have mass, but that was to try and find a space for all the prisoners to be together, and I didn't expect them to say yes. It was mostly just to bother them. Without waiting for my answer, the Major added, "I'll tell the chaplain to come. Don't worry. He's a priest. It will do you good to talk to him. I'm leaving. Excuse me, Luz."

The Major was a gentleman. He was more a fish out of water than I was. I felt like life was nothing but shit.

One afternoon a very young officer entered my room and asked me my name. I told him, and I thought I had seen him somewhere before. He asked me if I knew him. I told him the truth, that I didn't recognize him. Then he reminded me that back when I had been a track and field trainer at the Estadio Italiano, he had been an athlete there. I remembered him then. Years later I found out that he told a woman at the stadium about me, and that she called my mother to tell her that I was being detained there. Up to that day I had simply disappeared as far as my family knew.

Soon they changed my room from number 305 to number 303. I asked the nurse why I was being moved. He told me that I was less dangerous than the "new patients" since I couldn't get out of bed. I didn't know who they were at the time. The guards told me that the new room was where José Tohá had died, but when I saw the closet and the water and heating pipes, I knew that it would have been impossible for Tohá to hang himself in that room.[24]

THE CHAPLAIN AND THE EUCHARIST

The chaplain started visiting me. He was an older priest. He sat down next to me and asked me if I wanted to confess. I said yes without thinking. I had rejected Christianity for many years, but my desire to confess and receive the Eucharist that day was real. I clasped my hands together to pray and looked at the priest. I didn't see his face. All I could see were the two official insignias on the collar of his robe that announced his status as chaplain for the armed forces. I was very frightened. I was afraid he wasn't even a priest, and I immediately said, "Father, I can't speak. You're a military officer."

He was silent for a few moments and said, "I understand, child, I understand. Let's talk about something else if you wish."

I tried not to focus on it, but I was really emotional. My mouth was shut and my throat refused to emit any kind of sound at all. I started to cry. It was the first time something like that had happened to me, and I was afraid.

---

24. José Tohá was a central figure in Salvador Allende's government from 1970 to 1973 where he served briefly in several posts, including as minister of defense, minister of the interior, and vice-president.

The father said very softly, "Would you like to receive the body of Christ?"

I nodded yes, overcoming that strange silence that overwhelms me when I'm scared. "I think so, father, although it's been many years since I've thought about God. I would like to believe in him now. I don't even know what to do to make that happen."

"Have you been baptized, child?"

"Yes, father."

"God loves you, child, and for now that's enough."

I took communion and repeated what the father said. I felt strange. I couldn't accept that God loved me. You certainly wouldn't know it, I thought. I started receiving communion daily. The father would come and sit by my side. He held my hands on several occasions. Little by little I started telling him things, only personal things about my son, my parents.

One day the priest said, "What did you do, child?"

"I'm a socialist, Father."

"Did you kill someone?"

"No, father."

"Did you try to kill someone?"

"No, father."

"Child, did they rape you?"

I didn't answer. My eyes filled with tears, and I knew he guessed the answer.

"Do you know what will happen to you?"

"No, father."

I saw a lot of sadness in his eyes. He never asked anything again. He told me that I should try to arrange for them to take me to mass on Sundays. The chaplain gave a Sunday service for patients on one of the floors. But that depended on the DINA guards. Rodolfo Valentín González was the only one who agreed to take me a couple of times. I started feeling affection for that priest, and I looked forward to his visits. He was a sweet old man. We didn't talk much. He gave me the Eucharist and prayed by my side.

I wasn't quite sure what was happening to me. I just wanted to receive communion and have the priest come every day. The beauty of it all was that something appeared within me like a new friend, Christ, but I didn't see him as I did God. There was a cross on the wall facing my bed, and many times I said silently "You also suffered, didn't you?" That is how I began endless conversations with Him. . . . I felt like I had company.

58

7

NIGHTMARE IN THE BATHROOM

For a long time I regretted my decision to ask the doctor when I could start taking showers. I really just wanted to find out when I would get my foot out of the sling that kept me tied to my bed. I thought that if I could get out of bed, that I would be able to move around by hopping on my left foot. The doctor said he would order me to be taken to the hospital's hydrotherapy tubs.

A sergeant who had finished his duties came to my room and took me to the place where the tubs were located. They were made of cement. The sergeant turned on the water. It was uncomfortable since the sling forced me to hold my foot up in the air, over the edge of the tub. The sergeant started washing me with a huge sponge. I asked him to stop being so rough since I was scraping my elbows on the bottom of the tub, or to shut off the water because it was hard for me to keep my balance.

Without answering, the sergeant put his hand on my chest. Then he started touching me with the other hand, burrowing into my genitalia. I don't know what other women would do in that kind of situation. I started begging for him to stop, but I don't think he heard my pleas. I tried to sit up, to stop his hands with my own. He let go of me for a second, but only to free his penis. He started squeezing my breast again while he masturbated. He pushed my head underwater moments before he ejaculated.

More water entered my mouth and nostrils as I fought him. I felt nauseous like each time I was sexually assaulted, and I ended up vomiting.

I remember the sergeant's disfigured face through the water, and the feeling of suffocation. But above all the impotence, pain, the desire to disappear, to not exist, to be nobody.

It happened several times. I didn't dare tell anyone. I had learned in almost every case that retaliation was worse. The sergeant simply came to my room and said, "The doctor ordered me to bathe you, so I'm bathing you. . . ."

I asked the doctor every day to take off the sling and the drainage tubes so that I could put an end to that new nightmare. At last! They removed everything on Saturday, April 13th. I could put my foot on the bed and even turn it a little. They put a sort of wire mesh over my legs so that my clothes wouldn't touch my foot. Even the sheet brushing against it caused me immense pain. I suffered from hypersensitivity. It lasted for years, and my foot still aches. I noticed I could see the floor through the opening in my foot. The wound began to close little by little.

That was a great day. I asked for a trash bag to cover my foot and leg because of the cast. Then I tied it with a rubber band a guard gave me and started taking showers by myself.

Even though this was all going to end now, I knew that that period would affect my life forever. Today I feel like the hours fly by at lightning speed. There is so much to do and not enough time to do it all. Back then at the Military Hospital, each and every second crawled at a snail's pace. In the midst of uncertainty and fear, I had the opportunity to search my soul like never before. I had no excuses, no reasons, no arguments. None of that seemed to hold any value. I felt like even though I could have had the strength to bend the hand that held me underwater, or the cunning and wisdom to win the kinds of battles that don't require rooks or knights, bishops or pawns, nothing was of any use. It was as if one's own voice could not be heard, as if one didn't exist. I wasn't a person.

There, facing myself, I asked myself many times: "Who am I? What do I think? What's happening?" I realized that in the past, one still so recent, I had a lot of things that were so natural that I couldn't see them. I continued to rummage through my past. I forced myself to examine my relationship with my parents. I was able to feel for the first time how much I loved them, and I was moved. Healthy feelings were emerging from the deepest part of my being, like a river of love, without rational direction, without resentment, only love, uncontrollable love. And it hurt so much.

With the covers all the way over my head, I didn't want anyone to see me or talk to me. I needed to be alone by myself and with my memories. Silent, I was completely drenched in sweat and tears. I began reconciling myself with my feelings. I loved my parents, my son, and my com-pañeros like never before. At the same time, I knew that at a moment like that I couldn't count on anyone. If anything should happen, I had to face it all alone. Grouped according to similarities and differences, memories began collecting, emerging from my mind. I was pressed by a profound need to sort through and control them and to avoid suc-cumbing to a feeling of despair.

It was like an obsession to let out all the pain, even if it meant cry-ing. In that corner full of loneliness and abandonment, my voice rang out saying: "But it all happened already. It's all over. I can . . . I can keep going."

What had happened in the hydrotherapy tubs hurt me and so did what had happened at 38 Londres Street, but I tried to tell myself that worse things had happened, and I had survived.

RODOLFO, AIR FORCE SOLDIER

I can't say exactly how many different men from the DINA stood guard in my room at the Hosmil, but I will never forget Rodolfo Valentín González Pérez, a soldier in the air force who was a recruit from 1973. He is currently listed as one of the disappeared. He was from the Purén Unit of Military Intelligence (BIM). His direct commanding officer was Manuel Andrés Carevic Cubillos, at the time an army major, who was in turn under the command of army major Gerardo Ernesto Urrich González.

From the first day, Rodolfo behaved differently. He was more human, and this manifested itself in small details. He used to ask me how I was feeling. He followed the progress of my healing with interest. He never alluded—like the others—to the criminality of marxist ideology. On the contrary, perhaps because he was worried or because he trusted me, he told me that he had a brother who had sought asylum.

It pains me to have to admit that I didn't believe him. Moreover, I thought it was a dirty DINA trick to get me to reveal my "supposed party affiliations." When he asked for my advice, I told him what seemed honest to me. I suggested that he should tell his superiors his problem, if he knew and trusted them. I thought that it was still good advice even if it wasn't a DINA trick.

Rodolfo asked me if I wanted to contact my family, and he offered to take them a letter. I thought that the natural thing to do would be to accept. I limited myself to writing a short note expressing my affection. That brought me great joy. Rodolfo started going to my parents' house frequently, and they sent me things.

Rodolfo arranged for my family to start walking by on the sidewalk in front of the Military Hospital at three o'clock on Saturday afternoons, on Holanda Street between Providencia and Costanera. It was good to see each other, even though it was from a distance. So that no one would notice, I started to sit by the window at around that time of day. I started drawing the surrounding buildings and trees. My mom and dad went with my aunts and a cousin. They took my son too, but he never knew I was watching him. They were afraid he would cry or yell out for me, and that would have drawn the attention of the hospital guards. He was too little to understand that he could be so close, yet unable to come to my side or have me go to his.

During those days, I found out that Rodolfo was also carrying mail for other prisoners at the Hosmil. He was found out when two of Toro Garland's family members or friends caused a scene. Apparently the personnel on guard that day sided with Rodolfo and the matter never escalated beyond that. However, that supported my theory that Rodolfo kept the DINA informed about these activities.

Much later, when I was an employee at DINA Headquarters in 1976, I worked on organizing the Internal Intelligence archives. There I found a folder with photocopies of all the letters I had sent home. There were several letters from Toro Garland as well. From that day on I hoped that Rodolfo was still alive, but I lost that hope when I testified before the Truth and Reconciliation Commission. There they confirmed that he was also disappeared.

I think Rodolfo began to collaborate with the DINA out of fear, but later on his sensitivity made him get involved and he ended up giving out too much information. That is why they killed him, because he went too far in supporting the prisoners and their families.

Another of Rodolfo's efforts included agreeing to help my brother get into the Hosmil. He told me that Ricardo Ruz Zañartu had been detained in the AGA—the Air Force Academy. He also told me that "Tacho" had gone to the house to find out about my arrest. We talked for a long time since Rodolfo had stayed with the nurse on duty, so the nurse wouldn't go into the room. During the rest of our conversation, approximately twenty minutes to half hour, he told me about my family and my son. In spite of the nervousness I felt when I thought my brother could be caught there, I was truly happy to see him and hug him and listen to him talk about our family.

END OF THE FIRST DETENTION

Toward mid-May I realized that I was getting visibly better, even though the pain was so strong that I could sleep only with sedatives. With each passing day I was afraid they would discharge me. I knew my story was weak. I didn't know what Toño had testified, and I couldn't think of any way to justify the fake ID. They would never accept the truth, that I was a contact for the Socialist Party. My situation was definitely beyond delicate. They would never believe that the MIR had given me the ID just because a friend had requested it. If they agreed that it was Ricardo Ruz, it wouldn't cause any more problems for him because he had already been arrested by the AGA. But they wouldn't believe I didn't know anyone else from the MIR. That was something I could never say.

I knew that moment would arrive, but I decided to try and delay it. I did a number of things: I asked Dr. Elgueta to keep operating on me to help me prolong my hospitalization and to help me get physically stronger to face, as best I could, what was certain to come. The doctor agreed. He started giving me Calcibronat and vitamins and had me undergo another operation, which gave me a little more than a month.

Later on, since they weren't injecting me anymore, and without realizing that what I was doing put me at risk, I started emptying the contents of the antibiotic capsules. I was driven by a single objective: to buy time between the DINA and myself. When it was time to take my medication I just took the empty capsule. I passed my fingers along the sides of the bed and started putting dirt and grease in my wound. It was completely useless. My foot didn't get infected. However, the surgery wasn't effective and almost all the skin they had grafted died, which caused me more pain.

During the week from the first to the fifth of July, the two agents who had captured me came to my room along with the DINA guards. Later I would see them again in Purén de la BIM/Villa Grimaldi. They gave me a questionnaire, and I had to make another written statement. I did it, although I disguised my handwriting.

The moment was approaching. The doctor told me he couldn't postpone my discharge anymore. He brought me quite a bit of Calcibronat as a gift, which would help me stay calm. The countdown had begun.

On July 10, 1974, the doctor told me he had to authorize my release, that all he could do was give me follow-up appointments. The discharge meant that I was ready to continue with outpatient treatment, not that I was healed. It was just a matter of hours.

After a little while, the same policemen from the Purén Unit who had arrested me came and said I was being released. I thought, "Of course, they don't want to leave a trail. So their official version will be that I was released in front of witnesses. . . ."

On the truck, I stared at the streets eagerly, afraid they would take me to another detention center. That didn't happen, and soon I was home. The agents told me that if I chose to leave the house, my family would suffer the consequences. They said they would call to come and take me to my appointments at the hospital.

8

FREEDOM UNDER SURVEILLANCE

I stuck to the story I had given the DINA, hoping they would just accept the fact that I was a kooky chick who didn't know anything about anything. On that 10th of July I hopped around on my good foot and put my belongings in a plastic bag, things that Mrs. Puccio had given me and others my mom had sent. I looked around the room one last time, and I remembered José Tohá. I felt my mouth go dry and my heart start to beat a little faster, "Sir, where am I going?"

"Home. Where do you think?"

"May I say good-bye?"

"Only to the guards and the head nurse. Wait here." They returned with a wheelchair, hospital policy. I remembered the priest. . . .

"May I see the priest?"

"Yes, but make it quick."

I received the Eucharist sitting in the wheelchair. The priest blessed me. The head nurse informed them that they had to stop by the hospital administration to sign some papers. I took advantage of that moment to go to the room next door and say good-bye to Mr. Palestro. The problem with his blood pressure had returned and he was in bed. I said good-bye to Osvaldo Puccio, and he said to me slowly, "Are you sure they're taking you home?"

I told him that that's what they had said but that I wasn't sure. He put two beautifully carved stones in my hands that he had made on his farm on Dawson Island. I put them in the bag and walked away with my eyes full of tears.

A young man on guard in the hall, a soldier by the name of José, came over and said, "Lucecita, take this." Then he took off a very large silver cross from his neck and put it around mine. I tried to tell him not to, that it wasn't necessary, but he just said, "You are not alone. God is with you." I wore that cross until the DINA stole it from me. I felt my eyes full of tears and I closed them. After that all I felt were the swinging doors being opened by my wheelchair bumping into them and then closing behind me. I opened my eyes when we entered the elevator. Time felt like it was rushing by, and with each second I was feeling more and more lightheaded. Seeing the sky and feeling the breeze made me keep crying. They helped me into the truck since I was still wearing the cast with the opening on my foot. I felt nauseated and dizzy from the open space.

I remembered the flowers. Ever since my birthday, one of the nurses, the head nurse whose last name was Delgado, used to bring me flowers once every three days. He was a friend of the owner of the kiosk on the corner of Providencia and Holanda, and he brought the flowers that were still fresh but that could no longer be used in flower arrangements. There were a lot of flowers of every type and color. I spent hours arranging them into two bouquets that I put in the jars they use in the hospital for water. One was for Osvaldo Puccio and Mr. Palestro's room and the other was for mine.

The truck started going west. It was a light yellow C10 truck. I said to myself: "It can't be, it's a trap, my statement didn't explain how I got my fake ID. My explanation isn't even coherent. They can't be that gullible. Maybe they're actually taking me home. Of course there will be some kind of surveillance, in the hopes I'll contact someone from the party. I have to go along with the game. I'll just be with my family, after all, even if it's only for a day or a few hours. I'll be able to see them, hug my son, and tell him I love him."

"Lucecita, you're being very quiet," one of the agents said.

"I'm overcome with emotion, sir." More tears fell from my eyes; I was truly moved seeing the hill, Bellavista, Pío Nono, Perú Avenue. It seemed like we were heading toward my parents' house.

Since my father's retirement, he ran a business, a grocery store, from what had been my house. I entered through that door. My sister-in-law, who was nine months pregnant, saw me and exclaimed: "Wonderful! Now my daughter will be born. . . ." She hugged me first, and then my parents, my brother and my son too, who had just come home from school. We stood there holding each other close, silent. . . . What can you say to a five-year-old child? What is more real than a hug, than a caress? I didn't tire of filling his little head with kisses and he of being by my side holding hands.

I heard the agent telling my father, "Luz's detention was a mistake, as shown by her statements. The bullet wound was an accident, a regrettable accident. But we will see to it that she recovers. Don't worry. She has received the best medical attention available in Santiago. Right, Luz?" The man they called "Brindizzi" shot me a look that made everything perfectly clear.

It was a sunny July day. I was sitting in the dining area, in the veranda my father had built and the sun's rays streamed into the space. I sat by my son and thought: "How many days will they let me stay here?" All the pieces of the puzzle started coming together in my mind. It was like a game of chess, and their final move was more imminent than ever. This was a trick. I was trapped, that much was certain. They would take me to the Military Hospital. I would have to tell everyone there, the doctor, the priest, that I'm free. They know I can only move by hopping. And even if I left the house, I couldn't run away. Then my family would be responsible. They can arrest my father, my brother. . . . I must avoid all political contacts, even with people who just sympathize with the left. I am a live grenade, a danger to anyone who comes near me. Once again, I felt the sensation in my whole body and soul of being alone, like a leper. . . .

I looked at them. Mom insisted on bringing coffee, and they accepted. I thought: "Mom! Please don't insist. Let them go. I may only be able to stay for a few hours." It's sickening how they lie, how they play with my parents' love. All they know is that these are the men who brought me home. What do they know about how they treat us? I just have to keep playing along, even though there isn't even the slightest chance of winning, no chance of real freedom. What is freedom? I looked at my parents. Why can't they see beyond what's right in front of them? Mom opened up a box of cookies and dad brought some more coffee.

Mom, dad. . . . My parents. I remembered my life before my arrest. That life had been severed. Nothing would ever be the same. I was split in two: before my arrest and after. . . . The men were leaving. I was afraid. It seemed like they could tell what I was thinking. As I remembered the first night in Yucatán, I was overcome by a violent nausea and everyone could tell. I stood up and said, "I'm feeling dizzy. I'm sorry. It must be from riding in the truck."

I locked myself in the bathroom and looked at myself in the mirror. My hair had grown and it looked grayer. I made a decision. It doesn't matter. My fate has already been sealed, but at least I can fix some things. Christ, my friend! If you were God, I would say thank you!

Thank you for giving me this opportunity to make amends. Thank you, because I am now going to give my parents and my son all my love. I'll show it, speak it, feel it. The next time I come face-to-face with death I will go without owing anyone love. . . .

I remembered that night when I was feeling such pain, when I had thought how I would love to see my parents, to hug them and tell them I love them very much. . . . I would have given my life at that moment just to be with them. In the Military Hospital it was as if all of a sudden lights and sparks had shot through my head, illuminating the dark moments of my life. Then I was able to see my parents in a different light. I was able to appreciate, almost touch, their sacrifices.

Adita was born on July 11, 1974. She was my first niece, and the reality of birth seemed so beautiful to me. Everything was full of promise, with roads yet to travel, which contrasted with the knowledge that I would only be there for a few days. That seemed to sharpen my senses so that there were times I had to half close my eyes. The light, colors, and trees, the sky, the mountain range all seemed to penetrate my retina, and my mind captured them hungrily. It was an intense explosion of life, color, and warmth. I was possessed by love; it settled itself in my being.

I didn't get tired of saying "Thank you" or "I'm truly able to love my folks." I am greedily filling myself up with the marvelous beauty of my country and the perfume of my son's life. How could I have overlooked this before?

On July 12th they took me to the Hosmil. I remember the exact date because it was the day after my niece was born. I admit I was scared, but I tried not to show it. It was just like I had imagined it. Everybody who knew me came to the Trauma Center waiting room. The employees themselves had told everyone I was there.

All of the soldiers and nurses were saying, "Lucecita is free!" I greeted them. They were good people. Dr. Elgueta took the cast off my foot and gave me some instructions. I was going to have to dress the wound myself. As I was leaving he gave me an appointment for the following week and added, "Luz, are you really free?"

I told him that I had been up to then.

"Luz, if another doctor sees you instead of me, I wish you the best of luck. Really, I hope everything works out for you." Then he shook my hand.

For a minute I thought about sharing my doubts with him. I thought he might understand and that maybe he would help me think through it clearly. . . . No! I had nothing. All I could do was evaluate and accept everything that was happening. I limited my response to "Thank you, doctor. Thanks for everything."

That sergeant who took me to the baths appeared at the door, "Lucecita! I didn't believe it. It is you. So it's true you are free. . . ."

"Yes, Sergeant. I'm free."

I gave him a defiant look. I was afraid and thought, "Psychopath! I don't want to see you!" I tried to fight that memory. I felt waves of heat in my cheeks. I still feel a combination of shame, impotence, and rage. I wanted to say, "Please, doctor, throw him out. Do you know what he did to me?"

I was unable to say anything. For years I never said anything to anybody. I felt so humiliated. I didn't want to accept what had happened. I wanted to erase it. But there it was in my memory, and that moment remained very clear. I couldn't and still can't avoid blushing, I can't bury those memories. . . . He carried me from the stretcher to the bathtub. The only thing I managed to say once was, "Sergeant, why don't you ask a female nurse to bathe me?"

"Because the doctor is the only civilian allowed to see you. Don't worry. How many women do you think I've seen with their clothes off? Don't forget I'm a nurse." But his look seemed to harden. "Listen. Don't yell, or else. . . ." And he pulled me by my good foot. He pressed me down into the tub. The water kept rising, almost covering my cheeks. I was frantic and I closed my mouth. Water started going down my nose. I opened my mouth, more water. I reached out with my hands and tried to remove his, but he put the hose in my mouth. Water started filling my stomach. I swallowed it and felt like vomiting. I was suffocating. Suddenly he took me out of the water, held me, and started to kiss my thighs. I tried to breathe, to speak, to reason, but I couldn't. I wanted him to take away that disgusting mouth that was slithering all over my body and sliding between my legs like a sickening slug. I managed to sit up and grabbed him by the hair. I wanted to get him out of there. The water kept filling the tub. His damned tongue felt so cold, or was I the one who was cold? I kept vomiting water. I started hitting his head with my hands. He stood up. His eyes were red. . . . I started begging him, "Sergeant, please, please, you're hurting me. . . ." Again that face and he started touching me once more, searching for my clitoris with his hands.

"I want you to feel pleasure, did you hear?" he shouted as he bit me.

69

Then, looking at me, he added, "Stay still," as his hands reached my breasts.

"Enjoy it! I want you to see you feel pleasure!"

He bit me. I felt a sharp pain, and blood started flowing from my vulvae. I was crying and I kept begging, "Please, it really hurts."

"Does it really hurt?"

I was silent, petrified. He kissed me and asked me if it hurt. He left me for a second to open the zipper in his pants. Then he dunked me in the tub again and started masturbating. He only asked me again to tell him it hurt a lot, and he threatened to bite me again. He always added, "Careful not to yell! Just say 'it hurts. . . .'"

I repeated it over and over, "It hurts, Sergeant, it really hurts." At first my voice sounded hoarse and broken. Then I started to cry. After that he hugged me and said, "She's crying! My little girl's crying!" And on and on until he ejaculated.

Each of those occasions is imprinted on me. It wasn't just physical pain. I felt defenseless. I was afraid of that man. As a nurse, he was actually competent, attentive, and serious. Then, all of the sudden, he turned into a sadistic beast. I started to understand that he didn't particularly want to hurt me, since if I started begging him, almost crying, or really crying, he didn't even touch me. He just masturbated right away.

In those days I started turning into someone who just tried to struggle through each day with her share of hardship and astonishment. I felt like all men were in some way or other sons of bitches. Not even that. How are dogs to blame? After all, what do dogs have to do with anything?

I remembered all of that while the sergeant was there greeting me. It was almost as if he were happy to see an acquaintance. All I said was, "Yes, Sergeant. I'm free."

"I wish you the best," he said slowly, and he left.

I know I gave him a harsh look, and I thought I saw sadness in his eyes. But I came to my senses, thinking, "Luz, you're a stupid shit. What does that sadistic faggot matter to you? . . . ."

I returned home. Everyone at the hospital was convinced of my freedom. It was a step that brought me closer to what would take place. The days went flying by, faster than I would have liked. While I was at home I kept myself busy helping my mother in the kitchen. I tried to make things everybody liked: cake and cheese turnovers for July 15th, which was my father's and my brother's saint's day. . . . My son looked happy.

When I came home I went to the convent where the Santa Luisa de Marillac nuns lived, which was right across the street. They knew me from the time I was a little girl. I saw Sister Rosita, and she told me that another sister from the congregation was working in the Pro-Peace Committee.[25]

I didn't dare confess my doubts to her, and she must have thought that I had been released once and for all.

As she looked at my foot, which was still in a cast, she said, "You must try to forget everything. You have a son. Why don't you come to the school to work as a trainer and teacher? You could start working with us." I accepted. I knew it wouldn't last long, but it was a beautiful way to be with my son even more and to get to know his classmates. I had noticed how important it was for him to introduce me to his friends. His father was far away and practically didn't know him, having left when my son was barely a year old.

On July 13th, Luis Fuentes Riquelme arrived while my parents were gone and my son was at school.

"'Tacho!'" It was my friend.

"Luz!" We held each other for a long time. Then he looked at my foot and said, "Compañera! I love you so much!"

Once we got started, we couldn't stop talking. I asked him to tell me about Ricardo, how they arrested him, what he knew about him. He said they had been able to find out a little, that he had, in fact, been detained by soldiers from the AGA, the Air Force Academy. I told him my doubts about my own situation. He thought for a minute and said, "Let's go! I'll get you out of the country."

"I can't, Tacho. Do you know what would happen to my parents and my brother? They didn't just suggest it. They explicitly said it. I have to

25. The Comité Pro-Paz (Pro-Peace Committee) was an ecclesiastical organization created by the Archbishop of Santiago in October 1973. It was initially established to provide victims of the military coup legal advice. Later it began offering additional support to unemployed workers and defendants in legal cases. Owing to the organization's ties to some members and ideologies from Chile's political parties on the left, the repressive apparatus focused its attention on the Committee's efforts. In 1975, Pinochet himself demanded that the Committee cease its efforts, which occurred on November 27, 1975. However, some members of the Catholic Church, particularly Cardinal Raúl Silva Henríquez, were determined to replace it. This led to the creation of the famous Vicaría de la Solidaridad (Vicariate of Solidarity) late that same year and its official beginning in January of 1976.

71

stay here. I just hope they'll leave me alone when they see I'm not doing anything. My God! Go. I'm sure they're watching, Tacho. For the love of God, go."

My parents came and told him to go. He said he understood, and he hugged me. I didn't know it would be the last time, that we would never see Ricardo again, play chess, go to the pool, study, talk. He left. My friend, my brother. . . .

Even though I didn't want to see anyone who was involved with left-ist political parties, one day the wife of a compañero who lived in the area came to see me. I assured her I hadn't said anything, least of all mentioned them. We talked for a while in front of my father's business. A young man was sitting on the steps leading to the door of the convent, just a few feet away. Later, when I was at Villa Grimaldi, I recognized him there.

9

SECOND DETENTION

On Tuesday, July 23rd, one of my cousins got a student ticket and invited me to a concert given by Narciso Yepes at the Municipal Theater. On the way home, a block and a half away from my house, I realized they were waiting for me.

The sky was pitch black. It was one of those nights when the curve of the universe seems deeper, when you can smell eternity and feel the rhythm of time. For me, both the earth and sky stopped.

I recognized him from about fifty feet away. The young man standing there was a friend of Rodolfo Valentín González Pérez and, like him, he was also a soldier in the air force commissioned to the DINA. I started to walk more slowly and I remembered that he had told me he was married and that he had a baby who was just a few months old. Perhaps he just wants to tell me something, I said to myself.

My mind was racing. I couldn't do anything, not even try to run. Although the doctor had taken my cast off during my most recent checkup, I was limping badly. My wound was still open, and it required daily treatments. All I could do was keep walking toward my encounter with that future. In spite of the cold, I could feel sweat on my forehead. The previous hours resounded once again within me. Like a burst of music, I listened again to the Concert of Aranjuez. What a beautiful ending for my freedom, I thought.

The young man came toward me and asked, "Do you have a light?"

I instinctively moved to one side and said, "No I don't."

"Come with me! They want to ask you some questions."

"All right. I'll go home and wait for you."

He put a pistol against my left side. It felt like the barrel was sinking into my waist. I looked and saw it was a Colt 45. I imagined the hole

73

it would make when the bullet passed through my body. Resigned, I turned around. "Please let me say good-bye to my son!" I begged him. "Just a few minutes." I noticed two other agents on the other side of the street. When we got to the corner there was an old green truck a half a block away. "No, you can't go home," the young man replied. "But they know we're looking for you. They'll assume you've been detained."

"Detained?"

"Sorry, that you're in custody, because the boss wants to consult with you about some things."

"And right now? Is there someone at the barracks at this hour?"

"You're right, but it's you who's late. On that subject, where were you?"

I looked at Palermo Street. It was my final glance at what was my neighborhood. Resigned, I sat between the driver and a police officer and put the book my cousin Emiliano had lent me on the dashboard. I took off my earrings, heavy silver hoops, which could give me even more trouble if I were beaten. The police officer looked at them and let me keep them. They later stole them from me.

"I went to the theater."

"So she's watching movies, and we're here waiting."

"I didn't go to the cinema. I went to the Municipal Theater."

Silence. . . . The same square meter, the same vehicle, breathing the same silence that smelled of gas and the sweat of these people who seemed to ignore even the most basic hygienic practices. The air growing increasingly heavy, determined to fill your nose with that oppressive combination of filth, panic, the smell of blood being spilled, of raped women, of exhausted panting, of eyes covered by filthy blindfolds and mouths silenced by brutal beatings.

The dice! . . . Where are my dice? I smiled. I remembered the book I had been reading, the one Emiliano had lent me. I was never able to return it to him. . . . Someone from the DINA kept it, and that novel was never published in Chile. Now would have been a good time for the protagonist in the novel to throw the dice. If I get a six, I'll run. If I get a one, I'll kill myself. In either case I can be free.

I let my thoughts wander, trying to calm myself, "Hello, friend! It's been a while since you visited me. That's all right. Now we'll live together. You see? It's not you who's inviting me. I will come to meet you." Little by little, with fierceness, irony and abandon, I closed the doors to the present and decided to go towards whatever awaited me. That could be my last embrace with my friend, death.

"Stop the truck! Sorry, Lucecita, but I have to blindfold you."

I didn't say anything. There was no resisting. I looked and recognized the Rotonda Grecia highway loop. I was trying to guess where we were going, but they made several turns, and I lost track of where we were. They stopped after a little while. From the sound, I could tell they were opening a gate, and I heard the guards shouting. Months later I would realize that we were at the Terranova Barracks, otherwise known as Villa Grimaldi.

"May I take the blindfold off?"

"No, you can't, and I have to tie you up. But do you want a cup of coffee first?"

"Sir, I have some cigarettes in my purse. Can I smoke?"

"Sure, if you share them with us."

Once again I felt the same sensation I had experienced when I was at Tejas Verdes: smoking while blindfolded is like not smoking at all.

"I'll have to wait until tomorrow, right?"

"Yes, and now try to get some sleep."

I couldn't. What could it matter? . . . I remembered the previous days. I felt like I had followed their orders, or at least tried. My parents, my son. . . . They emerged like a painfully present absence. . . .

I went over my story again for a while, convinced I wouldn't be able to sleep, and I decided to think about other things. I wanted to be in good spirits the following day. Christ crucified emerged within me, and I said, "Friend, you are good. If you could, I'm sure you would give me time to be a mother. It doesn't matter to me anymore if you're God or not. I like talking to you. I like seeing you on this night of blindfolded eyes. You give me strength. You live in each and every dead compañero, in every being who suffers. Jesus, I know that no matter the pain, everything comes to an end. They may be intense, horrific moments. Friend, will there be freedom for me? . . .

Jesus, I know that the spear that hurts the most isn't the one that pierces your side, it is the fact that the one hurting you is a human being and that you can't hate him. That cross today can be an old bed where they rape you or a bed frame where they grill you.[26]

I felt calm. It had been months since I had received any news about my compañeros. They couldn't get any information out of me even if

---

26. For the burning pain associated with the effects of electric shock on someone tied to a metal bed frame, this form of torture is often referred to as *la parrilla*, or the grill.

I broke. I was foolish to think I had succeeded, that the bullet wound in my foot was my ace in the hole since it had given me enough time to distance myself from the possibility of being a traitor. Victory, even a fool could understand that, I thought. . . . How far I was from reality at that time. I was certain I still had a few cards to play, even though I knew them, and I knew that this would piss them off and that they might beat me even harder. However, I calmed myself down by telling myself, "All that can happen is that I'll die, and that doesn't scare me anymore. It's just a step from being to being no more. If I live, it will be like a gift, and I'll see my son again. If I die, I'll go happily." I felt almost at ease.

I remembered a time back when I was a little girl, when a horrible man grabbed me by the arm and took me to the room he rented with his wife, a woman who was so fat she looked like she was about to explode. They included me in their sexual encounters. I was four years old. I never dared tell anybody about it. It scared me at first, and later I began to interpret what had happened as something bad. I grew up feeling guilty, and I thought that God would burn me in hell for it. I spent my entire childhood with all that guilt, with my parents' constant demands. I felt like I was trying hard, trying to do well, but they never seemed satisfied. For some reason, for me, there was neither heaven, nor angels, and still less those places in pictures where sheep graze peacefully in the presence of God. . . .

I remembered my grandfather, and for the first time I thought, "It's better you're not here anymore. That way you don't know that your cherished granddaughter is in prison." I could never tell my grandfather about that childhood secret. I was afraid he wouldn't love me either. But you know what, grandpa? It doesn't matter. When I was older and I understood things, I stopped feeling so bad. How it hurts to grow up, grandpa!

MY GRANDFATHER

During my childhood, my grandfather was everything to me. He was creative, sophisticated, wise, intelligent, a musician, a painter, and a writer. He had the soul of an artist. He was a teacher and artisan by necessity, a union supporter by conviction, and a socialist at heart. His parents were from Navarra, Spain, from a village called "Los Arce." All of them went to Perú, but my grandfather came further south. He loved and taught me to love my country, Chile, deeply.

I remember summers in the big old house in the neighborhood of Recoleta. The countless adobe rooms, two patios, the grape arbor, and the fig tree, which was all mine. There were orange trees, lemon trees, and chickens. I would go with him to collect eggs and pick fruit among the bees and the aroma of lavender, and with the larks, who at dusk drew lines in the sky with their phosphorescent brilliance. He read me his poems and told me episodes of Spanish history.

When I was four, I listened to him practice the violin. It was something magical. I wanted to grow up quickly because he had promised me that he would start teaching me to produce those melodies as soon as my arm was long enough to take the instrument and rest it against my chin. And he kept his promise.

I asked myself many times: Grandpa, did anyone understand you? I felt like a princess by his side. I listened to his lullabies and Schubert's "Ave María." I stood for hours mesmerized by his clocks and crystal bottles where he kept his homemade liquors. The bottles were a variety of colors, and he prepared them just like he did his paints and brushes.

I remember his white hair, his walk, and the sparkle in his eyes as he stood entranced by the songs of the canaries and goldfinches in the cages along the hall in the old house. Soon they forbade me to go to my grandfather's house. My parents didn't like him talking about the Communist Party or the Worker's Movement. My mother would say, "Rotten child, go on. You'll end up crazy like that old man who wastes his time on nonsense."

By the time I turned fourteen, I had already become an athlete. My trainer suggested that I had to work really hard during my summer vacation that year if I wanted to win the national championship. My grandfather thought a while and said I should do what the teacher said, that it was about time I had friends my own age. Grandpa helped me break the ties that bound me to him. He said real love doesn't hold one back, it doesn't want to possess solely for itself, and seeks the well-being of the one who is loved.

Except for the days I spent with my grandfather, the rest of my childhood seems sad to me. I wanted to be a nun. I told my mother and, I don't know why, asked her not to say anything to anybody. She ignored my request and told one of the nuns. For my first communion I wore the congregation's habit, and a lot of things started to change for me. I think they started treating me differently. I often spoke with the sister who was the director, or the mother superior, and they talked to me about

77

what my life would be like. I would go to Rome at fourteen for the novitiate, and, when he was old enough, my brother would get a scholarship to attend the boy's school run by the monks of the order. I can't recall every detail clearly, but I remember feeling sad and scared when I heard these things.

The nun who taught our religion classes said that an angel watched over us on our right side and that the devil was on the left when we were asleep at night. I suffered every time I woke up facing the left. I felt like Satan had dominated my dreams, and I cried inconsolably.

As I grew up, I couldn't help contrasting my grandfather's teachings with all of that, and I started asking questions. The first was why they referred to our school as being for "young ladies." I asked if the little girls whose parents couldn't afford to pay for that school weren't young ladies. I knew my parents made huge sacrifices to make the monthly payments. I remember the number of times they only had bread with oil and vinegar to eat at the end of the month. I felt guilty for how much they spent on me, and it occurred to me to tell them I wanted to change schools to one where they didn't charge more than tuition. That's when I found out that if I left the school my brother wouldn't receive the scholarship. I felt a huge weight on my shoulders, and I said I didn't want to be like the nuns who differentiated between women who were young ladies and those who were poor.

Remembering my grandfather at Villa Grimaldi made me feel much sadness. But I also felt a sense of peace, that strange peace of knowing that life ends or that it will be drastically interrupted. I told myself, maybe it's better for my son to grow up without me. I couldn't bear knowing that he could be in a situation like that when he grew up. You can win or lose in life. From my family's point of view, I've lost. I accept that judgment. I'm not looking for what they call winning.

On the morning of July 24, 1974, they dragged me outside as soon as the officers arrived. I fell several times. The walk was a long one, and my foot still hadn't healed. I tumbled down the stone stairway at the entrance to Villa Grimaldi's main house. It had been days since my foot had hurt that much. I heard someone yell, "Bring that communist bitch now!"

There I was, standing there held up by a guard. I noticed I had lost the heel of my shoes, wide clogs that were comfortable for my bad foot. I felt my foot starting to swell again with a painful throbbing. I realized right away I was screaming. It was a reflex. My nose was bleeding. He hit me!

He punched me right in the face with a closed fist. I didn't feel in pain; I was confused. I felt myself falling. I thought I was going to lose consciousness. The man continued beating me when I was on the ground. My knees curled up and something lifted me, another punch that came from underneath me and smashed into my chin. I felt my feet in the air, and I fell on top of some furniture. I screamed again. It was metal, probably a desk. I fell on my back, and something sharp dug into my waist. The blood made me feel my wet pants. I don't remember anything else, just that I managed to think, "Why doesn't it hurt?" It was as if something were stopping the pain from reaching my brain. What incredible bodies we have!

I don't know how long I was lying there, but I reacted violently when they threw a bucket of water on me. It was freezing, and now I really was in pain. My blindfold had fallen off. I saw an officer who looked tall and thin from the ground. His hair was short, and he looked like a fierce animal. I was in an office. Months later I would find out that they were from the DINA's Purén Unit.

"So you woke up, you damned whore! Whores, whores, that's what communist women are, and the sons of bitches are all faggots. I hate you, you know. I hate you! Now you're going to see fascism in action. Isn't that what you call us? Soldieeeer!" he yelled, completely beside himself. "Did you know that's what they call us?"

"No, major, I didn't know."

"Yes. It's true. Go on, bitch, call the soldier a fascist so he can see that what his major is telling him is the truth."

He started kicking me. My ribs cracked. The officer, yelling like a crazy man, never stopped hitting me. I obviously couldn't articulate any words at all. I just heard the short, dry noise that the air made as it violently left me, as if I were deflating. I was shocked. The only thing he wanted was to hit me. "Say we're fascists! Say you wanted to kill us! Say you hate us!" he repeated time and again.

I lost consciousness several times, and I barely had any clothes on. He was ripping them off me, but I wasn't aware of my body. It was as if only my mind existed, thinking and reacting with infinite astonishment. I didn't feel my arms or my legs, nothing. I must have been completely swollen because my skin was taut. Suddenly, the officer knelt down and almost pleadingly said, "Listen. I'm going to leave you alone for a minute. Tell me you hate me. Now you hate me, right?"

I gathered my strength and tried to sit up. My eyes met face-to-face

79

with his. I could feel his breath. I couldn't raise my voice. Something seemed to strangle my neck, not allowing me to make a sound. . . . I slowly managed to say, "No, sir, I don't hate you."

I don't know why I said it. I didn't think. I guess because that's the way it was. I just remember that general feeling of pain, and just like when they raped me, the first time at the Yucatán Detention Center, it was like looking at everything from outside myself with a great sadness, as if a different level of consciousness had moved me several feet away from what was going on. It's like observing yourself from outside and whispering into your own ear: "Yes, Luz, it's you. All this is happening to you, and you just said, 'I don't hate you, sir.'"

The officer was furious.

"Get that dumb ass out of here! Throw her on the ground." I smiled, thinking, "Luz, you're going to your mother, she will take you in. . . ."

Two soldiers carried me in the air while the officer yelled behind me, "I'm going to kill this one! Look at her smile, like she's going to a party. This whore is tough! I bet they trained her in Cuba."

He started asking me when I had gone to Cuba. I just said, "Sir, I've never been to Cuba." Then I locked myself in a memory, the beautiful memory of Alejandro. I tried to picture him against the clear sky on that distant island. I needed to be certain he was safe by the sea.

The officer took my response as a mockery and started dragging me by the hair. My legs hit every one of the stairs. It was strange. I felt the pain. I recognized that it hurt, but nothing more, no crying. It was as if my mind had split in two, and the part that could feel had been blocked off.

I let myself go. . . . Alejandro, how wonderful to remember you! I could see the image of the mountains before me with the pink snow melting in the spring. I recalled their deep ravines, gray and greenish-black, with a beautiful maroon shade. I tried to open my eyes. I wanted to see the sky. I could hardly open them because they were so swollen. They threw me down on the ground on my back. At some point they untied my hands, or they came untied, and the palms of my hands were on the ground. I touched the earth, caressing it. I heard a vehicle moving away and the officer kneeling beside me saying, "Do you hear that? That truck is going to run you over now, first your legs, then each time a couple of inches above them until you talk."

At that moment they informed the officer that the colonel needed him. I heard the soldier say he was Major Urrich. Later I found out his complete name was Gerardo Ernesto Urrich González. The major gave the order to wait for him, and he left.

A soldier came over to me, and I recognized him. He had been a guard at the Military Hospital. "Lucecita, talk, do what he says. He's going to kill you."

"Do you want to help me, soldier?"

"You know I can't do anything."

"Yes, you can. Please, pray with me. Do you know how to pray? I have forgotten how, but I'll repeat after you. Please. . . ."

The guard closed his eyes and opened them again. He smiled and started: "Hail Mary, full of grace. Our Lord is with thee. . . ." Without realizing it, I started praying slowly, and little by little raised my voice. The prayers came from some part of my memory, intact, stored there since my childhood. I kept praying. I heard the sound of the truck again. The motor was roaring. Blessed art thou among women. The truck accelerated. And blessed is the fruit of thy womb. I felt something like a huge pinching on my left leg. . . . Jesus! . . . A shout: "Halt!" And I was far away, thinking. . . . How sweet it sounds. . . . Jesus! A combination of soft, tender love, like honey. . . . Jesus! I felt them dragging me. . . . And screams. I have not died! But it will happen soon enough. I want to die with my soul full of waves. Holy Mary, Mother of God, waves kissing the sand. Pray for us sinners. With dawn's awaking with caresses from the sun and flowers. Now and at the hour of our death, Amen. . . . I remembered how beautiful, and fresh pine forests are. . . . They opened a door and they dragged me up a narrow stairwell. It smelled moist, of mildew. It doesn't matter. I am carrying a new light within me, like a sun. Our Father, who art in heaven. The smell of wet earth, like clay. Hallowed be thy name, thy kingdom come, thy will be done. Union of father, man, and God. And forgive us our trespasses. Each tear made my skin more tender. As we forgive those who trespass against us. . . . That is how it will be as long as water comes from my being. And lead us not into temptation from violence. Water! . . . I'm thirsty! But deliver us from evil. . . .

Voices again, and people coming up the stairs.

I see a lot of legs all lined up next to each other. They look at me. I realize I'm naked, and I instinctively try to cover my breasts with my hands, but they're tied. "Bring her. Now I'm going to get it all out of her!"

"Sir, she can't stand."

"Bring her, I said! Hold her up, sit her down. No, better yet, hang her up."

I felt them tie my wrists and start tightening the rope. After a few pulls I was hanging. God! My shoulders cracked and I felt a series of deep sharp pains like red-hot irons. Then my joints gave way. At least all that exercise I did was worth something, I thought. There's no fracture. I'm strong. I remembered my mom saying, "You're running a race meant for men. Those 800 meters are not for young ladies. You go around exercising like the men do." And I remembered how I told her that being a woman didn't mean not playing sports. At least it was of some use now.

The major came over and said, "Lift your head up!"

I didn't do it. I couldn't. I felt really cold, and I was swinging like a pendulum. It didn't matter to me anymore that I was naked.

"Now you will say you hate me," he insisted.

"No, sir, I don't hate you."

"Why? Tell me why you don't hate me. . . ."

"Because I understand you, sir. Because I feel sorry for you, sir."

I heard laughing and murmuring. Yes, there were a lot of people and they kept coming. They were placing themselves in front of me, next to the major, everywhere. I felt like he was fighting with me, and I wasn't.

"Bring the traitor so she can see him! What's her name?"

"Lucecita," someone whispered.

"'Lucecita!' A pain in the ass, that's what you are. But I'll make sure you hate me. I promise you're going to hate me, you piece of shit whore!"

PRIVATE RODOLFO UNDER INTERROGATION

Two soldiers arrived. They were bringing Rodolfo Valentín González Pérez, the young man who helped the prisoners at the Military Hospital. He wasn't wearing any clothes except for some underwear that looked really white against his dark skin. His right leg was in a cast.

The major started to speak: "Look at this jackass! He was a soldier in the air force. He's a traitor! But we caught him. We captured him, and he tried to get away. He jumped through that window. The idiot broke his leg. We sent him to the clinic, just to question him." The major started laughing and added, "Of course he tried to run away! He knew what he was in for. Is everybody here? I want all personnel present for them to learn what happens to traitors and the whores who seduce them."

"What did that asshole do for you?"

82

"Nothing, sir." Laughter.

"You see that, soldier? She's defending you." More laughter. "When a marxist whore defends a soldier, it's because he's a traitor. So, you're not even going to tell us how you converted him? Did he sleep with you?"

"No!"

"Does it bother you when I call you a whore?"

"Your saying it does not make me a whore, sir."

"I'm fed up with you! This is the last time I'm asking you. What did this jackass do at the Military Hospital?"

"I don't know."

He asked for some paper and cut it in strips. He brought the lighter over and put the burning paper on my stomach. I started smelling the scent of burning flesh, like the smell of chickens when they're passed over flames to clean them. Only this time I was the one burning.

He beat me. He burned me. I don't know how to describe that moment. Just as I would regain consciousness, I would pass out again. I can't give a clear account. Could this be what dying is like? Urrich González kept insisting that I tell him I hated him in front of the personnel, that I hated them all. God only knows why, but all I could say was, "No sir, I don't hate you. I understand you. It seems like you haven't considered your options." And I added, "Do you have any, sir?"

At one point, I asked him how he could hate me so much, if he didn't remember that he had a mother, maybe a wife, a sister. Infuriated, he beat me even more, shouting that the women in his family were another thing entirely. They were ladies, and not whores like I was.

For many years, I thought no one would believe it if I told them what happened to me during those days. However, in 1991, in one of my trips to Europe, I was able to read the testimony of someone who was in the Terranova tower that day. That person remembered everything and told Human Rights organizations about it long before I did. I didn't know that person had been near me that day. I won't offer any more details, for now, since I don't want to interfere in the investigations of various cases where the testimony of this person is extremely important.

I have a foggy recollection of Rodolfo yelling, "Luz, tell them everything! I already did. I didn't resist. I confessed everything. Don't suffer for me."

"The faggot, he can't handle the fact that a woman could be braver than he is," the major shouted. "Do you all see that? I want you all to see. . . . Even a marxist whore is braver than a traitor. Look at this faggot.

He's a traitor! But you're going to see this one talk too! This bitch is going to talk too. I know everything. But you have to say it yourself."

Rodolfo was in a corner, half sitting on a mattress and leaning against the tower wall. He kept yelling incessantly, crying, "Luz, tell them what they want. Don't keep suffering, for your son, please do it for your son! Tell him what he wants! . . . Don't suffer for me!"

Urrich was beside himself with anger. He started shouting: "You, soldier, don't you get it? She says she didn't recruit you to the left."

I gathered all my strength and said, "Sir, I have not tried to recruit anyone. On the contrary, when the guards started talking in front of me, I asked them not to continue, not to talk in front of me. Please, ask them. There, beside you, are two of the guards. Ask them. You don't believe that I've recruited them all, right?" I looked right at the guy. He turned pale. He was Rodolfo's friend, the same one who had detained me the previous night. He looked distraught and frightened.

He lowered his eyes and, with an almost imperceptible nod, agreed. The major was bewildered. He turned around and looked at him. Then he started shouting: "Is that true? Did she ever tell you to be quiet?"

The guy hesitated. He looked at me and nodded affirmatively.

Urrich yelled, "Get the commanding officer of these assholes in here!"

I heard someone running down the stairs. During those minutes, Urrich looked at me without saying a word. He started pacing, and he said to someone behind me, "Let her down for a while."

They lowered the rope and left me with my feet touching the floor. My arms or my wrists were numb but they were no longer swinging in the air. All my blood seemed to be flowing into them. It was awful, as if thousands of needles were suddenly sticking me, making me feel a strange and painful tickling. Strong pains in my burnt abdomen caused me to let out a groan. I looked at myself; a yellow liquid was trickling from my burns. Lymphatic fluid, I thought.

Somebody said, "The cunt is attractive. At least this jerk got a nice piece of ass before dying. . . ." It hurt me so much when they called me a whore, but nothing I could say or do would have made them think any differently. Maybe they need to believe in their superior. It was as if I had hit bottom within myself. I had nothing. I was nothing.

A little while later, someone arrived and they hung me up again. Nobody said how to do it, and the soldier, perhaps with a trace of humanity, left me touching the floor a bit with the tips of my toes. It was less excruciating. They lifted my head. I saw someone who I would later know was Major Manuel Andrés Carevic Cubillos. "Raúl" is what they called him in the DINA. He was commander of the soldiers from the Purén Intelligence Unit who had been on guard in my room at the Military Hospital.

Then something incredible happened. Major Urrich González started interrogating Major Carevic Cubillos right there.

"Did you know that when the soldiers talked about the DINA she told them to be quiet?"

In a low voice, he answered, "Yes, they mentioned it to me several times."

Urrich looked at me and said, "And you, why did you shut them up?"

"Because I didn't want to know anything, sir, because what I have said ever since I got here is the truth. I don't know anything. Because I want to live, I want to be free, and I thought that knowing could be dangerous. I haven't tried to recruit anyone; I haven't converted anyone."

"But this fool told you he has a brother who got asylum."

"Yes, it's true, but I hope you know what my response was."

"And what did you say to him?"

"For him to talk to his commander, and that if he was loyal, his commander would understand."

Even more bewildered, Urrich looked at Carevic. He nodded that it was true.

Urrich gave me an intense look. Then he turned around and left. Before he started down the stairs, he shouted, "Take her down! Leave her on a mattress. Make sure a guard stays there!"

IN THE TOWER AT VILLA GRIMALDI

The personnel started to leave. A gray-haired man came over to me and asked if I knew him. I told him I didn't. He told me that he knew me, that he had married a friend of mine from college and that he remembered me because I was an athlete. Years later, he himself told me that in 1976, he was an army sergeant, the driver for Manuel Contreras.[27]

I don't know why he was there. Maybe the colonel was present. I don't

27. Colonel Manuel Contreras Sepúlveda was the head of the DINA and later the CNI. A close protégé of Augusto Pinochet, Contreras held one of the most powerful positions during the military regime. His fall from power and later criminal conviction came as a result of his connection to the Orlando Letelier assassination in Washington, D.C., in 1976.

know. There were a lot of people, and I obviously didn't take the time to look around to see who was there. There were moments when I didn't even have the strength to lift my own head unless they held me up by my hair.

I was held, or they say I was held, for twelve days in the tower at Villa Grimaldi. I can't remember the details. I know they were ordered not to feed me. Someone covered me with a thick black wool poncho. One day I woke up because someone was touching my legs. The guard gestured for me to be quiet.

"Quiet, he knows how to 'set' bones and he's examining you."

I didn't feel my legs. The truth is I didn't feel anything, except the inner edge of my foot and my right leg where I suffered from hypersensitivity. I looked at myself. I had scabs on my abdomen, and my pubic hair itched as it grew through my burnt skin.

The man spoke after a while, "It's not broken. Put her legs up, and don't let her walk. How does she go to the bathroom?"

"We take her."

I didn't even remember that. The guard gently lifted my head to give me water from a bottle, and again for a piece of chocolate and some bread. I cried when one of the men took a huge piece of apple out of his mouth and fed it to me, holding me so that I was half sitting up. He had hidden it in his mouth. . . . It was the most exquisite apple I had ever eaten in my life.

Days and hours didn't exist for me, only a permanent stupor. The few conscious moments were strange too. I felt like the guards did what they could, but I was incapable of anything. I just looked at them and said, "Thanks. . . ."

The pain was different too. I could feel its constant presence, but I wasn't suffering. It was as if the pain had crossed the threshold that a human being can endure, as if it had vanished, disappeared. I was beyond pain. One day I asked myself, is it possible to die from pain? I felt that more than anything I wanted to die, that a haze had taken over everything. A cloud took hold of me. I was lying on the floor, and I never felt it was hard. I wasn't there, it was as if I had traveled through some fissure inside myself and entered my own world, where I could see, remember, almost smell flowers and landscapes.

One day, they say it was my thirteenth there, they brought me food. I couldn't eat. My throat was dry and my lips were too. I was waking up, as if I were coming from somewhere. I started recognizing myself, and for the first time I saw the dust that was taking over the floor, the corners, the walls. I tried to fix myself up. I felt pain. I started to laugh. I was just starting to realize I was alive. My friend death abandoned me again. She wasn't there anymore. . . . I felt like yelling, "You bitch! You rotten friend! You ran from my smile as I saw you. Death! You're a fraud! Of course! It would have been easier to die so the traitor ran away. . . . Why not kill me?" It was just a question. I knew I would fight to live as long as I had even a flicker of consciousness. I leaned my back against the wall and looked at myself. In Tejas Verdes I thought I was as dirty as I could ever be. Now I really was. My abdomen hurt. It was an atrocious itch from the hairs in the blanket that got stuck between the scabs, but there was no infection. I moved a finger over my chest. I was covered with dust and earth, and I cried out happily. . . . You don't hurt me. I gazed at my foot, almost completely healed into a scar, and it too was full of earth and fuzz, with no trace of infection anywhere. I smiled again, and I felt like a child of the earth. Yes, I am made of earth!

Mother earth, my dearest mother, I came from your womb. I stopped suddenly. Am I crazy? God! In the worst moments, the mind could access an unlimited reserve of beauty. Everything seemed to help me understand that if I resisted the demented nature of the situation, I would end up stark raving mad.

The fantasy of my hands covered and crossed over my belly emerged from the desire of my mind to separate itself from that reality. It would take all the strength of my being to avoid these fantasies. I dreamed of this opening like a willingness to agree to see and to hear, to want to touch and smell whatever I could. I decided that this willingness would be a part of my life, whatever the situation might be.

Afterwards, I repeated to myself, trying to convince myself, "No, I'm not crazy. I'm protected by my instincts." Soon I was thinking again. I remembered Rodolfo. They said he was dead, that he had died for helping me. I couldn't understand how that could be true, that he could have died just for having taken a few notes to my son and my parents. I couldn't accept it. I thought it was another way of torturing me, of instilling even more terror in me.

Though submerged in a kind of energy-saving state of unconsciousness, my organism had to nourish itself during those days, and it had obviously fed off of what was stored up. I thought it would have been better if I hadn't been so skinny. I should have eaten more at home. . . . Any train of thought always led my thoughts home, to my son. I spoke to him as if he were present. . . .

"My dear Rafael, I hope you remember everything I told you, that if mom doesn't come home, it's because she can't. . . ." I remembered his sad little face. I couldn't prevent his suffering. I didn't know how that abandonment would affect him. I could only tell him: "I love you! Please don't forget that, I love you a lot." His childhood was different, as it was for so many other children. It would be years before I would know how those things affected him.

As I was thinking, I massaged my legs and I tried to move every muscle in my body. I was still naked. I could see my shoes in a corner, one of them missing a heel. I was really cold even though the blanket was thick. My shoulders and wrists were badly injured, and some kind of ring appeared on my left thigh. I don't know how it happened, perhaps from a hard blow or the rope.

One day, one of the guards stayed a while longer when he brought me something to eat, and he told me the other guards didn't want to go where I was being held. When I asked him why, he laughed and said he thought they felt sorry for me, and also because they were afraid that "what happened to González" could happen to them. I asked him about Rodolfo, and he said that they hadn't seen anything, but that the commander said that he was dead, killed because he was a traitor.

I explained that I had never tried to recruit him or anything of the kind.

"Maybe it's like you say, but the commanders told us we shouldn't talk to you, Lucecita. They said you're really smart, that you could 'screw with our heads' in whatever way you wanted, and that we could be 'made' into traitors like González."

"It's true he helped me, but he only took a few letters to my parents, nothing more, I swear to you."

"It must've been something more than that, Lucecita. If he helped you just like that, González must've done other things."

That night I heard some noises, and I could see that a light from a lantern was coming up through the opening to the stairwell. It was one of the guards bringing me clothes and a sandwich. I opened the bag. There were cigarettes and a thermos. It was coffee with hot milk. He waited for me to eat and then left. He said the clothes were his sister's.

I often thought I would never want to forget those days, not just the pain but everything I was feeling. I was discovering some treasures, the help from those on guard, knowing that human beings can always find each other anywhere. . . .

10

BACK TO THE YUCATÁN DETENTION CENTER

Around the end of July or the beginning of August, I don't know exactly, they put tape over my eyes again and made me get in a truck. Once again, it was back to the Yucatán Detention Center at 38 Londres Street.

The guards recognized me and assigned me the same number I had had in March. I was number fifty-four again. When they called roll, I realized that the numbers went beyond one hundred now. I sat tied to a chair like before, and my arms and legs swelled up again. I felt the same dull, painful throbbing in my feet and, especially, near the wound on my hand. I tried to get used to that position. My waist hurt and there was an awful smell. Of course! There were so many of us in the same room, and we couldn't wash ourselves. I stunk too. It was just that I had gotten used to it. They said the toilets didn't work, and that they only rinsed them with water once a day. I tried to tone my muscles by contracting and relaxing them one by one. It hurt, but I wanted to avoid atrophy. With no muscle tone, I was really thin. I had a well defined musculature before, but now it seemed to have disappeared.

My intuition told me that I still had a long way to go to survive that horror, and I knew that if I fell apart physically it would be impossible to escape the madness that lurked around my mind.

When I let myself think about the people I loved, I felt a sense of despair and anguish. I was frightened. The proximity of madness seemed worse to me than death. It occurred to me that, besides working on my muscles, I should try to maintain my ability to reason. I thought doing mathematical problems would help, and I tried to do some calculations. When the situation made it impossible for me to concentrate, I just counted by two's or five's. I kept myself busy trying and was able to block out that world of cries and pleas, of guttural screams.

It was good for me to feel that, despite everything, I was active; oblivious, but alert. I began compiling information, starting with identifying the different guards and officers by their voices, the language they used, the sound of their footsteps, and the different colognes they wore, which were strong and smelly. I recorded those smells and associated them with a feeling of rejection that I still maintain to this day. One of them smelled just like the sergeant nurse at the Military Hospital, and it still makes me feel nauseous. I tried to take in the situation rationally. I was able to hide my feelings of disgust and inner destruction. You couldn't tell how I felt, and being blindfolded really helped. But inside I was shattered.

Two days after my arrival at Yucatán, no one had talked to me. The wait increased the tension. It was hard to stay calm. Everything seemed to come back to me, filling my whole being with fear, more than fear, terror, panic. I couldn't get air. It was as if my chest were always tight, as though a hundred pounds were pressing down on me, making it painful even to breathe. Several sharp pains below my right collarbone practically immobilized my right arm. I tried to calm down. I felt agitated, as though I'd forgotten to breathe, and the more I tried, the more it seemed like there wasn't any air. I fought it by counting and visualizing the numbers, trying to regulate my inhaling and exhaling. I moved around trying to expand my rib cage. It hurt as if something inside were breaking. I felt faint and I had a fever.

It's an infection, I thought. Finally! I tried to figure out where it was located. Was it in some wound? It could be a urinary tract infection. The bathrooms were filthy. I discovered I was easily overcome by the same soporific state, the haze that allowed me to escape from the tower at Villa Grimaldi, just by bending my upper body and resting my forehead on my knees, especially when I got them to tie my hands in front. Once again only semiconscious, with that thick cloud crushing me, destroying every bit of feeling, I was left with the sense of resignation, that what was so horrible was reality itself. It wasn't a mental escape, but an escape from what was happening at that moment. I told myself, "Yes, Luz, it's you, and the ones who are yelling are other compañeros, and they're torturing them. The screams you hear, the ones that make every hair on your body stand on end, it's because they're in pain. And it hurts you too, Luz, because you know they're being torn apart. And you feel it because you're afraid and you're sweating. It's fear because you know you will scream like that again many times. It's adrenaline,

Luz." It was reality, but it seemed like, besides being real, it was madness itself. . . .

Like a ray of light, there emerged within me an almost triumphant "I've got it!" It was the key to the very thin line between sanity and madness. I was grateful for all those tools I was discovering that allowed me to keep going and feel safe from one minute to the next. Safe? How much you know! How much you don't know about your body, your mind, and what comes to the surface under pressure I must have always known all this, only I never needed it. . . . Accepting real reality? Real? It means crossing the threshold to stay within the sphere of reason. Denial, or floating somewhere in between, means going crazy, and I knew the limit. I've been on both sides. If the situation becomes intolerable, I just have to stop accepting that it's real.

Here, today, the memory emerges of the amazement, the anguish, the terror, and the growing desperation. It was like music that surrounds, moves, frightens, and distorts, like tumbling down the slide of the insane mind. I thought of those other places outside, and I told myself they also existed, but over there is the outside. Beyond these walls, in those houses that smelled of stew, beans, and salad. . . . They were next door, right across the street and, at the same time, infinitely distant. But they existed. I was sure of it, and it was a good point of reference. But here that's not going to help you, Luz. That is another dimension of reality, not yours.

I plunged into a delirious monologue where I called on Queen Madness and I said to her, "To know you is the only way to defeat you. This is your world. I will not be able to fight for my sanity unless I make room for you here. I welcome you without fear. Perhaps you will flee from me as death has. But it's a pact; it's a deal. We three are friends: death, madness, and Luz."

I returned to the present as if in a single bound. . . . Two guards sitting nearby were having coffee. "Why haven't they interrogated her?"

"Because her brother is giving his statement."

"Has he talked?"

"There he is. . . . They've just arrived with the weapons. They had them buried. . . ."

"Poor kid! So long and now this. . . ."

Those words penetrated me like a dagger. . . . It's my brother! A "Nooooo" spewed from the depths of my soul, and it was as if I had eaten glass and my entrails were being torn, ripped to shreds. . . . Everything seemed to vanish. I stopped hearing, thinking, being.

Everything started to fall apart. . . . My downfall, and I was being destroyed.

It was like being in a whirlwind, like a fierce wind against my face that made it impossible for me to breathe. . . . My brother! Why had they detained him? I never mentioned him. Surely someone else is talking. It's not fair! . . . But, is there a place here for justice? But who could it be? All the compañeros know he was a militant but that he stopped after the coup. All he could say are things from before September 11th, and what little he knows from me. . . . Another thought entered my mind, "The weapons!" It was as if I had just reacted. Without a shadow of a doubt, if they were referring to my brother, then those weapons were the ones he took out of the closet in my room. I remembered how I had waited out those three days of torture to give him time to realize I had been arrested and to clear the weapons out of the house. I remembered a conversation. . . .

"Where did you take the weapons?"

"To Grandma's house."

"How?"

"On the bike we use for the store. I loaded it with boxes of corn and onions, and I hid them in between."

Grandma! If he handed them over, they must have gone to her house too. Poor grandma. I hope my brother says she didn't know. . . . And my father? I thought I remembered that he was the one who got the weapons out, not my brother. Or did they go together? I don't know. I never knew for sure. . . .

A few hours later they took me to an office. A voice I didn't recognize interrupted my thoughts.

RICARDO LAWRENCE MIRES

"Sit down, Luz. Untie her and take off her blindfold. I can't talk if I can't see her eyes," said a sickly sweet voice. "Okay, Lucecita, the two of us are going to talk. Bring some coffees! Lucecita, what sign are you?"

"What?"

Of all the questions in the world, I would have never thought they would ask me that one at a time like that. He repeated it slowly, as if he were relishing each syllable.

"Y-O-U-R S-I-G-N, of the Z-O-D-I-A-C."

"Oh, that. I don't know."

"Oh, Lucecita! Every woman knows that."

"Not me."

I did know. I'm an Aries, but I was furious.

"Strange. On what day were you born?"

"March. March 31st."

"Aries. You're an Aries. That's why I knew we were going to get along ever since I met you. And now they've sent you to my unit. . . . Aries, Lucecita! That makes us compatible! Aries, Leo, and Sagittarius are all fire signs! I should have known. You couldn't be any other sign."

I looked at him. He seemed young, maybe my age although he had more gray hair than I did. He had attractive, greenish eyes with long eyelashes. I thought, "And who does this jackass think he is?" I kept looking at him, serious and quiet. I waited. I didn't bother answering. To tell the truth, I was annoyed and offended he would think I would like such a conversation. I'd rather have you hit me, you stupid, macho asshole. The perfect specimen of an imbecile! I don't feel like opening my mouth. He stood up, furious, and shouted, "Luz! Aren't you going to talk to me?"

"Of course. I have no trouble talking with you. It didn't look like you were waiting for an answer."

"Not an answer, of course, but a sentence, an opinion. I thought we were having a conversation."

"Forgive me, sir, but if you're interested in talking about horoscopes, you'll have to do the talking. I don't know anything about that kind of thing."

"Oh!" he said. He sat down, stretched his arms, and started looking at his hands.

They were horrible chubby hands with stubby fingers. As I remember him, he wasn't very fat, but he was the type who could be. He's got the hands of a lazy ass, I thought. He's never done anything with them his whole life except pick up pastries, chicken, and women, I suppose.

"Luz, the Aries. That sounds nice. You've got white hair, like me. You know what? I like you. Listen, I want to tell you something."

"Will you give me another cup of coffee?"

"Coffee? Of course. Guard! Bring two more coffees."

"Thanks."

"A cigarette?"

"Only if it's the kind I smoke. . . . Lucky."

"You see? We have a lot in common. I smoke Lucky too. Listen. I want

93

to talk to you and you keep shutting out options. But don't forget I'm an Aries, and stubborn, like you. We will talk. You will be here as long as it takes, as long as I want. You won't sleep. Neither will I. But we'll talk. Is that clear?" he said, raising his voice.

"Honestly, sir, not really. What are we going to talk about?"

"You can do as you like. I'm trying to say that I don't want to hit you. At this point no one wants to beat you anymore. Why are you resisting?"

"I can't answer what you're asking me because I don't know. I don't know where Miguel Enríquez is."

"You don't know? I don't believe you."

"Sir, you know everything. You know I'm not with the MIR. And even if I were with the MIR, do you think all the militants know where he is?"

"What I know is that you're a communist, a marxist. That's what you are."

I could see the trap. I thought that if my brother had already given them information, then they knew we belonged to the Socialist Party, and they wanted me to say it. Okay, fine, I'll say it.

"I'm a socialist, sir. Not a militant, of course! So even if you kill me, I couldn't tell you where Miguel is. And furthermore, sir, after so many months here, and please try to understand me, I can't say anything about the party because they've known about my detention for a long time. Nothing exists as I knew it. Besides, I was never a militant, just a sympathizer."

He took a long, silent drag on his cigarette. I did too. There we were face-to-face as if we were in a silent duel, looking at each other, smoking, thinking.

"Are you sure you have nothing to offer about the Socialist Party."

"Nothing you don't already know, sir."

He looked surprised. I was playing my last card. Could I use it as a bluff? I kept talking. "Honestly, sir, I don't understand you. You give me a cup of coffee, correction, two cups of coffees, and I'm on my third or fourth," I looked at the ashtray and after counting confirmed, "fourth cigarette. I'm grateful. But what's the point? To find out if I am telling the truth? You already know every card in the deck, sir." I was very calm and decided to continue. I stood up and looked at everything. I remembered how I had once had a meeting with Carlos Alamos in that same office on Londres Street. I imagined him in some other world smoking a smelly Tiparillo cigar. I looked at the officer again. "Why bother playing, sir?"

He put his cigarette out violently and muttered, "Shit! These guards! And here I am acting like an ass."

I automatically thought, "You're not more of an ass because you don't get up earlier." He stood up and yelled out the door, "Bring her brother in!"

I forced myself to remain calm. I was trembling. I wouldn't be able to smoke anymore. If I did, he would realize that I was shaking like a leaf.

COLLABORATION

My brother looked bad. He was dirty and covered with bruises. I looked at their color and figured they were about a week old. He was blindfolded. I asked myself where they were keeping him because I was pretty sure he wasn't in the large room with all the prisoners. Perhaps, deep in thought as I was, in that state of virtual absence, I hadn't realized he was there. I have to warn him I'm here.

"May I say hello to him, sir? May I take his blindfold off?"

"Let him go," said the officer, addressing the guard. I went over to him and we hugged.

"How are you?"

"Okay. And you?"

"Okay."

What an absurd dialogue! Our words could actually have been translated as "I haven't died yet and I feel like shit," but we kept going anyway.

"How is everyone at home? My son? And your daughter?"

"Fine, Fine. As good as they can be."

"Get over here, both of you! Sit down! This is against protocol, but I'm in charge here and I've decided to leave you two alone for a while. I'll be back soon."

He walked out, leaving the door open and a guard armed with a rifle in the doorway.

"Why didn't you go away?" I asked, although I had already guessed the answer.

"I couldn't. I felt guilty. The second time they took you it was my fault."

"Why?"

"Do you remember Navarrete?"

"Raúl?"

"Yes. That day you went to the Military Hospital, he went to the store and we started talking. I told him everything, that you had been released, that you had fooled the DINA."

"You told him everything you knew?"

"Everything. I'm sorry. I considered him a compañero. When I realized what I had done I wanted to die. He knew everything about you. I decided not to run away, I wanted to wait until they came for me. I knew they'd come for me even if you didn't talk. Raúl and I got involved in the party together. He knows more about me than you do."

I felt somewhat relieved. He didn't just hand himself over to the DINA. He had no way of resisting. They knew everything before they went to get him, but even so I would have rather seen him leave the country. Now both of us were prisoners and the burden and sadness for our parents would be greater. Not only was my son without his mother, but now my brother's wife and daughter were alone too.

"Tell me the truth. How are they?"

"Think about it. Mom cries. . . . She's hurting."

"And now even more."

It was so strange to talk to my brother under those circumstances. The officer brought more coffee when he returned. Actually, he hadn't finished with us yet. He hadn't even started. There was something in the air. It moved around inside of us, but I couldn't make out what it was. I was sure that at this stage in the game they wouldn't free me just like that. I was becoming a problem. For some reason they hadn't killed me yet. If they sent me to court, they would charge me with engaging in illegal political activities. And with whatever charges they might add to that, I would have to spend some years in prison.

But would they send me through the courts given what I knew about the DINA? I supposed they couldn't keep me there indefinitely. Someday they would have to make a decision. And it seemed like they had resolved not to kill me—yet. But why? The worst thing was that I couldn't think of any reason not to. Undoubtedly, that interview was crucial. The officer had shown himself to be excessively patient. Those officers, soldiers, and members of the permanent personnel in the police stations and detention centers were actually being directed from above, and with the explicit demand that they be rough. For them, we weren't people, just marxists, which they took to mean criminals and whores who wanted to kill them and their families.

"Okay, kids, recess is over. As things stand now, I should kill you both, but I don't want to," he said as he took the weapons, including Alejandro's pistol, out of the box. I shuddered. The "negrita" I thought, and I felt like my counting of the days was over. I tried to remember Alejandro's alias, the one I used when I called him at the airport. I rummaged through my memory. It had been erased forever. I never again remembered it, never, just his real name. Perhaps I intuitively thought Alejandro could use those documents and I blocked it from my mind forever. When I reacted, I heard the officer say, "I'm offering you the following, if you collaborate as much as possible, important things, information"—he said, slowly changing his tone—"I won't pressure you any further, and I promise you a small sentence, let's say, around three months, we could send you to . . . Frutillar, for example. You can go with your children. It's a beautiful place. . . ."

My brother interjected and said, "That sounds good."

I started saying that I hadn't been in touch with anyone for months and that I hoped they would understand that I didn't have any contacts, nothing current anyway.

"Good, let's go even further," the officer said, ignoring my words. "My name is Ricardo Lawrence, and I'm a police officer. I want a list of what you know. You'll be free if you comply. You can start all over again in the South. You could be a schoolteacher, for example, Luz. Think about it tonight. Try to get some sleep. I'll call you into the office early tomorrow morning."

"Guard! Blindfold them, but don't tie them up. Leave them together in a corner so that they can talk among themselves."

Moments later they brought in Alejandra. She had arrived at 38 Londres Street on August 1st, and we often sat next to each other. That night the three of us were there. My brother managed to sleep, or at least it looked like he did, and it took me a little while longer. I felt trapped. I had to give them something. The length of my detention worked in my favor. They can't expect my information to be current. I had to talk to my brother. Why say yes right away? I thought he must have had a plan.

I remembered Ricardo Ruz's advice, "If you have no other option, start by giving names of your compañeros you know are dead, then those who are out of the country or in prison, and if you have to go on, the marginal contacts. Given their minimal participation, they are compañeros who have little contact with the parties, and they're the ones who are more likely to get out alive. From then on, you have to live with your own conscience."

All I knew for sure was that I couldn't mention him. Although I knew

97

he had been detained, the fact that he was from the MIR would whet their appetites, and they would never believe I didn't know anything else. Everything Ricardo and I talked about seemed so obvious that I was afraid they would figure it out. The absurdity of my situation made me furious. All those months were for nothing. From one minute to the next I was on the road to collaboration in exchange for a light sentence. God! I was so confused. Even if I wanted to collaborate, even if it were the only thing I wanted, in truth I really couldn't do much. I felt everything was out of proportion, my present situation and everything I had experienced during the previous months. I couldn't understand what was happening. I thought about Raúl Navarrete Hancke. I remembered my conversations with him in the park near my parent's house and the tremendous support he gave me during my separation from the father of my eldest son. He got me a job at the Moneda when I didn't even have income to feed my son. He was the one who had brought me to the left, and now he had handed my brother and me over to the DINA. They didn't even ask me anything, not about the GAP or the Central Committee, or Gustavo. They knew everything, and things about my brother too. I thought about what he had been able to tell me and I pictured Raúl at home with his family. I was really hurt. . . . I came back to the present moment thinking that it was clear that, once we gave them the information, they would realize that the names were of people who weren't in Chile or who were impossible to locate. I believed I'd be able to convince them that I didn't know they were dead or refugees. After all, I had been there all those months. And my brother? I trusted Raúl to tell the truth, that my brother had been completely out of the loop after the coup.

As soon as my brother woke up, I told him that I'd been thinking that I wasn't arrested just for what he told Raúl, but that the information just confirmed that I was lying. I said I was sure they were going to come for me ever since they let me go. That seemed clear from the very beginning. I told him I had been arrested with a fake ID, that I still hadn't explained how I had gotten it, and that I was sure that now they would force me to clarify that point. I asked him again, "Are you sure Raúl is an informer?"

"Yeah, but don't worry, sis. I spent every day hoping they would come and arrest me. I wanted to get you out of here. I knew you'd let yourself get killed, but now we'll do whatever we can to get out together."

"We'll do anything?"

"Anything."

"At any price?"

"At any price. . . ."

He didn't say anything else, but I knew he guessed my thoughts.

"Look sis, you're my sister and we're going to get out of this one. Our life today is this. It's worse than hell. We have to get out."

I stopped talking and thought about what he was doing for me. I told myself he let himself get arrested struggling to convince me that everything was as he said it was. But I couldn't waste time trying to convince him. He won't listen to me anyway, I thought. I have to play my own cards. He doesn't realize that I could have faced anything alone. Now everything is worse with him here. Okay, I'll choose to try and live, but not at any price. I have to be sure he gets out of here, or at least to somewhere he can have visitors. I am worried about his health and his temperament. They would kill him without thinking twice about it. I was afraid because I knew I couldn't take seeing him tortured. Since he had been a cadet, and since we had personal friends in the army, it occurred to me that maybe that could help us. I remembered that Patricio, an officer and our neighbor for many years, had come to visit me while I was at home. He told me he could find me a job if I promised to give up my activities as a militant. I mentioned him once in passing, and years later I found out he was questioned just because he knew us. He was working at that time with someone I would know later as Colonel Orozco.

When Ricardo Lawrence arrived in the morning, he didn't seem to be in any hurry or anxious to talk. Sure, he's like a landowner of a country estate, the complete master of the situation. I heard the officer's voice at noon. I knew what time it was from the sound of the cannon on the Santa Lucía hill. A heavy silence emerged around and within me. They transferred us to one of the offices. When they took off my blindfold, I found myself fixing on a point past Lawrence, my mind wandering.

I felt that the saying I had adopted as my motto since the years I was a physical education student and that had remained with me during my imprisonment at Villa Grimaldi and 38 Londres Street still rang true: Save your strength. I thought about how unfair it was to have heart problems back when I was an athlete and not now. Why didn't my heart fail from the electric shock or the beatings? Now that it has been beating quickly for months it doesn't want to stop working. . . . I remembered back when I was an athlete, when, along with other classmates from the Catholic University, we repeatedly set and broke the South

99

American record for the 800-meter hurdle, and when I won the national championship. There, when Luz Arce was losing her potential was when my heart rebelled. How different life seemed to me at that moment! A few weeks earlier, I wasn't even sure if I would walk again. Now I could, albeit with a lot of pain, but I could.

That's what playing sports left me with, I thought, great physical strength and the ability to tolerate demanding situations.

"Okay, kids! What do you say we get a little work done?"

My brother and I looked at him without saying a word. Ricardo Lawrence Mires sat down in front of us and said,

"Names. . . . Let's see. Begin."

"Does that mean that what we talked about yesterday is a deal? Can we agree on the details?"

"Yes, ma'am. We can be more precise. The two of you are going to collaborate, and then you're going to be relocated. You can take your families, and I can get a job for you at least at the school. I know the director. You will be free after three months, but I think that it would be better for you both to start over far away from Santiago and from all of this. It's a beautiful place, but now I want names."

My head hurt. I had some coffee. I decided to alternate between people who were refugees, dead, and in prison. "The name of my superior in the GEA was 'Silvano.'"

"His real name?"

"I don't know, probably." He wrote the name on a sheet of paper. I thought about Raúl Navarrete and the possibility that he didn't know that "Silvano" was dead. I remembered that Raúl had been arrested in Til-Til a few days before the coup while he was transporting weapons from San Antonio in a party car he was driving. And to think that I had asked him to help me hide my books and weapons when I had been released! He refused. Maybe he didn't hand me over that day. . . .

"Where can I find this Silvano?"

"I don't know. I haven't seen him since before the change in government," I said, careful not to say coup. They had already beaten me for that before. "I think he was from the South, or at least his family lived in the South."

"And you. Do you know how to find this Silvano?" Lawrence asked as he looked at my brother.

"Well, I know him too. I think he was from Talca. Yes, he used to go to Talca. His family lives there."

I was just expecting to gain a few days' time. I knew they would check things out. That's why, when I saw they were going to disregard Silvano, I added, "You know, sir, I just remembered that he was a boxer when he was younger, a really good one. A few years ago he won against Bonavena in the youth division."

"Bonavena, the world champion?"

"Yes, when they were younger," my brother added. "I think it should be easy to find his last name."

Lawrence wrote it all down, but still wasn't entirely convinced. "Do you know anything else about him?"

"He was with the GAP, sir."

"Oh! . . . Then he's either in prison or dead."

"Sir, I don't think so because he wasn't in the GAP anymore by September 11th. He was in the GEA."

"Let's see. I understand what you mean by GAP, but GEA? What does GEA stand for?"

We started explaining a little bit about it without mentioning the compartmentalized structure. We talked about the Militant Training School.

"And they were? . . . Names. Let's see, names of the GEA members."

"Of course, sir, but there we only know aliases. We never knew anyone's name, much less his or her address. It was a compartmentalized structure. . . ."

"And your superior when you were detained in March?"

"His name is Mauro, sir."

"His real name?"

"I don't know, sir, but I don't think it was."

"This is useless. Nothing you have said is of any use at all! I need more. If you think you're going to jerk me around like this the whole time, you're both wrong. I'll put you on the grill again and see if you still want to joke around. Listen carefully. I'm bored so I'm leaving. I'll leave you alone. Here is a pencil and paper. When I return, I want to see a list of names."

He left. A few minutes later a guard came. My head, eyes, and stomach all hurt. I listened to my brother. . . .

"Sis, what's the matter?"

"I feel rotten."

I decided not to tell my brother about our compañeros I knew were refugees so that his reaction when he found out would be spontaneous.

I started by putting a girlfriend on the list. I knew she was in Canada because she even sent me a letter with five dollars in it. I put her at the top of the list, Carmen Sabaj. I didn't remember her address, but I wrote that I knew how to get there. I included two of her friends who were also with INESAL and who were either out of the country or ready to leave when I was detained in March. I don't remember their names now, but they were a couple. They lived on Juárez Street after the coup.

Then my brother told me we should put "Leo" on the list since he was free and had apparently made a deal with the DINA. He had given them Toño's name along with mine in March, and he remained free. I never found out what had happened to Gustavo Ruz Zañartu. My brother told me he had fallen into the hands of the AGA (Air Force Academy). I was able to confirm that years later, but I never discovered the circumstances in which he was arrested.

Now I know he was captured on March 12th, in other words, five days before Toño and I were detained. Since I needed to justify that someone else was in charge of the organization, I included my superior's name, "Mauro," on the list, and I added that I knew that he had lived with "Leo" at his house.

We pretended we hadn't realized that Raúl was collaborating with the DINA, and we included him on the list. We noted that he had been a member of the GAP and the name of the street where he lived. Then we wrote the name of a young man we knew had belonged to a MIR base. He and my brother were friends, and he was constantly seen with Raúl after the coup, which is why we suspected he was collaborating with the DINA too.

When Ricardo Lawrence returned, we gave him that list. He started reviewing it and read that my superior's name was "Mauro."

"This 'Mauro,' are you sure you don't know his real name?"

"No I don't, sir. I never met him personally, although I suspect he's a member of the leadership."

I was confident that even if "Leo" said that I had seen Gustavo, I could argue that I received written instructions from "Mauro" and that I thought they were two different people.

"The fact is, sir, that I think this 'Mauro' is the general secretary of the Socialist Party in Chile."

"And you say that he was at the house of this 'Leo'?"

"I suppose so, sir, but I'm not sure. Clandestine militants don't know where their superiors live. You just get messages at meeting places on the street, through your contacts."

"So the rumor about these contacts is true then?"

"Yes, sir, it's true. Toño and I were arrested because we had lost contact with our superior. I called 'Leo' to set up a meeting to reconnect us."

"And who is this Toño?"

"He's in custody, sir. We were arrested together on March 17th. The last I knew, he was at Tejas Verdes."

I had mentioned Toño several times hoping to find out something about him, but apparently they didn't have a list there of those of us who had been arrested in March. In spite of the fact that he said he would look into it, he never mentioned even the tiniest detail about Toño to us. I assumed they wouldn't tell me anything even if they did know something about him.

Those were difficult days. They interrogated us constantly, and then they started verifying the information we gave them. Sometimes they took me along, other times my brother, at times both of us. They soon learned that Carmen Sabaj was out of the country, and that the couple on Juárez Street had managed to find asylum, or at least that's what their family said. Then Lawrence handed me over to the unit assigned to Osvaldo Romo Mena. That was when I included compañeros on the list who I thought didn't have any party responsibilities, and in so doing, pretended at the same time that we were collaborating fully with them. I thought that would help us all get out of there alive, but it didn't happen that way. Some of them are still disappeared: Alvaro Barrios Duque, Sergio Riveros Villavicencio, Rodolfo Espejo Gómez, and Oscar Castro Videla.

I knew what Alvaro Barrios Duque looked like, from when I lived for several years in the neighborhood of Independencia. During the Popular Unity period, we tried to organize and operate a cultural center in the neighborhood where we lived. We were all from different leftist parties, and we didn't know the nature of each person's political activities. I saw Alvaro many times, and I knew he lived around Vivaceta, but that was all. I mentioned him and indicated the area where he lived. To find him, Osvaldo Romo Mena, Basclay Zapata Reyes, and the "negro" Paz took us in a truck and drove around the streets in the area. They were under the command of Miguel Krassnoff. This was during the first couple of weeks in August. We stopped by a house on Nueva de Matte where a girl lived who seemed to be friends with Alvaro even though she wasn't a militant. She said she didn't know exactly where he lived, but that another neighbor, Patricio Alvarez, could show us where. Patricio was detained and released after he gave them Alvaro's address.

When I saw them let Patricio go back to his house I breathed a sigh of relief. I thought this would happen to all of them sooner or later, and I was happy for him. When we arrived at Alvaro's house, they took me out of the truck and made me ask for him at his house. Basclay Zapata, known as "Troglo," was standing next to me, and "negro" Paz and Osvaldo Romo were farther back. Alvaro came out of the house unsuspectingly, and we walked a few yards toward the corner. There, Romo and "Troglo" made him get into the back of the truck. The vehicle headed toward Independencia to Carlos Rammsy Villablanca's house. He was also detained.

That day my brother and I were convinced that Carlos and Raúl Navarrete were collaborating with the DINA since, after kicking Carlos around a bit, they left to check on a few things and released him. In Raúl's case, they didn't make even the slightest attempt to find him, despite the fact that I said I knew exactly where he lived several times in front of Romo Mena's team.

We stopped by "Leo's" house the same day Carlos was arrested. Right up to the last minute I hoped my brother had made a mistake, but that wasn't the case. He was there, and he was also arrested, which confirmed for me that he had been released even though he had set Toño and me up in March that same year. I have to admit that I was enraged at that moment, a feeling that I would painfully learn to assimilate and understand over time. A few days later I found out that the agents who had made that so-called deal with "Leo" were members of the Purén Unit of the BIM. They were the same ones who arrested me in March, and they had released him without informing their superiors.

At least Krassnoff, Lawrence, and others at Caupolicán knew nothing about that, or so they said. The Purén agents who had released "Leo" in March were summoned to 38 Londres Street to explain the situation. That was why they made sure to give me a beating before they left the Yucatán Detention Center, since I had brought "Leo" in and called attention to them.

I never saw the compañeros they arrested again. They didn't even bring us face-to-face, maybe because they knew each other better. Lawrence said he was going to keep interrogating us the following day, that he thought we had given him very little information. He kept saying that it was our last chance. In those days, there was a lot of movement by units that were responsible for capturing and interrogating the MIR's militants and supporters. They were being detained in droves.

104

FURTHER AND FURTHER

I felt horrible. I couldn't eat. I asked the guard to take my food to my brother. They made fun of us, but they gave it to him. I remembered that we were one of two identifiable couples there at that time. Erika Hennings and her husband, Alfonso Chanfreau (detained and disappeared), and my brother and I. I didn't know them, but I will always remember Erika. She was a young woman with large, expressive, dark eyes, olive skin, and curly black hair.

I now know that I spoke to her during my arrest. I can't recall all of that conversation, but I remember asking her to call my parents if they released her, and I gave her their telephone number. Maybe that's when she told me about her daughter, and she and Natalia remain etched in my mind.

Ricardo Lawrence was tired and annoyed. A couple of days went by and no one called us. It seemed as though they had forgotten about us, which was welcome news under the circumstances. My brother and I had agreed to cough every once in a while so we would know if we were in the same area. Alejandra realized this and coughed too so the guard wouldn't notice that it was a sign between us.

I passed the time dozing, and I started having nightmares that incorporated all the surrounding sounds, the screams of the prisoners who were being tortured, the begging and crying of women claiming their innocence, and the yelling of the guards. In one of those nightmares I knew it was nighttime because of the sounds: I could hear them taking the prisoners to the bathroom. Then they would take our chairs and make us throw ourselves on the floor, really close together. "On your side, you assholes," the guard used to say.

We wouldn't fit any other way. They kept the men tied up really tight, and some of the guards tied the women a bit more loosely. They even left us with our hands untied sometimes. I remember waking up really sore the first few days.

It was late, but there was more activity than usual. I heard some of the officers arriving. It was Krassnoff Martchenko and Lawrence Mires, and after a while you could hear Romo Mena's voice. It was clear that they had brought new prisoners from the MIR who apparently had some degree of importance in the organization's structure. I heard my brother's voice by my side. He talked to me slowly and confirmed my suspicion that new prisoners had arrived that afternoon while I was sleeping.

They were really doing a job on them. . . . ." They would leave us alone for a few hours. That kind of peace feels as painful as the torture itself since you're able to rest only because the "rack" is occupied. We were interrupted by the shouts of a guard who realized we were talking. He was yelling loudly and he shook me by the arm: "What's the matter with you, bitch? Shut up! I'm new here. They sent me because I'm really mean!" Pretty soon we began to hear screams, heartbreaking screams, the kind that tear your soul apart, that make you relive everything all over again, that are forever etched in your mind. Now that I think about it, I have never in my life had occasion to feel, touch, smell, and hear so many expressions of pain.

Around that time in August 1974, I felt I had drifted further and further away from that Luz who thought she could face anything without betraying what she so cared about. I felt like they had ripped from me more than just bits of my skin, but also bits of my soul. I felt that they had taken away any possibility to remain who I was. I can't explain it clearly. I didn't just feel full of pain and unease. I was beyond desperation. I was as if every scourge and disease had taken possession of me. The feeling of being lost often emerged within me. My nightmares attacked me even when I was awake. I think all that horror was driving me insane.

11

NIGHTMARES

They kept me sitting with each leg tied to a chair leg. Sometimes my hands were tied behind my back, and other times they were tied in front of me. My eyes were covered with tape and a piece of someone's dirty shirt. I shivered from the cold, and my sweat froze on my skin.

I didn't think about keeping my muscles active anymore. I was defeated, shattered, broken, although I wasn't openly collaborating. I was still defending many things. I didn't turn in any compañero who had an important role in the party or in the MIR. I told myself that as I tried to find some way to breathe in that feeling of death. It was as if a desert of hard sand and nostalgia had grown from within me. I felt like thorns and knives were tearing me apart from one day to the next. Each scream, each howl multiplied into thousands of echoes in my mind and seemed to make my head explode. I wanted to get up and untie myself. I imagined a nail or a knife. Anything seemed good to rip open my veins that were swollen from the strain. They gave me a kind of hope I could turn my life into a river flowing over the dirty, filthy floor in that evil place that one day was like a home for me: 38 Londres Street.

When I managed to sleep, I couldn't fend off a recurrent nightmare I had had since I was a little girl.

I was nine years old when I got a really bad case of tonsillitis. I felt awful, and I must have had a fever. One night I had the first dream I can remember, and it started to recur. All I had to do was close my eyes, and the railroad tracks appeared before I could even fall asleep. I had to walk on them by jumping from one wooden tie to another. A man's voice shouted "one!" and I had to obey and jump over one tie. Then he would say "three!" and I jumped over three. But the voice kept getting faster and faster: "Five! Fifty! One hundred!" I kept running and sweating, but

I realized I couldn't do it, and that no matter what I did I was defeated. And the voice did not stop. On the contrary. Finally exhausted, I always fell. Then I woke up feeling dizzy and seeing stars. My arms felt heavy and I didn't understand anything. It was the same thing every night. At dusk, as the sun was setting, I started dreading that anguishing dream. The nightmares recurred until just a couple of years ago.

I remember that one Saturday, possibly August 17, 1974, a few days after I had started collaborating, they took me to an office tied up and blindfolded. I sensed that the situation was different from all the previous ones. There was a lot of silence. I realized that my brother was next to me, apparently in the same condition I was, tied up and blindfolded. He must have heard them bring me in so he coughed several times and I knew he was there.

I felt him beside me. I fell forward because of my bad foot, and they had fortunately tied my hands in front of me. I instinctively stretched them in front of me, and I was able to perceive that we were in front of a desk. There were at least three other people sitting there, which I could tell from the different voices even though I only recognized one of them, Miguel Krassnoff Martchenko's. They questioned me about Rodolfo González. I kept insisting that he took some letters to my parents and my son, that nothing else had happened, and that it was true.

Krassnoff Martchenko insisted that this was the investigation where they had to establish whether the recruit González Pérez was a traitor or not.

Since I refused to state that Rodolfo had told me about some of the detention centers and how the DINA functioned, they hauled me out and took me once again to the second floor where Osvaldo Romo Mena and a police official tortured me again. The police official had long black hair with a few strands of gray, blue eyes, and he was drunk. They applied electric shock to me again. They wanted me to sign a statement saying that I had seduced Rodolfo at the hospital with the intention of recruiting him to the Socialist Party. I told them no a million times. I begged them to believe me. They told me that what I said wasn't the least bit important. They had a statement already written affirming that I had slept with Rodolfo at the Military Hospital and that all the guards from the Cavalry School and the nurses would sign it. They said that refusing to sign it wouldn't do me any good, and they took my hand and stamped my fingerprint on the document.

They kept torturing me, saying I would have to learn to behave myself. I was raped again by at least three agents. I must have lost consciousness because the next thing I remember was waking up tied and blindfolded on the first floor. I was on a mattress in a corner. I stayed there all night awake and crying, overwhelmed by an indescribable pain. I was exhausted, and I kept having one nightmare after another. I must have been really confused because I felt like I needed to hold someone's hand, to feel someone beside me, someone whose presence could lessen the feeling of abandonment. I heard Patricia Barceló and Osvaldo Romo's voices. I knew she was a doctor. Her voice sounded different to me, maybe because she was a woman and a compañera. I never heard her beg and plead like the other women. The truth is, I don't know. . . . I don't remember exactly what I said, but I do know that Patricia came over to me and took my pulse. It seems she said something to Osvaldo Romo because he asked the guard to leave me alone on the mattress that night. Patricia checked my pulse with her hand on my neck. I remember her hand being soft and tiny. I didn't even see it because I was blindfolded, but I perceived it like that, almost like a caress. That small contact with someone who wasn't from the DINA was enough to make me start to cry.

I can't say whether I slept or not, maybe intermittently. In the morning I could hear all the prisoners getting up and the guard screaming, moving the lines toward the bathroom. I remember I couldn't get up, or I refused to. . . . I stayed there until the guard noticed I was still on the floor. He started yelling at me to stand up, and since I didn't, he started piling all the mattresses on me. Then he stood on top of me. He lifted the part of the mattresses that covered my face and said, "Open your mouth. I'm going to give you some coffee!"

Then he put the barrel of his pistol in my mouth until it touched my palate and pulled the trigger. No bullet came out. Apparently, it wasn't loaded. Then he started walking on the mattresses on top of me, ordering me to get up. Since he didn't get his way, he got bored, and he jerked me around until I was left half sitting on the mattress. It seems that was the moment I started saying incoherent things. All I remember is that I thought I had my son in my arms, and I sang lullabies and described some beautiful landscapes I was seeing. My mind was far away. . . .

They taunted me in the DINA for years because of what I said that morning. I could never remember what I said, but Alejandra told me about it months later. It seems that I was describing a place with some hills at the edge of a beautiful valley and little black fish swimming in a clear stream. When she told me that, I remembered I had been to a place like that near Santiago several years earlier. . . . Maybe I remembered Ralún and heard the melody again that the wind was wrenching out from between the thorns of a cactus at the top of a hill. Perhaps, in all my despair, I walked again through the tall grass, and maybe I dreamed again of the birds gliding overhead.

That morning, as soon as he realized what happened, my brother asked to speak to Ricardo Lawrence. He complained about how I had been treated the previous day and that morning. I wasn't afraid when the guard shot his gun. I so wanted death. . . .

Officer Lawrence had them take us to his office and told us that his superior wanted to speak with us. He handed me the telephone, and I heard Marcelo Moren Brito's voice for the first time.

Today, I wonder: What was that investigation all about? Was it just a charade to try to tear a signature out of me? Could Rodolfo possibly still have been alive? What did the DINA tell the air force about what had happened to Rodolfo Valentín?

MARCELO MOREN BRITO

I don't know whether what happened to me lasted two days or three, but on a certain day in August they had me speak to Marcelo Moren Brito. I remember clearly that I listened to a voice on the receiver that was saying—correction—yelling, which was how he expressed himself, something about sending someone to get me so we could talk at his office.

I was transferred to Terranova a few hours later. I still didn't feel well. I was dizzy and it was hard to think. They put me in a room with a cement floor, which was far from the main house. That was when I saw a young man there. He was short, with a dark complexion and straight dark hair. I can't remember his facial features because there was a blindfold over his eyes and the fabric covered his face. As I passed by him, I tried to see the floor through a tiny opening in the lower part of my blindfold, and I was able to make out clearly his straight black hair and his shoes, which looked like the safety shoes that industrial workers wear. He was sitting on the floor with his legs stretched out.

The guard was inside the room, and it seemed like he was bored or that he had orders to get more information from the prisoners because he kept trying to strike up a conversation. After a while, I pretended

I had fallen asleep. I was too nervous. I wouldn't have been able to talk or explain anything to anybody. However, I did hear the conversation he had with the other prisoner. The guard called him "Huaico," and I heard that "Huaico," whose real name is Joel Huaiquiñir Benavides (detained and disappeared), was working up north in Cobre Salvador on the day of the coup.

A few hours after I arrived, they took me blindfolded to meet "Jefe Ronco," that is to say, Marcelo Moren Brito. When I was at Yucatán, I had heard it was terrible to fall into his hands. At that moment, he didn't seem aggressive or violent, except for his voice. On the contrary, he seemed like he was in a good mood, and he kept making jokes. He asked me for details about the daily routine at the Yucatán Detention Center and about my personal life. Our conversation was a little forced since it wasn't easy for me to talk with him. He reiterated during our conversation that what Officer Lawrence had promised would be done.

He never spoke specifically about the way I would start collaborating with the DINA. I thought it was better that way. I knew they only wanted one thing: that I turn people in, and I hoped I could find some way to redirect my collaboration toward another area and do the least damage possible. The DINA wanted what they called "important prisoners": leaders in charge of military, information or communication structures. They called this "pulling threads to unravel the structural framework."

During my conversation with Moren Brito it became clear to me that one of his principle goals was to justify the existing repressive measures, in addition to legitimizing the DINA as the most important "security force."

There was a special effort in those days to outdo the AGA's Air Force Intelligence Service. Moren Brito started from the premise that I would collaborate and guaranteed that my brother's and my life would be respected. He ended the conversation saying that it was late and that he would send me back to Yucatán the next day.

When I left Moren Brito's office, they took me to another room at the main house. I realized there were several other prisoners there, and I recognized Doctor Patricia Barceló among them.

I was able to see her from under my blindfold because I was lying down on the floor when she came to the room after I was already there. I don't know her personally, but I remember she was delicate and thin and had black hair; she was wearing a green skirt or dress. That night was the first time they put handcuffs on me instead of tying my hands. The handcuffs had some kind of hooks that clamped tighter when I moved my hands. I freed one of my hands, trying not to move to keep them from tightening, and so I could doze without hurting myself. When I could see the sun coming up under my blindfold, and when the guard began to move around, I very carefully put my hand in again.

AT THE YUCATÁN DETENTION CENTER AGAIN

The guards gave us some coffee and then made me get in the vehicle. From underneath my blindfold, I could see someone lying on his back on the floor of the truck. A guard came over right then and yelled, "Okay, honey, hurry up! Sit in the back against the cab!" Then he turned to someone else, who could have been Paz since Basclay Zapata was driving, and added: "You go ahead and get in back, don't worry, the other guy's a stiff."
"'Emilio?'"
"Yeah, the asshole died before he talked."
"Isn't he the one they're complaining about in France?"
"Yeah, it's gonna hit the fan. I guess the bastard's French. . . ."
I spent years thinking that Alfonso Chanfreau Oyarce, whose political alias was "Emilio," was back there dead. I was overcome by silence. I guessed it was the only tribute I could make to a compañero who died defending and protecting the people he loved, his family, his compañeros. . . . Before we left Terranova, the guards said they had run him over with a truck.

In time, I started realizing that talking about horrific forms of torture in front of us was part of the process they subjected us to in order to soften us up. However, I really thought it was true at the time. Now I'm not sure. I still haven't been able to pinpoint the exact day I saw Alfonso Chanfreau—if it was really he—on the floor of the truck. It was sometime in August 1974. All I know is that the last day his wife, Mrs. Hennings, saw him alive was on Tuesday the 13th.

Every time I returned to the Yucatán Detention Center, the guards had fun assigning me the same number: prisoner fifty-four. I realized they were nearing number one hundred and fifty when I heard them call roll. A guard told me that they had started counting from one again, and that I was number fifty-four from the first "batch" of DINA prisoners.

I've wondered for years about the exact date I returned to Yucatán, and I've never been able to determine it precisely. The rest of the time I spent there at 38 Londres Street is really hazy. I just remember bits and pieces of that period, which was the most awful in my life. I felt like I had been destroyed, and I was in a constant state of semiconsciousness. I had few moments of lucidity, which is when I smelled the fetid odor of our bodies.

Yucatán was a permanent hole of horror and terror. Everything smelled of blood, shit, and death. I know there were times when the compañeros would tell jokes, but those moments were the saddest for me. I remember they used to give us coffee in the morning if a compañero had money to pay for it. One day they asked everybody if we had any money. The guards kept insisting, and it was hard to come up with the amount we needed. The guards made the coffee and insisted we all drink it.

The coffee was strange, but then everything there was really dirty, disgusting, and slimy. I drank it. It was warm, which made me feel better, but my mouth was peeling and full of sores after a few days. Other compañeras near me complained of the same thing. Dying of laughter, the guards told us they had made the coffee with everybody's urine. The small bathroom on the first floor wasn't working at the time, and they took us to urinate in a can.

Days went by like that. By the end of August, so many compañeros from the MIR were still being arrested that they left me alone for a while.

A COMPAÑERO FROM THE PARTY

I have remembered through some real soul searching. All these years, it was impossible for me to remember that I turned in another compañero from my party. Maybe since he's alive, and since I didn't see him on the lists of the disappeared, I never stumbled upon that memory.

I'm not going to identify the compañero. I think he will give important testimony if he decides to go public. I just want to say how my desperation crossed paths with his. The responsibility is all mine.

After the coup, this compañero, who lived in an apartment, gave me his keys so we could use his place for meetings during the day. That's what I told Osvaldo Romo Mena. I didn't see them arrest him, but I do remember perfectly the instant they came and got me out of my chair in a corner of 38 Londres Street. Next to Krassnoff Martchenko's office, he and Romo Mena made me repeat that Guillermo had lent me his apartment so we could hold meetings there. Guillermo insisted that he had lent me his place so I could sleep with someone there. . . . I desperately denied it. I was so traumatized by what had happened to me that it was impossible for me to see that had I said yes I could have spared him a lot of pain. I realize now how desperate I was. I was unable to realize at that moment that it would have been a thousand times better for them to call me a whore than for them to torture my compañero. I don't know what happened to Guillermo. A short time before my trip to Europe, I found out that he apparently had collaborated, and that he later left the country.

I am implicated in this compañero's supposed collaboration. I just want to state here that a lot of what happened took place in the midst of terror. Although I tried my best to preserve all my sense of reason there, that day I was unable to see that I could have attenuated Guillermo's problems if I had just said, "Yes, I'm a whore."

MARIO AGUILERA SALAZAR

Besides on the compañeros who are disappeared, I informed on others who survived. I remember one of them vividly. For years I only knew him as the compañero who was arrested on Grecia Avenue. I never knew his name until I returned to Chile and met him. He welcomed me warmly, and it made me incredibly happy to see him in the courts with a microphone in his hand. His name is Mario Aguilera. He is a television reporter on the news program "24 Hours" on the National Station. We talked an entire afternoon trying to reconstruct those painful hours. I asked him again if he had forgiven me. He said he had. Through him I found out about some details that I didn't know or some I had forgotten. I've been able to bring some things to mind about the terror of August 1974, but to this day I have been unable to recover others. I couldn't help but laugh when he starting laughing and asked me, "Do you remember the little seal sounds?" Of course, how could I forget the compañero whom the guards forced to make those cute sounds? I didn't know it was Mario Aguilera who tried to find ways to stay active and give the compañeros a breath of fresh air in the midst of that inferno. I thank God I didn't even know Mario's name in 1974 since he was much more important in the party than the DINA imagined. He didn't break and inform on any of his compañeros. He survived and was exiled to France.

As Mario kept talking, my memory recovered bits and pieces. He told me that making the seal sounds started when the guard caught him talking to someone and punished him by making him act like a shark. Mario said he didn't know how imitate a shark, but that he did know how to be a seal. The guards thought it was funny. And since there were also brief moments of relaxation in the midst of all that horror, especially when the officials weren't around, Mario made his seal noises and Alejandro Parada sang tangos.

I hadn't been able to identify Alejandro Parada until the day I talked with Mario. When I testified before the Truth and Reconciliation Commission I referred to a young man by that name. I knew he had been arrested because he was the son of a coworker at my father's office. I found out about Alejandro Parada's arrest just a few years ago, but today I came to the conclusion, after talking to Mario Aguilera, that I met Alejandro Parada and saw him after he had been arrested. It's just that I always knew him as "Cano" or "Jano," and that's how he is referred to in my testimony before the Rettig Commission.

There was another thing Mario told me that I could not have known, given that the men and women in Cuatro Alamos were locked up in different rooms, and which really moved me, especially since the two people involved are both alive. It's about the underground message service.

When they took all the prisoners from 38 Londres Street to Cuatro Alamos, they locked Mario and Christian Van Yurick in the large room. The only thing separating this room from the Tres Alamos sector, where the prisoners could have visitors, was a door. Christian and Mario sent messages under the door, which were then passed from the prisoners at Tres Alamos to the families of those in Cuatro Alamos. That's how they started an underground message service. The compañeros at Tres Alamos could receive visitors and things, and they passed on cigarettes that often ended up all crushed and broken after going under the door. When they took Christian out for more questioning, Mario made sure he stayed close to the door so that the message system could continue.

One day there was an inspection at Cuatro Alamos and when the agents checked Mario and Christian's room they realized that that door had always been open. They could have even tried to escape. But they would have never imagined that, and they hadn't checked the door. . . .

Another story Mario reminded me about was the "stupidest taxi driver in Chile." That same month, in August 1974, they brought a prisoner in and brutally tortured him. A rumor started that he was one of the instigators of the first bank robbery that had occurred during the dictatorship.

The case was tragic because they found out the truth only after the man was tortured and his wife and a female friend of his had been captured. He was a taxi driver, married, but he also had a girlfriend. He couldn't use the excuse of having to work at night because of the curfew the government had imposed. He was a little late one night, and as he was going home the following morning thinking about what he would tell his wife he saw the news about the bank robbery in the paper. When he got home, trying to avoid his wife's reproaches, he told her that he couldn't ignore the situation his country was in and that he had been one of the bank robbers. As proof he showed her the paper where they mentioned that the thieves had escaped in a taxi. His wife was really proud and couldn't keep her promise not to tell anyone, and so she told someone else who told someone else until the news reached the DINA. When they found out the truth, they started calling him the "stupidest taxi driver in Chile" the whole time he was in custody.

12

ANOTHER DETENTION CENTER

It seems strange, but it's true. It never occurred to me to think about or try to find out how my compañeros were disappearing, not even during my most lucid moments. I don't understand it. I realize that a lot of questions I ask myself today, or that others ask me, weren't part of my thought process at the time. There are those who have asked me: "Didn't you ever think about saying no?" And I realize that I didn't, and the reason is simple: Say no to what? Don't rape me, don't ask me that, don't torture me, don't reduce me to trash. . . . No to what? Did they even ask me anything? I'm referring to the fact that I never decided anything based on a question and a few minutes to think about it. No, it wasn't like that. . . .

In those days, not everything that happened was clear to me at the very moment things were taking place. With time, and as I've been writing, I've started to understand. Having perspective and being in a different situation and time help. In those days I never imagined it would be useful for me to familiarize myself with the DINA structure. For example, I never thought that "Extermination Units" existed, in other words, people whose only mission was to kill and dispose of prisoners who had been condemned to die. I knew that death was there waiting for us around every corner. I imagined that there were people who made the decisions, but I never stopped to think about how. I thought that those who made it to the Cuatro Alamos prison survived, but that wasn't true. Even compañeros who made it to Tres Alamos, where they could have visitors, later disappeared.

Today I know, for example, that even stranger things happened, like the facts surrounding the disappearance of John MacLeod Trever—who was apparently connected to the MIR—and his mother-in-law, María Julieta Ramírez. They both went to Tres Alamos on November 30,

1974, he to visit his wife and she to see her daughter. John and his mother-in-law were stopped by the guard and charged with taking documents given to them by prisoners. They are both disappeared to this day.

Only after a long time, starting in 1991, did I start to suppose that there must have been an even more secretive unit within the DINA that had the gruesome task of eliminating people in Chile and abroad.

One August afternoon, "Troglo" took me from the chair where I was tied and led me to a green vehicle. He sat down behind the wheel. At the same time an officer got in and sat to my right. I would later know him as Juan Morales Salgado. (The day of the coup he was in charge of the repression in Constitución and other cities in southern Chile. There is testimony that shows him to be responsible for numerous crimes: kidnapping, torture, and the disappearance of people in that region.)

It was a short trip, not more than fifteen or twenty minutes at the most. The truck stopped and turned right. Then it stopped before we entered an underground parking garage with at least one curve to the right. There, looking through the tape over my eyes and sunglasses, I could make out the reflection of something that at that moment looked like an illuminated red and green sign.

They took me out of the car when we arrived at that new detention center. I remember a stairway and then an elevator. I entered a spacious room where you could hear phones ringing and several people talking. A man asked me if I needed anything. I asked him for some cotton pads because I had been bleeding a lot since the last time they tortured me. I heard him complain loudly: "Another one who's come in bleeding! These dumb soldiers don't know how to do things right. . . ."

I thought they might be civilians, and I felt really frightened. Who were they?

They took me to another room and had me sit in a chair. From his voice, I could tell that this was the same individual who had met me when I arrived. He sat down in front of me and put some keys in my hands. Before I could think about anything I felt an electric shock run down my arms and through my whole body, and I let out a scream. I fell forward and I heard the man say: "That's so you don't forget what it feels like. . . ."

Then he ordered them to take my blindfold off and I could see him. He was a young man, tall, with short blonde hair, light eyes, and metal-rimmed glasses. He was wearing a shirt and beige pants. There were other men, but they were younger. All of them were in shirtsleeves, and had their shoulder holsters in plain view. That was another way they were different from the DINA's agents who wore their weapons on their waists.

YOU ARE LUZ, I WILL BE SOMBRA[28]

The blonde man's holster was a light color, made from pigskin. I saw a guy with a small machine gun sitting on a sofa a few steps away. He was polishing the weapon with the barrel up in the air and his finger over the trigger guard. He kept breathing on the metal and rubbing his shirt-sleeve on it. Then he held it out in front of him looking at it from a distance. Satisfied, he repeated the same procedure over and over again until the blonde man in front of me shouted at him, "Leave that weapon alone, you idiot! You're making me nervous." The guy kept looking at the gun with a stupid expression on his face.

"Luz, forgive me. Sometimes they seem like a bunch of children." Then, returning to the previous moment, he added: "But don't be fooled. They are trained like hunting dogs. . . . I just have to give the order and they kill. Excellent boys. My name is Javier, Luz. Some of my friends recommended you. That's why you're here. You have some qualities I admire, above all obedience. That's why I think you should live. Because you're young, healthy, and strong. For you, I'm going to be 'Sombra.'"

Then he repeated: "You are Luz. I will be Sombra. Do not forget it. When you least expect it, I will approach you slowly and say "Sombra" in your ear. Then you will know it is me and you will do as I say. . . ."

A man with a very white face entered the room. He had big, dark eyes that bugged out, and straight, black hair that covered his forehead. He was carrying a drawing pad and several pencils, and he started drawing me. I tried to understand what each of those individuals was doing there. Everything seemed really strange. At one point he came over to me and, looking at my face, took hold of my chin. I could see a tremendous disdain in his eyes and a strange smile on his face when he said, "You look like a frightened deer sniffing the air. You sense danger and that makes your hair stand on end. I can see it in your eyes." Everything

28. The agent's name "Sombra," meaning shadow, is a play on words since "Luz" means light in Spanish. I have left all proper names and aliases in the original Spanish throughout the English translation.

seemed surreal. I looked at him, intrigued. He seemed sad. Something in his gaze was crying out. Then I tasted blood in my mouth. I had bitten my own lips.

They brought some sandwiches, coffee, cigarettes, and a package of cotton pads, which is what I valued most.

The office was plain but elegant. "Javier" stood up and invited me to sit in an armchair upholstered in beige, brown, and white striped chenille. He sat down in front of me. We were separated by a coffee table. I noticed that there were some bronze lamps on end tables by the armchairs that matched the decor. I looked at everything as I ate. The man had good manners. Everything was bewildering. "Javier" put on some classical music, and they served some more coffee. I thought it had to be one of those coffee substitutes that taste weird.

"Javier" drifted back again to what he had said at the beginning, that the DINA didn't know how to do its job, that they were brutes. I started feeling strange, a little light-headed, and I stopped eating. "Javier" said: "Go ahead and eat."

I heard a voice behind me when we finished our sandwiches and coffee. I was petrified when I heard it, and I didn't dare turn my head. I knew that voice.

"Lucita! What a surprise to see you. I saw your son a little while ago. He was riding his bike. He's just fine."

I was obviously surprised. The man came closer and stood in front of me. My doubts disappeared. It was Daniel, the accountant at the factory next to my parents' house. I remembered that there was a rumor in the neighborhood that he belonged to Patria y Libertad. I didn't manage to say anything. The man kept talking, saying things like, "Behave yourself. 'Javier' is a friend, a great person." Then he started telling him how he knew me from the time I was a child. He told him about my athletic career, about my son, my parents. He turned to me from time to time saying things like, "You see what happens, Lucita? I told you over and over not to get involved with those communists."

That was true. Every time we ran into each other he told me to stop getting involved in politics, that it would bring me trouble.

"Javier" observed everything and asked, "So you have a son?"

Daniel replied: "She sure does. He's blonde, smart, and really friendly."

I was angry. I started feeling worse, strange, like I was getting drowsy. I was scared. "Javier" kept talking. I was really nervous. I started trembling, and I felt cold. . . . The blonde man talked and talked, but I don't remember what he said. I tried to concentrate. My eyes were burning, and people's faces, things, everything became blurry, as though I were seeing double. I had never felt anything like that before. I was scared. They must have put something in the coffee. I tried to convince myself it wasn't true. I felt a pressing need to urinate. Then it became an obsession, and I asked them to let me go to the bathroom. I felt that I was bleeding, and I remembered that a guard had given me a sock he found lying around that morning. It was so dirty I wrapped it in a page from a magazine that was on the floor. I had put it between my legs. . . .

I stood up and said, "I'm going to stain the couch if you don't let me go to the bathroom." My head was spinning and my tongue felt huge, as if it were growing and didn't fit in my mouth. The guy with the gun stood up and helped me. I leaned on him. "Javier" ordered them to blindfold me and take me to the bathroom. Once we got there, the guy made me touch where the toilet was and then turn to the left. Then he counted the steps to show me where the sink was. I thought I was alone, but a voice told me: "You are only authorized to use the toilet and then go to the sink. Then you need to call us."

"Sir!" I exclaimed—I was used to calling the DINA guards that— "Could you lend me a jar or a bottle?"

"And what for?"

"To wash myself, please. . . ."

"Don't screw around! Be thankful for the cotton."

"Please, some paper."

"For what?"

"Sir, I'm bleeding and I want to get rid of the mess." I was embarrassed and wanted to cry. . . .

"Shit! These women are so complicated. . . . Wait. I don't want you to get everything dirty," the guy said. It seemed like he hadn't left.

I said again "Sir!" It was hard for me to talk. I heard a sound like a badly tuned radio and a voice. . . .

"Are you going to use the bathroom?"

"Yes, sir, sorry," I answered mechanically. I pulled my pants down and thought . . . "'Sorry?' What's wrong with me? Are they watching me?" The blood was still flowing. I wrapped all the mess in paper and left it next to the toilet. I heard that voice again, like from a radio, and noise.

"Stand up!" I did and I almost fell. Then I heard another order.

"Put the cotton pad between your legs." I did this and tried to move forward. I was able to, but I had to hold onto the sink. I heard the voice again.

"Turn around! Walk. . . ." I did it, telling myself, "I can, I can disobey." Then I started to walk. Then I hit my foot on something on the ground and backed up. The voice said, "Kneel down and feel it. . . ."

I did, and it felt like the first time I wore glasses, as if the floor were a lot further away than I anticipated. I was scared because my hand touched something that felt like a man's hairy leg. I remained kneeling. . . .

I obviously wasn't acting normal, notwithstanding the fact that nothing was normal there. I could think, but it was hard. I felt like someone had turned a microphone off, and someone there came over to take me out and back to the same office. They took my blindfold off there. I remember soft music. The volume kept getting louder, and I heard a voice resonate inside and outside myself.

"Luz. Are you all right?"

"Yes, everything's fine. . . ." I thought, "fine?" I felt my head fall forward, and my arms felt like they were hanging. . . .

"What are you thinking?" someone asked.

"I'm sad, very sad. . . ."

"Just sad? Nothing else? Some anger? Do you want to cry?"

"No, I don't want to cry." That wasn't true. I wanted to cry. . . .

"Don't you think that's strange? When someone is sad, they cry. Tell me about it, Luz. . . ."

I started to talk. "It's like a dream, a blue dream about the ocean. I see someone covering herself with a huge shawl. It's a woman letting her hair down and walking. Then she sits down in the sand. It's fall and it's cold, so cold it hurts your skin. That woman captures what she sees and hoards it inside."

The man changed the cassette. I felt very tired. Before he could continue asking me questions, I said, " And you, sir, who are you, what are you thinking, and what am I to you?"

The man laughed loudly and yelled, "Take her, and let her get some sleep. We'll work tomorrow, and early at that."

They took me to a small room. Only a bunk bed fit in there and an armchair, where the same guy who was cleaning his gun before had been. María Teresa, a compañera from the Socialist Party, pretended she was sleeping in the bottom bunk. She was with Toño's group. Her compañero, Claudio, was from my group, the GEA. I closed my eyes and tried to sleep. After a while, something suddenly happened, and I've never been able to determine if it was real or if I dreamed it. Whether I was asleep or awake, whatever the case may be. . . . I lived it and was absolutely destroyed by it. . . .

I heard a noise and some voices. It was "Javier" and a little boy. . . .

"What's your name?"

"Rafael."

"I'm going to break your finger, Rafael"

"No, No!" and some horrific screams from the boy. . . . Then begging and pleading, and crying. . . . I felt like I wanted to get up. My hands were tied and my head was spinning. I tried to tell myself it wasn't my son's voice. I repeated it over and over a hundred times. It's not my son's voice, it's not my son, it's not even a boy, it's a recording. It seemed like the same thing kept repeating itself at intervals. . . . I tried to convince myself it was a tape. It all continued, and, in spite of the fact I tried to convince myself it wasn't my son, that monstrous dialogue suddenly seemed to overcome me. I heard, "Now I'm going to break another finger. . . ." And more screams, and I was trying to get up, trying to understand. Why doesn't anyone else seem to hear voices? I kept telling myself. . . . No, it isn't. No, it isn't my son. But pretty soon I was crying. It seemed like I could see my son writhing in pain with his little hands reaching toward me, saying: "Mommy! Help me mommy. It hurts, mommy." And I kept repeating, "Calm down, Luz, it's a tape recording. They want to scare you. . . ." I don't know if it lasted a few hours or all night. In spite of the fact I was sure at times that it was a recording because everything kept repeating over and over, it was enough to leave me feeling destroyed. . . .

I could tell day was breaking when the light filtered in through the painted glass. The voices were still and I had a strong pain in my throat and chest. I felt anguish, the need to see my son, to hold him in my arms, to cradle him, to watch over his sleep.

I started hearing noises. They were coming. They took me out of the room. I could go to the bathroom, and I took a shower. The water was freezing, but it felt great to me anyway. This time there weren't voices or people close by. I took the blindfold off. I looked at myself in the mirror and saw my pale, emaciated face. But my heart was worse.

After I left the bathroom, they took me to an office. It was a different one, larger, not elegant at all, with several desks. Pretty soon "Javier" appeared and started saying that he was interested in the information I could give him about the Socialist Party. I told him the same story, that I had been in prison and away from the party for six months, and that I had already told the DINA everything.

I realized that, in addition to the girl I had seen the night before, they were trying to find Luis Peña. I don't know if they ever managed to arrest him. I didn't see him. I have no idea how they continued the investigation, but they had a meeting scheduled that morning where Alejandro Para, "Jano," was supposed to arrive. I saw him when they brought him in blindfolded and tied. Although I had seen him before, I didn't know what role he played in the party. I only knew he had arranged some meetings with Toño. They didn't bring me face-to-face with him.

Captain Juan Morales arrived and told "Javier" that the DINA wanted me. He said he was taking me back to 38 Londres Street. There was a heated exchange between "Javier" and Juan Morales, and then they took me back to 38 Londres Street. I saw María Teresa again there, and we sat together. When we could talk without the guard noticing, she asked me if I had said anything about Claudio, her compañero. I told her I hadn't, and she asked me to please not do it. I promised her I wouldn't just to calm her down. I didn't know where he was anyway. I didn't even know his real name. I know María Teresa spent at least one more night at Yucatán and survived.

OSVALDO ROMO

The day after I returned to Yucatán, Ricardo Lawrence sent for my brother and me. He said we would each start "working" with a unit. He assigned me to Osvaldo Romo Mena and my brother to a police lieutenant who called himself "Marcos." Later I would find out his name is Gerardo Ernesto Godoy García.

The first thing I need to confess is that it's hard for me to just keep focusing on this one individual. That doesn't mean that Romo Mena should be acquitted. He undoubtedly will be since everything seems to indicate that the cases of the detained and disappeared will all end in amnesty.[29]

Thinking of Romo Mena today, I can see that he was the man in 1974

29. Author's note, July 28, 1993: In less than twenty-four hours the second military court found Fernando Lauriani Maturana not guilty for his participation in the kidnapping and disappearance of the Andrónico Antequera brothers, given lack of evidence.

who had the power to take anyone his superior, Miguel Krassnoff Martchenko, ordered, and drag him to hell. Today, he is the only one in custody. It's hard for me to understand how Romo is guilty and the others aren't.

Osvaldo Romo seems very different to me today from the man he was in 1974. In my mind, I always pictured Romo as massive and greasy, a ferocious dog sicced on opponents and militants. He terrified me. I managed to see him again in 1992 a few days after they brought him to Chile. It shocked me. He seemed shorter than I remembered him when, hunched over and dragging one leg, he asked me with tears in his eyes, "Have you forgiven me?" With that single gesture, I realized that the disgusting, filthy, vulgar man I remembered, the Osvaldo Romo with gnawed fingernails everyone knew, the indisputably ruthless torturer and implacable rapist who caused me so much pain and disgust in 1974, was the manifestation of the "disposable man" the DINA needed for its goals of annihilation. Since he arrived in Chile, Osvaldo Romo has been receiving adequate medical treatment, and every time I see him he is thinner, more fit, and he still retains the shrewdness that characterized him during the time I knew him in the DINA. I have to confess that his request for forgiveness coupled with the fact that he is now the scapegoat, a civilian without special privileges, makes me inclined to forgive him, and I have. I feel like Osvaldo Romo, with all his negative traits, was used and abused by the DINA. He is undoubtedly responsible for many things, horrendous things, but it is hard for me to accept that he is the only one who has been convicted. It is hard for me to accept that his superiors remain unpunished. Osvaldo Romo's abilities, such as his innate shrewdness, had made him Krassnoff's right-hand man. During 1974 and 1975, the DINA supported and celebrated him as one of their "best" agents. His fierceness answered directly to the demands made by Krassnoff, Ferrer, Wenderoth, Moren, Espinoza, Contreras, and others in the DINA.

On that day in 1974, they took three of the prisoners who were collaborating to the Terranova Detention Center: Alejandra, my brother, and me. I went in the truck with Osvaldo Romo, Basclay Zapata, and "negro" Paz. My brother went in the Austin Mini that belonged to Lieutenant Colonel Gerardo Godoy García, which, as I understand, had previously belonged to a prisoner. That day the officer gave my brother some gray pants and a green shirt. The clothes he was wearing were terribly dirty and in shreds, and the two men were about the same size.

125

I found out that Alejandra was going with us during the trip with Romo Mena and his unit. Romo started a conversation that really bothered me. I didn't dare say anything. I just listened. I remember him referring in a very disparaging way to Alejandra and Muriel. I couldn't block out the odor that that disgusting man gave off. Every time I had my blindfold off, I couldn't take my eyes off his disgusting fingers and his dirty fingernails bitten down to almost nothing.

When we arrived at Terranova, I was able to see under my blindfold the place that I would recognize months later as the driveway next to the main house. I also recognized Alejandra. She was very thin, and I remember she was really cold. Besides the men who had taken us, officers Lawrence Mires, Krassnoff Martchenko, and Moren Brito were present. I know there were more people there, but I couldn't see them. I just heard their voices.

On that occasion, I heard the names of the special units for the first time. I found out that Krassnoff Martchenko commanded Halcón, that Lawrence Mires was in charge of Aguila, and that Godoy García commanded Tucán. We were told that from that day forward we would start "fishing." In other words, we would go with our assigned teams looking for militants on the streets of Santiago and identifying them.

Moren Brito said that this was a new type of work and that what would happen with us depended on the results obtained. After that, they transferred us back to 38 Londres Street. They took me out several times. One day I spotted a compañero on Estado Street, and he was arrested. I knew him as Walter Contreras, and I've looked for him for years on the lists of the detained and disappeared. I haven't found him. I remember that when we arrived at the Yucatán Detention Center with him that day, Romo Mena and Zapata Reyes forced me to tell him that I had been working with the Army Intelligence Service for years. I suppose he believed it. I never saw him again.

"Javier" came twice while I was at Yucatán, and he did what he promised to do. He came close to me and said "Sombra" in my ear. A guard came for me right away and took me to an office. Then he would ask me how I was and would give me some cigarettes. Another time he put a piece of chocolate in my mouth. Each time he said he was taking steps to get me out of the DINA's hands. I thanked him and hoped it wouldn't work. That man terrified me more than Krassnoff or Lawrence or Moren. Maybe it was just a ploy to get me to collaborate more with Krassnoff. I don't know. . . .

I remember a guard at Yucatán who was short, with white skin and curly, dark hair. He always offered to take us women to the bathroom where, according to him, we could wash up a little bit. The first time I "fell for it" and thankfully accepted, I let him lead me there. As soon as I took off my blouse to wash myself, he approached me and grabbed my breasts. I was able to dissuade him from going any further, and he gave me my clothes back. Since it was during the day I started to yell, and I think he was afraid an officer would catch him. I was blindfolded. Those were very depressing situations. After that I never accepted his offers again, and whenever I could I warned the girls who had just arrived about what that guy was doing.

One day, Basclay Zapata Reyes, "Troglo," asked me if I wanted to take a shower. I told him I did. He got me out of the chair and took me in a truck. He explained on the way that they were going to raid an apartment and that I could use the bathroom while they searched the place. I thanked him. Up to that point I didn't think he would have assaulted me.

When we arrived at the place, even though I was blindfolded, I could see if I lifted my head a little. I recognized the neighborhood near the Providencia Theater on Manuel Montt. I don't remember the exact apartment. As I was taking a bath, "Troglo" came in and tried to start touching me. Just like Moren Brito, there are testimonies about Basclay Zapata's brutality and cruelty, but I don't know if he tortured me or not. That day he asked me to sleep with him. When I refused, he insisted. He even brought me clothing as a gift. I imagined, and I later confirmed, that he had stolen it from the apartment that was being raided. Refusing to have sex with him, I gave him back the sweater and the blouse that he had handed me, and he didn't insist.

Now that I remember it, the situation seems incredible to me. There I was, naked, begging him not to be raped, and there he was trying to touch me. He suddenly stood there, looking at me, and said: "All right. You can keep the clothes anyway." Then he left the bathroom. I rinsed off the shampoo and the soap quickly and got dressed. I spent the rest of the time trying to untangle my hair, which had grown a lot, but I didn't dare leave the bathroom.[30]

30. Author's note: In 1992 I found out that this was Adriana Urrutia's apartment and that the clothes they gave me were hers. She survived, and I gave all the clothing, except for a maroon sweater, to the compañeras in room number 2 at the Cuatro Alamos Detention Center.

I don't know if it was at the end of August or the beginning of September when they took me to Cuatro Alamos along with the other prisoners. They were clearing out Yucatán, apparently because it had already been identified as a DINA detention center. Some relatives had even come knocking at the door asking about their family members.

CUATRO ALAMOS

Cuatro Alamos was a secret detention center. It was located next to the Prison Camp that belonged to SENDET, the National Prisoner Service. This prison was on Departamental Street, and the prisoners could talk to each other and have visitors. Cuatro Alamos was different from the other detention centers. The men and women were kept separated in rooms with bunk beds. We could take showers, and they fed us regularly. They gave us beans one day, lentils the next, and chickpeas the third day. I don't remember if there was any other food. We were locked up, but we weren't blindfolded as long as we stayed in the room. At the time I arrived there, the police were in charge of the camp. The DINA later assigned the command of "Cuatro," which is what we called it at that time, to prison officer Orlando José Manso Durán. Only Tres Alamos remained in the hands of the police, and Conrado Pacheco was the officer in charge there.

Those of us who were at Cuatro Alamos were still prisoners who weren't recognized as such. In other words, we could disappear at any time. The most terrible part of it was the uncertainty of knowing they could come for us at any hour of the day to take us to other detention centers again. During my stay at that camp, I remained under the impression for quite some time that the prisoners who were taken from there were then distributed to different detention centers throughout the country. I had this idea because the DINA units put people they were taking into different lines and assigned each one a different city name.

When we arrived at Cuatro Alamos, several of the female prisoners complained that they had symptoms of vaginal infections. When the doctor came, I asked them to take me since I still had severe pain in my foot. The doctor said that the wound was healing well, but that the hypersensitivity continued. It was even uncomfortable when my pants or my pajamas brushed up against it, but especially my shoes.

Rosseta Pallini González was one of the compañeras in my room at

128

Cuatro Alamos. She was the wife of one of the MIR's leaders. She died in exile in Mexico, and was survived by a son.

Mónica Chislayne Llanca Iturra was another compañera in Room Number 2, and she is, to this day, one of the detained and disappeared. I met her there. Now I know that she had connections with the MIR. Back then she told us, perhaps out of fear, that she was a socialist and an employee at the Social Security Office. Early in September 1974, she was taken from our room by one of the DINA units, Halcón Uno. Osvaldo Romo Mena assigned her the code "Puerto Montt." Today, that is known as one of the terms that meant death.

I'm not going to go into great detail about Mónica because the cause of her kidnapping and her eventual disappearance are currently under secret judicial review in Santiago's Third Court. The judge in charge of that case is Mrs. Dobra Lusic Nadal.

I had forgotten the names of these women for many years. Then, in 1991, when I was living in Europe, I found a photograph of Olivia Monsalve de Becerra and recognized her story as I was reading some old newspapers. I realized that I had met her, Silvia, and Alejandrina in Cuatro Alamos. I was deeply moved.

THE UNBORN ONE

One night, early in September, Silvia started to have sharp pains in her abdomen. We banged on the door asking for a doctor. She lost the baby she was carrying because of the tortures she had undergone. There was a page from a newspaper and some cardboard from a box in the closet in the room. That is what we used to wrap the one who would have been the youngest child of DINA agent Miguel Angel Becerra Hidalgo. It was horrifying.

It was cold, and the bloody mass of the dead child and placenta gave off a kind of steam in the air. I put it in the middle of the little path between the two bunk beds and sat down on the lower bunk next to Alejandrina. I couldn't stop looking at it. We were all shaken. A few hours, even just a few minutes earlier, it was a live human being. He or she does not figure on any list, but is one more killed by the DINA. We didn't cry very loudly, perhaps because we were more focused on the mother at that point, trying to calm her, to help her get dressed, to keep her warm, and wipe the tears from her face. When the guard on duty came back to the room and saw the fetus, he also reacted. They took Silvia, and a few days later we found out that she had been transferred to the Police Hospital. When she returned she remained in a state of determined silence that we didn't dare interrupt.... That other child who belonged to Miguel Angel Becerra, the one who was never born and who never had a name, lost his incipient life in a cold room at Cuatro Alamos. I didn't sleep that night. No one did.

During Silvia's absence, Alejandrina told us her story in a moment of deep sorrow as we all passed around a cigarette. I realized that, in those days, they were facing what was just the beginning of a long process of different stages of pain. I found out from Alejandrina that the DINA agent they found dead on a road near Parral was Miguel Angel Becerra Hidalgo. They were related by marriage, and his wife was María Olivia Monsalve Ortiz. She also said that their eldest son, Miguel Becerra Monsalve, is still at the Dignity Colony.[31]

He was separated from his family by a judge's order issued in Parral that gave custody of the boy to the Germans in Villa Baviera.[32]

31. Colonia Dignidad (Dignity Colony) was a closed society created by Germans who immigrated to Chile after World War II. In recent years, there have been several accounts of links between the colony's religious leader and founder, Paul Schaefer, and the Chilean repressive apparatus, including the DINA and even Pinochet himself. Some former prisoners have alleged that the colony became one of the DINA's secret torture centers, and the Rettig Report, created by the Truth and Reconciliation Commission, documents some of these stories as well. The colony changed its name in 1991 to Villa Baviera (Bavaria Villa) when it began to feel political pressure following Chile's return to democracy. Furthermore, there has been additional testimony regarding the sexual abuse of young boys by Schaefer, who became a fugitive after accusations were made against him in 1997. These stories make Arce's reference to the Parral judge's decision to grant legal custody of Miguel Becerra to the Germans at the colony after his father's death and against his mother's wishes especially poignant.

32. Author's note: During my stay at Cuatro Alamos I was able to see that Muriel Dockendorf Navarrete was in another cell. She was the wife of one of the MIR's leaders, and she remains disappeared to this day.

Part 2

13

OLLAGÜE DETENTION CENTER

A new stage in my captivity began when I was transferred from Cuatro Alamos to the Ollagüe Detention Center, which was located at 1367 José Domingo Cañas. The DINA grew in terms of personnel and material resources. More officers arrived, and the presence of female agents became permanent. There were changes for me as well. I was kept in a different place from other prisoners. However, the small size of the premises brought the suffering of the compañeros who were being brutally tortured much closer to me. In spite of the fact that I was collaborating with the DINA, my status continued to be that of a prisoner who had not officially been recognized as such. The DINA was convinced I wasn't with the MIR. That was why I was no longer a prisoner of Krassnoff's Halcón unit, and I began to report to the commander of the prison, Captain Ciro Ernesto Torré Sáez.

The day after the first anniversary of the coup, a little before noon, I was taken from Cuatro Alamos and transferred to what I would later learn was the DINA's new detention center, Ollagüe, which replaced Yucatán.

Up to that day, my status as a prisoner depended on the Halcón unit led by Miguel Krassnoff. When the guard at Cuatro Alamos handed me over to the agents in Halcón One from Caupolicán, Basclay Zapata Reyes noticed I didn't have any eyebrows or eyelashes left after having my eyes taped over so frequently. In an act of human kindness, he just put some really dark plastic glasses on me and made me promise to close my eyes when they told me to and not to open them for any reason.

When we passed the corner of Bustamante and Irarrázaval, they ordered me to close my eyes, and I did. When we arrived, we entered the building, and they took me to an empty room. In front of the guard, Basclay Zapata Reyes removed some kind of blindfold from my eyes. Then, adopting a harsh attitude, he yelled, "Stand still, you piece of shit!"

I stayed seated in an armchair, the only piece furniture in the immense room. Everything was covered with dust. The house had apparently been empty for a long time, either that or no one bothered to clean the place.

Approximately fifteen minutes later a guard entered and ordered me to follow him. He was one of the ones I had seen at 38 Londres Street. He greeted me as though he were meeting up with an acquaintance. He looked at me. Curiously, he found me different. I told him that I had been able to take a bath every day at Cuatro Alamos and that I had cut my hair.

"You lost all your hair again!" He remembered the incident with the wig and my very short hair when I was arrested in March. He made a gesture for me to follow him. "Captain, here is Lucecita."

"So this is Lucecita. Sit down," he said as he pointed to a chair. The man kept talking. "I'm a police chief. Ciro Torré is my name. It isn't an alias. I'm the commander of these quarters."

By that time I had learned enough to know not to trust anyone, even someone who, like that officer, was smiling and exhibiting a friendly attitude. He was the perfect example of the image you have when you picture a rural police chief: someone you see at public celebrations, baptisms, and weddings, a kind of godfather, a good guy, and a good talker.

"Let's talk, Lucecita, because you're going to work with me. Tell me everything. Who are you? How were you detained? Why?"

I began, weighing my words. Up until then, no one had figured me out yet. Captain Torré looked like he had all the time in the world. He either didn't have or didn't show any personal opinions regarding current issues or political parties. He constantly asked me to clarify what I was saying and the words I was choosing carefully. What he did flaunt was his knowledge of the current situation and the fact that his wife was a lawyer.

Without knowing whether his attitude was genuine or not, I started using more unusual words. Many of them were improvised on the spur of the moment or were just unusual synonyms. Either way I was still in his hands and in a very strange situation. I wouldn't have been able to give him any information even if I had wanted to. I didn't know anything. More than six months had passed since my arrest. By that time,

134

I was the prisoner who had spent the most time with the DINA. The oldest, they used to say. There was no possibility that I might be allowed to have visitors. I had seen practically everyone. I knew many of their real names, especially those of the officers, and I knew where several of their detention centers were located. Somehow I had to keep buying my life from one minute to the next.

I was starting to catch a glimpse of a remote possibility. I couldn't think of anything else. After all, I thought, officers like Krassnoff and Lawrence already used that kind of marxist jargon, at least the kind the MIR employed, and they did so well.

I tried to pique the captain's interest subtly. I tried to imagine what might be going on in the country as I talked about my life, my studies. . . . I remembered that, during the time I was free, I had heard about some nuns who were already mobilizing efforts to support the prisoners' relatives.

Suddenly the captain mentioned something about intelligence work. I decided to take the offensive and said, "Captain, do you really believe that the left is a threat to the government? Don't you think there are other relatively 'untouchable' institutions and political parties that could cause you more than one problem? You know that I haven't read the newspaper or heard anything for months. However, I will venture to say that the Church and the Christian Democratic party, at least some factions of each of them, must be stirring up trouble.

This seemed so obvious to me that I was surprised when I saw the captain's reaction, and I thought, "He's jerking me around. Pretty soon, when he gets tired of this he is going to beat the hell out of me and stop me right there. . . ." But he seemed genuinely surprised.

"That's incredible. I think you must have read or heard some news at Cuatro Alamos. How do you know about this?"

I kept talking, resorting fundamentally to common sense since I didn't know anything about the issue. I talked about logical things, about how events develop over time based on facts and relations of cause and effect.

My life started depending on what I had learned, read, and thought in the past. I had only one weapon: my brain. And there was also one fortuitous fact: the officer was more ignorant than I was about those matters.

The captain realized that we had talked way past the lunch hour. He said he would leave me alone in a room and that he would give the

135

materials I needed to write down everything I knew because he wanted to learn everything.

I was in a real bind. What was I going to write? . . . Without realizing it, the captain had given me clues about how to formulate what I was doing instinctively. I couldn't avoid remembering what I had been thinking about at Cuatro Alamos. Living in that violent atmosphere definitely sharpened one's senses. I decided to try and seem like an extremely rational person. The alternative was to fall completely under the DINA's control.

Captain Torré Sáez interrupted my thoughts when he commented that he was reading *Orquesta roja*.[33] I remembered Ricardo Ruz for a few seconds and felt tenderness. We had read it together. Without thinking, I told the officer, "Captain, the first thing I'm going to write for you is a marxist vocabulary and then a communications manual." The captain looked pleased and intent on becoming an intelligence officer. I encouraged him to keep reading books about espionage, telling him that it would be a good way to learn.

Torré Sáez took me to what would be my room for the next few months. There was a mattress on the floor. He called two guards and told them to bring a table, two chairs, a typewriter, and office supplies. "I'll have them bring you a bed and some pajamas," he said as he left.

Feeling brave after the apparently successful day, I asked him, "Captain, may I take a shower?"

"A shower? We'll see. I don't know if there is a shower, but we'll see. . . ."

They closed the door. It was a small space, a place normally used to store brooms, mops, and other cleaning equipment. I took a deep breath. I sat down on the mattress and started thinking about what had happened. I smiled. It was undoubtedly fortunate that this captain was the detention center's commander. It was yet to be seen what would happen when Krassnoff found out. . . . The guards, "Jote" and "Rucio," returned quickly with the rest of the things. "Jote" laughed and said, "Your hair is growing, Lucecita. Now you even have an office. That's great! I'm going to have to be nice to you. After this, pretty soon you're going to be giving me orders. Where do you want the table?"

33. Arce is referring to the spy thriller *The Red Orchestra* by Gilles Perrault. It was originally published in French as *L'Orchestre Rouge* in 1967. It recounts sociohistorical events and espionage in Europe during World War II.

I laughed. There wasn't very much space.

"That's right! Only the table and the mattress fit. But we can move them around if you want to, and put the mattress and then the table. . . ."

He was a good guy. He never treated me badly, on the contrary.

"Thanks, 'Jote.'" I hadn't laughed in a long time. "Thanks."

"Okay, okay, now you're acting emotional and getting all sad. Okay, now, calm down and have a seat at the table because I'm going to bring you some soup right away. Then, afterwards, if you want to get outside for a while, I'll let you wash the pots and pans."

I looked outside and realized it was a really beautiful day.

"And, the way things are going, I'm sure the captain will give you permission to leave the door open a little when we are out here standing guard. Look at the pool. Look how beautiful, Lucecita. Oh! And just so ya know, 'Rucio' and I are going to stand guard in front of your door every other day. Here's a Lucky for you. I asked 'Clavo' [Hugo Clavería Leiva] for it since he likes the same smokes you do."

Those feelings hurt me so much! Not just morally. It was hard for me to breathe. It was a physical pain that cut my throat like a knife. I couldn't avoid them. I decided I had to try and control my expression and learn to always maintain the same face and attitude. That's it. I had to stop being someone and be something. "Jote" was waiting for an answer.

"Yes, 'Jote.' I'll wash the dishes and the pots."

I ate the soup, broke the bread and ate some of it. I smoked the cigarette and hid the matches under the mattress. I had the impression that something had changed within me. It was tangible. I wasn't cold anymore, and I didn't feel any pain. I thought about how people try to relax under difficult circumstances, and that I, on the other hand, had to make the best of that permanent state of stress. That stress would give me the energy I needed.

"Jote" took me to a water pump in the yard, and I washed the dishes. He laughed at me, and hard, when I asked him for detergent. He taught me how to wash with dirt. It worked. The mud got rid of all the grease. I almost gleefully stuck my hands in the earth and scoured the pots. That became a daily activity, a way to enjoy spring, with its cool mornings and evenings flirtatiously interrupted by the resplendent midday hours.

"'Jote,' do you think I could wash my blouse here?"

"I should have known! That's not up to me! That's how women are.

137

You give them an inch and they take a mile. As far as I'm concerned, you certainly can but you're better off asking the captain."

I went back to the room and started working on the marxist vocabulary. Sheets of paper began to pile up, and the captain went twice a day to see how my work was progressing. But soon what I had feared happened. Krassnoff said my work was "a bunch of bullshit" and that I—as always—was mocking them. The worst of it is that he was right. My work was bad.

Fortunately, Torré attributed Krassnoff's attitude to what he defined as a conflict between the army officers and the officers from the police force. According to him, the rivalry was heightened by a kind of "injustice" caused by differences in the access to promotions in the two institutions. At that time, it was normal for it to take longer to be promoted to captain in the police force. It was also the case that officers from the same rank in the army had a higher status because the army was the oldest branch of the Chilean Armed Forces. Therefore, there were times when a police captain who was thirty-five years old or more would be the subordinate of an army captain who, if recently promoted, might be just twenty-seven or twenty-eight years old.

Ciro Torré talked to me about this. He was convinced that police captains were more qualified for intelligence work because they had maintained greater contact with people. I suppose there was an implicit criticism of the DINA's tactics in his comments.

After I was settled in the room, Krassnoff ordered Alejandra to be taken to the same place. We would sleep there together.

It seems that Torré felt responsible for me, in his own way. Of course! I experienced that unpleasant feeling several times in that world ruled by a brutal machismo. Officers tend to express their paternalism in a wide variety of ways that range from changing your name to even acting like a kind of father who has given you life.

One day he stood there looking at me and said, "'Diana!' That's it. 'Dianita' is your name. You look just like the naked huntress Diana on my calendar."

When I looked at him, I felt frightened. There he was, in front of me, staring at me with his face glowing, his eyes all lit up, his lips half opened, and his greasy, piggish face. I felt repulsion. I wanted to run away, but I sat there, calm. . . . Struck dumb. I just looked at him with my expressionless face, which was one of the things that bothered them the most. That feeling of humiliation shot through me like a bullet, then

I heard, as if I were listening to someone else speak, "Captain, I would appreciate it very much if you could think of another name. 'Diana' sounds like the name of a whore to me. . . . I prefer my own name. My name is Luz."

"We aren't going to talk about it anymore." Torré replied. "You're going to be 'Diana.' 'Dianita,' that's it. It fits you much better."

He started laughing and walked out. From that day on the captain called me by that name. The guards continued calling me "Lucecita."

A few days after arriving there, I realized that there were at least five more officers at Ollagüe than I had met at Yucatán. At 38 Londres Street I had known Krassnoff Martchenko, Lawrence Mires, and Godoy García. At the Ollagüe Detention Center, besides the officers in charge of the individual units, there was the commander, Ciro Ernesto Torré Sáez. I reported to him. He also had a second man with him, Fernando Eduardo Lauriani Maturana, alias "Pablo." Other officers answered to him as well: the Second Lieutenant of Police Palmira Isabel Almuna Guzmán, alias "Pepa," and Jiménez Santibáñez. The last officer to arrive at Ollagüe was Captain Francisco Maximiliano Ferrer Lima, alias "Max."

Krassnoff Martchenko sent for Alejandra every day. I kept writing in the room, and the vocabulary list was growing. The captain was now calling it his dictionary. Torré had authorized me to take a shower every morning, but I had to ask for permission to do it every day. That was probably an order from Krassnoff Martchenko or, perhaps, a form of harassment. Krassnoff began a kind of game. I asked the guard at the door to ask him if I could take a shower the following day. Sometimes he sent for me, and each time the conversation between us was more or less the same. They left me at the door to his office with a blindfold over my eyes. After a while he would say, "Oh! There's Lucecita, sorry. . . . Diana. Is that your name now?"

I remained quiet.

"Answer, you piece of shit! When I ask you a question, you have to answer me! Do you know with whom you are speaking?"

"Yes, lieutenant. I know your name."

"Oh! You know my name. And who told you my name?"

"You did, lieutenant. You told me your name is Lieutenant Miguel Krassnoff."

"Yes, damn it. . . . Krassnoff. Krassnoff Martchenko. . . . A Russian of the white kind. A white Russian, got it?"

"Yes, lieutenant."

"Good! And now that you understand that the communists massacred my people, what do you want?

"Permission to bathe myself, lieutenant."

"What time did you take a shower today?"

"At five o'clock in the morning, lieutenant."

"Authorized, but at 4:45. . . . Yes or no?"

"Yes, lieutenant, 4:45 is fine."

It didn't matter to me if he gave me permission to take a shower ten or fifteen minutes earlier every day. In the end Krassnoff Martchenko got bored, or maybe he was busy, and I got to take a shower every day until they took me to Villa Grimaldi.

I don't know if there were other reasons, but for me it was important to be clean. I didn't want to give them the satisfaction of seeing me even more crushed in that place where I didn't have any rights.

Even though I had been reduced to shreds, the DINA would only see me in one of two ways: on my feet or dead. I had chosen to fight for my life and my brother's as well. That was deeply ingrained in me. Ever since then, whenever I'm tense, I take a shower or wash my hair without even realizing it, even if I already did it that morning.

I remember that in July 1975 María Alicia, Alejandra, and I went to live in tower 12, apartment 54 on 77 Marcoleta. As soon as I could, I shut myself in the bathroom and took a shower. I spent more than an hour in there. I couldn't come out. All the soap, shampoo, and water in the world weren't enough to make me feel clean. The filth of the DINA's detention centers was inside me. I continued feeling it. It was impregnated in my mucous membranes and in my mind. It's one of the things I'll never be able to forget.

During that time at the Ollagüe Detention Center, the shower had its quirks but I learned how to deal with them well. Only "Jote" and "Rucio" let me bathe myself alone and with the door closed. The other guards not only left the door open but stayed inside the tiny space and bothered me. They applauded when I took off my clothes, saying, "I'll lather you up, sweetie." Then they acted like they were going to come closer.

I tried my best not to show any fear. I knew that a soldier is programmed to obey a commanding voice. So, besides the occasional groping I couldn't avoid, which always cost them dearly, I was able to keep them at bay. I was determined not to stop bathing myself, and I yelled at them, "Come closer, asshole. Try to come closer. I don't even need to tell the captain about this. I can take care of you all by myself. I dare you to try me."

Krassnoff Martchenko had prohibited the guards from talking to me since Yucatán. He told me in front of Lawrence, "That bitch is intelligent, and she's got a way of talking that can really mess with these guys."

They told one another a lot of things about me. Saying that I'm very intelligent was an exaggeration. Maybe I have an innate survival instinct, but the rest of their comments were half-truths, like that I knew karate or that I had special training.

I took some courses, sure, like just about everybody from my generation, nothing special. But I never clarified those things. In some way, that image served as a deterrent for those guys who, from one day to the next, came to feel so powerful. They had embarked on their quasi-divine mission to rescue the fatherland from the marxist plague.

They concluded from my attitude that I had some special training, that I had made some secret trip to Cuba where they had prepared me, that I was not simply a woman with leftist ideas but a kind of computer. That is what Marcelo Moren Brito christened me when he alluded to my ability to memorize things. All of that held the guards off, at least a little. There was always somebody who would say in those moments, "Leave her alone. That bitch knows karate, and one of these times she's going to knock your balls off." And they laughed.

I don't know if it was worth it or not. I developed an enormous capacity to act coldly and aggressively, even though I was really torn up inside. I shivered constantly, and the trembling still reappears whenever I feel tense. In those days I thought it was worth it. My objective was to make them believe that their methods of psychological torture were effective. I needed to believe I could take them to the realm of language, that I could speak calmly and quietly even about my own death.

My greatest fear was that they would pressure me with my loved ones, with my family and my compañeros. I tried to show them I didn't have any feelings, and they were willing to believe anything evil about those of us they classified as criminals and marxist whores.

14

TRAITOR AND WHORE

Krassnoff said to me once, "You know you're a traitor, don't you?"
It was incredible how their cruelty cut to the quick. I realized that something very vulnerable could break within me. I couldn't let them penetrate so deep inside me. I stood there without moving a muscle while I heard horrific screams, while I watched someone twisting and turning as they were tortured on the "grill." Only God knows how hard that was for me. I was able keep myself from showing my emotions, but they were getting louder inside me every day. I needed to subject myself to a strict routine. I entered the shower every morning with determination, even though it was terribly cold and my lungs were in bad shape. The guards kept saying, "You'll die all by yourself. We won't even have to kill you." I would answer, "But if I die, I'll go clean. . . ."

No one seemed to understand, except Lumi. I was so obsessed with not letting them control me entirely that I ended up losing the ability to feel the effects of heat and cold. That lasted for years. Many years after leaving the DINA, I was still able to distance myself from my surroundings and their effects. Apparently, of course, it all came at a very high price.

That day, when Krassnoff Martchenko mentioned betrayal, I told myself, "Luz, your real triumph is being able to face anything. They must never get the truth out of you. . . ." Then, without even blinking, I answered him, "Yes, Lieutenant, I know. It's something I decided to be at a specific point."

"Tell me, and what does a traitor feel?"

"Lieutenant, all I can tell you is that, in this war of yours, I am on the losing side. From a loser to a winner, you only gave me two options: To live or die. I chose to live. How do I feel? That is my problem, sir. If you want to know, think about it. Try to imagine this same war that you're referring to, only reversed. Try to put yourself in my place and tell me this: What would you have done in my situation? . . . I suppose your immediate response will be 'Who, me? . . . I'll never be a traitor.' I believed that too for a long time. I ask you again. You, what would you have done?"

He looked at me and leaned back in his chair. He chewed on a pencil with his typical gesture of twisting his lips. An angry look flashed across his eyes. He took the pencil out of his mouth and looked at it. Then he came toward me and yelled, "Don't make me laugh. . . . A marxist whore comparing herself to me? To an officer? What do you know about what it means to be an officer?"

I ignored the part about being a whore and answered him. Now I had him where I wanted him, "That is correct, Lieutenant. I don't know what you are, or Lieutenant Lawrence, or Lieutenant Godoy, or Lieutenant Lauriani, or Captain Torré. But I do know what the army says an officer is. A man of honor. . . . A man with a profound vocation for service who has dedicated his life to. . . ."

He yelled at me to shut up and ordered a guard to get this whore out of his presence.

I walked. The guard pulled me by the arm to make me move faster, and I crashed loudly into the frame of the door. I hit my forehead, saw a flash of light, and felt like I was going to fall down. Then I heard Krassnoff's voice saying, "Get her out of here, lay her down somewhere. Give her a cup of coffee and a cigarette." When the guard was practically dragging me away, the Lieutenant came over and spoke to me, "It didn't hurt, did it? You didn't cry. No, you're not going to cry now. You're brave. I know you're brave. . . ."

I didn't say anything, but I thought: "You're right, Lieutenant. It doesn't hurt anymore. . . ."

Desperation, pain, and anguish were the scar tissue encasing my soul, solid like a shell. The bump on my forehead swelled into a big knot that lasted for months, turning a wide array of colors: purple, greenish-gray, various hues of yellow. And I still have it to this day, a little bump you can feel when you touch my forehead.

I suppose Krassnoff didn't forget that incident. Later, as a DINA employee, when Manuel Contreras promoted me on August 16, 1976, from the category of female civilian employee to a civilian employee with the status of officer, this fact was a hot topic everyone was talking about at the club. I ran into Krassnoff by chance as he was leaving a meeting at Headquarters and he congratulated me, "Congratulations, and I want you to know that I really mean it. From a winning officer to a losing officer." He shook my hand. I felt as though someone had punched me as I listened to his compliment. I heard him add, "Although in my opinion, I still think you're holding back way too much."

At least twice between 1974 and 1975, Krassnoff reprimanded me for what he called my holding back. On many other occasions he yelled at me, "Get that idiot out of here. She isn't broken yet. She's still holding back. . . ."

Krassnoff knew I had a few things left of my own. He didn't know how few. . . . He gave me a military salute by clicking his heels together and acting as if he were standing at attention, and he smiled with his twisted mouth.

I went to the office, and a strange, ambiguous feeling swept over me, like something heavy taking hold of me without pleasure or pain. Being promoted to the status of an officer had been one of those "social conquests" that María Alicia fought for so we could differentiate ourselves from the female employees who had secretarial and administrative duties. And since everything that one of us achieved was applied to all three of us, María Alicia, Alejandra and I were included in the category of female personnel along with the professional women who worked for the DINA. We were still "the package" even though we worked as analysts at Headquarters. And, besides, it was a sort of defense for us against the DINA personnel who questioned our presence there.

Many people still thought we should be eliminated. In those days, I think the three of us felt that our only alternative was to be employees or die. At least, that's how I saw it. Nevertheless, the greeting from Krassnoff, by then a captain, and his reference to my "holding back" shook me.

I shut myself in the bathroom for a few minutes and thought that, on one hand, it was true. I was holding something back. Several things. At that moment I felt like I was virtually at the point of no return. Each step, each battle, each day, was making me shrink inside, reducing me. I felt like I was becoming less and less of a human being. My feelings had become as basic and as primitive as my answers were precarious. Suddenly, they grew within me and said to me in unison: "We are all you have, we are your very essence, and we are dying. Leave room for us. . . ."

144

I returned to the office. I was in a no-man's-land. It was like walking through a desert, and behind each difficult and painfully climbed hill or summit, there was nothing but another valley, even more arid than the previous one. There were no set paths. With nothing to hold onto, without precedents, without a history or a guide to turn to, I felt lost, orphaned. I didn't know which paths to seek or how to build them. If they existed, I didn't know about them. I couldn't see them. I repeated incessantly: "Luz, Luz, it's not important. If there isn't a road, you'll have to build one." I was walking a tightrope where my balance was so precarious that only extreme rationality would allow me to carry on. Or so I thought.

Something interrupted my thoughts. I had to keep going. I hadn't gotten this far only to give up now. As I came back to reality, I thought, "It's temporary. God! It's only temporary. . . ." I needed to believe that it was, and I appealed to my familiar defenses. . . . I said to myself, "Calm down. You have a son, and you have to raise him and feed him. You have to get away from the Church and the courts, and the DINA too. You have a lot to do. . . ."

Getting back to the days of José Domingo Cañas in the Ollagüe Detention Center, I remember that Monday, September 16th, I was talking with Captain Torré. The subject of the prisoners' living conditions came up. "You know, 'Dianita,' I passed by the prisoners' room, and there was a terrifying smell."

"Captain, wouldn't it be possible for them to take a bath? I believe you'd be able to decide those things as commander of the barracks."

"Yes, but you know what the shower's like."

Of course I did. The old, dilapidated bathroom was only three feet by five feet, and the shower didn't have a drain. The water soaked into the cracks, and it all turned into a muddy mess. Nevertheless, I insisted. "What about a short, voluntary shower, or they could wash themselves in the sink?"

"No, there aren't enough guards."

We drifted onto the subject of the blindfolds. I had realized that the captain wouldn't do anything he couldn't justify with some argument in front of Krassnoff Martchenko or Lawrence Mires. In front of the "star officers," he didn't want to appear to be "soft" on the prisoners. That's why I added, "We see anyway because sooner or later you cry and the tape comes loose. That isn't very safe for you."

The captain called in "Pepa," Second Lieutenant of Police Palmira

145

Isabel Almuna Guzmán. She bought fabric and thread, and together we made new blindfolds. It didn't help much since pretty soon they were just as dirty as the other rags had been.

PALMIRA ALMUNA GUZMÁN, "PEPA"

I knew her as "Pepa," but I found out her real name in the press after she was identified during Justice Bañados's investigations into the Letelier case.[34]

Palmira Isabel came to the Ollagüe Detention Center in September to be Captain Torré Sáez's assistant. Palmira was a second lieutenant in the police force. She treated me with respect.

Palmira Isabel was a young, happy woman. She was thin, even though she was large boned, which made her look very solid. She had dark hair, and she wore it long and straight with thick bangs framing her round face. She had regular features and almond-shaped eyes.

She asked me to accompany her once on an errand. She brought me a reddish wig, and the two of us left with a driver in a car from the barracks. She took me to someone's house, but I don't remember many details. One thing that did stick in my mind was that we went to have tea at a café. Much later, when the DINA closed the Ollagüe Detention Center and transferred us to Terranova, she stayed on as the assistant to the commander there, Pedro Espinoza Bravo.

In those days she went quite often to the area where the prisoners were held. She even had a "favorite," a guy from the MIR. The officer took him out of his cell and let him sit in the sun on nice days.

In 1975, Major Rolf Wenderoth Pozo told me that Palmira had taken it upon herself to take a little boy who had been detained along with his father to a children's home. He didn't give me any more details, but I think it's important to mention it since now we know that at least one boy was found by his grandmother in one of those homes after the DINA killed his father. That's the case of Iván Montti Cordero's son.

Perhaps he wasn't the only child separated from his family. Speaking

34. Orlando Letelier had served as President Salvador Allende's foreign minister. He was assassinated along with U.S. citizen Ronnie Moffit in a car bomb in 1976 in Washington, D.C. It is one of the most frequently discussed cases of the DINA's repression. Manuel Contreras was sentenced to prison in connection with this crime, along with Pedro Espinoza Bravo. The U.S. government has continued to release previously classified CIA documents regarding the case in recent years.

of that, no one has explained yet what happened to the children of the pregnant women who were arrested. I want to ask those who were the DINA's directors in those days: Where are the women who were arrested by the DINA when they were pregnant? María Cecilia Labrín Sazo, Gloria Ester Lagos Nilsson, Cecilia Miguelina Bojanic Abad, Jacqueline Droully Yurick, Michelle Peña Herreros, Nalvia Rosa Mena Alvarado, Elizabeth de las Mercedes Rekas Urra, Reinalda del Carmen Pereira Plaza. And what about their children? Were they born? Were they killed too? . . . .

LIEUTENANT "PABLO"

On the morning after I was transferred to Ollagüe, Captain Ciro Torré arrived a few minutes before eight o'clock. I know because the guard hadn't changed yet. A very young officer accompanied him. I recognized him as soon as I saw him. He had been one of my brother's classmates at the Military School.

"Good morning, 'Dianita.' This officer is my assistant, Lieutenant 'Pablo.'"

Torré explained that the lieutenant would supervise the progress of my work whenever he couldn't do so himself. Once I had recognized him, I didn't look at Fernando Eduardo Lauriani Maturana again. I wanted to avoid having him identify me. One of the things I was most careful about was not mentioning my brother. I wanted the DINA to forget he existed. There would be better opportunities to fight for his freedom. The few times I was able to see my mother, she told me that they had been able to see him as soon as he was allowed to have visitors.

As soon as the captain left, the lieutenant made himself comfortable in a chair. His joyous attitude surprised me given everything you saw around there. That was the only thing missing, an out of place snot-nosed boy. I remained silent, put a sheet of paper in the typewriter, and set out to type.

The lieutenant kept talking: "You know? I know you. I know that's what you always say when you want to approach a beautiful woman, but I'm sure we've seen each other. . . ."

I looked at him. He was young and flirtatious, in a way I might have found desirable on more than one occasion. I smiled, not at him, but because an image came to my mind. He looked like a rooster in a hen-house showing off all his feathers, puffing up his chest, and stretching his legs, as though he were saying, "Look at me. I'm standing right here. . . ."

I corrected my image to one of a peacock opening his tail. He was the kind of man who needed a woman to be his mirror. He doesn't see her, just the effects of opening and displaying his attributes. He wasn't looking at me. That kind of man doesn't see a woman. He just admires himself. He feels likes he's the owner of an attraction that should supposedly fascinate us. "Stupid macho man," I thought, ready to promptly put an end to that situation.

"Yes, Lieutenant Lauriani", I said calling him by his real name, "we know each other. At the Military School in 1965 you were in the Third Section of the Third Company. Your instructor was Lieutenant Enrique Leddy. You and your classmates used to call him 'jackass Leddy.'" I continued telling him about events that had occurred in that course year by year.

He looked at me more and more surprised by the minute. I answered all his questions. Anyway, my brother had already told Ricardo Lawrence all about it. He stayed in the room talking nonstop while I wrote. Toward midmorning, I was the one who was surprised. The lieutenant looked at his watch and said, "Luz, I always have coffee at this time. Will you come with me?"

"Where?"

"What do you mean where! To the cafeteria, of course."

"Lieutenant, do you realize I'm a prisoner?"

"Luz, don't you realize I'm an officer?"

"I know, lieutenant, and if your invitation surprises me and I refuse to go, it's for your sake. What would Lieutenant Krassnoff Martchenko say, for example? I have enough problems, lieutenant."

"Problems. That's all right. I'm an officer, and I'll take complete responsibility. I order you to go with me. Guard! Take the lady to the club. I'll be there shortly."

The guard shrugged his shoulders and ordered me to go, "Come on, hurry up, or they're going to yell at me."

That wasn't all. The truth is that the lieutenant never stopped surprising me. What he called the cafeteria must have been the kitchen in the house. There were a couple of tables. He ordered coffee and continued talking about himself, his life, his love affairs. Then he asked me some questions about my family, and he was interested in hearing about my son. At one point he took my hand and started caressing me. He

148

tried to kiss me, ignoring my objections, and he started talking in a really exaggerated way. He said I looked so fragile and alone, that I must be so lonely, that he could imagine the drama of a young woman and her child mixed up in these stories about marxists, and that he just wanted to show me affection. . . .

I had already heard this before from the guards at the Military Hospital and at the DINA, this exonerating me of any responsibility for having leftist political ideas. It was a kind of justification that made it possible for them not to be hard on me.

I freed my hand from his and told him that the reality at the moment was that I was there as a prisoner, that I was worse off than a criminal since they can at least serve a prison term that supposedly includes some basic rights. I told him I didn't even have the hope of going to court, that I would rather avoid additional problems, and that at that moment, officer or not, he was putting me in an awkward situation. I asked him to order me to be taken to my room, and I thanked him for the coffee.

From that day on I no longer bothered trying to figure out why things like that happened. The men from the DINA thought they had rights over me. I was part of their property. They looked like stupid macho men with a Don Juan complex to me. It was just another way to try to subjugate me completely.

I never managed to understand them. The most frequently asked question was how I dealt with sexual desires, if I masturbated or not. What I truthfully never felt was the desire to have a sexual relationship with anyone. I needed affection, warmth, companionship, and to feel understood. I needed that a lot.

The lieutenant was practically a kid, and, because of the way he acted, his subordinates soon began calling him "Inspector Clouseau" and "Pink Panther." He never reprimanded me, and it took me years to fathom how I could end up liking that young man who was a DINA agent.

Every day at Ollagüe was pretty much the same. Each day started with a shower in the morning. Lauriani, with Torré Sáez's permission, had brought me an electric heater, the kind with coils. I used to turn it on when I returned from my shower shivering from the cold. The guard had turned a can into a mug for me, and, after a while, someone brought a little teapot. I heated water and drank coffee that my mother sent through some DINA agents who secretly went to the house. They took my notes to her, and, from time to time, they brought me coffee, soap, toothpaste, and detergent. Mom sent cigarettes and cookies too, but I didn't always receive them.

I found out from my parents that some people were taking advantage of our situation. They said they could get things to me, but I never received anything they sent. And I'm not only talking about people in the DINA.

Alejandra and I were still sharing the room, and in spite of the fact we didn't talk much, I started caring about her. I didn't feel alone when we were together. Since I had paper, I started to draw. Alejandra surprised me once when she did it too. Years later I saw some really remarkable drawings she had done. Alejandra also had a beautiful voice. She made us feel nostalgic when she felt like singing.

15

MY LUNG INFECTION AND MY LAST MEETING WITH MY
BROTHER

I began to feel a strong headache. I couldn't sleep. I couldn't open my
eyes. They were swollen, and the light bothered me. When Lauriani
Maturana saw me, he decided to take me to the emergency room after
asking his superior, Torré Sáez, for permission. They instructed me not
to mention anything except my health. They didn't ask much. The nurse
gave me a sedative, which helped me sleep a few hours, and she let me
take a strip of aspirin with me when I left.

On Monday, September 23rd, I couldn't get up. Not only did my head
hurt, but the pain was localized on the right side of my head. My head,
my swollen eye, my gums, and my eardrum were all throbbing. I was
going crazy by the time Torré arrived. I told the captain I needed to
know how my brother was doing, and that I wouldn't write another line
until I could confirm he was alive.

They brought my brother on September 24th. They kept him a while
with the prisoners. Then they brought him to my room. They refused to
leave us alone, untie him, or take off his blindfold. I couldn't even hug
him. But he didn't look like he'd been beaten. They had told him I was
sick, and he was worried. He tried to talk to me about our decision to
become informants. He wanted to trade places with me and have me go
to Cuatro Alamos. I refused. By that time I was sure I had a better chance
of getting out of there alive than he did. It had nothing to do with abilities. It was a road already traveled, and I was certain it was all over for
me. He could still go to a detention center where he could have visitors,
and then . . . freedom. I sensed he could go back to his old life, and I
felt like that path was closed off to me. I remembered the words Romo
said to me once when he took me from Cuatro Alamos to Ollagüe,

"We're going to have to kill these women because we've all slept with them. . . ." Of course, the language he used was much lewder.

With all that in mind, I flatly refused to let my brother take my place. I thought the obvious machismo there would give me more freedom to do things that would be strictly forbidden for my brother. I wasn't even sure what I was betting on. It was just a possibility to buy his life and my own.

My brother accepted. My argument was reasonable. He told me indirectly that they were already saying terrible things about me at Cuatro Alamos. I asked him to never defend me and to take care of himself because nothing I was doing would make any sense if he didn't. We were really sad when we said good-bye, but I knew I could trust him to do his part.

When my brother left, Lieutenant Gerardo Godoy arrived, although at that time he called himself "Marcos," "Captain Manuel," "Mano Negra," and, just like Urrich, "Cachete Chico." He asked me about the work I was doing. I thought it was strange. He gave me the impression that he wanted to see what I thought about my future and about what my brother and I had talked about. I would have liked to put off that moment, but I wasn't in a position to say something like, "Lieutenant, as soon as I get it straightened out, we'll get together and talk about it."

I said, "Lieutenant, I'm sure that besides wanting to know what I'm doing, you are also interested in why I do it. I'm making a marxist vocabulary list and a communications manual. If I'm writing this it's because I know you aren't going to release me or send me to a prison where I can have visitors, because of all the prisoners who are still alive, I am the one who knows you and the DINA the best. I chose to live. From that perspective, I believe there are only two options. It is going to seem premature, but I can't think of anything else. Either you'll give me a job someday or you'll kill me. The lieutenant looked uncomfortable. I realized that my straightforwardness had caught him off guard, that he hadn't thought that far ahead. He quickly said good-bye and left.

THOUGHTS AT OLLAGÜE

I was really worried. Perhaps I had spoken too soon, but, on the other hand, I felt relieved. Now it was their turn. If they didn't kill me soon, I would know that it would be possible to survive. I felt worse, more in pain and more emotional after seeing my brother, and I didn't even have the right to have a headache. It doesn't matter, I told myself. I have to keep going, pain or no pain. I sat on the bed and looked at my foot. My wounds had healed, and there was new skin there that was really red and shiny. The funny thing is that the rest of my foot and leg were numb, but right there it hurt more every day. I was learning how to take the pain. It didn't distract me. It didn't sap my strength, except when I was run-down. It was strange, but I thought I could face any other kind of suffering. Now I've lost that strength, that capacity for rising above the pain, riding on the crest of a wave. Now, when I let my guard down, I'm more at the mercy of physical and moral pain. I started learning how not to cry during that time at Ollagüe. Not crying caused me physical pain. I'm not talking in metaphors. When I was sad I felt a deep pain in my chest, in my neck, and under my left collarbone.

I had changed. I couldn't gauge what was happening to me, and I was frightened. I just had my intuition. Consciously or not, I was making choices and decisions. Whether they were appropriate or not is another matter altogether. But they were my choices, good or bad. I wasn't indifferent. It was my responsibility. I took a look around. I thought that only Alejandra was in a similar situation. I knew that my collaboration had happened during an extreme situation and that it wasn't entirely my decision. Other people and factors intervened that weren't entirely clear at the time. But something told me I had to enter into it completely. I felt like I would never be able to keep going if I started down the path of feeling like a victim, even if everything changed at some point. I knew that others took different paths. The guards talked about "the fanaticism of those who died without talking." I always admired the MIR's militants for their bravery. Even in the worst of conditions, they got organized and found ways to get documents out of the prisons. I was never able to do that.

I knew Krassnoff asked all the informants about others who were in the same situation. He asked me several times about Alejandra. I told him each time that I trusted her even though I didn't know her, and that I cared about her.

Now that time has passed, I know that perhaps I could have trusted some of the guys from the MIR who survived. But I chose not to take even minimal risks back then. I'm not trying to justify my actions. I've actually thought a lot before making these assertions. I'm saying this because it's the truth just like it's also true that a couple of people who survived have attributed their own collaboration to me, and I've taken their actions upon myself as well.

153

I believe that María Alicia, Alejandra, and I tried to do the best we could with the minimal tools at our disposal. I often felt like I was at the breaking point. I tried to get over it, at whatever cost, only because I knew I would go crazy if I succumbed to it. I lived without trusting anyone.

HUNGER FOR BREAD

Those days at Ollagüe were difficult. One Monday they didn't come for Alejandra. At around ten o'clock in the morning Krassnoff came to our room for the first time at Ollagüe. He was happy. He sat down in front of me in the only available chair. The lieutenant asked us how we were and how our weekend had been. Alejandra talked with him almost the whole time. He seemed different, more open and relaxed, so much so that for the first and only time in front of me he asked, "Is there something you would both like to eat?"

Alejandra and I answered in unison, "Bread."

The lieutenant laughed and said, "Unbelievable. . . . Bread? I thought you would say cake or a sandwich. . . . You really want bread?"

Alejandra told him she was hungry. She said that the two of us had mixed water with some milk and cereal and eaten that for a day. The lieutenant kept laughing at our story and told us about psychological hunger. A little while after he left, a guard came with a bag full of bread. It had been a long time since we had eaten fresh bread, and it tasted especially good. That fresh-out-of-the-oven smell reminded me of the aroma of my childhood, of all the days I had lost and that seemed further away every day.

SEEING MY FAMILY

On Tuesday, October 1st, Lauriani found out I still had a headache and asked me what he could do. One molar and my jawbone hurt very much, and I thought it might be a cavity. On October 2nd, he took me to a dentist at the Military Orthodontic Center. I needed a root canal. Lauriani explained to him that I couldn't return. The dentist suggested cleansing the area, but I thought that would just be a stopgap measure that was of no use to me, and that pretty soon I would be in pain again. So I told him to remove the tooth. I couldn't consider things a normal person thinks about, such as keeping my own teeth until my old age.

154

All I could do was eliminate a possible source of future pain. Lauriani offered to take me home, and I accepted right away.

My parents looked happy when they saw me. Lauriani told them he had gone to the Military School with my brother as he pointed to a picture he saw sitting on a table. It was of the day they handed out the ceremonial swords. My mother started to cry. My son asked me over and over if I was going to stay. One of my aunts came and started telling me how she, my mom, and the family had suffered, that my mother was really shaken up. She told me about their financial problems. I remember feeling an ambiguous sensation that bordered on happiness at seeing them and sadness because of the deep pain my actions had caused the family.

I wanted to stay there hugging them. At the same time I wanted to run away. I knew what my mother was referring to when she talked about how happy the mother of the lieutenant must be with her son, and about how sad she was, and how my brother had looked so handsome in his cadet's uniform when he was at the school. . . . That he looked like a prince. . . . All I could think of was the image of him dirty, tortured, haggard, and covered with enormous bruises on his face the day he said to me, "Sis, I had to come find you and get you out of here. That's why I stayed, waiting for them to arrest me."

FEMALE PERSONNEL AT OLLAGÜE

Female personnel became a permanent presence at Ollagüe. I had heard women's voices at the Yucatán Detention Center, but here I saw them every day. I heard them laugh and talk as they sat in the sun near the pool. I saw three women the most: Rosa Ramos Hernández, María Teresa Osorio ("Marisol"), and María Gabriela Ordenes ("Soledad").

As of Monday the 16th there began to be quite a lot of movement. I could tell whether there were more prisoners or not by comments the guards made or because the grease line in the soup pots I washed went up or down. I also knew from the sounds I heard when they took them to the bathroom.

In those days a lot of people from the MIR were being arrested. They belonged to the information apparatus, and one of them worked for LanChile.[35] In April 1993 I managed to find out his name: Germán

35. LanChile refers to the Chilean national airline.

Larrabe. He survived and lives in exile. I saw the young man from afar. They apparently let him sit outside in the sun while he was tied up and blindfolded. They often tried to make prisoners suspicious of one another by giving some of them special treatment even though they hadn't done anything to receive it. I remember him because he wasn't wearing the typical clothes people wore at the time, at least the people I knew. He was wearing snow-white pants, a pink shirt, and a red cashmere V-neck sweater.

I was washing something at the pump in the yard when Romo Mena came over and started talking about his favorite subject: "That woman from the MIR is driving me crazy. She's got some cunt! If you knew what a cunt she's got! I used a key to electric-shock her. The bitch swallowed the whole thing with the line and everything in her!" I kept washing in silence.

They arrested Laurita Allende around the same time. Captain Torré told me she had cancer and that they had removed one of her breasts. He said she transported explosives in her prosthesis. Using those kinds of comments, they desensitized the guards to her. The comment that she was as dangerous as Pascal kept the guards from feeling sorry for her. I never saw her.[36]

Torré Sáez told me of his progress in reading the spy thriller *Orquesta Roja*. I continued writing about "communications and the political left" and I knew the time was coming when they would have to face that decision: And now what do we do with her?

One day I told the captain not to dial a telephone number in front of a prisoner even if he was wearing a blindfold. Back in those days we didn't have push-button phones in Chile. When he asked me why, I told him we had learned to count the number of seconds it took for the dial to move. He got excited and told a guard to bring him a telephone. The guard hesitated. I have to admit there was malice involved on my part, and I really got a good laugh from the situation that followed. The captain didn't seem to understand the guard's hesitation so he repeated the order. When they brought the phone, they left the cord unplugged, the captain made me close my eyes. I explained that it had been quite a while since I had practiced, that I was "out of training," and that practice was essential for

36. Although Arce does not mention his full name, she is clearly referring here to Andrés Pascal Allende. He served as the MIR's secretary general until 1986 and was especially famous for being President Salvador Allende's nephew. He lived his exile throughout Latin America, including Argentina, Mexico, and Cuba.

that kind of thing. He started to laugh and cheerfully assured me he was going to learn. When he left he muttered under his breath something like, "These guys from the MIR are incredible."

Torré was happy with his progress. One afternoon while he was reading what I had been writing about clandestine communications, he told me that he was going to have his own operative unit. I was shocked. He said he wasn't going to ask for facts or crumbs like the others. I suppose he was referring to Lieutenant Godoy García or Lauriani Maturana. Then he added what I dreaded the most: that I would help him. I repeated that I had given Krassnoff and Lawrence all the information I had. He said we would still talk and that we would go over everything again.

I started talking to the captain and repeating the information Romo had already "checked out" in August. I didn't know what he was involved in at that time. The captain was especially interested in knowing exactly where Gaspar Gómez, the director of INESAL, had his residence, and they took me in a car to point out his house to them. I calmly went along since I knew from Romo Mena that he wasn't living there anymore. They had information about a militant I knew from INESAL. They had his ID, but they just showed me his photo. I knew him as Leonardo Moreaux, but I told him I didn't recognize him. I remembered Krassnoff had shown me the same ID at 38 Londres Street in March.

They assassinated Miguel Enríquez a few hours later, and Captain Torré was removed from his post.

16

LUMI VIDELA MOYA

A few years ago, when I began to feel that I was a daughter of God, I asked Him over and over as I cried: "Why did you let me live and not Lumi?"

More than a friend, Lumi is my sister who lives in me. What she gave me is priceless. The understanding and affection she gave me are unforgettable, and she continues to be an endless source of energy in difficult times.

I told myself many times that I'm indebted to her. Remembering Lumi helped me confront the worst of everything. I'll even go so far as to say that she knew she would die anyway. Even so, she stood her ground to the end. She was a great woman who touched me deeply, like Ricardo Ruz, "Tacho," and "Tano." In spite of our short time together, she realized what I was trying to do and, in her own way, she let me know about her plans. Opening up to her was my only transgression in my feelings and actions. And even though we didn't talk very much, it wasn't necessary. We were naturally in tune with one another. Lumi was a brave woman with the ability to step outside her own limitations and see what was going on around her without prejudice.

I tried to tell her, "Lumi, whether you do it or not, you'll die." She refused to change her attitude. My heart was the first to sense Lumi's death, and I was deeply, and forever, shaken when I later confirmed it. I was hurt. I knew that even if I couldn't face myself or my actions of that period, I would still find a way to say that Lumi died while in the DINA's hands.

When we were together at José Domingo Cañas she told me she had a son. Dago is about the same age as my eldest son, and in December 1990 I asked to talk with him. They told me that it was premature,

158

maybe sometime in the future. At that moment, Lautaro Videla, Lumi's brother, was out of the country. I left Chile postponing something that I felt was necessary, trusting God to allow me to give them my, to me, vital testimony some day. I wanted to tell them about my days with Lumi and what I know about her husband, Sergio Pérez Molina.

Today, on June 12, 1991, in Austria, I have just read the Chilean press and discovered that Dago Pérez Videla has filed an action against Juan Manuel Contreras Sepúlveda for the death of his mother, and that he will do the same for the disappearance of his father (*Fortín Mapocho* and *La Epoca*, May 28, 1991).[37]

When I read Lautaro Videla Moya's testimony in the magazine *Apsi* No. 381 (27-III to 7-IV, 1991), I wrote to him. A year and a half later I was able to meet Dago, thank him for his support, and tell him that everything I know about Lumi and Sergio is already in the courts.

I met Lumi when Ricardo Ruz had us get together so I could work on disguising her physical appearance. This was at the beginning of 1974. She was a leader in the MIR, and she belonged to the National Organization Commission, the same structure where her husband, Sergio Pérez Molina, also worked as a militant.

That January afternoon was special in many ways. The conversation between us was spontaneous. I explained that we needed to decide if she wanted a more or less permanent change or if she wanted to learn how to change her appearance whenever she needed to. I said we could try both ways, but that the most important thing was for her to feel comfortable and natural.

We talked about hair, makeup, and clothes. She showed me warmth and acceptance. We empathized with one another, maybe because we were the same age. We went to a café and decided that, since she had already cut her hair short and had decided to change the way she dressed, a wig and learning some makeup tricks would be ideal.

We laughed and talked about a million things we didn't allow ourselves to talk about as militants. I realized that the streets stopped seeming hostile for a few minutes. We bought a wig and went to a salon. We spent quite a while that afternoon looking at potted geraniums and spider plants on people's balconies on Merced Street, almost right across

---

37. *Fortín Mapocho* and *La Epoca* were both alternative newspapers in Chile that disappeared during economic difficulties in the 1990s.

from the Santa Lucía Hill in downtown Santiago. There, we went our separate ways.

On Saturday, September 21, 1974, I heard the guard mention how they had arrested Lumi. I was alone in the room thinking that it wasn't a common enough name to hope it could be somebody else.

That night on the 21st, I felt feverish and went to bed early. At about nine-thirty I was half asleep when the sound of the door woke me up.

It was a guard who told me Lieutenant Krassnoff had sent for me. That was out of the ordinary for a Saturday, especially given the time of day. The scene is clear and imprinted in my mind. There was a round, white, lacquered table. Lumi and Alejandra were there too. Krassnoff had me sit down when he saw me. Sergio Pérez was in front of me. He looked bad, and his half-closed eyes opened when he turned to look at me face-to-face. His hands were tied with a thick rope. He smiled at me. Krassnoff said: "You see that it's true? She looks good, doesn't she?"

Sergio opened his lips. I noticed his mouth was really dry and that little patches of blood had dried and hardened around the corners of his lips. When he talked, he tried to wet his lips with the white foam that told me he had been tortured with electric shock. He had his hands on the table, and, ignoring what Krassnoff had said, he asked me, "How are you?"

All I could say was, "Fine."

He knew it didn't make sense to ask. I knew that nothing I said could summarize how I felt. I realized immediately that Krassnoff was in the process of convincing him to collaborate. Krassnoff gave me a pack of cigarettes. I took it and offered one to Sergio. I watched "Chico" Pérez breathe the smoke in deeply. I knew all too well how you feel at times like that.

I was shocked when I saw they didn't have him blindfolded. That usually implied the possibility of death. Krassnoff talked the whole time about how well I was doing. Lumi and Alejandra kept quiet. "Chico" Pérez spent almost the whole time with his head down. He lifted it from time to time and looked at Krassnoff without saying a word. When Sergio finished his cigarette, Krassnoff Martchenko said I could go. He called the guard, and they took me away.

They brought Lumi to my room a few days later around midmorning. We hugged when the guard shut the door. I stopped typing, and we both sat down on the bed. We sat there holding hands for quite a while. Lumi asked me some questions about the guards and their schedule.

160

She asked me about me. Without hiding my situation, I told her, "I'm collaborating. I'm writing some things about the party."

Lumi picked up the pages that were stacked on the table. She read some of them and smiled while she looked at me with a funny gesture of complicity. She said, "I know what you're doing. . . . Listen, Luz. I've been around and I've had a chance to see some things. I'm doing my own thing too. I'm also 'collaborating.'" She looked at me with the same expression of someone who knows they can't say anything else, but I understood her complicit smile, and I was afraid for her.

I knew that Lumi had been able to get some things from Krassnoff quickly since she had arrived. She had money with her when they arrested her, and they gave her permission to buy deodorant, soap, toothbrushes, toothpaste, and even cologne for all the prisoners to use. I told her I thought it wouldn't last long and that the price for her was enormous. I wasn't referring to the material value, just that they would never believe she was collaborating with the DINA. I told her that there were more important objectives, that there were so many of us that the soap would only last a few days, and that this might undermine her effort to convince Krassnoff of "her collaboration."

She just pretended to collaborate with them. I don't know if she was actually compelled to reveal anything. I've always felt she wasn't. Perhaps it's just a hunch, or maybe it's my affection for her. But I'm sure she had only one objective in trying to convince them: to get as much information about the DINA as possible for the MIR's leadership. She started trusting me with things little by little. She didn't explain in detail. It was as if she were talking to herself out loud, ignoring my presence. The guard told me that Lumi had also bought coffee, sugar, and chocolate, because she was worried about the prisoners. He said that Krassnoff wanted her to stay in the room with Alejandra and me, but that she had refused. She thought that her being with everyone else and sharing their fate would help them keep their spirits up. It was obvious that this was a way to stay in touch with those who would be able to go to Cuatro Alamos. That way, she could be sure the information would get out.

I told her what I had tried to do at Tejas Verdes. I told her about the blindfolds, and that all of that came and went in the blink of an eye. Then I asked her if she knew anything about Ricardo, "Tano," or "Tacho." She told me that as far as she knew, Ricardo was still alive, but that he was still being held captive.

Lumi returned several times. She always asked me for information about the DINA personnel. I told her everything I knew about each one, and I added: "Lumi, don't trust any of them. It is one thing for them not to beat you and give you a cigarette, and another thing altogether for them to do something for you, something that would go against the DINA."

I told her about my experience with Rodolfo, the guard the DINA murdered because he took mail from prisoners at the Military Hospital to their families, and that I thought he was dead. Without agreeing with or denying anything, she said, "You're from the Socialist Party, and I'm from the MIR. We are both trying to do something. I realize we can't both win. We are doing two very different things. I can't do anything else. I've thought about it, and I can't."

"Lumi, you're acting with a short-term goal. And you'll die whether you achieve it or not. You're committing suicide."

She took me by the hands and said, "I don't have anything else, and I have to do what I have to do."

I saw a sweet, sad look in her eyes, not one of resignation. I also knew she was referring to her romantic breakup with Sergio. I knew about it because the guards and the DINA personnel had made remarks about it. We talked about that and about our children, about all the pain we could cause them by being near them. . . . As I looked at her I knew I couldn't say anything to change her decision. She would keep going to the very end. I stopped talking. I looked at her big, dark eyes. They were shining, but she held back the tears. We hugged, and she said, surprised, "You have a fever!" Then she stood up, took off her leather jacket, and added, "Give me that black thing you wear." I didn't have anything to keep me warm, just a wool knit sweater that was full of holes. It didn't make any difference whether I wore it or not. I gave it to her. She put it on, tied it around her waist, and jokingly said: "How do I look? . . . Here, put the jacket on. It will keep you warmer."

I refused. It was a beautiful brown leather jacket. She wouldn't take no for an answer, and she put it on me herself. As she left, she added, "When we aren't together anymore, it will be like a hug from a friend."

She was just like that. Lumi remained with the prisoners, but she arranged for the guard to bring her to talk with me. One of those times, she only went to tell me that "Tacho," Luis Fuentes Riquelme, had been arrested. She knew we were friends. "Tacho" had resisted arrest and had a bullet wound in his buttock. I asked her to send him my love. I was sure who it was because we had a secret code, and Lumi gave me the message without knowing what it meant.

162

On October 4th, Sergio Pérez died. For years I was convinced that it had happened and that Lumi knew about it. We never talked about it. I admired her ability to help everyone without stopping to think about her own suffering. Many times when we were together, we held hands and listened to Sergio's screams coming from the building next to where we were. She held me tightly, and we lapsed into total silence. We couldn't do anything except support and hold each other. We didn't say anything because there are no words to describe what happened to Sergio or to alleviate Lumi's pain. I felt powerless because I couldn't even comfort her. . . . What do you say at a time like that? What?

I can't forget that the same day, perhaps after confirming Sergio's death or ordering him to be transferred somewhere else, the doctor examined María Cristina López, alias "Alejandra," and me. Then came Miguel's death and Alejandra's suicide attempt. Then they sent me to the place where the prisoners were held. That's where my pulmonary infection peaked. I have very vague memories of that month. I know that Lumi sat beside me sometimes and helped me eat soup or drink coffee. But I remember perfectly that the day Lumi died, we happened to be next to each other in line to go to the bathroom. She took me by the arm. I felt really weak and a guard came over to tell me that I had to go for a while to the room where I had stayed before. He said I had to get all the papers I had written because he needed to take them to the office. The guard let Lumi help me. I'm sure she already knew then that she was going to die because she gave me a very special good-bye. She buttoned my jacket and lifted the collar as if she wanted to keep me warmer. Then she said, "I wish you luck! With all my heart, I hope you can do it." Then she hugged me harder than ever before. . . .

Our eyes were brimming with tears when we said good-bye. I heard her say, "Listen, Luz. Krassnoff asked me if I trusted you and your collaboration. I told him that I didn't like people from the Socialist Party and that I didn't know you, which is why I couldn't trust you." Then she repeated, "Good-bye. . . ."

I remembered that a few days before Sergio died, she revealed to me that she was recruiting a DINA guard. When I felt that strong hug and saw her eyes full of tears, I knew that soldier had betrayed her and that she had realized it before they took her to be killed. But, even so, she had the courage to worry about my health and take the time to say such a marvelous good-bye. I was plunged into an endless terror. In a fever that

163

kept me in a state of constant drowsiness, I wanted to hold onto her, to not let them separate us, to yell loudly: "LUMIIIIII. . . ."

I was really anxious that night, but it seemed like my body was winning the fight. I felt like I could think more clearly than during the previous days, or perhaps the impact of my encounter with Lumi made me more aware. I could measure it because the physical pain reappeared as soon as I felt more alert. Early one morning I begged the guard to take me to the bathroom. I really needed to urinate because I had drunk a lot of water the day before. They took me. My eyes were blindfolded with a light blue handkerchief that my mom had given me when Lieutenant Lauriani had taken me to the house. I had sewn an elastic band in it, and I could see underneath it. I was horrified when I walked outside. The guards were shooting dice and betting on Lumi's clothes.

I closed my eyes in the bathroom and cried. Lumi had died.

"Chico" Pérez had resisted until he died, and Lumi tried to pretend to collaborate. They both died approximately one month apart. I found out years later that Lumi Videla Moya's naked body was found early that morning in the garden of the Italian Embassy.

SERGIO PÉREZ MOLINA

Sergio was a member of the MIR's Political Commission, and he was the movement's national director of organization. They called him "Chico" Pérez or "Chicope." I never saw him again after seeing him with Captain Krassnoff Martchenko on the night of September 21st, but I heard him every day until approximately eleven o'clock in the morning on October 4, 1974. All these years, I have always believed he died that day. Maybe he hadn't died at that time, and they took him in agony to die somewhere else.

I saw María Cristina López, Sergio's girlfriend, for the last time on October 4th. I am absolutely certain about these dates because I know it was one day before Miguel Enríquez Espinoza's death.

Lumi, María Cristina, and Sergio were arrested along with several others on September 21st. I heard rumors about these arrests from the guards. They were talking about hidden weapons and money from the MIR, and about the personal affairs of the Pérez-Videla marriage. I didn't know María Cristina. She seemed like a sweet and pretty girl to me, although she seemed to be in fragile health. Even though she spent much more time with me than Lumi had, we didn't share any

164

kind of personal contact besides what was necessary to live together in such a small space.

We only spent two nights with all four of us together in the room, and we really couldn't sleep because we only had a twin mattress and we couldn't get comfortable. The only thing María Cristina and I experienced together was when the DINA doctor examined us. I thought they had taken her to Cuatro Alamos when she didn't return. I still thought it was possible to survive when you weren't a party leader, and she had admitted to an unimportant position. What I don't know is whether María Cristina died because she was Sergio's girlfriend or because someone revealed her real position in the MIR.

Sergio survived fourteen days of atrocious torture. The guards talked near the door to my room about how they had beaten his testicles to pieces. We heard his screams when that happened. His agony began on the morning of September 22nd, just a few hours after Captain Miguel Krassnoff called me into his office where I had been able to say hello to Sergio. I awoke startled by a hoarse, monotone moaning. It was horrifying to listen to it. God, what it must have been like to experience it! . . . For a while I wondered if it was a sound my mind had invented, but the guards yelling "Shut up, you bastard!" or telling each other "This asshole is really screwed" told me that his screams were real. During that time I thought I could differentiate between the screams that come from being shocked with electricity and the way people yell when they're being beaten. Sergio suffered much more. The only time I couldn't hear him was when they came for him to keep torturing him. I realized they dragged him out. He was almost crying as he pleaded with them, "Please, please . . . kill me . . . please, somebody shoot me." I can't write this without crying. . . . At about eleven o'clock on the morning of the 4th, his groaning made me think he was unconscious. Suddenly, I couldn't hear him for a few seconds, and then I heard a kind of loud gasp, like someone gasping for breath but unable to breath, as if he were drowning . . . and I never heard him again.

He was really close. There was a kind of closet next to our room. That's where they kept Sergio. My eyes filled with tears. I was overcome by silence, powerlessness, pain, and respect. His begging and crying remained with me for months, and I can still hear it when I remember him as a brutal testament to what my friends in the MIR suffered.

165

17

THE DAY MIGUEL DIED

Each October 5th, year after year, I'm forced to remember the past. On that day in 1974 Miguel Enríquez Espinoza, the MIR's Secretary General, died. It started out like any other day, fighting to get a shower. However, I soon found out that that day would be different. The Ollagüe Detention Center was full of different kinds of sounds, which was an indication that something was going on. They closed the door to my room, and I complained. Leaving the door open during the day was a "right" I had earned that was very important to me since it meant I could breathe a little looking at the mountains and a bit of sky, seeing the grass that was so green it didn't even look real, or listening to the birds singing in the treetops. They seemed so far away from everything that was happening there.

Due to the unusual commotion, you could tell there were more people than usual there. Marcelo Moren Brito's voice stood out, among others. He shouted orders, dispatched vehicles, and called different units. I sensed the smell of death. About ten minutes after they closed the door, three guards came: "Jote," "Rucio," and another one who took Alejandra.

"Lucecita, I have to tie you up and blindfold you."

"'Jote,' I haven't been tied up for a long time, and why the blindfold if I'm locked up in here all alone?"

"Those are the orders. Let's go. Lie down on the bed."

I put the blindfold on myself. I realized he was tying me down carefully. He knew my foot hurt, and when I put my hands together in front of me he agreed not to tie them behind my back.

"Thanks, 'Jote.' Is something going on?"

"Yes, must be something pretty big. All the officers are here. I'll untie you when they leave. Try to sleep. Can I get you a pill?"

I heard people racing around and unfamiliar voices. They turned on "the frogs" (military radios). They had installed a kind of communications center in the rooms at the end of the yard. Using international code, the agents transmitted orders and coordinated the movement of the vehicles. The DINA didn't have radios in the cars back then, which is why they obtained military radios.

"Ollahue to Rojo, over."

"QAP in QTH, over."

"QSL."

There were metallic sounds, no doubt from checking and loading the guns. Vehicles came and went. I listened to all the instructions. They mobilized helicopters. This was clearly a big maneuver.

The last thing I heard was Marcelo Moren Brito yelling. I was sure there would be more prisoners within a few hours.

The commotion stopped moments later. All you could hear was the radio sending messages from time to time, indicating that different mobile units were converging on a certain part of the city. I must have fallen asleep since I woke with a start when they opened the door. They were bringing in Alejandra, and they tied her up next to me. She looked like she had been crying a lot. I asked her what was wrong, and she said sobbing, "Miguel died. He died fighting. . . . Miguel died."

I tried to comfort her. I was really upset too. I knew who he was. I tried to talk to her. All I could say was, "I'm sorry."

She didn't say anything. She lay down on the bed next to me, and they tied her up too. I closed my eyes. My heart wept. We all knew they wouldn't arrest Miguel, that they would kill him instantly. Miguel Krassnoff Martchenko, Osvaldo Romo Mena, and Marcelo Moren Brito had said that over and over.

Out of that context, in a different time and place, and from different perspectives, Miguel Enríquez would be a controversial figure. But Miguel Enríquez wasn't just the MIR's general secretary. He was an icon of the entire radical left of that time. He was even a symbol for the DINA. They feared him and pursued him viciously. They were sure that destroying him would be the end of the Revolutionary Left Movement. I never saw the officers and the DINA personnel at Ollagüe so happy. One of the guards commented that they celebrated the event with a barbecue at one of the numerous houses the DINA had seized, one in Cajón del Maipo.[38] Many people bragged during those days and afterwards that they had Miguel's

38. This refers to a town near Santiago.

weapon, as if it were a trophy. The only thing I can say about that is what Rolf Wenderoth told me in 1989, which is that Colonel Manuel Contreras had it in his possession for years. It's the weapon that his son, Manuel Contreras Valdebenito, used to kill the CNI agent Joaquín Molina years later.[39]

ALEJANDRA'S SUICIDE ATTEMPT

For years I was convinced Alejandra tried to commit suicide the day Miguel Enríquez died. She says she didn't, that it happened a few days later when they took her to see Claudio Rodríguez, alias "Lautaro," another youth from the MIR who was fatally wounded during a clash with the DINA.

In any event, I had already been diagnosed with a pulmonary infection when that happened. I had a headache that hadn't left me in peace since September and a fever. We were both lying on the bed, tied down. I was half asleep. A noise made me look up. It was Alejandra, who was sitting up. Instinctively, I took off the blindfold and was stunned for a few seconds. I called a guard and tried to open Alejandra's mouth. An empty bottle of barbiturates fell on the floor. A guard and I put water in her mouth. Using our fingers, we started extracting the half-chewed pills. We didn't know how many she had managed to swallow.

While "Jote" went to see how he could get them to send a doctor, I tried to talk to Alejandra. I wanted to keep her awake. I knew that in such cases it was better for the person not to fall asleep. I said something to her about trying to hang in there and not cry. She asked me to let her die. The doctor came, and they took me out of the room. They blindfolded me and put me in with the other prisoners. They sat me down in a corner on the ground with my back against the wall. I couldn't sleep. I heard "Jote" a few hours later. "Listen, this is a mess. I'm leaving at eight, but they know you're here. They'll give you something to eat. It's my turn again tomorrow. Depending on how things are going, I'll come get you so you can take a shower."

"'Jote,' have you heard anything about Alejandra?"

39. The National Information Center (CNI, Centro Nacional de Información) was established in 1977 to replace the DINA. It fulfilled many of the same repressive functions during the remaining years of the dictatorship as well as additional duties that included intelligence gathering and administration. With the return to a civilian government in 1990, the CNI was disbanded. However, many agents continued to work for the Directorate of National Defense Intelligence (DIDN, Dirección de Inteligencia de la Defensa Nacional), the intelligence service that replaced the CNI.

"No. I don't know anything. The doctor took her, to the clinic I think."

That was the first time I heard them mention the clinic. Several days went by, and I lost all notion of time. I returned to that dreamlike state of being neither awake nor asleep. All I remember is that suddenly "Jote" or "Rucio" made me stand up and walk a few steps. They gave me coffee, and one day they gave me milk. I had fallen into a daze. I had my hands in my pockets, and I clung to the pictures of my son that I always carried with me in my jacket pocket. "Jote" said to me, "Let's go, Lucecita. You have to keep going. Besides, you owe me some drawings."

I had a fever, and I suddenly felt like I was returning from somewhere. Those were brief moments, and then I went back to sleep trembling. Some guards made me take analgesics. I was out of it, feeling the kind of calm that precedes the storm with a reddish sky and warm air. All I was able to remember clearly were some things about Lumi Videla. I also remember that Captain Ferrer spoke with me twice and that "Jote" told me that Ciro Torré wasn't the commander of the Ollagüe Detention Center anymore, that Ferrer Lima was.

CAPTAIN FERRER, ALIAS "MAX LENOU"

Captain Francisco Maximiliano Ferrer Lima arrived before Miguel Enríquez died, while Captain Ciro Torré Sáez was still commander of the Ollagüe Detention Center. He took over command while I was sick and was being held with the prisoners.

He was one of the first people in the DINA with whom I established a more personal relationship. When I met him, he made a deep impression on me. The growing mistrust that I had to keep cultivating constantly reminded me not to believe what the DINA personnel said. . . . "Just observe and record every comment, every gesture," I frequently repeated to myself: "I only have one tool, my head. This is the place where everything will be. Everything else, personal experience, is just additional information and must therefore be entered and processed. It doesn't matter if it hurts."

"Max" talked about treating the prisoners differently. Literally, he said "not to massacre them" like he said Krassnoff and others had done. It was clear that "Max" played the role of the good interrogator with me, but I liked the fact he talked to me like that. "Max" was the kind of man I liked to look at. I found his blue eyes attractive, which was sufficient for his excessive concern about dressing like a secret agent not to bother me.

169

He was courteous, mild mannered, and refined, unusual qualities in a place like that. He was also intelligent, shrewd, and, above all—something that is very hard to find and that I am grateful for still today—he was loyal to me in what he promised. When I say loyal to me, I mean he kept specific promises. Nothing more. "Max" promised to tell me if the DINA decided to kill me, as long as he was the officer in charge. And I trusted that it would be as he said. That didn't mean that he was going to save my life.

I know it sounds strange, even crazy, but in places where the most vivid imagination is entirely superseded by the reality of suffering, humiliation, and degradation, it's a blessing to know that death isn't going to surprise you, and that you'll have a few minutes to say good-bye to the people you love, even if it's only in your own thoughts.

I experienced something similar years later when I worked in the CNI with Manuel Provis Carrasco. If the DINA ordered him to kill me, I knew he would at least say something like, "Sorry, sweetie, but I have to kill you."

It sounds crazy, but that's how I lived. That's why, when they killed Lumi Videla Moya and they considered killing Alejandra and me at Ollagüe, I was sure he would tell me. When Captain Ferrer ordered the guards to remove me from where the prisoners were held in November 1974, he asked me, "Luz, do you trust me?"

I said I did, and then he added, "It's all over. We are going somewhere else in a few days. It's gorgeous, full of beautiful gardens. You'll be fine, much better." Then he described the place to me in a really beautiful, almost sweet way.

I knew it was true, that the DINA had decided not to kill me yet. That doesn't prove anything, I know. But, anyway, to this day I am grateful to "Max" for those words. Perhaps it was like unfurling a banner that said, you're not going to die yet.

I knew that Lieutenant Krassnoff Martchenko thought my collaboration was useless. And Captain Torré, who thought I could be useful, had been removed from his post. That's why Ferrer Lima's opinion probably sealed my fate at that point. I don't know.

"Max" called me into his office every day. He confided in me about his ambition as an intelligence officer. He was already talking back then at Ollagüe about creating an intelligence school and defining the profile of an agent. He knew that the DINA was not actually performing intelligence work, and he knew there would be consequences in the future for the repressive tactics they were using then.

He seemed genuine in his approach. Given his seniority in rank, he should have been getting ready to apply to the War Academy. He started to do it, but he wanted to be an intelligence officer.

He later told me about his conversations with Colonel Contreras. He made a choice. He decided he didn't want to be a high-ranking officer. I sensed his happiness when he found out that Colonel Contreras would support him in his training, and he sent him to Brazil to take a course at the Intelligence School.

I know it's strange for me to say that I was the depository of some officer's private confidences, but that's how it was. Perhaps there were personal characteristics, mine and those of others, that played a role. The fact that I was the prisoner held by the DINA for the longest time was also a deciding factor. I knew everyone, and word had it that I wouldn't get out of there easily. That made me a useful confidante. They considered me almost human.

"Max" never made any amorous overtures while I was a prisoner. He knew I trusted him to some extent and that it was easy for me to talk to him. He was undoubtedly one of the most important people in my life then. I don't know how to label that feeling. I would rather define it.

He occupied an important part of my thoughts. I didn't try to understand why back then, and even less now. Perhaps the reason is obvious. I am still grateful for his kindness. "Max" gave me a dog when he saw I was clearly lonely. He noticed I liked music and lent me a tape player and cassettes. He saw how the tape had left me without any eyebrows, and he gave me an eyebrow pencil. He knew that the food was lacking, so he bought me sandwiches and gave me cigarettes. There were other priceless things like talking about children, about life, without ever assuming the role of the critical father. He had a different role.

A few days after "Max" told me that the Caupolicán Unit would move to a different detention center, there was a transfer to Terranova/Villa Grimaldi. The only relevant event prior to that move was that María Alicia Uribe Gómez, alias "Carola," was detained in November. After being brutally tortured by the Aguila unit led by Ricardo Lawrence Mires, she started collaborating with the DINA and sharing the little room where Alejandra and I lived.

I returned to the Ollagüe Detention Center in 1992 accompanied by a National Television crew from the news show "24 Hours." I went with the journalist Mario Aguilera Salazar and his cameramen. Going through that house was really incredible. It's almost unchanged, except

171

the white walls with blue borders have been painted a different color. There is another wooden building in the yard now. The rooms that used to be above the brick wall in the back aren't there anymore, and the trees, including the palm tree next to the pool, have all grown. Today you can't see the National Stadium's light tower or the bit of mountain range that saved me from despair.

After walking through the place, and once Mario and his crew finished taping and showed the scenes to those watching the show, we left with broken hearts.

18

THE TERRANOVA/VILLA NOVA GRIMALDI DETENTION CENTER

When we arrived at Terranova, they took María Alicia, Alejandra, and me to a room that was a lot larger than the one at Ollagüe. I recognized the place as soon as we entered. It was the same place they had taken me on July 23rd. Some things improved for us and others got worse. The good part was that the bed where the three of us slept became my bed, and they brought the other two women a bunk bed. Everyone had a place to sleep. There was a chair, a small table, and a plush, golden-colored armchair that had seen better days, in which Pedro Espinoza Bravo often sat. I remember a closet, and a few days later they brought us a television.

We were much more comfortable. However, there was no water at Terranova. They brought it in water tanks. We had to ration the water again. They gave us a teapot each day with water to wash ourselves.

Once we had settled in, Captain Ferrer Lima came to our room with a young man. The captain said he was a doctor who would be in charge of attending to the prisoners whenever necessary. He introduced him to me. Then he said that, since I had some knowledge of first aid, I would be in charge of what they called the "canteen." In military jargon, that refers to the trunk where all the medicines and other paramedical instruments are kept.

The doctor gave me the medications, which consisted of some analgesics and chlorodiazepoxide (Librium). He also gave me syringes and needles. It wasn't common back then to use disposable needles in Chile so there was also a metal container to sterilize them in and metal cases for storage. I mentioned to the doctor that it would be a good idea to have antibiotics, and he promised to bring some. He gave me some instructions regarding sedative dosages, and he authorized me to distribute them among the compañeras who were very nervous or upset.

I started treating minor emergencies.

One day that summer Krassnoff Martchenko asked me if I knew how to start an IV.

"I've never started an IV, sir. . . ."

"It doesn't matter. The prisoner is a doctor. He'll talk you through it. . . ."

He took me personally to the metal bed frame where a young man was. On the way, Krassnoff told me the prisoner suffered from ulcers and that apparently one of them was hemorrhaging. I didn't know if it was true or if it was something the young man said to stop the torture for a while.

The man was naked on the "grill." They were in the process of removing the wires when I arrived. He had been tortured until just moments before. I was afraid. I still wasn't sure if it was true that you would die if you drank water right after electric shock torture. The guards had orders not to give us water after torturing us, and I thought this guy was going to die if I gave him fluids intravenously.

I knelt down by his side and told him I had never had to find a vein in order to give someone an injection, much less inserted an IV. The young man told me what to do. It seemed to me like he was asking for a very fast drip, and I thought he wanted to die. I agreed, but I thought I would be held accountable for obeying those instructions if he died. Krassnoff went to the torture room and told me to hurry up. I didn't pay any attention to him because I was really nervous. The young man talked to me about Concepción even though he felt sick.

For many years I believed that young man had died. I remembered him without knowing whether that IV had helped him to live or die. When I testified before the Truth and Reconciliation Commission, I asked the lawyers, Carlos Fresno and Gastón Gómez, to please help me look for him. I know the lawyers looked through all the folders, and I wasn't able to identify him in the photographs that were shown to me.

When I returned to Chile in 1992, Viviana Uribe Tamblay called me from CODEPU.[40] She told me a doctor had returned from Italy just a few

---

40. The Committee for the Defense of People's Rights (CODEPU, Comité de Defensa de los Derechos del Pueblo) was founded in Chile in 1980. Its primary goal has been to offer legal and psychological assistance to victims of human rights abuses and their families. It continues to be one of the leading human rights organizations in Chile today. CODEPU's current president is Paz Rojas Baeza.

days before and that, when he testified, he mentioned that he had been administered fluids intravenously in the summer of 1975 at Villa Grimaldi. I was able to see him some days later, and it was touching. His name is Doctor Patricio Bustos Streeter.

There was another room to the north of the room I shared with the other women. That's where they started building what the DINA called the "dresser drawers" and the prisoners called the "corvi houses" or the "Chile houses."[41] The black humor in Chile is incredible. They were like tiny boxes where a man of about six feet could fit sitting down with his legs curled to his chest.

I remember María Alicia's situation was particularly difficult even though our material situation had improved. She had arrived just a short time before, which is why the pressure from the Aguila unit, the ones who tortured her, was very strong. She would return to the room utterly broken and immensely sad. Alejandra continued with Krassnoff Martchenko's Halcón unit, and, theoretically, I still answered to Captain Ferrer Lima. However, he was no longer commander of the barracks.

Terranova was not only the base for the DINA's Caupolicán unit, which was led by Major Moren Brito, but the Purén Unit was also there, which was commanded by Major Raúl Eduardo Iturriaga Neumann. The Metropolitan Intelligence Brigade (BIM) was also located there. The commander of the detention center was the most senior officer there, Lieutenant Colonel Pedro Espinoza Bravo.

I remember that all three of us were considerably thinner than we had been before. Alejandra's weight loss was so excessive that when she was lying down on the bed with a pillow next to her, you couldn't see her. Whenever María Alicia and I saw her sleeping like that we used to say she was "hiding."

Captain Ferrer told me that he would be busy for a few days and that I should draw him some maps showing movements and positions of the opposing armies in every battle of World War II. He didn't want me to sit around doing nothing. He brought me some enormous atlases from the Military School Library, textbooks on the topic, and paper for the situation maps. He also gave me appropriate pencils and pens. I found out later that they used to steal the paper and the watercolors during raids.

41. The term "corvi" comes from the Corporación de Vivienda (Housing Corporation), a social program that was created in the 1950s in Chile to aid lower income families with affordable housing. The very small size of Corvi houses led prisoners to make a joke about their tiny cells.

A few days before Christmas, Francisco Ferrer Lima, "Max," went to the room I shared with María Alicia and Alejandra, and gave me a puppy. The puppy bit my hands playfully when I picked him up. I wanted to name him Kim, but the guard insisted on calling him Bronco. He was a faithful companion the whole time I lived at Terranova.

On Monday, December 23rd, Espinoza Bravo, alias "Don Rodrigo," told all three of us that we could be with our families for a while on December 24th.

ANOTHER CHRISTMAS PRESENT

A little before Christmas, they told us they would give us a stipend of 100 pesos a month. I remember we were supposed to use it for deodorant, soap, and other little things, and they bought us clothes. The three of us had nothing but the clothing on our backs, the majority of which had come from raids where they had robbed things for us. Even though we were getting many things, we gave them away too since it was common for other compañeras to lose their clothes as a result of being tortured.

I remember I bought myself a skirt with a beige-colored, safari-style jacket, some sandals, and a purse. Alejandra was more practical and bought herself jeans. María Alicia got handmade clothes. After a few days, commander Espinoza said he had given two officers permission to take us out, and that the three of us would go with the two officers so no one would get the wrong impression. One of them was Rolf Gonzalo Wenderoth Pozo, and Captain Manuel Abraham Vásquez Chahuán was the other.

They took us to "Caledonia" where they bought us some punch and took turns dancing with all three of us. I didn't know that place, but I guess it was a popular place back then. Obviously, the officers' intentions to initiate some kind of relationship with María Alicia and me became much clearer there.

The fact that they bought us clothing and that we went out with the officers generated a lot of hostility from the female personnel who made every effort to spread the news. I think that's where the stories originated suggesting that we modeled for them and things like that, which wasn't true. What I won't deny is that even though I only had one outfit to wear, that outfit and I would always be clean and look as presentable as possible. I don't think Alejandra, María Alicia or I ever walked in

176

front of the prisoners like models. The only time I was among them was to administer some medicine.

We often saw female agents who had our belongings when we arrived at Terranova. They had robbed anything that hadn't been broken during torture sessions. María Alicia protested, and Rosa Humilde Ramos Hernández had to return her dresses and an arrow she wore around her neck. Obviously, complaining was just for the principle of the thing because none of us wanted to use those clothes again. Clothes from the prisoners, yes, but anything those agents had worn, no.

It wasn't an ideological issue. We knew our compañeras and we didn't know anything about those other women, about how they lived or what habits they had. It was a question of hygiene. . . .

CHRISTMAS 1974

On the morning of December 24th, they told us they were going to take María Alicia and Alejandra to see their mothers, and that they would bring my mother and my son to Terranova.

They asked me to write my mother a note saying that they would bring her to see me. At about three o'clock in the afternoon a guard came to get me and took me to a terrace next to the staff cafeteria at the main house. When they came in, they gave me an ice cream and some wafer cookies. My son played with Kim-Bronco. Rafael had grown. He was going to turn six in a couple of months. I was so happy I could caress him. I told him to behave for his grandparents, that I would be working far away for a while. That is what my mom had told him, that I would return like I had before. I said I would try to call him at least once a month.

My mom told me about the family. She talked to me about how sad she was. I tried to calm her saying that I would do everything I could to resolve my situation. I wanted to instill in her a confidence I didn't have, but I told her I thought it was going to take a long time. I asked her to be patient and thanked her and my father for taking care of my son.

My mom told me they had put tape over her eyes on the way and that my son had noticed it even though she had worn dark glasses.

When they took them away, a guard took me to my room. The other girls hadn't arrived. I looked at my hands. I had stroked my son's little head just a while before, and now it seemed like I could touch the emptiness in them, an emptiness that permeated my entire being. I couldn't

177

believe it would be a long time before I would have him again by my side. I remembered the enormous number of times when I would have wanted to see him even for a second, and, although we had been together almost an hour, it was so little.

Just think how wonderful it was to have had them by your side, I told myself. I sat at the tiny, white table. I took a piece of paper, asked the guard for a glass of water, and started painting a landscape. Any place, part of a road flanked by golden poplars, and in the background, the silhouette of the mountains and a bit of sky. I could feel wings of freedom rustling in the bushes. It was my dream of a golden fall. Almost in the horizon, the road disappeared at some bend in a distant place I was unable to see. But I hinted at it. Other days will follow these, I thought, and I signed the painting.

NEW YEAR'S EVE AT TERRANOVA

These kinds of parties and celebrations meant taking a break from the daily routine. At different hours during the day, the officers found a free moment to stop by the room and say good-bye to us before they left.

"Don Rodrigo" and Rolf Wenderoth Pozo came in the afternoon. With their chubby cheeks looking a little more flushed than usual, they were both in a festive mood. They were more talkative and cheerful after the drinks that preceded their visit, and they accepted the usual: black tea for "Don Rodrigo" and an herbal tea for the major.

"Don Rodrigo" started with his usual chatter as he talked to us about the future. I gave him my idiotic smile as if I were listening devoutly. I looked at María Alicia and Alejandra as I sat down, and I asked myself, are their smiles the same as mine? I started feeling furious even though I had only listened to the beginning of "Don Rodrigo's" prattle.

"Don Rodrigo . . . ," I said to myself with mock solemnity, separating each syllable, "DON RO-DRI-GO, THE RE-DEEM-ER!" The son of a bitch thinks he's the savior himself. I listened to him for a few seconds. There he was lecturing us about how we would live each day to come.

I felt an unspeakable fury. To them, we were the "package." Just like always, the double standard. On the one hand, we were supposed to buy our lives by being nothing and having no will or life of our own, but watch out! We had to be efficient. On the other hand, we were all females of the same age. We were all born in 1948 and twenty-six years old at the time, and, according to them, we had committed all the sins of

178

women our age. In other words, we were marxist militants and therefore whores. In my case, there was also my "disgraceful" condition of being separated from my husband.

The rage inside me was fighting to be heard. I had to control myself. How hard it was while I was faced with that sorry excuse for an authority figure.

When I came back to earth, it was like crashing on the ground face-first. . . . "Don Rodrigo" was on the same subject, talking about how someday maybe we could even be . . . ladies! . . . They left. I had heard the same lines before. All the officers who came that day pontificated about how one year was coming to an end and that the new one would be better, and that they would wait to give us hugs until the new year, so we would have good luck.

I thought about it. When I really didn't know what to say or when I realized it was impossible to truly get inside a person, I resorted to these same expressions. I thought that this is what happens in situations when culture abandons us. When you're faced with facts devoid of logic or reason, and feeling becomes inexpressible, or when you realize that no matter what you say you won't be able to alleviate someone's pain or give them what they need. . . . Like at funerals, for example. Yes, it wasn't December 31st. It was another funeral, a masquerade, the funeral of my soul. . . .

A guard came with our dinner at about eight o'clock. He had his fingers in the soup, as usual, but I was already used to it. It was what in prisoners' lingo we called "farm fresh." Chicken soup. It was delicious, or at least I thought so, finger and all. We had just finished eating when there was a knock at the door. . A man I had never seen before entered. He said he was the officer on duty. He asked us if we had enjoyed the dinner, and he added that he would send for me later because he wanted to talk to me about some things.

I was worried. . . . The three of us decided to go to bed and leave the television on. Later, a guard came and said that the officer on duty needed me in the office. I was overwhelmed by a feeling I knew all too well: a combination of apprehension and feeling like I was on red alert.

I got dressed quickly. I decided to go voluntarily. I thought it would be easier for me to control the situation if I didn't refuse. If I resisted from the beginning, he could still have them remove me. He had the power to do it, at least for those hours while he was still running the detention center. I kept my spirits up by thinking about how I had gotten out of worse situations.

When I got to the office, he took out a bottle of liqueur and offered me a glass. I accepted so I could avoid arguing about it, and I tried to take the initiative in the conversation. I thought it might be possible to make out all right if I could shift the subject to something about his work.

"Lucecita, I know about you. About what they say, that is." He took a sip of liqueur. I told him that even though I was still a prisoner at that time, I was sure that would change at some point. I said that my professional relationship with Captain Ferrer was excellent, and that I was sure Commander Espinoza was interested in the situation that Alejandra, María Alicia, and I all shared. I spoke well of both officers, letting a couple of phrases slip that suggested a vital dependence within the unit. I thought this would make him have a more "professional" attitude. I made my first mistake when I mentioned what time it was.

"Sir, I would like to know if there is anything specific you would like to talk to me about. The captain has been working on a project and he came to the conclusion that he has been able to identify an important part of the MIR's structure. He gave me his rough drafts so I could rewrite them. I have to give them to him tomorrow, and I haven't finished yet. I would like to be excused."

He didn't even consider what I said: "Look, Lucecita. The New Year was half an hour ago. Come over here and give me my hug."

I tried to act really natural, but I was disgusted when he hugged me. That man had a terrible smell. His jacket was covered with dirt and so much dandruff it looked like snow. I felt the nausea that never left me well up in my stomach like a wave. I tried to hit on a reason that would allow me to get out of there. I decided to have a drink. "I'm strong," I told myself. I remembered how I hadn't even felt tipsy on the rare occasions I had had a drink. And, given the tension I felt at the moment, it was even less likely to happen! And then I got an idea all of a sudden. I would get him drunk. I didn't know how to avoid the situation, but I could try to postpone it. I poured myself a little more liquor and walked toward the door with the glass in my hand. I wanted to see what exactly was going on. I heard a woman screaming and I was terrified. The prisoners! There were more screams, gunshots, yelling, and crude jokes. There were conversations close by and laughter.

"Let's go, Lucecita. Come on. Don't spoil the party. Look, everybody

180

out there is having a good time. I gave the boys a few bottles. They're young and have really stressful lives," he said as he came closer again.

I continued walking toward the door. I said "You're right, Pedro." Then I opened the door.

There was a guard there a few feet away. That night none of the guards I knew or who were nice to the three of us were there.

"Do you need something, sir?"

I hurried and answered him. "Nothing, just that you should celebrate too. Isn't that right, sir?

"Of course. Here you go man." He gave him a glass. The young man looked on. . . .

"Drink, man, drink! Until you see the bottom of the glass! Let Lucecita see."

I turned that phrase into a playful dare and said, "But I haven't seen you drink like that, sir."

"We'll fix that right away, then . . . ," and he downed another drink.

He suddenly looked happier again and said to the guard "Go on. Take a look around and then find yourself some amusement." Then he closed the door and turned toward me. "You're going to lock it, right?"

He went to the desk. That's where the keys were! He locked the door and put the keys back in the same place.

He put his arms around me. Trying to contain the repulsion the man inspired in me, I managed to get away from him. Then he got violent. He grabbed me by the hair and, pulling it until it hurt, pushed me down on the armchair and threw himself on me.

All I remember is that I felt almost indifferent to everything. I didn't even have any thoughts. As soon as I could, I went to the bathroom next to the office and fixed my clothes. When I walked out I saw him standing there adjusting his pants. He had his back to me. I picked up a metal trinket that was on the desk, the DINA's symbolic fist, and it felt cold and heavy in my hand. Everything happened in the blink of an eye. He didn't even turn around before I whacked him over the head with it. I put all the anger, powerlessness, and humiliation I had suffered all those months into that blow. . . . He fell on the floor without making a sound. I dragged him over to the armchair. Nothing mattered to me. It was as if the violence had all gone into that blow. I sat down for a minute and thoughts began to emerge slowly. I was calm, as if I didn't feel anything. I looked at the cabinet, and I caressed each one of the AK submachine guns with my eyes. There were clips and surely there was ammunition

181

somewhere. The screaming had stopped. It had been a while since I had heard gunshots. The beasts are sleeping or resting, I thought. For an instant, I imagined taking out the guns and freeing the prisoners. Would I be able to get to Tobalaba? I glanced at the officer who looked like he was sleeping. I was afraid he was dead. I went closer and saw he was breathing. Maybe the blow really hadn't been so hard and he was sleeping because he was drunk.

I went over to the desk. I saw an address book as I grabbed the keys. I went through it and found the officers' telephone numbers. The officer on the sofa moved and groaned. I picked a blanket up off a chair and covered him up, not to keep him warm, just so he wouldn't wake up. I heard some noise as I left the room. I instinctively turned to the left. There was a kind of sofa there, and one of the guards was with a woman. I assumed she was one of the prisoners. I was shocked. She was pregnant. Her clothes were on the floor, a wrinkled dress with beige, white, and lilac colored flowers. . . .

I gestured for the guard to keep quiet. I assume he understood the officer was sleeping since he gave me a sly smile. The woman and I looked at each other, and I walked out of there confidently. As I was walking down the stairs, the cool morning breeze blew through my hair. It was morning. . . . As I felt that cool air, I told myself that maybe the rest of the year would be better.

I felt like I was drugged. I felt my face growing progressively harder. Something was tearing me apart inside, and I clenched my teeth harder. When the officers arrived, Lauriani Maturana came to our room and sat down beside my bed. I told him what had happened, omitting the parts I would have wanted to forget. He told me he would inform his superiors with all the details.

A doctor came and talked to me for a while. I insisted I hadn't been raped. I was ashamed. I was completely incapable of admitting it, much less to those people. I knew I was indirectly protecting someone who didn't deserve it, but who deserved what went on there? For what? I thought, besides, nothing could erase from my being what had happened. What would it change? What would it matter to me if they threw him out of the DINA or not? Or if he were arrested or not? There were a lot of officers like him left. I would still have all of that imprinted in me forever. . . .

I don't know if they believed me or not. What I could say or feel really mattered very little. The doctor gave me a sedative, and I slept for a while.

I woke up for lunch, which I had to force myself to swallow. I had a crazy idea while I thought about people "on the outside." I thought about going out on the street, approaching the first people who walked by, and saying to them, "Hey! You, Mrs. Normal, you with the right to walk down the street. . . . You know what? They raped me!" Suddenly, an image flashed before my eyes of someone saying, "It's your own fault! . . . You asked for it. . . . Didn't you like fixing yourself up? Didn't you like wearing miniskirts? . . . I smiled silently. Surely, that's how people thought. I had listened enough times to things like, "Didn't you like being a communist? Well, there you go. . . ."

A while later the guard at the door told me that Espinoza Bravo wanted to talk to me, and they took me to his office.

INVESTIGATION

Espinoza Bravo explained that there would be an internal investigation. After he was off duty, the officer left as if nothing had happened. The others started questioning personnel and some of the female prisoners. Espinoza Bravo told me in a note that the officer was being held in the solitary confinement cells. He said they had beaten him and that they were going to discharge him from the DINA. He took the opportunity to continue talking about dignity and honor. He said he understood my situation, but that he needed my statement for the preliminary investigation. I told him everything, leaving out the part about how he raped me. I suppose that man realized I hadn't reported everything. Perhaps he'll never understand why. It took me fifteen years to accept what had happened to me as a woman in the DINA. Nevertheless, I was able to articulate it when I spoke before the Truth and Reconciliation Commission.

On the way back to my room, the guard had me take a look at the "corvi houses." I saw the officer. He was apparently under arrest, and they were beating him. I realized I didn't like seeing him. I didn't want to see him. . . . I tried to flee, but I just stood there feeling like I didn't want to exist. . . .

They told me a few days later that the officer was discharged from the DINA along with some of the guards, and that they had taken the pregnant prisoner to the institution's clinic. I suppose to the one located at 162 Santa Lucía Street. After that New Year's Eve, my personal situation improved in the eyes of the officers at Villa Grimaldi. I had had the weapons within reach, and I didn't try to escape. I didn't do it because I was a coward. I confess that for a minute, I thought about freeing the male compañeros first, but I didn't dare. . . . Where would we have gone? Besides, I knew they wouldn't have believed me, not just because I was an informant, but because of another night when Rolf Wenderoth ordered that the doors be left open where the male prisoners were, and had an armed guard hide to kill those who tried to escape. Another guard warned the compañeros, and that's how they avoided that trap.

Now I knew I wasn't the strong woman I tried to show everyone I was. I found myself very close to the edge. I had learned something that New Year's Eve. I would never kill anyone, at least as long as I was able to think. But the way I struck that officer with the metal object scared me. I was blind at that moment, I told myself. . . .

I was continually giving in to that pressure that screamed at me from within, "You've come too far. All you can do is keep going. There is no going back. You are a traitor, Luz Arce," resounded within me. I had gone to hell. It was as if I were falling. No one had to push me. I was going straight to the bottom. I thought to myself, I can only stop this destruction if I die.

19

MY SON AND FAMILY COURT

During one of Espinoza Bravo and Wenderoth Pozo's visits in the first week in January, they informed us that we would be allowed to call home at least once a month. They told us we could start the following day. When I went, Krassnoff Martchenko ordered me to tell my father to stop petitioning the Pro-Peace Committee on my behalf or they would kill me. I had to use those exact words. When I talked to my mother, she was desperate because my ex-husband was trying to get custody of our son. They had already set a court date, and, if I didn't show up, they were going to hand my son over to his father. He was alleging, through his lawyer, that I was disappeared.

I was crying as I hung up the phone and left. What could I do? How could I go before the court and say, "Here I am. I'm the mother." I shut myself in the closet when I got to our room. I wanted to cry in private.

After a little while Espinoza and Wenderoth heard about what was happening. They came to the room and made me come out. Then they asked me if I was ready to pledge my eternal loyalty in exchange for my son. All I could say as I was crying was yes. A few days later they had me get dressed up. I fixed my hair and makeup very carefully, and I went to Family Court with a team of DINA lawyers. Someone had talked to the judge beforehand, which is when I lost all respect for my country's judicial system. However, I was thankful because they gave me permission to keep my son with my parents. That way I could live with him when I was released. . . . The DINA had arranged everything. My ex-husband and his lawyer didn't have any alternatives. He tried to speak, and the judge said, "How could you say that your ex-wife is disappeared? I have no trouble seeing her. . . ."

185

CREATING THE VAMPIRO GROUP

Given how the year had begun, anything seemed better by comparison. There was a lot of activity, and they kept busy hitting the MIR hard. Captain Ferrer Lima was taking a pilot's course in the army's Aviation School. He obtained some manuals, and I made drawings for him to help him study.

Ferrer Lima was convinced that I was able to remain "stable" as long as I kept busy. I told him that myself. It was easier to for me to escape that way. From time to time Krassnoff Martchenko asked me to redo his rough drafts of the MIR's militant structures, based on statements prisoners had given or other information he had obtained from documents they found during the raids. That is how I knew what the Halcón and Aguila units were doing. It was shocking to see how the compañeros went from the list of the wanted to the list of those who had been detained. And after he arrested someone, Krassnoff tried to determine which compañero would assume the duties of whomever was arrested.

In December 1974, Lieutenant Fernando Lauriani Maturana had made so many mistakes in his actions as a DINA agent that Krassnoff, indignant, reprimanded him. He shouted at him in front of prisoners and subordinate personnel. Lieutenant Lauriani was really depressed after that. He came to the room where I stayed. I realized he didn't understand why things weren't working out for him. I limited myself to listening.

He talked as if he were talking to himself. He listed his problems one by one, like the time they stole his vehicle with the unit's weapons inside when the agents were out setting a trap or on a mission. Similar things happened to "Inspector Clouseau," like the time he couldn't find his car. He used his DINA identification to make all the passengers and the driver of a bus get out so he could use it. That's how he arrived at Terranova with his prisoners, by public transportation. If he hadn't seemed so upset, I would have laughed. I was silent as I listened to his long list of problems. I only intervened when the lieutenant grabbed his weapon and said that he should kill himself.

I told him to explain everything he had told me to Commander Moren. I knew that Moren Brito liked him, and I thought maybe he could calm him down. I panicked at the thought he might shoot himself right there.

In short, the lieutenant didn't kill himself. He spoke with Moren Brito, who decided to create a new unit to give the lieutenant another chance. That is how "Vampiro" was born. He assigned some of the oldest and most experienced men to work with Lieutenant Lauriani, to keep him from making too many mistakes.

ROLF WENDEROTH POZO

A new situation arose that would profoundly change my days at Terranova. I met Officer Rolf Wenderoth Pozo as "Don Gonzalo." He was a major, thirty-six years old, and had recently graduated from the War Academy as a high-ranking officer. He would accompany Pedro Espinoza Bravo when he would come to our room before leaving Terranova in the afternoon. I didn't even notice the major's presence at first. I didn't know his duties either, but he looked older than the other officers who were in the DINA.

One of those afternoons Rolf said, "I have an upset stomach. I brought some herbal tea. Could you make me some?"

I stood up and answered him harshly, "The tea leaves are covered with dirt. I'll need permission to go to the bathroom to wash them, and you'll have to order a guard to take me. That's if there's any water left, of course!"

It really bothered me that they acted as though they were in a tearoom. The other girls, Alejandra and María Alicia, complained about how I made everybody coffee, especially during the night shift when it was really cold, no matter how late it was. However, Espinoza Bravo's mere presence pissed me off. He was always giving lectures. He had bestowed upon us the great honor of taking us under his wing. He had the "package" with three piles of shit and trash, and he was going to turn us into "upstanding women."

Wenderoth ignored my manners since he was always very polite. One day he asked me to leave the room with him. He led me down a dirt path, and a few meters on I saw the rose garden. I was amazed. I knew it was there. "Max" had described it to me at Ollagüe. I had never seen so many roses in my whole life, and they looked so beautiful!

They came in every shape and size. There were some little white and pink ones, and further on there were huge ones with thick petals that looked like they were made of velvet. My eyes devoured the beauty that could coexist with that gloomy place. I stopped suddenly. There was a strange, cold flower that stood out among all the others. It was a white rose that also had various shades of blue. I have never again seen those roses any other place. I felt afraid as I looked at it, and Wenderoth said, "Are you cold? Do you want to go back?"

"No, sir. I was just looking at that blue rose. I've never seen one like that."

"Go on, look at them and take as many as you want," he said as he offered me a white and yellow one. I took it and walked in that sweetly perfumed tide.

I forgot the major's existence. I ran around ignoring the pain in my foot. When I regained consciousness and saw Rolf Wenderoth, I felt ridiculous. I was agitated and sweaty. I felt embarrassed. I wanted to disappear, to run away, to yell, to insult him.

He pretended not to notice and just said, "It's late. Should we go?"

I walked toward the room. They closed the door behind me. I stopped and stood there holding the flowers. I leaned against the door, looking at María Alicia and Alejandra who asked me many questions and made fun of me.

"Come on! What happened? I knew it! Gonzalo only has eyes for you when he comes here," said María Alicia.

Alejandra, who was sitting in the top bunk added, "When you talk to him. . . . He can barely control himself as he nods his head back and forth with his cheeks all red . . . , " added Alejandra, who was sitting on the top bunk. She laughed as she imitated the major's movements.

I laughed with them. All I could talk about was the roses. I hid my rage because I couldn't understand it. I didn't tell them about the fear I felt when I saw the blue rose that looked to me like a cup filled with pain and suffering. And it was so beautiful. . . .

From that day on, María Alicia and Alejandra teased me about the major. María Alicia would say, "I'm glad. That way you won't act so silly whenever that boring 'Max' stops by." I teased María Alicia about Espinoza Bravo, and we both joked about Alejandra with Krassnoff Martchenko. It was a game. None of us was involved with anyone at the time.

Pretty soon Rolf told me that I was no longer assigned to Captain Ferrer Lima, and that I wouldn't go to "Max's" office anymore. I would go to his. That bothered me even more. It didn't just bother me to see that the girls were right. Sooner or later I would have to face his demands, and I wouldn't see "Max" anymore. Well, I did see him, but he rarely spoke to me again.

Major Wenderoth didn't seem to be in any hurry. He apparently just wanted me to be there, sitting in front of him at his desk. He occasionally dictated a document for me to type, memos or fliers for the staff concerning management and the daily routine at Terranova.

On a daily basis he put together the report on the prisoners of the brigade, which was then forwarded to Headquarters. I got used to reading backwards while I looked at it. That's why I remember the names of prisoners I never saw. The messengers at the barracks delivered the report every day. At that time they were Avalos and Rubilar Ocampo, who would be a CNI agent years later and who appears to be involved in Federico Renato Alvarez Santibáñez's death.

I felt horrible. It was obvious to everybody that I was just the major's new plaything. I was livid at the staff's mocking laughter. I knew how ruthless they tended to be when talking about women.

One day when Major Wenderoth Pozo went to a meeting at Headquarters, "Max" called me and said very seriously, "Please, Luz, continue doing what you have been doing until now. Don't give in to the major's hints. I'm not saying anything against him. I don't know anything about him. He's my superior. I know he doesn't give you any options. But think of yourself. I'm sure you have a future. I'm sure of it. At least, you deserve one. . . ."

I listened to him without saying anything. I neither confirmed nor denied anything. With a curt "Will that be all, Captain?" I left and said, "Thanks for the advice."

Even though there still wasn't any water at the detention center, the roses kept blooming beautifully thanks to an irrigation ditch that bordered the property. Tons of baby Chilean snakes were born there. The guards would pick them up to scare us. I had to make a huge effort to overcome the phobia I had of those animals since childhood and of anything like them. The guards picked them up and handed them to me trying to see if they scared me. They knew the other girls were afraid of spiders, and that I picked them up and set them on the plants outside our room. When they handed me those snakes, I took them and shuddered from the contact with their cold bodies, but I learned to hide the disgust and the fear they caused me. I ended up accepting them, and adopted one as a pet for quite a while until Wenderoth, disgusted, made the guard remove it. They never bothered me with the snakes again.

I kept it in a flowerpot from the office, and I carried it around in a box of matches in the pocket of Lumi's jacket. It was a baby snake. . . . It had beautiful skin. It was more yellow than the others and had pretty, dark markings and a smooth, white belly. When someone else picked it up, it used to wriggle all over. I got over my phobia completely.

The major often took me with him to walk in the rose garden. I took the opportunity to walk my dog, Bronco-Kim. He loved it when I threw sticks and stones for him to fetch. The dog knew my voice, and more than one guard got a nasty growl from him.

Little by little I started letting go of my serious attitude with Rolf Wenderoth. It wasn't premeditated. First it happened, and then I realized it. He protected us, and he was earning my gratitude. One day he showed me a "little house."

Several soldiers were building a hut beyond the roses, next to the tower. He said it would be for the three of us, and that it would be ready in a couple of days. He explained that it would have two rooms, and that he thought we should have our room facing east and that they would bring us a table and chairs for the other side.

It bothered me that Rolf was always observing me. It wasn't like the way some of the people from the units looked at us and always told us they knew all about the three of us and made comments about our skin or our breasts. Nor was it like Krassnoff Martchenko's contemptuous half smile with his twisted mouth, as if he were looking for something hidden in our attitudes. The worst part was that I was beginning to realize that each day I seemed more and more like one of those stray dogs that are thankful for a pat even though you might kick them. The more Major Wenderoth protected us, the more frequently I was spontaneous with him. I felt like I was lowering my defenses. Rolf didn't ask for anything in exchange—yet—not even a drawing.

I continually felt like I was becoming more and more relaxed with him. I already knew very well that I was explosive when faced with yelling and aggression. But like this it was impossible for me to maintain a distant or confrontational attitude. I had such a huge need to have some contact that would make me feel human. I wasn't even looking for affection or support. It was enough for me just to exchange words without violence. . . .

I was uneasy all the time. I kept telling myself, "The major's going to make you pay up any day now."

One day he said, "Luz, I'm going to be out of the country for a little over a month. I've been thinking that it wouldn't be good for you to spend the whole day in the house. I think it's good for you to get out, even if it's just to go to my office. I'll make everything about this official, even the tiniest details. I want you to help me with this. Nobody can tell me your problems like the three of you can. I'll be sure everything is clear regarding the routine at the barracks and anything I can control." Then he added, "Luz, I would like you to type my memoir for the War Academy. That way no one will object to your presence in my office. But only if you want to."

I told him I knew how to type, but that I had never written a memoir or anything like that. He replied that it didn't matter, that it would be fine however I did it. I said, "Major, if you want to take the chance, I'd be delighted."

He said he would try to find a suitable typewriter. I remembered that when Lieutenant Lauriani Maturana took me home and I was in my room, I realized that they had taken a lot of things in the raids, but they had left Ricardo Ruz's typewriter, perhaps because it had been taken apart. Wenderoth asked me to write my parents a note asking them to give the messengers the typewriter.

My parents had a package for me. They always hoped someone would take me to see them or come on my behalf. Besides the typewriter, they sent a box with food and a pair of beautiful tall boots that my mom knew I liked a lot.

I cried. I knew that their financial situation was bad, and even so they made sure to send me things. I thought the boots were beautiful. They must have been really expensive. I felt they were a luxury, which made me feel worse. The armor I wore to defend myself hid numerous cracks, and a flood of tears streamed through them. I started to lose control and repeat slowly, as though approaching a kind of catharsis, "Shit, life's a real bitch!"

It had been a long time since I had cried. When I came to myself I saw the major sitting in front of me. There wasn't anyone else left in the office. It was late, and I thought the world was a piece of shit. I looked at the typewriter. It would be one of life's sick jokes. If he were still alive, it's owner, Ricardo Ruz Zañartu, was most probably still at the Air Force Academy. Maybe he was in exile, I thought. I hoped so. And now I had his typewriter, and I would type the major's memoir with it. The BIM from the DINA would fix it.

That outburst had the merit of taking me away, to nothingness. I was relaxed, as if nothing existed.

"Major, forgive me."

"Don't worry about it, Luz. What can I do?"

191

"Nothing, Major, it's okay. It's over. It was just a passing moment. May I go?"

"Yes, of course. It's late. I'll take you. Now, if you think it would do you good to have a cup of coffee or to talk. . . ."

"Thanks, Major. And would you like a cup of herbal tea?"

I walked outside. The major had given me permission to walk around Terranova's interior paths between the little house, the offices, and the bathroom. It was a triangle, an enormous space compared to the little rooms where I stayed for over a year.

When I first started walking alone around the property, I felt abandoned. My eyes almost hurt as I gazed out over the distant horizon. I felt even more orphaned without walls close by.

It was getting dark and cold. I went to get Lumi's jacket from the little house where we lived, and I brought the tealeaves for the major. It was as if the cool air had penetrated me through my nose, and I felt a mixture of fear and emptiness. I drank my coffee, and the major asked if I thought it would do me good to see my parents and my son. He said he would arrange it as soon as he got back from his trip. I thought about my brother. I hadn't seen him since September at Ollagüe.

The rest of the time I didn't say anything. Rolf Wenderoth always respected my moments of silence. He's the kind of person I couldn't argue with, not because I hadn't tried, but because he didn't get annoyed with me. He waited until I felt ridiculous ranting and raving all by myself, and all I could do was calm down.

Wenderoth walked me to the house. It wasn't necessary, but he always did it. That day it was a long, interrupted walk.

"Do you like walking, Luz?"

"Yes, Major, and I'm supposed to. The last time I saw a doctor about my foot, he recommended walking, but it hurts a lot."

"It hurts? Why didn't you say so? A doctor should look at it."

"There isn't a cure, Major. I suffer from hypersensitivity. The hope is that it will go away with time. Years maybe."

"But couldn't you take something for the pain?"

"I've tried every painkiller, Major. I have messed up my stomach from taking so many."

"Even so, a doctor should take a look at you. Please tell me what's happening. I'm not a mind reader."

"I have a bunch of physical ailments, Major. I could spend every waking hour with a doctor."

"No, it's not a bunch of ailments. What it is, and don't get angry, is a bunch of bad habits." I looked at him. His prematurely gray hair—like mine—and his smile were shining in the light from the tower they used to turn on at night. I realized I had never looked at his eyes before. They weren't attractive; they were rather small. But there was a lot of tenderness in them. I laughed without feeling scared.

"What do you mean bad habits? Name one. . . ."

"Um. . . . It would take a long time. Don't worry. I'll tell you all about them one by one. You might scratch me if I tell you about all of them at once. But some other time. Look at your eyes, swollen from so much crying."

He took out his handkerchief and started wiping off my mascara that had run. When he finished, he folded it and stood there looking at it.

"Major, I'll wash it if you want me to. Your wife may not understand why you were consoling a prisoner. And I'm sure she won't believe you if you tell her you were near a steam engine."

He smiled and handed it to me, "Thank you for thinking of that."

We arrived at the house, and the major said good-bye as he caressed my hair and said, "You have pretty hair, Luz. It looks good like that. Don't cut it."

Everybody knew that I used to grab a pair of scissors all of a sudden and cut my hair really, really short. I felt an urge, the one I always felt, to put a complete end to that situation, but I held back.

I remembered that when I was arrested and began to realize all I would have to face I tried to find ways to look as ugly as possible. Then at Ollagüe, when I decided to "sell" the image of an implacable, cold, professional Luz, I started using makeup. But I had to adopt other defense mechanisms. It never bothered me. I had been trained since I was twenty-two years old, when my husband and I separated. I found out from all those friends who approached me, supposedly to offer moral support, which according to them, of course, began with a quick tumble in bed.

I remembered how indignant I used to feel when I handed an essay or a report over to some character and he looked at me and undressed me with his eyes. I walked in the house. It was hard to be a woman, at least for me. I thought about my son, and I was glad he was a boy.

A few days later there was an incident with the major. My spirit was fading, like I was drowning. I felt uneasy and irascible, tired and depressed. I gave Krassnoff Martchenko angry looks as he walked through the offices showing off his twisted mouth and his phony smile. Whenever he had that attitude, everybody knew that something was about to work out for him. María Alicia and I looked at each other and exchanged a knowing "he got lucky last night," but we were sure that whatever he had up his sleeve had to do with the MIR.

There were raids almost every day. They brought their loot to Villa Grimaldi and stacked it in piles. One day they left a bunch of records, books, and everything you would need to set up a darkroom in the main office. Many years later, I would find out that they had come from the homes of MIR militants who were arrested en masse in the Valparaiso Region, in mid-January 1975. I took a closer look when Krassnoff's men left. I knew they would burn them. I picked up some records. I just wanted to see them, hold them. . . . The music was by Peter Ilich Tschaikowsky. I remembered my house and my son, and I saw myself in that lost past. . . . Running, studying, dreaming of utopias. . . . Wenderoth came over, took the records from me, and started breaking them. He was smashing them angrily on the edge of a desk.

I yelled at him, calling him a brute, an animal, a stupid, ignorant soldier. I said he was a monster, worse than that. . . . I ran all the way to the house where I threw myself on the bed and started to cry. I asked myself what was happening to me. With everything I have lived through, and now over some records. . . . I heard a noise, and I sat up, frightened. It was Rolf standing at the open door. "Luz, please forgive me!"

I was troubled. I expected him to say, "That's the last straw," or "Go to hell," or something like that. I felt uncomfortable. I tried to talk, but I had no voice. I remembered how I often lost my voice when they interrogated me, just like every time tension gets the better of me. I remembered the stories the major told me, the ones about how he had set a record when he was a lieutenant. If a soldier made some mistakes that exposed him to the officers' wrath, it was his kick in the ass that could send that soldier flying farthest. Of course he's an animal, I thought. I still felt awful.

I returned to the office. The staff were looking at us out of the corner of their eyes, and they laughed behind the major's back. When Rolf went to the cafeteria, one of the other officers came over to me and said, "Well done, Lucecita. This major really is an animal. To be honest, we were afraid for you. But when we saw him leave here all quiet, like he had his tail between his legs, we knew he was going to look for you and that he wouldn't hurt you. Don't give in."

20

A COMPAÑERO: "JOEL"

I have wonderful memories of "Joel," his wife, and their baby. I know he has been challenged, just like Alejandra, María Alicia, and I have. Although it doesn't count for much, especially coming from me, I'll do more than just defend "Joel." I'll take it upon myself to say why the DINA was able to manipulate him. I will only give an overview of the situation, which will allow me to shed some light on the nature of his case, because I trust and believe that he himself is the one who should speak up.

Like the majority of the compañeros in the MIR who appear in this story, I met "Joel" in the DINA. But before I saw him, I saw his young wife with his daughter who was just a few months old. The DINA took both of them to the Terranova Detention Center. They held his wife in our room on a few occasions. She was always blindfolded. I remember her as if it were today, with her long, dark, wavy hair. There was a bag next to her chair, the kind every mother buys with love and hope to carry things for her newborn baby or for one that is about to be born. They left her daughter with us. Alejandra, María Alicia, and I took turns feeding her, changing her, and rocking her. It meant a lot to us to be able to give that baby a little love.

I know that "Joel" renounced his loyalty to his party only after he was badly tortured and in order to obtain freedom for his wife and daughter. The little girl was sick when she was born, and at the time they predicted she would have a short life.

I don't have the words to express what I imagine were his feelings back then, nor did I have the option to support him. I don't know if I would have dared. Given how things were back then, I think neither of us would have trusted the other, even if the possibility existed. It wasn't just a lack of trust. It was also a kind of mutual protection. We had already paid too high a price for our past mistakes to make them all over again. We were alone and at the DINA's mercy. "Joel" survived, and I'm happy about that.

I was there when Captain Ferrer Lima brought him to our room so they could put a remote control explosive device on his testicles before they took him somewhere. They took me too that day. "Joel" had convinced them that Nelson Gutiérrez would arrive at a particular place. He was the leader of the MIR's Political Commission. Ferrer asked me if I knew "Guti," Nelson Gutiérrez's alias. I told him I did, although it wasn't true, but that way I would not be able to recognize him.

I remember seeing "Joel" from the window of a house as he walked down a street. No one arrived. I always thought that he took them there to warn someone in the area that the DINA had him.

I later spent several hours with "Joel." Since I knew how to draw and he had an extraordinary gift for tracing letters and numbers, they put us together. While I made false IDs from the Telephone Company, the Gas Company, and the Electric Company (Chilectra) so the DINA agents could enter any residence whenever they wanted, they had "Joel" paint Argentine license plates to put on the DINA cars.

BILL BEAUSIRE ALONSO

One day, toward midmorning, Krassnoff came to our room and ordered me to flush out a prisoner's ears.

I took the largest syringe I had and boiled it. Then I prepared some warm water with a disinfectant and stepped outside. They put a chair next to the door and brought in a young man. He was wearing blue jeans and a blue shirt with white dots or some really intricate design.

I told the guard he at least needed to remove the dirty rag over the prisoner's eyes in order for me to unclog his ears. I started applying the water as carefully as I could, and I asked him who he was.

I remember clearly that he said, "Bill Beausire Alonso." I pointed out that even though we didn't know each other, that I knew he was Mary Ann's brother. I told him I had a wicker basket that had belonged to her and that they had stolen it in some raid and given it to me. I told him it was really pretty and that it had makeup and false eyelashes. He confirmed that it was his sister's. When I mentioned to him that there were a lot of cosmetics I didn't recognize, he explained that his sister had been a ballet dancer, which is why she would most likely have had unusual kinds of makeup.

I told him I knew they had raided a place where she and her compañero, Andrés Pascal Allende, were supposed to be, but that they didn't find them there. I flushed out his ears until the guard thought it was enough.

I asked Bill why he needed the treatment for his ears, and he said he didn't know if it would do him any good or not, but that someone who had seen him that morning and claimed to be a doctor had prescribed it. His right ear hurt him a lot from the beatings. I mentioned to Bill that I had seen some pictures of him where he looked really fat, and that I would have never recognized him the way he looked then. He said that the hardships of prison had made him recover his figure. I asked him if my treating his ears didn't make the pain even worse. He said it didn't, and that the warm water made him feel better. And he said he could hear better since I managed to remove a lot of wax. When the guard had me go back to my room, saying this wasn't an opportunity to chat, Bill thanked me with a smile. . . . I never saw him again. He is still disappeared to this day.

HUGO MARTÍNEZ, ALIAS "TANO"

In early January 1975, Hugo Ramón Martínez González arrived under arrest at the DINA's Terranova Detention Center. I remember that, as usual, I was sitting across from Wenderoth when Krassnoff came into the office and mentioned to the major that the new prisoner belonged to the MIR's High Command and their Central Committee. He didn't say anything else. He probably even mentioned his name, but that didn't tell me anything back then since I only knew him as "Tano."

I knew very little about him, but I did remember that Ricardo Ruz had once told me that he belonged to the High Command and that he had relatives who were in the armed forces. I listened as I pretended to review what Wenderoth had been dictating to me, but I started really paying attention when Krassnoff mentioned that the prisoner had relatives in uniform. There were already two coincidences. I counted the hours until the unit commanders sent their reports on their prisoners. Those were the reports Wenderoth used in order to write the document he sent to Manuel Contreras Sepúlveda. I needed to see the box where they wrote the alias. I was horrified when I saw it said "Tano." It was my

197

friend. I supposed it would be too much of a coincidence for there to be two people called "Tano" in the High Command.

I would take a chance. I asked Rolf Wenderoth to please let me see him. Krassnoff had mentioned that he was wounded, and I asked Rolf to let me give him antibiotics, especially since the lieutenant had said they didn't plan on calling a doctor. Wenderoth Pozo refused, but I begged him so much that he gave me permission to go. A guard escorted me to the solitary cells. "Tano" was all curled up in the first one. In spite of the small space, I got inside and sat down next to him. I told him I had permission to give him penicillin. He smiled when he saw me. He recognized me right away. A bullet had pierced all the way through his right hand. The wound looked like it was infected with some kind of green mold. I was really sad. As I prepared the penicillin at his side, I showed him another jar and explained that it was an anesthetic. I said it would alleviate the pain.

When I gave him the injection, I asked him if he really hated me for collaborating. He reached toward me the best he could with the arm of his wounded hand and motioned to me to come closer. He hugged me very tight. I cried with my head buried in his chest. He started caressing my hair with his good hand and held me very tight, all the while telling me, "You're an angel. I know the pain will go away. But I also know I'm going to die." I stood up and told him it wasn't true. I said I would go every day to give him antibiotics with a painkiller. I tried to show him my foot, and I told him that for a long time I could see right through the opening but that, even though it still hurt, there I was, alive and walking. . . . But I knew I had never had such a serious infection. However, I wanted to believe he would live. I decided to try and go at least once every twelve hours to give him penicillin. When the guard made me leave, "Tano" hugged me again.

I thanked Wenderoth for letting me go. I told him he needed penicillin every eight hours. He said that every twelve hours would be fine.

I left my room the following morning at eight o'clock sharp. The guards still escorted me to Rolf's office. I was carrying the box with the syringe, the penicillin, and the tube of anesthesia in my hands hidden in my pocket. As we approached the trees in the garden near the main house, I saw my dog coming to say hello. He was playing with something he had found in the bushes. I was petrified. It was one of "Tano's" sandals. I knew it was his because I had seen them the day before and they weren't a common kind of shoe. I practically ran to the office

198

and told Wenderoth I was going to give the prisoner his antibiotic. He wouldn't let me and said the doctor was going to go soon. I kept begging him, and he refused to the point where he became angry.

A few hours later, after he had compiled the list of prisoners, I looked through it. That day my friend wasn't on it. They had taken him out during the night. I never forgot that that day was January 13, 1975.

For a long time I kept hoping that they had taken him to a clinic or to the hospital like they had me. When I testified before the National Truth and Reconciliation Commission, I found out that the only respect the DINA showed his relatives, who were officers in the armed forces, was to throw his body in some Santiago neighborhood and mention in the Crime Section in the paper that his death had been a payback between rival gangs. That's not how it happened. I saw him after he had been detained and wounded under Miguel Krassnoff Martchenko's command, while he was being held in the DINA's solitary confinement "dresser drawers." The report issued by the Legal Medical Institute affirmed that Hugo Martínez had died from two blows to the thoracic region, which had nothing to do with the wound I saw on his hand while he was being held at Villa Grimaldi. In other words, my friend was executed.

THE EIGHT FROM VALPARAÍSO

In January 1975, they arrested the girlfriend of one of the leaders of the MIR's Valparaíso Region. She was a young woman who had previously managed to escape the repression in another of the MIR's regions in the south. This is how the Caupolicán Unit was able to obtain the address of the leader of the Valparaíso Region.

The recently promoted commander, Lieutenant Colonel Moren Brito, traveled to the city of Valparaíso with Lieutenant Lauriani Maturana and the Vampiro Group. They had complete authorization to dismantle the MIR's structure in the region.

The DINA agents arrested nearly all of the MIR's militants who were linked to that structure. When they raided the house on Agua Santa Street where the MIR's leaders lived, they obtained a list of the upcoming meetings with other militants and set up traps there. On one of those occasions, Fabián Ibarra, who had answered a call from Lautaro Videla Moya from Santiago, was forced to try to get Lautaro to travel there. Fortunately, Lautaro realized it was a trap and didn't go.

Moren Brito and Lieutenant Lauriani Maturana drove the prisoners to the Maipo Regiment. After some discussion with the commander of the aforementioned military base and Captain Heyder, on January 28, 1975, they proceeded to transfer approximately twenty prisoners to Santiago, eight of whom disappeared. These eight are listed below:

Sonia del Tránsito Ríos Pacheco was arrested on January 17th in Viña del Mar along with her husband Fabián Enrique Ibarra Córdoba. Carlos Ramón Rioseco Espinoza and Alfredo Gabriel García Vega were both arrested in Viña del Mar on January 18th. Horacio Neftalí Carabantes Olivares was arrested on January 21st. María Isabel Gutiérrez Martínez was arrested on January 24th in Quilpué. Abel Alfredo Vilches Figueroa was arrested on January 25th in Viña del Mar, and Elías Ricardo Villar Quijón was arrested on January 27th.

Their relatives started taking steps to find their whereabouts. At first the DINA denied having made these arrests. However, faced with the overwhelming evidence presented in the courts, the DINA's very own director had to appear before the Santiago Appeals Court in July 1977. He recognized that the DINA had carried out the maneuvers on the aforementioned dates, but he added that all the militants had been freed immediately, with the exception of Horacio Carabantes, who supposedly asked to be released in Santiago.

What the Truth and Reconciliation Commission's report fails to mention (since that report was forbidden from mentioning agents' names) is that the person who wrote these answers for the DINA's director was Rolf Wenderoth Pozo.

On that occasion, it is probable that the DINA felt forced to admit that it had carried out that operation since the very commander of the Maipo Regiment had stated as much in his official response to the courts. He denied any responsibility on his part or on the part of the soldiers in his regiment, stating that the DINA had led the maneuver and that the participation by his regiment was limited to offering logistical support.

Once the prisoners had already arrived in Santiago, another name stuck in my mind since I had to take him off the MIR's structure list. I knew a prisoner named Erick Zott had arrived. I would soon hear his name again early in February when Ferrer Lima mentioned him in front of me and said he was one of the prisoners they were taking to the German Dignity Colony.

Back then I never knew if Zott returned from the Colony or not. That is why, thinking he was disappeared, I thought to mention him to the Truth and Reconciliation Commission.

LAUTARO VIDELA'S ARREST

I never spoke with Lautaro at Terranova. Today I know more about his life, his innumerable anecdotes, the sad things. He isn't a young man anymore, but he still looks like he is. In spite of all he has lived through, he exudes great joy. He is the eternal defender of the weak, and he has earned my respect and my affection, and not just for being Lumi's brother. Lautaro has managed to rebuild his life. His partner is a wonderful woman, and his daughter is beautiful.

I remember that all of the prisoners heard when Lautaro was arrested. It was a big event for the DINA. He was the most important prisoner of that time, as Officers Krassnoff and Lawrence said. Lautaro Videla was a member of the MIR's Political Commission, and he was in charge of organization. His nickname, "Chico Santiago," was on the lips of guards, agents, and prisoners alike. With his record, it's a miracle he survived the DINA.

When they arrested Lautaro, they kept him in the solitary confinement "dresser drawers" whenever they weren't "grilling" him or beating him. We knew they had arrested his wife first. I only saw her once. The guard who was escorting me to Rolf Wenderoth's office told me who she was. They were leading her very slowly along the paths in the Villa Grimaldi garden. She was having trouble walking. She kept touching her stomach and leaning all her weight on the guard who was leading her. I assumed she was in really bad shape. It was very painful for me to see her. You could tell she had been tortured a lot.

I never saw her again, but I did see Lautaro. I had known him for several years. He didn't remember that, which was obvious because I doubt he even noticed my presence. I had met him during the Frei presidency when the MIR took over some land in the Cerrillos sector, calling it Camp 26th of July.[42] It was next to the University of Chile's School of Architecture. I had some friends from the MIR who participated in that event, and they asked me to go paint some banners.

While I was there, two important MIR leaders arrived who were living

---

42. The MIR's use of the name "Camp 26th of July" is a direct reference to the Cuban Revolution and specifically to the 26th of July Movement. On July 26, 1953, Fidel Castro led an insurrection at the Moncada fort in Santiago de Cuba against the Batista dictatorship. Although the revolutionaries lost this battle and many were imprisoned, including Fidel Castro himself, it was a major historical landmark in the revolutionary movement that would later succeed in overthrowing the Batista dictatorship in 1959.

undercover at the time. They were Lautaro and María Alicia. Time and the DINA would bring the three of us together again under different circumstances.

I knew when Lautaro was at Terranova because I saw him appear on the list of prisoners. I knew general things, like where they were keeping him, or that he refused to cooperate at the press conference, the one in which four of the MIR's leaders participated. I saw Lautaro standing by a window once. When he saw me he said, "That was my sister's jacket. . . ."

I answered that yes, it was, that she had given it to me. That time I felt the urge to stop for a moment and talk more with him. I didn't have the courage. . . .

MARCELO MOREN BRITO'S NEPHEW

Meeting Alan Bruce Catalán had a deep effect on me. I saw him as he left one of the offices of the Caupolicán units and walked down a hallway toward the support office of the BIM Command at Terranova. I saw him at the same instant I heard Moren Brito's horrendous yelling. I had to stand back against the wall to let them walk by me. Moren Brito looked like a madman as he was saying, "You can't even save your own family from the MIR's infiltration. . . . But I'm going to kill this one, nephew or not."

Once they had passed by, I walked silently to Wenderoth's office. I asked him if it was true that the young man was related to Moren Brito. Wenderoth said yes, that he was in fact somehow related to the commander. I never saw Alan Bruce again, but Moren Brito was in a terrible mood for several days. Alan is one of the disappeared.

THE PRESS CONFERENCE

In the summer of 1975, they ordered us to turn on the television, and we listened intently to what the compañeros from the MIR were saying. The three of us knew they had been planning this news conference. On many occasions, Krassnoff Martchenko, Espinoza Bravo, and Ferrer Lima mentioned they were preparing this program.

María Alicia, Alejandra, and I listened in silence. We knew the compañeros didn't have any other choice. A short time ago I found out we only saw a part of it. We neither heard nor saw the list that was read on the air of compañeros who were being held at Terranova and who were said to be in exile or to have died in shootouts. The three of us didn't discuss it. Since I knew some of the compañeros from the MIR's leadership during that period, I assumed that "Marco Antonio," "Lucas," "Nicolás," and "Cristián" were in a very delicate situation. I couldn't help but feel solidarity with them. I only saw them a few times, and they were always with Krassnoff or some other officer.

I had never met any of them before Terranova. The first time I saw them was when they took me to Cristián Mallol's cell to give him an injection of antibiotics. He had a bullet wound. I periodically saw them when we were allowed to keep the door open, when they were being taken blindfolded past our room on their way to the main house. And on one occasion, Krassnoff Martchenko brought all of them to our room, according to him so we could socialize.

It was a strange situation. We didn't talk much. I can't even remember what we said. Marco Antonio spoke to me a couple of times. I thought he was trying to be nice.

THE LITTLE HOUSE NEXT TO THE TOWER

A little while after this—I had been detained for almost a year—they moved us to the little hut they had built for us.

I suppose I started calling that place "the little house" as a way to make the ugliness of our daily lives seem more palatable. Actually, it was little more than a wooden shack with cracks that let in the cold air during the winter. But simply being further away from where they were torturing our compañeros gave us some kind of peace of mind. Although we still knew what was happening, not having to listen to the howling of people being tortured was one source of pain we would not be forced to endure. Even though we were right next to the tower where at least I had been tortured before, it was still better.

During that time, they arrested a journalist and member of the MIR's Central Committee, Gladys Díaz. I don't remember speaking with her back then. Rolf Wenderoth mentioned that there were numerous international attempts to demand Díaz's release, especially from Germany. He said they would have to release her at some point.

I also knew they were holding her in the tower at Villa Grimaldi. However, I didn't know the details surrounding her detention and imprisonment until I heard them in 1991 when I lived in Europe.

21

MAJOR WENDEROTH'S TRIP

The major went on a trip with his class from the War Academy. Despite the fact that, as he promised, he left everything in order, they started bothering us again. Some guards entertained themselves by throwing rocks at the hut, especially when the officers were gone for the night. We couldn't sleep, and we were very scared.

I think it is fair to underscore that they didn't just taunt us because some of the officers protected us. There were guards who did it because, to them, we were still three marxists. The called us "Mirists." There were others, more than just a few, who supported the prisoners. I don't know whether María Alicia or Alejandra noticed that fact, but that's how it was. I found this out when Rolf Wenderoth made a comment praising María Alicia for denouncing some of the soldiers on guard who gave extra food to some prisoners. The guards who received reprimands were obviously repressing the three of us.

Nights and weekends started seeming like they would never end. We never knew what was in store for us in the coming hours. Everything depended on who was on duty. I started feeling very afraid again, and I realized that Major Wenderoth's mere presence diminished the problems. I put a lot of effort into typing his memoir, trying to make the hours pass without thinking about the coming minutes.

I started feeling extremely tired, just like when I was at Ollagüe. I tried to stay calm. Wenderoth had asked a doctor to come a few weeks before he left to evaluate the pain in my foot. He said the only thing he had that he could give me was some Valium 20, which could be injected.

I asked Rolf and the girls to learn how to administer the injections. They refused. Lieutenant Lauriani Maturana was the only one who had the courage to do it. I showed him how, and I had him give me the injections when I couldn't bear the pain any longer. Pretty soon I had a bunch of bruises and welts on my arms until the lieutenant learned how to give an injection by practicing on me.

When the pain was unbearable at night, or when the lieutenant wasn't there, I gave myself the injections in my thighs. That helped my foot, but not my headache.

One Monday, I was unable to get out of bed. At about ten minutes after eight o'clock, a guard came to tell me that Ferrer Lima wanted to see me. I told him I wasn't feeling well, and that I wasn't going to get up. The officer came to see me.

He asked me what was wrong. I told him I didn't feel well, but that everything that was bothering me wasn't the real problem. The worst of it was that I felt like I couldn't go on anymore, that my situation had to change somehow. "I need to get out of here, 'Max,'" I told him. "I'm going crazy."

"Luz, Luz. . . . The Luz I know is strong and brave. Try."

"I can't, Captain. I can't" I told him. I was absolutely convinced I had never felt this way.

"All right, get some rest. You'll feel better tomorrow."

I didn't even wake up the next day. I remember that the captain returned with a doctor. The diagnosis was pneumonia and fatigue. Five months before it had been pleurisy.

Those days have been erased from my memory. I remember that "Max" came to see me, but that's all. All I remember is waking up sometimes and seeing him sitting there. He asked me how I felt and tried to encourage me. I talked, but I'm not sure what I said exactly. I don't know if they gave me tranquilizers so I would sleep. I vaguely remember telling Major Ferrer Lima that the DINA wouldn't have to kill me, that I would die from a lung infection just as the guards had predicted, and that better yet I would go insane before that. He just said, "You're going through a bad time, Luz. That's all. It will pass, like all the others. . . ."

When I wasn't sleeping, I felt like I was floating. I couldn't even say exactly how long I was like that.

Early one morning I opened my eyes. I felt like I was returning from somewhere. I felt better and took a shower since they had connected the water. I knew it was rash to use it. Sometimes a kind of hail spurted out when I turned on the tap, and the drop hanging from the showerhead froze in midair. But I didn't care. I got under the freezing water because I knew that afterwards my body would react by turning red and numb.

205

I started typing the memoir again, but I wasn't able to finish it before Wenderoth Pozo returned. Somebody from High Command finished it. I went back to the same routine, and Rolf started taking me to the Military Hospital. I started feeling better, and they gave me a fairly complete physical at his request. They tried to find the source of my headaches, which continued in spite of the fact I had recovered from the pneumonia. They gave me a prescription for glasses, and they detected what the doctor called mild diabetes. They couldn't do anything about my foot. I would have to wait for the pain to subside over time.

I continued injecting myself with sedatives everyday so I could stand the pain that any kind of shoe gave me. I learned to walk without limping, but only for short distances.

GENERAL BONILLA'S DEATH

The day of March 3rd is forever etched in my mind. That afternoon, when the radio and television stations had already announced that General Bonilla had died, Wenderoth Pozo told me about it. He didn't give me all the details. But he did suggest that the officer had become a problem for the DINA, and that he suspected that the accident had been provoked.

I don't know if he said that because he was sure the DINA didn't accept "burrs under its saddle," if it was simply a suspicion he had, or if he had evidence. I was afraid it was a trap to measure just how much I was interested in knowing things about the DINA. All I did was listen without asking any questions. I knew that this attitude often made the officers doubt me, even more than if I had asked them something. Major Wenderoth only added that the general had too many connections to militants in the Christian Democratic Party who didn't agree with the military government as much as had been hoped.

No matter what the actual cause, this wasn't just something that Wenderoth said. The personnel even coined a gruesome saying. Whenever anyone did something that could elicit a reprimand from his superiors, the guards and agents at Terranova used to say, "They're going to throw you out of a helicopter."[43]

43. According to Arce's testimony, which was echoed in a denunciation by Eduardo Bonilla Menchaca, the general's son, General Oscar Bonilla was murdered by the military in a helicopter on March 3, 1975, in Chile's Seventh Region. The military's official position, however, was that his death was the result of a helicopter accident.

ALFREDO ROJAS'S ARREST

Osvaldo Romo Mena came to get me very early on March 4, 1975. They took me out of there quickly, saying that we had to go look for someone who left his house before eight o'clock in the morning. They told me that I would have to go with Basclay Zapata Reyes to look for Alfredo Rojas, the ex-director of Railroads. I told them I didn't know where he lived.

Osvaldo Romo told me, "It doesn't matter. We know." I couldn't believe Alfredo would still be living at the same house as always, with his mother and, as I later found out, his son.

They took me so I could identify him. It wasn't necessary. Everything was too easy for Krassnoff Martchenko's unit. Both armed agents got out of the truck and took me with them. Osvaldo Romo knocked on the door. A woman answered saying she was Alfredo's mother. What is more, she had us come in, asked us to have a seat, and called upstairs to her son. Alfredo came running down and asked what was going on.

He gave me a sincere hello, and he agreed to go along with Osvaldo Romo. He went with him in his car, a Yagán that was kept at the Terranova Detention Center as an additional DINA vehicle assigned to one of the units.[44] I know that another DINA agent who had gone in the back of the truck drove the car on the way back.

Once we arrived at Terranova, they took me to Wenderoth Pozo's office. He was upset because they had taken me without asking for his permission. I used that to allow myself to ask him to please let me see Alfredo. As usual, he started by refusing and asking me why. I insisted that I had known him and that I wanted to know how he was. In the end, he agreed. He took me himself to the bathroom near where the prisoners were held. As soon as the guard opened the door, I went in. I couldn't be alone with him. He didn't have his glasses on. He was blindfolded and sitting on the floor with his back against the wall. He looked upset, and I realized they hadn't tortured him yet. Wenderoth tried to use my presence to give him a sermon so he would collaborate. When he heard that, Alfredo put his head down again and just added, "I'm not in contact with anyone from the party. Everybody knows the DINA arrested me last year." I didn't know he had already been detained, and I asked

---

44. The Chilean Yagán was actually a French Citroën that looked more like a military jeep than a car.

him on what day it had happened. He wasn't able to answer me since Wenderoth immediately took me out of there.

I was never able to find out anything about Alfredo even though I asked Rolf about him several times. I managed to figure out what had happened to him years later. While I was living in Europe, I had the opportunity to hear the testimony of another compañero who survived. It was true. Alfredo had indeed been arrested at some point during 1974 and taken to the Ollagüe Detention Center. He apparently succeeded in convincing the DINA that he would collaborate, and they let him go with the "duty" of finding and handing over some of his compañeros from the Socialist Party. Alfredo didn't give them anyone. Moreover, at some point he met with some of the compañeros the DINA had ordered him to find, and he warned them to leave, that the DINA was looking for them.

One of these compañeros was then arrested by the DINA. When they asked him if he knew they were looking for him, he said yes without weighing the consequences. He said that a compañero had warned him, and he mentioned his conversation with Alfredo. According to what I heard, Alfredo and this compañero met each other again in the tower at Terranova, and the compañero asked for his forgiveness. This is the last anyone knows of Alfredo since he is disappeared to this day.

There is additional testimony subsequent to mine about Alfredo's detention at Terranova made by Gladys Díaz Armijo. The content is heartbreaking. Gladys has published her testimony in accordance with her professional mission as a journalist, and also as part of her own personal experience with the Defense of Peoples Rights and against Impunity.

I've chosen not to write Alfredo's second last name on purpose. When I was his secretary, he told me over and over that he liked to just use Alfredo Rojas as his signature on documents. Therefore, I respect his decision one more time.[45]

DELIA

During the time I was at Ollagüe, when Captain Torré decided he would also run an operations unit, I tried to avoid handing "Delia" over to him

45. There is no further explanation regarding Arce's decision not to offer the full name of Alfredo Rojas Castañeda. According to official documents, he was detained at his home on March 14, 1975, and freed from the Cuatro Alamos Detention Center on March 26, 1975. Several witnesses, however, including Arce, mention having seen him at the Villa Grimaldi site from March 4, 1975, to as late as April 16 or 23 of that same year.

by telling him that "Delia," a member of the Socialist Party Central Committee, lived in the Tajamar Towers. If I were caught in a lie, I could always say that I had confused the name of the buildings because she actually lived in tower number 10 at the San Borja Complex.

I spent several days going up and down the floors at the Tajamar Towers with members of Torré Sáez's unit. I comforted myself with the thought that I was either going to die from all that walking or I would withstand the physical workout and get stronger. I had told them that I didn't know either the tower or the apartment where she lived, so they made me go up and down with them in case we found her.

Since the agents had to go with me, and since they tired quickly, they thought that this was surely a false trail. However, when Germán Jorge Barriga Muñoz from the DINA arrived, he called me immediately. According to what he himself said, I would work on the Socialist Party. Around that time, Major Wenderoth was getting ready to go on a trip, and either he didn't do anything or he couldn't. The fact is that Germán Barriga brought me to his offices on several occasions. He asked me for the names of my compañeros from the Central Committee and from the Socialist Party's Political Commission. I insisted over and over again that another unit had already unsuccessfully searched for the only person I knew. I repeated my story about the Tajamar Towers. When I finally thought that captain would stop calling me, he showed me Fidelia Herrera, alias "Delia." Then I found out that he had taken the time to ask for the lists of owners and renters in all the towers, and that he had obtained the names and address of her and her husband through the Social Security Bureau.

All I could do was identify her. I didn't know anything about her work. Germán Barriga made me watch some interrogation sessions. For example, one day when she was sitting in a chair in the front hall near the Commander's door, Barriga started pinching her breasts really hard. Another day they had me stand next to her on a street corner. No one came. I didn't know if it was a made-up meeting or if they saw us from a distance. I didn't say much on that occasion because they had put a tape recorder in my bag.

When we were sitting in the truck, there was a guard in the driver's seat, which meant that I could only talk to her "officially." She asked me why I was collaborating, and I told her what had happened to me a short while ago in relation to my son. That fact didn't justify my collaboration, but I had to tell her something.

209

Barriga Muñoz was really perverse with "Delia." They made her elderly husband suffer a great deal. I won't give any more details out of respect for him.

ARIEL MANCILLA

While Wenderoth was absent from Terranova, I went to his office to type his memoir. I saw the report on prisoners sitting on his desk. Even though another officer, Eugenio Fieldhouse, had temporarily assumed the major's duties, and even though his desk was on the other end of the office next to the door, the clerk continued to leave the document to be signed in the same place, on Wenderoth Pozo's desk. I remember seeing a compañero from the Socialist Party on the list. I never met or saw him, but I didn't forget his name. When I saw his name as I passed by the report, it looked like it was spelled incorrectly to me. I told the typist that Mancilla was spelled with an *s*.

The soldier took the document and left, undoubtedly to check with the unit that was holding the prisoner. When he returned to the office, he told me, "Lucecita, there is Mansilla with an *s* and Mancilla with a *c*. This criminal's name is with a *c*." I never forgot his name: Ariel Adolfo Mancilla Ramírez. Unfortunately, I cannot say anything more about him, except that a group from the Purén Unit was "working" the Socialist Party at that time and the officer in charge of that group was Officer Germán Jorge Barriga Muñoz, alias "Don Jaime." Furthermore, in honor of the memory of this compañero, it is fair to say that if Ariel had admitted his position in the party and collaborated with the DINA, he could have caused the Socialist Party as much damage as Estay Reyno caused the Communist Party.[46]

PEDRO ESPINOZA'S TRIP

At the beginning of 1975, Commander Pedro Espinoza Bravo left the BIM and Chile. He was nominated as a military attaché to Brazil. He came to the "little house" before he left.

He came one Sunday at noon to have lunch with us. It was the soup

---

46. Miguel Estay Reyno was a young militant in the Juventudes Comunistas (Communist Youth) who was detained and tortured in December 1975. Estay Reyno, known as "El Fanta," became a collaborator and participated in detentions and interrogation sessions.

they served at Terranova, but it was better since he and Captain Manuel Abraham Vásquez Chahuán made an effort to bring some other things.

Although I never liked him, I have to confess I was sorry to see him go. Wenderoth Pozo wasn't there, and the commander, who personally looked after María Alicia, acted as a kind of deterrent to the guards and agents who took it upon themselves to repress us. That day I found out from the commander that they weren't going to send another officer from the BIM. He said Moren Brito would assume command of that DINA structure since he had been promoted to Lieutenant Colonel. I told myself, "better the devil you know." I was afraid a new commander would come who would make things worse. However, I chill ran down my spine when I imagined what Terranova would be like under Moren Brito's command. Espinoza Bravo made sure he maintained a minimum of order. After all, besides taking preventative measures, he even punished some acts, like what had happened on New Year's Eve. And those measures in some way kept the personnel in line. Although it wasn't much, it was better than nothing at all.

Of course Espinoza Bravo reiterated his idea of our future in the sense that we could become "women of class," which I translated as the kind he liked, and he gave each of us a gift. He gave Alejandra and me a little painted mushroom made of wood, which I suppose was for good luck. María Alicia got a silver pendant with a necklace.

Espinoza told us that if we wanted to write to him we could give our letters to Major Wenderoth, who would pass them on by diplomatic pouch. I wrote to him a couple of times, and he answered me. All his letters were full of recommendations like the ones in his "sermons." All I could ascertain was that the envelopes were from Brazil, but I told myself that that didn't prove anything, and I didn't write to him again.

22

THE CIGARETTE CASE

Major Wenderoth gave me a leather cigarette case for my birthday. I was alone at lunchtime when "Julia" and "Marta," two female agents from the Purén Unit, walked by. I knew by their attitudes and from the guards that they didn't like me.

I always thought it was a kind of "jealousy." They saw me as Lauriani Maturana and Ferrer Lima's "friend" because they talked to me, especially Captain Ferrer Lima, who always kept a certain distance from the female personnel at Terranova. The women in the DINA thought both officers were very attractive.

When I walked by them, they always said, "It's not their fault. It's that these whores seduce them." They were referring to all three of us: María Alicia, Alejandra, and me. I didn't even turn to look at them.

These girls were a lot younger than I was. I guess they had less experience in life than I did. Lauriani Maturana came over to me more than once to say, "Stay here with me until they're gone. These little girls make me sick. . . ." I used to kid him about it, and that's how I found out that he had dated one of them. And, on more than one occasion, he used to find little notes she had left for him under his door when he got to his apartment in the San Borja Complex tower. The situation was well known, but that day, in my opinion, they crossed the line.

"Julia" came up to me and started saying that the cigarette case I had was hers. She said that not only was I from the MIR, that I was a thief besides. She said she would report me and that I would be sent where I belonged, this time to a prison for common criminals, which is where I should have been in the first place. A guard who was standing close by watched the scene with curiosity, and he apparently didn't know how to react.

212

I could have easily shown she was lying, but I felt the vulnerability of my situation more than ever. All any of them had to do was say something, and, if I couldn't prove otherwise, it was obvious no one was going to believe me. Someone warned the major about what was happening, and he came out of the officers cafeteria and over to me. The major spoke with the girl who stuck to her story at first. Rolf picked up the cigarette case and said, "Miss, do you smoke Lucky?"

She looked disconcerted and said that she didn't.

I left. I didn't want to watch the scene or, worse yet, humiliate her. The major went to the office with her. All the personnel were watching as they pretended to eat. I returned to the table with my coffee, and a little while later Rolf came back and sat down beside me. The corporal, who was in charge of the cafeteria service, came over and asked his superior if he would like something. It was unusual for an officer to have coffee in the staff cafeteria. I realized that simply having coffee with me was an act of support for me in front of the troops.

We talked about what had happened. He said he would let Human Resources handle the employee's situation, since the armed forces were paying her salary. I asked him not to be too hard on her, that she was practically a child.

"And besides, nothing happened," I added.

"Nothing happened. Of course nothing happened. But that's because the guard who was there is fond of you, and another one came to warn me at the cafeteria. Because they know I won't allow anyone to abuse you or anyone else. But even though you're right, that it was a 'typical little girl's tantrum,' here, with the duties she has now and those she may have in the future, this is simply not acceptable."

At times like those, I thought the major really believed what he was saying. I could never understand that split in his personality, that double standard that on the one hand prohibited certain abuses and, on the other, was so permissive when it came to repression, assault, torture, and robbery. Although, in all honesty, I should add that from time to time they questioned the robberies that occurred during raids, especially if there were consequences. Now and then some of those affected had connections to high-ranking officers, and the complaints came from high up in the chain of command. Then measures were taken and someone was punished.

I know there is often a kind of identification between victims and their victimizers in these types of situations. I cannot respond regarding the hidden realm of my own consciousness. But one day I asked Rolf

213

Wenderoth how they could stand the at-times degrading treatment they received from their superiors. He answered me matter-of-factly, that it was with the hope of being promoted so they could do the same thing someday.

It has taken decades to rid myself of a kind of alien, invasive presence, the stuff of panic, of the fear that governed and guided my behavior to the point of making me obey when it came to not talking, not speaking out, not remembering. That mental escape of wanting to live on the sidelines, to remain safe in a world where nothing is far enough from harm's way. . . . In those days all I could feel inside of me were the symptoms, the shudder that crawled across my skin and overpowered my mouth, leaving me speechless. That is why I believe my expressing and revealing what happened isn't important only for me: just as in the past repression and torture were an affront to society, today we remain assailed by impunity. An impunity that extends the terror beyond the dictatorships, a kind of institutionalized impunity that is a vast form of repression.

After what happened with the cigarette case, Rolf gathered the unit's personnel together in the cafeteria and told them he wasn't going to accept that kind of attitude from anyone. He referred specifically to the three of us. He asked them to be polite, and he said they should treat us like ladies. I was uncomfortable. I knew that situations like that created even more problems. Members of the staff who didn't accept us considered themselves "humiliated" in front of us and, sooner or later, when the officers weren't around, they would make us pay for it.

Rolf never listened to my entreaties that he not put us in that situation. I never managed to get the officers to understand that things happened when they weren't there, and that we were the ones who were affected. They seemed to believe that their control and authority were permanent. Perhaps, according to their military structure, that's how it should have been. But it wasn't like that in practice.

Years later I heard Contreras Sepúlveda make similar comments about absolute power. He used to say, "Bring me the person who is offended! I'll *unoffend* him right now!"

After a few days Rolf told me he wanted to talk to me, that for quite a while he had wanted to run some things by me. But not there. He wanted us to talk quietly and without interruptions, and afterward he would take me to my parent's house.

I feared that moment. I have always been really clumsy about how I say things. I hurt people unintentionally. I thought I clearly understood my feelings. I didn't manage to express them without wounding him or saying things that could hurt him. I knew I didn't love Rolf, but I had developed a deep gratitude and affection toward him. It felt good to be with him. He took his time and gave me what I most needed at that moment: affection and to feel almost human. Now I know that was the plan. I have never been able to avoid experiencing things and at the same time observing what I'm experiencing. I asked myself everyday, could this be premeditated? If it was, he had hit the mark. When he was far away, I felt defenseless and utterly vulnerable. We had formed a bond. Despite my constant struggle against it, I somehow depended on him. There was no denying it.

There were times when I managed to survive only with the help of his tenderness. I gave in to many needs. Now I know what was happening to me. In that world of madness and cold that freezes your soul, I needed to feel close to the only source of human warmth there. I'm not talking about sex or even touching. I came to feel a deep affection for him. It was an affection mixed with a growing feeling of suffocation.

But that day, as I left with him, I was unable to express my misgivings. I gave in when he told me, "All I'm asking is that you let me love you."

I felt defenseless.

The car headed toward downtown Santiago. He parked it and showed me some keys. He said they were for an apartment. I agreed to go. From that day on, and although I've denied it over and over again, I found out it was essential for me to receive affection. I suffered enormous contradictions from then on, from feeling moments of happiness, to an obsessive need to end the relationship.

Rolf stood by me patiently for years. He won me over with affection. Intentionally or not, he kept me safe from many unforeseen events. He gave me what little stability I had during those years. For better or for worse, and considering that relationship over the years, it was good for me in spite of everything.

However, the thought of ending all that was always compulsively inside me. I tried to do it many times in several different ways, but I never could. I felt imprisoned twice over, by the DINA as well as by Rolf's affection. Our breakup only came when the military put more than 60 miles between us and sent him to Tejas Verdes. Then everything changed. The feelings and the years we shared remained very important. He

215

continued to protect me as much as he could with what power he had, but from the CNI, not the DINA.

Through that relationship, which was not between equals, because we were never on a level playing field, I started realizing that Rolf wasn't aware of how much institutional culture he had within himself. I realized that he also seemed to divide women into two groups. The first group included the officer's wives who were "serious and respectable," and who had undoubtedly been investigated and later approved when seen to fulfill the institution's requirements. The "other women"—in other words, all the ones who for one reason or another did not meet the requirements—were what they superficially called "whores" and, as such, for sale, easy to persuade and use.

Rolf never put it in such brutal terms, but through his judgments, comments, and behavior, he acted exactly like the others, just like the majority. No, Rolf Wenderoth was not aware of his own contradictions. He lived according to a strict "outward moral code" that could be summed up as "It's not important how one is, but how one appears."

Despite being a married man, Rolf used several arguments to justify his relationship with me. His main reason was that he was controlling someone who could be a danger to the institution in the future while also keeping them from killing me. Rolf often pointed out the difference in our relationship, saying that if he didn't commit to it or make it legal, it was because of circumstances beyond his control. Of course! He couldn't leave his wife until he was at least a colonel. He asked me several times to wait the ten years that he had left to be promoted to that rank so he could retire and marry me. He told me he didn't want to leave his wife in a vulnerable position, that as soon as he could he would buy a house in her name, and that his daughters were still too little.

I would look at him, trying to guess how much of that he really believed. I told him several times that I wasn't interested in getting married. With time I have come to the conclusion that Rolf believed his own excuses. I thought he sold himself those justifications to be able to live with himself. That is how he came to terms with his "reality," feeling like a victim of his circumstances, which allowed him to avoid taking responsibility for his infidelity.

He probably experienced some moments of crisis in his personal life. What couple doesn't have them! From his point of view, the situation was unbearable. I don't know how his wife felt. I don't know how she experienced or experiences these situations. At the time I sided with him. Today, now that I'm much older, I regret having intervened in their lives.

That experience with Rolf Wenderoth meant that I was able to accumulate experiences and knowledge that I can consider to be positive. Let me explain. It would be impossible for me to have that type of relationship now, even though it seemed so normal to me back then. My life has changed. Of course! I can now fathom how insignificant I was and felt back then. Perhaps that was the basis for me to reevaluate things like family, or a couple as a "couple," with two people who come together to share everything, to support each other, and to build. . . .

Back then I succumbed to necessity—which I experienced in an anguishing way—of feeling loved, supported, and protected, and of believing for even just a few moments that I wasn't alone. And by that time I was old enough to know that when you let someone touch you, what comes next is sleeping together.

Back then, when I tried to convince myself that I was a lot better off than I could have been, I told myself, there are women who have been raped once in their lives and are scarred forever. I have been repeatedly raped and humiliated. Not just that, I have also been tortured and destroyed. I have scars, yes, but in spite of having been reduced to an inhuman condition, I still believe that love exists. Maybe not for me, but I was sure it existed somewhere. And then I thought that far away from those beasts, sex could be something natural and beautiful. I told myself that more than a thousand times.

When I remember those days, in spite of the pain I feel, I realize that those experiences were of great service to me, even though I wouldn't recommend them to anyone as a learning experience. I realize that what I learned the hard way has settled deeply within me.

LEONARDO SCHNEIDER, ALIAS "EL BARBA"

Even though he was detained by the AGA, the Air Force War Academy, I met Leonardo Schneider Jordán. I only saw him once as he was entering the BIM Command's support office at the Terranova Detention Center. He had just left the Caupolicán offices escorted by several guards. A noncommissioned officer from the support office told me that he was "el Barba" and that "they had taken him from the air force."

Some time later I heard what happened directly from Wenderoth too. Indeed, the DINA kidnapped the young man, who had begun a process of collaborating with the AGA. At that time I was still unaware of the rivalry between the DINA and the AGA, which intensified with Leonardo's kidnapping.

23

DINA EMPLOYEE

On the afternoon of May 7, 1975, Wenderoth told me to go to the "little house" and for the three of us to fix ourselves up because we were going somewhere. He refused to say anything else. María Alicia, Alejandra, and I changed our clothes, and I guess we put on makeup. With a certain amount of nervousness, we talked and tried to imagine what was going to happen.

Wenderoth took us in his car. For a fraction of a second I thought they were going to kill us and dump us somewhere. When we entered what I would later know was General Headquarters, located at 11 Belgrado Street, Wenderoth escorted us to the offices of the DINA's director, Colonel Contreras. We met the director's assistant, Captain Alejandro Burgos De Beer, and the second in command at the support office, Lieutenant Hugo César Acevedo Godoy.

Major Wenderoth entered the Colonel's office alone. When he came out, he had me go in. They continued placing value on "seniority," in other words, the order in which we were arrested.

Colonel Contreras informed me that from that moment forward I was going to be a DINA employee. He added that it would ensure my security since the MIR had given all three of us a death sentence. He said we would all live in an apartment nearby where Alejandra, María Alicia, and I would be comfortable and well taken care of since it was right across from Headquarters' guardhouse on Marcoleta Street.

As soon as I entered the office, I knew he was the man who had been in my room one day at the Military Hospital, the one who had told me, "I am the boss of all the prisoners in this country." I listened to him. I have to admit that once I got through the initial moments, I couldn't stop thinking about the statement "From this day forward you are free

219

and. . . ." Nothing else mattered. At that moment I really thought I could be free. . . . Time would soon to teach me otherwise.

I imagine the return trip to Terranova must have been torture for Major Wenderoth. All three of us were talking at the same time. In my case, after more than a year, it was frustrating to know that I had been released and that I couldn't leave right away. According to what Contreras Sepúlveda told us, they were in the process of fixing up the apartment since some lieutenants who had lived there previously had left it in bad shape. With a promise of freedom that was not really freedom, and with a naïve sense of hope, we continued living at the Terranova Detention Center. I'm not sure if we were there until the end of June or the beginning of July of that year.

"MARCOS'S" ESCAPE

On May 15, 1975, Captain Germán Barriga Muñoz went to the BIM's High Command. He was angry. He was one of the DINA's "tough guys." When I saw he wanted to speak with the major, I tried to leave, but Wenderoth Pozo ordered me to stay and listen to the conversation.

Barriga Muñoz told the major "the prisoner had escaped." When I heard his name and alias, I knew he was referring to "Marcos-PS" from the Socialist Party. That day I found out his real name: Sergio Iván Zamora Torres. I have not spoken with "Marcos," so I am only going to refer to what I remember about that day and the testimony of a surviving witness, one of the compañeros Sergio handed over to the DINA, perhaps trying to pretend he was cooperating, or because he was exhausted from the torture. In any case, as far as I have been able to determine, all of them are still alive.

I learned the details surrounding his escape. "Marcos" gave Barriga false information regarding a contact. He said he was going to meet a compañero on Santa Mónica Street. Once he arrived, he ran and sought shelter at the Pro-Peace Committee's offices there. Under the Archbishop's protection, and when credible doctors certified the torture he had been subjected to by the DINA, he remained hidden for a long time until he received the necessary documents to go into exile.

The situation added a new element to what I considered in those days to be a situation of latent conflicts between the Church and the State. I witnessed Barriga Muñoz's agitation, and the constant telephone calls made by the brigade's director. I heard that Contreras Sepúlveda himself tried to seize Sergio from the Archbishop's protection. In the end, Sergio caused the DINA a lot of trouble. The sad thing about that situation is that apparently the same protective measures were not extended to the other compañeros who fell into the DINA's hands.

THE ARRESTS OF RICARDO LAGOS, EXEQUIEL PONCE, AND CARLOS LORCA TOBAR[47]

When I saw Ricardo Lagos Salinas's name on the list of prisoners at Terranova, I again pleaded with Rolf Wenderoth to allow me to see him. It was the last time he agreed and he let me see a prisoner.

They took me to the yard near where the prisoners were held. Ricardo was sitting at a small table. His white shirt was very dirty, with the collar bent inward, and his blue suit was wrinkled and covered with dirt. He looked very haggard.

I only managed to talk with him after promising Rolf Wenderoth that I would ask him to collaborate with Germán Barriga Muñoz's team. Since there was a guard near me, I just asked Ricardo if he would collaborate. He responded with an abrupt "No." I didn't keep insisting, both out of respect and because all I was interested in at that moment was seeing him and trying to find out if I could help him in some way.

Ricardo returned the questions, "And you? Why do you do it?" He was referring to my collaboration with the DINA. I knew that nothing I said would change his position. I simply answered that I had been unable to resist. He told me that Ponce Vicencio and Lorca Tobar had been arrested. That was a surprise to me. I didn't know. I asked him if he needed anything, if there was something I could give him. He told me, "If you can get something sweet, I would appreciate it." Since I didn't have any money, I returned to Wenderoth's office and begged him for some change. When he found out what it was for, he looked upset and gave me twenty pesos. They gave me twenty pieces of candy at the cafeteria for that amount. They were small, square, and came in all different colors. Ricardo just said "thanks" and they took him away. . . .

I never saw him again. Every time I asked Rolf Wenderoth, he said he was there, and that it looked like he was collaborating. I wanted to

47. It is important to note that Ricardo Lagos Salinas is not a reference to Chilean president Ricardo Lagos Escobar. See note 51 for more information regarding this possible confusion in Arce's testimony.

believe it was true. I was never able to find out anything about Ponce Vicencio or Lorca Tobar.

AT THE SAN BORJA TOWERS

I don't know if it was the end of June or the beginning of July when Rolf Wenderoth informed us that the apartment was ready. We gathered our belongings and moved them in the major's car. It looked like we were coming from far away, from out in the country. We were carrying everything we owned in plastic bags and cardboard boxes tied with ropes. We must have looked like quite a spectacle, to say the least, because the concierge looked really surprised when he saw that collection of bundles.

The apartment was number 54, and it was in tower 12 of the San Borja Complex on 77 Marcoleta. It was pretty. Everything seemed like an incredible luxury to me after having spent over a year in different DINA detention centers.

Wenderoth said he would come back the following day to take us to Terranova.

As soon as we were alone, María Alicia told us that she had been in that apartment before. It belonged to the family of "Ariel Fontanarosa," which was Max Joel Marambio's alias in the MIR. It was poignant and sad for her. I also knew Ariel, but only by name. I knew he had been the director of the GAP in the beginning, before the Socialist Party took over leadership of that group.

Each of us had a bedroom, and a new series of experiences began for us, like having a decent bathroom, or being able to walk down the street. However, it took a long time for me to decide to go out on my own. I had lost the habit. I felt dizzy the first time I did it. I felt intoxicated by the space. I had felt something similar when I left the Military Hospital, or when I was able to walk around Terranova, but that day I went to the Forestal Park was overwhelming. The open space seemed enormous to me. I actually had to lean on something so I wouldn't fall down.

I started seeing my son much more frequently. Rolf made the effort to take me to my parents' house on weekends to be sure I would arrive without any problems.

The rest of the year was much calmer, with the exception of some minor incidents here and there. I realize it's really difficult to understand how I could live, survive. I remember that everything seemed "new" to me, being able to see, wanting to see everything again. But my life

222

wasn't connected to reality. I was even more disconnected now from the surrounding world than during my clandestine life. When I speak of feeling intoxicated with space, I am trying to express the dizziness of finding oneself in a place that seemed to have no boundaries. I could gaze deep into space without seeing anything but the horizon. Beyond the city skyline, the mountains, I could perceive other lands. It was incredible. But aside from feeling I was lost in a place that had once been my city, there was another different dimension that helped save me from nostalgia, pain, and guilt, and it was like living outside, on the fringe, anesthetized. It was as if all I could do was breathe, gaze, smell, and touch everything with awe and eagerness. It always seemed I was seeing things for the last time: a sense of transience, of passage, of an eternal wandering, of angst from not knowing where I was going. Everything was familiar, the streets, the places. . . . And yet, everything had changed.

Nothing was my own. It was all there, like a gift, only to be gazed at . . . for as long as I was alive. I often repeated to myself that life is like that. . . . You keep on going but without knowing for how long.

THE 119

I remember that one of the biggest shocks I had that year was when I bought the newspaper *La Segunda* on Wednesday, July 23rd. There was an article there about the list of "The 119." It was my first real encounter with the disappeared. It was like an enormous closed fist that struck at the heart of my conscience. The three of us read the article, and we were speechless. It couldn't be. María Alicia, Alejandra, and I had seen almost all of the people who appeared on the list. . . . I was overcome with emotion. We looked at each other, and passed the newspaper to one another. . . . I don't know if I couldn't understand or if I didn't want to understand that Rodolfo Espejo Gómez was dead, and Oscar Castro Videla, and so many others. I couldn't accept what the newspaper was saying. I always thought that they had spent some time at the Cuatro Alamos Detention Center and that from there they had been sent to a prison camp and that they would already have been released or would be out of the country now, safe.

It was the first time I knew for sure that people had died. The apparent peacefulness of those days began to evaporate once again. I started feeling a new sense of urgency and knew I needed to live with my son again.

I told Rolf that, and he suggested I wait, that it was too soon after such a huge step, and that I shouldn't risk losing everything by being rash. It was clear that we weren't living in the world of "normal" people. . . .

During that time, Officer Lauriani Maturana lived in tower 6 at the San Borja Complex. He was living in the apartment where a compañera from the MIR who was connected to the Valparaíso Region had been detained in January 1975. He came to see us somewhat frequently, especially when he didn't have any shirts to wear and would bring one for me to iron for him.

I told the lieutenant that I was afraid to walk alone in the street, and he lent me an enormous and very old pistol. But it fit perfectly since I carried a large handbag. The weapon made me feel safe, even though I knew that if someone wanted to kill me I wouldn't even have time to open my bag.

AN INCIDENT WITH FUENTES MORRISON

One day Alejandra left early. She didn't want to wait for Rolf to take her to the apartment, and she went alone. A little while later she called Wenderoth to inform him that she had run into trouble. When she arrived at the apartment, she told us that some men had tried to kidnap her. According to the descriptions Alejandra gave of the individuals, the DINA said that they were from the air force and that "Wally," Fuentes Morrison's alias, and other agents were with them. This was in retaliation for the DINA's "kidnapping" of "el Barba," Schneider Jordán, who had been collaborating up until that time with the Air Force Intelligence Service.

In September of that year, they took us to watch the Military Parade with the whole unit. As soon as the event began, we realized that an individual sat down in front of the three of us in the grandstand, and he was staring at us a lot. Pretty soon Rolf Wenderoth came over to where we were sitting. Up until then he had been somewhere else with his family, but another DINA agent who was near us recognized that man. Once again, it was Fuentes Morrison. Then Rolf spent the rest of the afternoon with us and later gave us a ride home.

When Fuentes Morrison saw the major, he said hello to him cordially, and he left a little while later. Wenderoth told me about the conflicts between the Air Force Intelligence Service and the DINA so we would increase security precautions. I don't know if everything he said was true, but whether it was or not, it terrified me, and the most immediate response was for the three of us to stay even closer to him.

BATTLE ON MALLOCO STREET

As the days passed, I was getting to know the people around me even better, and my confusion grew. It was so difficult to imagine being out of the DINA that I often fantasized about how people must have felt in the past when they believed that the Earth was flat. I felt exactly like I was at the edge of that abyss, like I was fighting not to fall in the torrent that would carry me who knows where.

My steps had taken me to a dead end. None of those officers seemed aware of what was happening to us. Or were they pretending? It was as if they were trying to seem very tough when, in reality, they were nothing but a bunch of insensitive, loudmouthed neurotics.

I could only think as far ahead as the next day. "Today isn't even mine," I thought to myself. It's not that the road looked difficult or steep, hard or complicated. You just couldn't see it. One day Major Rolf Wenderoth told me, "Luz, what do you want?"

"Major, I don't know. It seems like hopes and dreams have ceased to exist. I was a militant, and now I'm not. I was a prisoner, and I stopped being one. Technically, I am a government employee. I was recruited through very original means. Of course! I need to believe there's a future. It's the only way the present can make any sense. . . ."

During the day, sitting at Rolf Wenderoth's desk and looking beyond him, it seemed like I could only see his silhouette against the light behind him. I escaped by looking out the window that was behind him, and I ran my eyes continually over a fragment of the mountains. I came to recognize each detail in the hills, absorbed by its contours and colors.

Living in the apartment and working at Terranova was a routine that was interrupted from time to time by visits from Colonel Contreras, Alejandro Burgos, and Juan Morales. One day in October 1975, the three of us were having dinner. We were eating leftovers from a stew I had made for lunch with Rolf Wenderoth, since from time to time he would tell me not to go the Villa Grimaldi and to wait for him at home until he finished his meetings at Headquarters. During the dinner, the intercom in the apartment rang. It was Captain Juan Morales who had come to inform us that Colonel Contreras was on his way. He sent someone to buy sandwiches and something to drink for the director.

We were sitting at the table with the colonel, Captain Morales, and Captain Burgos, and we had almost finished dinner when they called from Headquarters to inform us about a clash on Malloco Street.

We were told that Inspector Jiménez had been wounded, which I would find out years later wasn't true. That day the colonel asked what personnel they had available. At that moment, and with the desire to know what was happening, I said, "Colonel, if you do not have enough personnel, we can be your bodyguards. Remember that I was once part of a security team."

The colonel asked us if we had weapons. I asked him if we could forget he was the DINA's director for a moment and answer him as Manuel Contreras. He smiled and said yes. Then we told him that María Alicia and I had weapons, that Pedro Espinoza Bravo had given María Alicia one and that Fernando Lauriani had lent me another one. The colonel ordered Alejandro Burgos, "Make sure they issue them weapons tomorrow. Let's go!"

We raced off in the cars that escorted Colonel Contreras. They gave us rifles when we arrived at Malloco Street. We began advancing hunched over and took cover in the brush that lined the road. You could still hear shooting. The officers went ahead of us. Alejandra, María Alicia, and I lagged behind and were really shocked when we saw the body of a man by the side of the road. We approached him, and the girls recognized Dagoberto Pérez Vargas. I didn't know him. We turned him over on his back, and I tried to find a pulse in one of the arteries in his neck. A shiver ran through my entire body. There was no doubt about it. He was dead. I kept my hands there a few seconds and felt that his skin was still warm. I brushed the mud from his cheek, and I don't remember if it was María Alicia or Alejandra, but one of them helped me close his eyes.

The officers looked at us a few feet away. All they asked was "Who is it?" One of the girls said, "Dagoberto Pérez." I noticed her voice quivered. The officers were pleased, and we kept silent. When we arrived at the main house at Terranova, Colonel Contreras asked me if I knew Nelson Gutiérrez or Pascal Allende. I lied and said I did. I had heard they needed to identify them, and I wanted to be sure to be there if that happened. The colonel approached another officer who had arrived in a helicopter, and they greeted each other warmly. They were obviously friends. All I found out was that the officer was called "el Zorro" in the army, and that he had studied with Contreras since the time when they were at the Military School.

Colonel Contreras ordered María Alicia and me to go in the helicopter and follow the MIR's leaders who were apparently fleeing toward a road behind the plot of land that led to another highway. The colonel, "el Zorro," told me to get in the cockpit and for María Alicia to sit in the back. She felt sick and was vomiting during the entire flight. I spent the entire time talking to the officers through some headphones that also had a kind of microphone that went under my mouth since the noise of the helicopter made it impossible to hear.

The helicopter had a spotlight that illuminated the ground below. I didn't see anyone. We didn't do much searching, and pretty soon all the colonel was doing was showing me the fancy moves he could do in the helicopter. I had succeeded. It was easy to keep the search from being thorough. I couldn't forget Dagoberto lying at the edge of the road, and, even though I knew María Alicia was suffering, I was relieved. She couldn't see below either through the hole they had left open in the belly of the helicopter. I realized what it had meant for her to see Dagoberto Pérez dead. It is always harder emotionally when the person is someone who was one of our compañeros. However, at that moment, the important thing was to not see anyone from the helicopter. Of course there wasn't an opportunity to express one's own feelings. Besides being dangerous, it would have ruined everything we had achieved up to that point by gritting our teeth, clenching our fists, and wiping any tears and expression from our faces. During those days I thought it was a thousand times better for them to trust me. I couldn't identify the people for whom they were searching anyway. I knew that that night they would shoot at anyone who was walking in the brush. That's why, as I buried all my pain within me, I worked at trying to avoid having us look downward and have the officers show me their skills as pilots. . . .

We returned to the main house after we had flown quite a while. They had set up a kind of operations center in the dining room. They offered us coffee, and I could see that they had detained an elderly woman and an adolescent male. They either worked at the house or on the land. A lot of personnel were arriving. The hunt would continue.

When Colonel Contreras saw that María Alicia was sick, he assumed it was from the flight and ordered Rolf Wenderoth to take us home. He excused us from working the following day since it was already morning.

Days later I found out that the MIR leaders and their female companions had indeed managed to escape. Major Wenderoth told me so himself, and he also told me about the events that led to Doctor Sheila

Cassidy's arrest, and the conflict with the Church following a battle and a series of raids.

There it was again, the situation of permanent latent conflict. On occasions such as that one, it lost its latency and was transformed into a kind of struggle between the regime's armed power and the Church's moral power. In fact, the actions taken by the Christian Churches, Helmut Frenz, Cardinal Monsignor Raúl Silva Henríquez, and what was then called the Pro-Peace Committee were a constant thorn in the DINA's side. The DINA tried to remove them from power and intimidate them. If they weren't able to do so it was only thanks to Monsignor Silva's courage and that of some religious leaders and personnel in the institution who, following their Christian beliefs, fought for people's rights and defended life.

24

CHRISTMAS AT TERRANOVA

On December 23rd, the personnel at the Terranova Detention Center left at noon. They gave me a little basket with fruitcake, liqueurs, canned food, and all the ingredients to make a Christmas cocktail. The truck with a deliveryman and driver, Avalos and noncommissioned officer Rubilar Ocampo, had been arriving with packages for the personnel from Headquarters since the early morning hours.

The major dropped us off at the apartment, and we said good-bye. He was going to spend the holidays with his family in Osorno at his wife's parents' house.

I went to help a cousin at her business and at noon on December 24th I bought a small bouquet of roses and took it to my mother. We had an argument, and I took my son with me when I left. I had a talk with Alejandra and María Alicia. Alejandra said she didn't have any problems with my son staying with us. María Alicia said that it wasn't a problem for her if he stayed occasionally, for a weekend, but not for an indefinite amount of time. She said the presence of a child bothered her.

Without knowing what to do, since at that time we received a monthly salary that wasn't even enough to rent a room, I tried to find Rolf before he left to go south. I was able to speak with him, and he told me he would make some arrangements. He told me to call Captain Burgos De Beer. I did what he said, and he ordered me to go to Headquarters immediately.

I went with Alejandra. The colonel received both of us, and she confirmed that she didn't mind living with my son. The colonel said that, in the meantime, while he found a way to resolve the impasse, he would send me along with my son to a campground the DINA had at Las Rocas de Santo Domingo. He said to wait for instructions there, and that

229

he would be in touch with me at some point. The colonel spoke with Major Jara Seguel so he would receive me. He commanded the DINA unit there at that time.

On the morning of December 27th, Contreras's driver came to get me. I had only been there a couple of days when I asked Major Jara Seguel if I could call my parents' house. He said that it would be all right to do so once a week. When I spoke with them, they were very worried and said that I had received a summons to appear in court. They didn't know any details, and when it arrived they just repeated the instructions that I had given them myself at the DINA's orders: that I had been arrested, that they had apparently released me, and that I had sent them a note to say good-bye and that I was leaving the country without saying where I was going. They said they knew nothing about me.

When I finished talking with my parents, after calming them down and asking them to stick to that story, I told Major Jara Seguel what was happening. The officer spoke with the director, who was vacationing at his house in Las Rocas de Santo Domingo. The director told me not to worry, and that he would make arrangements to avoid problems for my parents after his vacation.

I knew I couldn't do anything more at that time. I was very nervous, but I didn't have any choice but to wait. . . .

PATRICIO

I met Patricio during my stay there. He was a DINA employee in the unit stationed at Las Rocas de Santo Domingo. He was nice. Patricio used to play with my son sometimes, and we started to talk. We often stayed to listen to him sing after dinner, and that's where we talked and had coffee together. I soon realized that Patricio knew about my relationship with Rolf Wenderoth. We were never indiscreet, but we never hid our tracks either. People were talking about us long before the relationship between the major and me even began because it was obvious that his relationship with me was more personal, even though he protected all three of us.

Patricio told me he wanted to start seeing me. I was honest with him. I told him the only thing I could promise him was that I would talk to Rolf when he returned from Santiago, which I did. I traveled to Santiago on February 27th. Rolf cried. It hurt me to see him so sad, but I knew that if I wavered I wouldn't be able to end that relationship. I made the mistake of telling him everything. Rolf insisted on going with me to the bus

230

station. He said he would forget everything I had told him, that he would never mention it again. He said we would talk about it some more when I returned to Santiago, and that maybe it was just some passing thing, that it was summer, and that the time of year is favorable for those kind of romances, etc. . . . I ended up crying too. My feelings were so conflicted that I couldn't define them. That same day, when I returned to Las Rocas de Santo Domingo, I saw Colonel Contreras. There was a barbeque to celebrate the end of the summer. The colonel told me that the following day I was supposed to go to Santiago with my son, and that on Monday, March 1st, I should report to Headquarters. He said I wasn't going to work at Terranova anymore.

I returned to Santiago. At Headquarters I found out that Rolf had also been transferred, and that he would continue being my boss. I wasn't sure how to respond. I wanted to stick to my decision, but I didn't want to be on Rolf's bad side. I was really grateful to him. The first days went well. Rolf asked me about Patricio, about our relationship, etc.

I started going on weekends to Las Rocas. Major Jara gave me permission to go whenever I wanted. I returned early on Monday morning in time to go to work, but soon Rolf started asking me to reconsider. He said, "Just think about it, Luz. I'm not asking for anything more. I love you. If what you need is for me to guarantee a future for you, I promise that once I'm promoted to colonel (he had ten years to go), I'll retire, and we'll get married."

I tried over and over again to explain to him that I didn't want to get married, that I was truly thankful to him and really cared for him, but that I didn't love him. I started living in a situation where I was doubly pressured. On the weekend Patricio asked me thousands of questions about Rolf. We always ended up fighting, and he went to be with his unit while I cried. Major Jara Seguel told me, "You have to decide soon or you're going to cause a problem." I told him that I didn't have doubts, that it was the major who wouldn't leave me in peace, and that Patricio on the other hand was jealous. Patricio always came back and we made up. Then Rolf started again on Mondays.

I kept trying to explain to him that I wanted to have a relationship with Patricio even if it only lasted a week or a day, that no matter what I needed to break up with him. I felt so pressured that I thought it would be better to tell them both to go to hell. Rolf kept repeating, "Luz, he's not right for you. He's a boy. He's very young and immature. You are too much woman for him. He's going to make you suffer."

It's true he was four years younger than me, but I wasn't looking for a husband. I just wanted to see if I could have a relationship or not.

One day we were arguing when the phone rang. Rolf answered it and handed it to me, "Take it. Here he is."

It was Patricio. He was at Headquarters. He told me to come downstairs for a minute. Rolf gave me permission to go. Patricio embraced me in the middle of the yard. He hugged me so hard that it hurt, and I backed away. He seemed strange. He said, "Let me hold you. Let all these bastards see us together." He kept repeating, "I love you, Luz."

I asked him what was going on.

"They're a bunch of bastards, Luz. Every one of them. They called me from the director's office." We walked toward the door with our arms around each other. We went to my house, and Patricio started to tell me, "It's very simple, Luz. Either I break up with you or they kill you."

"What?"

That's the only word I managed to utter. I remembered Contreras's voice when he told me in his office on May 7, 1975, "You can sleep with anyone you want, Luz, with any of my officers. But don't fall in love."

Patricio was indignant. I saw he had bruises on his forehead.

"Patricio, what happened?"

"I'm under arrest. My superior told me everything at the barracks. I escaped. I took one of the trucks and ran it into a wall. I put it in reverse and hit it again. I don't know how many times. That's when the colonel decided to tell me himself. I begged the major to let me tell you. They know I'll tell you the truth. All they care about is for us to stop seeing each other, but I don't have much time. I want you to know that I love you. Trust me. Wait for me to call you."

I was dumbfounded. We had a cup of coffee and returned to Headquarters. Major Jara approached us and stroked my hair.

"Let's go, Pato. . . ."

"Just one more minute, Major."

Patricio held me tightly for a few moments, but I was no longer there. I went up to the office. Rolf was waiting. He said he knew how I felt, that he loved me, that what we had wasn't over, that I should let him take care of me.

I asked him if he knew what was going on.

He said he did, that he had expected it, that an immature boy would have left me sooner or later. I interrupted him asking him if he knew they had forced him to break up with me by threatening to kill me.

232

He said, "Is that what he told you? How unoriginal. I don't suppose you believe that. Surely he must have found himself a teenager, and he felt bad telling you. . . ."

An absurd world. Lies and deceit. Who lied? I don't know. Who was Rolf? Who was I? Who was each DINA agent? Was anyone free in that web of intrigue?

No matter what the situation was, I decided to believe Patricio and act accordingly. If he lied or not was one thing, but it was something else altogether if they hurt him. I would take the initiative to protect him and myself as well.

I wrote him a note to say I was back with Rolf, that I was sorry about what happened, and that I had made a mistake. I asked Rolf to please be sure to get it to him so he would receive it that same day. Having done that, I hoped they would consider the case closed, and that Patricio would think I didn't have the guts to defy the DINA. I wanted him to see that our relationship wasn't worth fighting for. Rolf agreed to send the note.

I felt sick at the office the next day. I hemorrhaged severely. Rolf took me home, and they gave me the day off. I was in bed when Patricio came. He stormed into my room angrily and stood there looking at me.

I was pale, and my eyes were swollen because I had cried so much. He had my letter in his hand. He took his pistol from his waist and held me, saying "I came here to kill you, but I can't."

I didn't say anything. I knew there was no future for us. He left.

The babysitter I had at that time to take care of my son while I worked came to my room and started to say, "Ma'am, forgive me for intruding. Did you break up with that young man? Tell me and I'll chase after him. You two look so good together. You know, I'm older, and I can tell that you love him. Mr. Rolf is really good to you, but I've never seen you so happy as with the young one. Tell me to call him. I saw where he left the truck. He hasn't left yet. Ma'am. . . ."

I looked at her. I could tell she was worried and that she was doing this because she cared about us. I told her, "No, María. Don't worry. Everything is fine as it is. It's just that I don't feel well. I have a headache and menstrual cramps."

She came over, fixed the bed, and said she would bring me some coffee with hot milk.

I agreed so she would leave. I wanted to be alone. I was miserable, and I knew that what was happening would mark me for life. Maybe my relationship with Patricio wouldn't have lasted long. It's true he was immature, and so was I.

I could never find out the truth because even though I could walk around outside, that was the only freedom I really had.

Years later I heard that Patricio got married. I was happy for him.

HASBÚN AND CONTRERAS

While I was at DINA Headquarters, I witnessed some unusual events. One thing I had a hard time understanding were Father Raúl Hasbún's frequent visits. Even though their meetings weren't public knowledge, the personnel in the cafeteria told me that they had to make some sandwiches for them even when the cafeteria was closed. I heard the same thing from some of the members of Contreras's group of bodyguards and from Wenderoth himself who mentioned it to me on one occasion. I have no doubt whatsoever about the priest's friendship with Contreras and his admiration for the dictatorship. I saw him myself on a few occasions as he got out of his car to enter the building heading toward the DINA.

TESTIMONY BEFORE THE UNITED NATIONS

I saw Major Ferrer when I arrived at Headquarters on March 1, 1976. It had been months since I had heard anything about him. He showed me a thick file and told me he was studying the documents for the defense he had to present on behalf of the military government before the United Nations regarding allegations of human rights violations that had occurred since 1973. The family members of people being called "presumed disappeared" were constantly making these accusations.

Captain Ferrer was going to advise the government spokesman who was going to Geneva. Rolf Wenderoth was one of those in charge of coming up with answers to each of the allegations. I remember that he had the lists of the people's names. Since I was still sitting across from his desk, I realized that the major was carrying files with background about them. I noticed that in some cases they simply answered that the person had never been detained, especially when there were no witnesses present. When there were, the answer was that the person had been released or given permission to leave the country. I was even able to hear that in some cases they denied the militant even "existed." Several times I sat there astounded when I heard, "Upon investigating the individual in question, his existence is not confirmed by records at the Social Security Office." Then on the next line they suggested that this "supposedly fictitious person" was one more invention of international marxism to discredit the military government.

At Headquarters, I told Rolf Wenderoth about the subpoena they had taken to my parents' house. Rolf spoke to the director who ordered a lawyer, Rafael Alfaro, one of his legal advisors, to contact my parents. My parents had to appear in court accompanied by the lawyer. There they confirmed the version the DINA had ordered.

25

ANALYST AT THE DEPARTMENT OF INTELLIGENCE

Wenderoth was in charge of setting up the Department of Internal Intelligence during that period. Since the DINA had been restructured, and since it had decided to decentralize the files at Headquarters, we had to forward the documents to each of the respective departments. I found out that there was a foreign intelligence department. I started organizing a file. There was a little bit of everything there: news clippings, magazines, and, most of all, criminal allegations.

Wenderoth Pozo told me which areas the department was supposed to cover. Little by little, the staff grew in size that year. Once the recently promoted Colonel Pedro Espinoza Bravo had returned from Brazil, he was again assigned to the DINA. He assumed control of the Undersecretariat of Operations, which then became the Directorate of Operations. When this change occurred, the Department was transformed into the Undersecretariat of Internal Intelligence. Since the first days, Rolf Wenderoth and I had to issue a daily press release, in addition to organizing the files.

María Alicia continued working at Terranova. She complained that it was really far away and that I only had to cross the street to get to the office, etc. As a result, she was soon transferred to the Tucapel Unit, which at that time operated at a barracks on Pío Nono Street, just a few blocks from home. Alejandra was sent to Internal Intelligence as an analyst for Division C-2. When Alejandra arrived, the Undersecretariat of Operations had been divided into five divisions to coordinate declassified or public information. C-1 concentrated on "subversive movements." C-2 worked on the Christian Democratic Party and the MIR. C-3 was in charge of unions. C-4 focused on professional societies, and C-5 was in charge of businesses.

Wenderoth Pozo was the assistant director, and he chose Division C-1 for himself. My position was that of a C-1 analyst, which meant I focused on everything concerning leftist political parties, except the MIR. In addition, since no one wanted to work on issues involving the Church, I took that file and started to reorganize it.

During that time, despite the fact I didn't feel I was a Christian, I loved Christ the man. However, I had a huge irrational fear of the Pro-Peace Committee's legal actions. I knew they had supported the same court proceedings I was being sought to appear in, and I was terrified. When I started reorganizing the file, I discovered the recent creation of the Vicariate of Solidarity. According to Wenderoth, numerous documents had been stolen by DINA agents who had entered the Pro-Peace Committee's office through a hole in the roof. I don't know if this is true or not.

As I started reading about the Vicariate of Solidarity, I was favorably impressed by their actions, but I was still terrified of them. That is why I decided to find out as much as I could about the Vicariate of Solidarity so I could get away. It was a huge contradiction for me as I started understanding their logic and seeing everything Monsignor Silva Henríquez, Monsignor Tomás González, Monsignor Jorge Hourton, Monsignor Carlos Camus, and many others were doing. That was when I discovered the first documents that referred to Liberation Theology, and I had the opportunity to read writings by Gustavo Gutiérrez and Leonardo Boff.[48] I had never heard of this church before. It was very different from the one I knew as a child, which had instilled such fear in me as a young girl that I fled from it as an adolescent. I just read it in silence when I happened to come across it.

Sometimes I bumped into Father Horacio Spencer at Headquarters. He was a Police Chaplain, and he always said, "They're making such a stink because these communists are getting knocked around and grilled! And when have they ever expressed such concern for common

---

48. Gustavo Gutiérrez and Leonardo Boff are two of the founders of liberation theology. Gustavo Gutiérrez is a Roman Catholic priest from Peru who has devoted his life to helping the poor. His most famous book, *Teología de la Liberación,* was originally published in Spanish in 1971 and has been translated into other languages. The English translation was published in 1988 as *A Theology of Liberation.* It was edited and translated by Caridad Inda and John Eagleson. Leonardo Boff participated in the development of liberation theology in Brazil where he worked with the poor and where he has linked poverty to issues of ecology and land reform. Although he is no longer a Roman Catholic priest, arguing that the church forced him out of the clergy for mixing politics with religion, he is a key member of the group of founding theologians who developed this marxist reading of the Bible and the life of Jesus Christ.

prisoners?" I looked at him and thought that perhaps that priest didn't know what happened in the DINA's detention centers.

This priest is the same one who signed a kind of "certificate of honor and good conduct" in 1991, a document for Brigadier General Pedro Espinoza Bravo, who presented it when he asked to be freed on bond during the legal proceedings in which he was involved. These were part of the case Minister Bañados is investigating surrounding the assassination of Orlando Letelier and his secretary, Ronnie Moffit.[49]

Father Spencer often stopped by the office to talk with Rolf Wenderoth. The priest greeted me very cordially, and he said that he would hire me as a secretary when he became a bishop. I was scared of him.

EDGARDO ENRÍQUEZ ESPINOZA

When Rolf and I arrived at Headquarters, we were assigned an office on the second floor in the DINA's building. Then we moved to the second floor of another building that was also part of Headquarters. A few days after we arrived at this new location, Ketty, Rolf Wenderoth's secretary, distributed that day's documents in the wooden boxes that were on our desks. I started going over what she had left for me. I wanted to finish it quickly since I was trying to get the press release ready before lunch. I found a telex, and, when I read it, I thought there must have been some mistake. I was sure the document had come from Foreign Intelligence and that it should have been sent to the head of the Directorate of Operations. The document had come from an Argentine intelligence service affiliated with the Cóndor Unit, and it was informing the DINA about their detention of a Chilean citizen, Edgardo Enríquez Espinoza, Miguel Enríquez's brother, whom they were placing at the DINA's disposal. Rolf had arrived, but he was in some other office. I was trembling in fear as I left the document in the major's box, and I returned to my desk.

As I look back on that event, now that I have much more information, I think that perhaps Ketty's mistake was leaving it on my desk when the document was for Wenderoth. Maybe Rolf really was part of the DINA elite that planned operations abroad.

I had a lot of free time back then, and I had started studying about the cold war and the politics of détente on my own. That year Rolf Wen-

---

49. On May 30, 1995, Judge Adolfo Bañados sentenced Manuel Contreras to seven years in prison. Pedro Espinoza Bravo received a six-year sentence.

deroth was appointed as a part-time professor at the National Intelligence School, the ENI, and he gave me the task of planning the entire course class-by-class.

It was hard to pick up the books on marxism again. I couldn't read them at first. I felt conflicted. I felt nauseous. Something inside of me made me reject them, and I suffered without understanding why. I forced myself until I managed to read them again. It was painful for me, under these new circumstances, to read books that had been my favorites at a different time. I decided to try, as best I could, to make the course on marxism objective, and under no condition to study political parties from the Chilean left. The guidelines Rolf gave me for designing the course were very general, which allowed me to include just the history of marxism on a very superficial level.

I thought it was important to show, as far as I could, that it was a different ideology, and that being a marxist did not imply being a criminal or a whore.

That task allowed me to request books and magazines that had topics of interest to me. Rolf and I often stayed at the office many more hours than what was required for staff, and I took advantage of that time to study.

Everything concerning prisoners was absolutely out of my job description, except in unexpected situations like the telex with information regarding Edgardo Enríquez's arrest. I was only allowed to know what the press said or what the Vicariate of Solidarity published.

OAS MEETING IN CHILE[50]

A few days before the OAS meeting took place, Rolf received a memo that really upset him. It informed him that he had to make the Undersecretariat's female personnel available for security duties while the different activities took place during that meeting.

Rolf was annoyed, but we still had to attend and be ready to take orders from Major Juan Morales Salgado. The day I went, nothing out of the ordinary happened in the room where I was. Rolf was able to arrange for me to go only on the first day. He was angry because the majority of

50. This meeting of the Organization of American States took place in June of 1976. Henry Kissinger was present at this meeting and met privately with Augusto Pinochet at the Moneda Presidential Palace. Recently declassified documents from the CIA show that Kissinger offered his support privately to Pinochet during that meeting. The CIA's involvement in the military coup in 1973 is well known.

his staff were women. He had managed to exempt me because of my bad foot, but the other girls continued their service until the OAS meetings ended. I think what really bothered him was that the work still had to get done and that, according to him, the secretaries were not trained for those duties. He was more talkative than usual, perhaps because of his state of mind. He told me that the DINA had contracted several seedy motels and that they had selected female personnel to "escort" the diplomats and foreign delegates.

CARMELO SORIA

In mid-June Captain Lawrence Mires came to talk with Major Wenderoth. I started to leave, but Rolf told me not to. I overheard the captain telling him about how they had forced someone to drink a bottle of liquor, and that then they put him behind the steering wheel of his car. He also said that an agent had then started the car and sent it racing down the street. I immediately imagined the car flying over a cliff. I gave Wenderoth a terrified look. Wenderoth told me to go ahead and go to the cafeteria if I wanted some coffee, and that he would be there soon.

Rolf never said anything about the matter, and I never dared ask him anything. The next day, as I read the newspaper, I saw that they had found Carmelo Soria's body. The details that appeared in the article matched Lawrence Mires's description.

I wanted to escape the DINA, but fear kept me from taking the necessary steps. My relationship with Wenderoth was becoming unbearable. Every day I asked myself with increasing frequency, What does he know about the DINA? And I was afraid for my son. I knew I couldn't keep him locked up all the time. I tried to act naturally and encourage his relationships with his classmates, but I couldn't relax until he came home and I saw him. But a second fear immediately emerged. It was that if his presence gave me my only true happiness—I would say the strength to not go crazy—I felt that having him with me meant dragging what I most loved to the same fate that awaited me. The same uncertainty, the same routine of panic and anguish. . . .

THE DINA BEHIND CRIMINAL ACTS

What I remember being most relevant in July was an incident that took place on the 15th. It happened at the airport when Chilean bishops En-

240

rique Alvear, Carlos González, and Fernando Ariztía arrived from Río Bamba, Ecuador. They were greeted by protesters who were insulting them. I read about it in the newspaper. A week later Rolf showed me some pictures that the DINA had taken, and I could see that the protesters were BIM agents. I was able to identify Basclay Zapata Reyes and other agents from the Purén Unit among the people in the photographs.

I looked at the pictures and I said to Wenderoth, "You mean that the BIM organized the protest?" The major answered yes, but not just the Purén and Caupolicán Units. Other agents from other units like Tucapel and Ongolmo had also participated. I realized that the DINA was still growing, and not just at Headquarters. Now there were units that I didn't know except by name and sometimes by their leaders.

Each of those events made me evaluate the press in a different way. And although I was never able to confirm some cases, I couldn't read about any crime in the newspaper's crime section without suspecting that the DINA had been behind it. My insecurity was growing each day.

The months went by, and the papers I had to read to do my job started becoming hostile objects. I didn't want to see them. They increased my fear. Everything seemed to indicate that the DINA was growing, that it had more influence every day, and it was as if nothing could stop it. . . . I felt lost, trapped. During the first days of September I found out that Mr. Orlando Letelier del Solar's citizenship had been revoked. I read about his death only days later. . . . People talked about the incident, and there were a lot of rumors floating around. Everybody made Orlando's death look like a crime of passion.

What had begun as an easy job, reading the press—something I had always liked—summarizing it, and then commenting on it started to turn into torture. I couldn't maintain even a precarious state of balance. I was afraid of my own shadow.

MY SON'S VISIT WITH HIS FATHER

In 1976 I asked if I could take my vacation in December to be able to work during the days before Christmas at my cousin's business in order to earn some extra income. My son studied at a private school, and since I tried to make our home as normal as possible and I had a babysitter to be sure my son was with an adult, I had to do some fancy footwork to make my salary stretch. Quite often, we were barely able to count on having the bare minimum we needed by the end of the month. Rolf helped me. He gave me money for my son's bus fare every day. I always ate lunch at the cafeteria at Headquarters, and Rolf bought my breakfast and a snack every day. That way all I had to pay for at home was food for my son and his babysitter.

I remember that while I was working at my cousin's business, I looked through the window and saw "Joel," the guy from the MIR who was made to paint Argentine license plates. My heart started beating faster. I had heard a rumor at Headquarters that he had been released, but by then I questioned everything and everyone more and more each day. I was afraid they had murdered him. Seeing him made me feel a mixture of happiness and fear. When I finished helping the client, I went over to the door. "Joel" was walking several feet away. He looked good. My first impulse was to call out to him, but I didn't dare. I was afraid. I don't know of what. I remembered that "Lucas" and "Marco Antonio" were dead, and I was afraid to talk to him. I was afraid of knowing, of speaking. . . . With immense sadness, I watched him walk away.

During the Christmas holidays, my son's father came to Santiago. He spent some time at the apartment with Rafaelito, and then we went to my cousin's house to a family reunion. My son was happy. Since Rafael had been very young when we separated, he was practically meeting his father for the first time. My son used to ask me questions about his father. I didn't even have a picture to show him. That night he looked so happy. I remember feeling overcome by a deep sorrow. I remember that around mid-1976 I had written my mother-in-law a letter telling her to please tell her son that Rafael was asking about him. I said that he could write to him if he wanted or visit him if he came to Santiago. I wanted my son to have a concrete image of his father, a different reference from the world of the DINA in which we were engulfed. His father answered, and my son looked so happy.

I had made all the arrangements to go into the Military Hospital on January 2nd. They had to remove some veins in my right leg. That is why my son went on vacation with his father after Christmas Eve. I went with them to the airport. When they walked through the doorway leading to the boarding area and disappeared from my sight, I felt an enormous solitude. I calmed myself down, thinking that my son would be fine with his father and I checked myself into the hospital.

Alejandra and Mirtha, a secretary at Headquarters, donated blood for my operation. I was operated on on January 3rd. When I awoke in the recovery room, the doctor came over to me and told me that he had operated on both my legs.

The postoperative period was painful. At the Military Hospital I started feeling the fears I had in the past during my other stay there. All I wanted was to leave. Alejandra and my mother came to see me. When they discharged me, I was alone at home until Rolf Wenderoth returned from vacationing in the south. Since I couldn't walk, he was going to keep me company, taking turns with my mom.

They gave me a long sick leave, but I returned to work before it was over. The lonely hours at home made me feel worse. I went to the London Clinic, which was run by the DINA, for postoperative treatment until the doctor removed my stitches and discharged me.

My son returned just before it was time to start the school year. Rolf and I went to pick him up at the airport. Our home was filled with happiness again.

26

NATIONAL INTELLIGENCE SCHOOL

After I returned to work, I found a memo in with other papers, and the signature on it caught my eye. It was "Max's" name. It gave information about the courses that were going to be offered at the National Intelligence School (ENI) starting in the month of February. I read it attentively. I was tired of the work I was doing. The course would last until August. I always liked studying, and I thought it would be a good change of pace even if only for a short time. I talked with Rolf Wenderoth, and I asked him to send me. The memo explicitly stated that employees who attended must have the permission and the support of their superiors. At first, Rolf refused outright. I insisted until I got him to promise me he would look into it. Since there was a deadline to apply for a spot at the ENI, I asked him about it practically every day. Finally, Pedro Espinoza responded. He had talked about it with the director, and he had agreed, adding that all three of us, María Alicia, Alejandra, and I would go. We were still seen as a single package.

We were at the ENI from the beginning of February until August 1977. In personal terms, it meant I would see María Alicia again. We had grown apart since she had gone to live in another apartment because she didn't want to live with my son. I understood that neither she nor anyone else had any reason to put up with the presence of someone else's son. But her attitude had hurt me, and, since we worked in different places, we didn't see each other for over a year.

Seeing each other at school led to the inevitable. Regardless of the path each of us chooses, there was a very important period in our lives that will link us forever. And sharing those seven months as classmates tied us together again, maybe more than in the past.

Something else that was important for me was that that period became a true parenthesis in my life. An evasion? Yes, we were students again even though we were studying things like secret service, search and seizure, intelligence and counterintelligence, marxism, foreign relations, surveillance and description, karate, explosives, shooting, secret codes, and makeup. It's incredible how I managed to escape reality. I think it didn't make any difference what we studied, and the fact that it was a course for officers was something I wasn't conscious of. Being a student again was something marvelous.

I saw "Max" again there, and he looked happy. There was a school, and he was the assistant director and then the director. He was my professor for secret service and surveillance and description.

During my first term at the ENI, a bus from the institution brought us to Santiago and left us at the entrance to Headquarters. Then I would work with Rolf for a while.

In June Colonel Contreras confirmed he was coming to the house to celebrate his Saints' days (Juan, Manuel, and Guillermo). I told "Max" about it and invited him because I knew he needed to arrange a meeting with the director. "Max" didn't want to go. He didn't like gaining access to the director that way. He accepted when I told him that other officers were going too.

The foreseeable happened. Wenderoth got angry with me and left early. "Max" was able to talk to the director, who showed interest and had Captain Alejandro Burgos—his assistant—make a note in his agenda for a meeting with "Max." As was the general custom in military circles, when the colonel left, so did all the officers.

María Alicia, Alejandra, and I were sharing our impressions of the meeting when the doorbell rang. It was Juan Morales, Marco Antonio Sáez, and Ferrer Lima. We were surprised. Marco Antonio started talking with Alejandra, and Juan Morales with María Alicia. I was sitting on a sofa talking with "Max" when he suddenly tried to embrace me. I pushed him away. I have to confess that I felt attracted to the major, but I was afraid. It was instinctive and fortuitous since it helped me realize several things, and I was faced with new questions about the DINA's procedures.

To be honest, I didn't tell him no. I said, "No, not as long as I'm involved with someone." He tried to convince me by saying literally that my attitude was "prudish," and that it wasn't what he expected from the strong-willed, brave woman he knew. He said all these things that are supposed to make a "lady" feel obligated to give in so as to avoid being labeled a "repressed fool."

I laughed when I heard that. "Repressed fool" was the least offensive thing I had been called in recent years. I was amused by the fact that the wise, intelligent officer would use arguments that I had been hearing since I was a teenager. All I said to him, thinking out loud more than giving an answer, was that he knew what I was. He knew I had many shortcomings, but that I wasn't going to be able to resolve them just like that, by sleeping with someone. I also said I wouldn't be more of a whore or more "prudish" just because someone said so, and that I looked at relationships in a different way. I said that sex for me was something more than simply being together to take advantage of a situation, and that I felt like I should start to act according to my thoughts and sense of self, at least in that respect. I said that was the only thing I could allow myself at that moment, and that I hadn't even had that in previous years.

I added that if what he wanted was to thank me for giving him access to the colonel, that it wasn't necessary. I pointed out that I had done that because I was thankful for what he had given me in the past.

"Max" looked at me very seriously. He was obviously uncomfortable, so I simply changed the topic since I didn't want that either. We talked pleasantly, and we drank some champagne until the lieutenant and the captain announced that they were leaving. "Max" took advantage of that opportunity, and all three of them left.

I must confess that, in spite of the fact that everything I said was true, what fueled my rejection was fear. I was afraid of traveling unknown roads at that point, such as really becoming involved with someone in the DINA. In those days nothing made sense. Nothing seemed right. For example, I know that what I said to him about ending a relationship before starting another one still holds true for me today. A relationship with two people at once would cause me extreme confusion. I wouldn't be capable of keeping that up, and I would feel as if I were using someone. And on a more personal level, I'm absentminded, quite forgetful, so what would probably happen is that I would get someone's name wrong or something like that.

In spite of believing this about myself, I did have affairs, sometimes parallel ones. They were a complete disaster. And finally, although it sounds like an obsession, if there is one thing that disgusts me, it's promiscuity. Perhaps I saw and experienced too many things.

I realize now that my fears about the issue, in addition to an inability to have orgasms, influenced me so that I unconsciously set traps for myself. The "I will or will not go to bed" with someone "if I want too," allowed me to consent to only those relationships that I intuitively knew wouldn't be traumatic. That was the only way for me to receive affection, which I needed a lot. It wasn't an interest in sex, and I'm not even talking about feelings. I wanted someone to be there who could chase away ghosts and fears. I wanted the illusion of someone showing me some affection, even if only for a few minutes.

The knowledge that I was having difficulties led me to tell myself: sex is just another form of communication, something I can choose to practice or not. Then I made up or adopted a saying as my own, "I'll give myself to someone, if I want to, but I won't sell myself."

The first time I said it was to the DINA's director, Manuel Contreras. He asked me to dance with him at a reception, and he started talking to me.

"Luz, you are the most beautiful of my prisoners."

"Thank you, colonel. But I thought I was an employee, and to be frank with you, I would rather have you say I'm the most intelligent," I said laughing.

"I meant to say the most beautiful of the prisoners who came through the DINA, and also very intelligent. And you really are, I don't know about beautiful, but you are very attractive, and you can have anything you want. Just ask."

"Thank you, colonel. I suppose you are referring to material things."

"Of course! Everything that makes life enjoyable. Clothes, money, and everything money can buy."

"And tell me, colonel, what's the price? Because I imagine there is one."

"That you be friendly and affectionate."

"You know what, colonel? I'll give myself to someone, but I won't sell myself."

"Are you rejecting your director, Luz?"

I knew I was walking on thin ice. So I tried to seem very happy and practically flirting I said,

"No. I'm not rejecting my director. My director changed hats, and he started behaving like a man. That's why I can say no, as a woman."

He laughed, and feigned an excessive cordiality and cheerfulness, which of course I didn't have inside of me, while we continued dancing. A few minutes later the colonel asked all three of us to sit around him. María Alicia was at his left, Alejandra was on his right, and I sat down on the ground in front of him. The officers were standing around us when the colonel toasted the three of us and said something about how he had given us life, that he was like a father to us, and that we had nothing to fear under his protection.

I looked at him thinking. . . . Does he really believe his own story, or is he saying that so the three of us will believe it? In fact, his statement was true. He had assumed power over life and death. It was after that toast that I dared mention to him that I had seen Ricardo Lagos Salinas at Villa Grimaldi, and that I thought he was dead.

The colonel said to me, "Of course it's possible you talked with him. He was arrested, and he collaborated. That is why we freed him. He helped us a lot. And now he's traveling around Europe saying all kinds of strange things! These marxists are very ungrateful. . . ."

Since I kept looking at him without saying anything, he asked, "Are you doubting your colonel, Luz?" He didn't give me time to answer, and he added, "I understand you, but I want you to believe in me, and I'm going to show you he's alive." He continued talking about other things as if the topic had never been mentioned.

A few days later I found a file in my office with photocopies that referred to some publication in which Ricardo Lagos had answered some questions by a reporter. I looked at them without imagining that Ricardo Lagos would someday be the Minister of Education in the first Concertation government.[51] I felt like I wanted to believe it was true, that Ricardo Lagos was in Europe.

But that wasn't the only thing that happened that night. The three of us realized that the colonel had said the same things to María Alicia, Alejandra, and me about improving our situation if we had a relationship with him.

He received three identical answers, unequivocal no's. Over time, a number of things began to strike me. Now I believe it's highly probable

51. The reader is reminded that there seems to be a confusion in Arce's testimony regarding Ricardo Lagos Salinas and Ricardo Lagos Escobar. They were both members of the Socialist Party in Chile during the Allende government. When the coup occurred, however, Chilean president Ricardo Lagos Escobar—who also served as the Minister of Education in the first Concertation government—was the Ambassador to Moscow in 1973 and later went into exile in the United States. Ricardo Lagos Salinas, however, is disappeared along with his compañera, a Spanish citizen named Michelle Peña Herreros, who was eight months pregnant when she was detained. Although some witnesses claim to have seen her at Villa Grimaldi and suggest that she gave birth to a baby at the Military Hospital (Hosmil), there is no further information regarding their child.

that if one of the three of us had accepted, they would have automatically recruited us into the female units that searched for information through the sex market. This is a conclusion I came to later. At that time it seemed like an attempt to judge our behavior. I was sure the night the three officers returned wasn't just spontaneous.

Trying to find out more, I told Rolf what the colonel had said to me. Rolf laughed and attributed it to confusion on the colonel's part.

I always suspected the DINA of fomenting the disagreements María Alicia, Alejandra, and I had. I never mentioned it. I didn't think it was my place to judge how they were developing their own professional and personal relationships with their superiors and others. I know this is mere speculation, and perhaps a lack of modesty, but I believe that if the three of us had worked as a team, we could have caused them more than one headache. I never dared find out.

My struggles were very basic: to survive, to elude the Vicariate of Solidarity, and to not be completely at the DINA's mercy. All that effort was wearing me down. It was an unstable life with a lot of loneliness, and I feared my situation was irreversible. I continued to try to not succumb, while at the same time I tried to convince them of my loyalty and maintain some of what they called "Luz's quirks."

It is so hard to always mistrust everyone! I made minimal exceptions so I wouldn't go crazy. It seemed like it would be so easy to die, and I tried to find strength by saying, "Luz, even if you only live one more second, that second is the rest of your life. There you have your future. That is the worst that can happen to you, and you already have that. Every additional hour of every day is a triumph, a gift, a reason to be happy."

It's not like I automatically believed it just because I thought it, but it was good for me to feel that I wasn't entirely defeated. In my emotional life, my Achilles heel, there were times when I consented to a request or I encouraged it just because my fear was so immense or because I knew I wouldn't be able to face those hours alone. It wasn't just a need to be with someone. I suppose it was that I couldn't be with myself. I couldn't avoid my own questions. Curled up in bed and hopeless, I couldn't see a way out. I couldn't rely on my family. I felt that they had suffered so much, and I tried to act happy whenever I was with them. It seemed like they didn't understand the situation. It seemed like they were expecting me to tell them I was fine, and I told them I was fine.

It was more difficult with my son. He seemed to sense my terror. I had to ask him for a lot, and I felt very guilty asking him to follow security measures. Sometimes he asked questions, and I tried to tell him the truth without making it too severe or difficult. I didn't want to lie to him, but I didn't want to hurt him either. . . . For years that guilt guided the way I behaved with him, and I overprotected him. I tried to give him a stability I no longer had.

While I was a student at the ENI, being in classes and studying made me remember my militant past, like when I stayed at Tomás Moro or Cañaveral, or when I was at INESAL and Socialist Party Headquarters. Sometimes I remembered Alejandro, and other times Ricardo Ruz. It hurt me to imagine what they surely thought of me.

One morning in the search and seizure workshop we were beginning a practical phase. Each of us had to create a set of picklocks for all types of locks and keyholes. Standing in front of the emery wheel, I was having trouble making what we called a pig's tail, which is used to open cars and the kinds of locks you close from the inside by pressing a button.

I was hot, and tiny metal splinters were pricking my hands. The goggles I was using to protect my eyes kept moving around because they were too big for me. I was uncomfortable, and on top of everything else, it was one of those days when my foot hurt. A classmate came over and offered to help. I knew his name and rank, but we hadn't spoken before that day. So I turned down his offer to help, but he insisted, saying "I'll teach you, and then you can do the other ones." I handed him the metal and the goggles. He had the key ready in a few minutes. "Now it's your turn. Cut the metal."

He got behind me and guided my hands with his, the typical game of the innocent embrace. If you complain, there's always the excuse that they just wanted to help. I decided to act like the guy wasn't even there, ignoring his attitude. He got bored pretty fast and stood next to me. He helped me with all the work, and he gave me the ones he had made for himself too. From that moment on the young man became a member of our study group that included Alejandra, some officers, and myself.

This young man had a truck he could use, and he offered to pick me up everyday. We stopped taking the bus to school. Soon I started having a relationship with him. He was really nice. He showered me with gifts and attention. It was like living on borrowed time and experiencing maybe what I should have experienced at another time, when I was free, when I was young. It was an uncomplicated, open relationship without any kind of problems He was so sweet!

One weekend we went to the Jahuel Hot Springs. We went horseback riding and hiking. I breathed deeply. We enjoyed the food and played foosball, ping pong, and billiards. Time seemed to fly. I noticed it was hard for us to say good-bye. It took us longer to say good-bye in the parking lot than it took us to drive from the Hot Springs to Santiago.

On Monday, after classes, "Max" sent for me and asked me very seriously, "Luz, what are you doing?"

I supposed immediately he was referring to the relationship, but I answered as if I didn't know what he meant.

"You know what I'm referring to. I want us to talk about the officer."

"Oh! The lieutenant," and I added laughing really loud "Major, to the rescue! Whom are you trying to save, Major? Me, from the claws of a cynical, womanizing lieutenant? Or the poor, defenseless boy from the claws of this evil woman?"

"Don't joke, Luz. I want to know what's going on, what's going on with you. It isn't consistent at all with the Luz I think I know. And the only thing I know is that the officer's wife spent all weekend crying and asking if her self-sacrificing husband's mission was very dangerous. And I think he was with you."

I thought to myself that either they had already gotten to him or Counterintelligence is working wonderfully well. Some people knew about it though, like Captain Pedro Tichauer Salcedo, the officer's friend, and another officer who was his neighbor. He had asked him to take care of things if there was some emergency at his house.

I knew the officer's wife. She was like a spacey teenager. They had two beautiful children. I felt bad. "Max" knew how to present things to me. I thought, "Such a scandal. Who knows how many other women he's been with or he'll be with in the future." I answered a little angry, "Fine, 'Max.' You asked me an honest question, and you at least deserve an honest answer. Why all this drama? They were just a few days of fun. Or is it that I'm the problem? You know how well I know all of you. Are you by chance a monument to faithfulness? What do you think I'll do to your lieutenant?"

"Oh, what a woman! No, that's not it. Get it in that thick head of yours. You are the problem, but in another way. The officer is no saint. Agreed. No one is. Agreed. But he always stayed within some boundaries. He never missed a night at home. And now he goes on a long weekend with you. I know him, Luz. He's falling in love with you. What will you do then?"

I thought about Patricio. I didn't even believe half of what "Max" was saying. It was his style. He would get me to end my relationship with the officer, and as a result I would feel "great." But I got the message. "Okay, 'Max.' It's over. There won't be any more problems, at least from me.

251

"I never expected anything less from you, Luz. I want you to know that the wife of. . . ."

"Max," I interrupted him, "Don't go on. I've always been honest with you, Major. It's not because of his wife and their beautiful children, nor is it because you asked. It's not even about him. It's about me, Major, because I don't want any problems. That's why. Permission to be dismissed, Major."

He gave me a kind smile.

"I understand you, Luz. I know you're angry. You have my permission to leave. We'll talk soon."

The relationship ended. The officer called me several times, but the High Command could relax. Their man was safe.

That allowed me to see clearly how the playing field was marked. There was no problem if María Alicia, Alejandra, or I had relationships with officers who were, according to them, "mature." However, if it happened to be an officer our own age or younger, then they intervened immediately. I was somewhat lucky. "Max" was always a gentleman and even elegant in the way he presented things. Rolf acted before anything could happen. If some officer approached me, he arrived minutes later and questioned him, "Tell me, Captain. Do you need something? I am this lady's superior. You can ask me anything you need to know about work." Obviously no officer challenged him openly.

What I used to call the "young officers rescue squad" didn't affect other female employees at Headquarters. There was a kind of overestimation of the three of us, and a lot of distrust!

During my class at the ENI, on one winter day we were sitting in the sun during our break. Jorge Marcelo Escobar Fuentes, then head of the Counterintelligence Unit, called me over and took me to one of the yards behind the school. He told me, "A friend of yours wants to see you."

I was frightened. Raúl Navarrete, the guy who had given the DINA all the information he knew about me, was sitting in the captain's Austin Mini. He got out of the car, gave me a big hug, and just said, "It's so great to see you're all right."

I smiled quietly. When I saw him, I thought it was possible to be worse off. An empty feeling came over me, and my smile was more sincere. I think I connected with him, tacitly, but deeply. We were made of the same kind of shit. We were both surviving, which at that time seemed like a good thing to me. I felt like he looked at me relieved to see me alive. I never saw him again.

252

27

AFTER THE NATIONAL INTELLIGENCE SCHOOL

I don't remember how María Alicia ranked in our course at the ENI, but Alejandra was second and I was fourth out of twenty-four officers. Returning to Headquarters made me feel bitter inside. After I had that brief relationship with the officer, which was cut short, I was with "Max" a couple of times. It felt like an unresolved issue. During those years I thought I could have loved that man. However, "Max" simply passed through my life. I think what impressed me most was how he acted while I was a prisoner. I fancied I had been able to erase my feelings, and that he didn't even matter to me. There was just emptiness and pain. Nothing else fit inside me. I learned that I could be with anyone and still remain who I was, just more empty. . . . That is something you never forget. . . .

There are difficult transition periods. That period was like that, when you feel like you can't live anywhere, but even so you still want to live. What little I had left of myself struggled to come out. I still felt deeply wounded and at the mercy of a foreign, empty, hostile environment. So I said to myself, "Without roots to hold you down, it is easier to move on. There will be another time, other days, to sink into the earth and, perhaps, blossom."

The year I spent at the ENI was a "good" year in terms of work. In mid-August, they confirmed my position as a Public Information Analyst in Internal Intelligence. I was informed that I would become part of the group of part-time professors at the ENI, and that I would teach on marxism as a teaching assistant to Commander Wenderoth, who was in charge of the subject. They gave all three of us the status of civilian staff. We were promoted to the rank of officers, and my record was wiped clean. And there I was more distant, sadder, and more lonely every day.

"CHATY," ARMY SECOND LIEUTENANT

I didn't know "Chaty" personally, but I knew who she was when I saw her go to Headquarters. I don't know how to describe her duties exactly. What little I know about her comes from what I heard from Rolf Wenderoth and from a captain she had an affair with.

One day, Rolf Wenderoth was very upset. He told me he was angry because Colonel Contreras had changed a lot. His frustration seemed genuine to me. He told me he wasn't the same friend he had known for years. He was hurt because he had been at Manuel Contreras's house with his wife the previous weekend, and the colonel hadn't even come out to greet them. He said they had spent some time with María, the colonel's wife, and that she seemed unhappy since she also evidently resented the changes in her husband. Rolf had been one of the officers closest to Contreras since he began his career. When Wenderoth was a lieutenant and got married while he was assigned to the Engineers Regiment at Osorno, the Contreras-Valdebenito couple had been in their wedding, and he had given away the bride.

When Rolf arrived at the DINA, he was one of the officers who had immediate access to Contreras. According to him, he was "marginalized" little by little by Vianel Valdivieso and Pedro Espinoza.

That day Rolf told me, "Do you know what I heard? That little 'Mamo,' Contreras's son, was apparently having trouble having his first sexual encounter, and the colonel asked 'Chaty' to sleep with him." Rolf was indignant. He talked about the way people were being used, and about the "lack of class" of some of the female personnel. He added some things like, "What can you expect from these girls when the Female School is the Military's whorehouse?"

I thought about "Chaty." Maybe she didn't realize what was happening. Maybe she felt like she was between a rock and a hard place, even though she was an officer. She was younger than me, maybe five or six years younger. I knew how much a woman changes over a period like that. On a subjective level, since I barely knew her, I felt like she was like a sister. I thought, "She probably knows too that there is no way out." I shivered as I felt a deathlike cold run through my body. How many underworlds were there yet to uncover?

Rolf looked angry. I thought that maybe what bothered him more than he admitted was that the boss had marginalized him from the group of officers that surrounded him.

URUGUAYAN IDENTITY

When I finished the course and returned to the office, I noticed that Rolf was more worried than ever about my safety and about how I would have to live in the future. Up until then, the constant pressure coming from the courts that were summoning me to appear as a witness in cases of "presumed disappeared"—which is how the cases were classified back then—hadn't constituted a serious risk for me. But everything seemed to indicate that the pressure from the Vicariate of Solidarity was far from diminishing, and that it would continue to grow and become permanent.

The institution's instructions were clear. No one must testify. During 1991, the year when I had the opportunity to review a lot of old press and put what had happened in order, I realized that the decree regarding the change from the DINA to the CNI was dated August 13, 1977. In other words, the officers, at least the high-ranking ones, knew what would happen long before the personnel at the institution did, which included me. I imagine this influenced Commander Wenderoth's special preoccupation with finding a way to avoid what was turning me into a weak link in the institution.

According to the report I received, Colonel Contreras authorized a mission in which I would assume a foreign identity. This was to allow me to live in Chile after obtaining a temporary resident visa and enable me to maybe request Chilean citizenship one day, in accordance with the legislation for foreign residents that was in place at that time.

Wenderoth Pozo planned everything with the assistant director of foreign intelligence, Commander Arturo Ramón Ureta Sire, who died from a heart attack in July 1992 at the Military Hospital. Ureta Sire contacted the man from the DINA in Buenos Aires, Captain Christoph George Paul Willike Flöel, who was also the DINA contact for the Uruguayan Intelligence Service. They asked him to see if it would be feasible for them to give me that identity. I traveled to Montevideo, Uruguay on August 19, 1977.

I left Santiago with identification in the name of Ana María Vergara Rojas, and I returned from Montevideo as Graciela Susana Miranda López or López Miranda on August 30th of the same year.

Rolf took me to the airport, and then we talked on the phone fairly regularly to coordinate my return and to keep him informed regarding the way the process was going. At the airport in Carrasco, Captain

255

Christoph Willike met me as planned. He immediately put me in touch with a man he said was Roque Vergara, who was with the Uruguayan Intelligence Service. He, along with Captain Willike Flöel, took me to the Hotel Ibicuí, which was on the street with the same name. It was just a few yards from the Cagancha Plaza in Montevideo. He told me he had some things to do, but that I should trust the Uruguayan officer since he knew him.

In Montevideo I took advantage of the opportunity to see the most picturesque places and learn what I had to in such a short time to be able to pass for a Uruguayan citizen, such as adopting the accent and local idioms. I bought a newspaper to learn about general things you would assume a citizen knows about his or her country.

The officer talked to me about relevant aspects of Uruguayan history. I memorized the names of soccer players at that time, cities, streets, newspapers, magazines, etc. They took pictures of me for an ID and for a Uruguayan passport. When I returned to Chile, Rolf Wenderoth was waiting for me at the airport. We stopped by the apartment to drop off my suitcase, and from there we went to the cafeteria at the Police Officers Club. They had a reception there to celebrate the assistant director of foreign intelligence's saint's day and Rolf's birthday.

Before I left for Uruguay, I followed orders and gave the fake ID in the name of Ana María Vergara Rojas to Officer Vergara. He then sent it to Christoph Willike, who in turn sent it back to Chile through means unknown to me. When they gave it to me, they said it had come by diplomatic pouch.

With my Uruguayan passport in the name of Graciela Susana López Miranda or Miranda López—I don't remember exactly—Rolf Wenderoth Pozo began to take the necessary steps to find out how I could request residency to live "legally" in Chile. As usual, he asked agents Carlos Estibil Maguida and Aníbal Rodríguez Díaz for assistance. The agents pointed out that it wouldn't be difficult for me to receive Chilean residency provided that I could show I had a work contract. Rolf Wenderoth and I went to talk with the officer that directed the DINA's computer unit. He told us there wouldn't be any problem since that unit functioned using a computer company as a front.

Once the application had been completed with my personal information and I had obtained the necessary signatures, I went to the offices of the International Police, which at that time were located in the old Social Security Office building on General Mackena Street. Wenderoth

Pozo and Estibil Maguida accompanied me. Pretending to be Uruguayan, I began the necessary process to obtain residency in Chile.

When the DINA changed to the CNI, the dynamic that developed within the institution made it impossible to complete the necessary steps. I didn't dare present that situation to the CNI either, which is why I don't know what happened to those documents.

CHANGE FROM THE DINA TO THE CNI

The DINA changed its name. Manuel Contreras Sepúlveda still commanded the institution. During the second half of September, the CNI started trying to resolve some issues that the DINA had pending. One of them affected me particularly.

During the time when we were at school, Alejandra moved and rented a small apartment. A short time later, Miguel Angel Poblete, a lawyer for the Judicial Department, informed me that in a little while I was going to have to return the government apartment where I lived in tower 12 since it was going to be given to a ministry in exchange for some office space. It seemed like an attempt to avoid legal problems with the owners of the property since a few days earlier we had found out that a relative of the owner, Max Joel Marambio, who was in exile, was taking steps to recover the property.

I started looking for a place to rent. When I realized I didn't have the resources to pay rent, on top of the cost of educating and caring for my son, I talked with his father. I asked him to take our son for a few months while I found a place to live. He sent me a ticket for the boy. At the airport, a stewardess took him and promised me that the airlines, Lan-Chile, would accept the responsibility for giving him to his father when they arrived at their destination.

The information they were starting to publish about the Letelier case generated a series of changes within the institution. I would say that the colonel lost part of his omnipotence and influence to Jaime Guzmán Errázuriz and others in the government. All this translated into the DINA's attempt to avoid having the repressive organ disappear, which is how they invented the name change. In reality, that's what happened. Everything else remained the same.

The day the situation was made public, there were a lot of meetings between officers and Director Contreras, and there was also one for all the personnel that took place in the Officers Club. The DINA's assistant director at the time, Colonel Gerónimo Pantoja (retired from service), led the meeting. He said that because of maneuvers by international marxism, the institution unfairly had to face scrutiny from the outside. He said the DINA was not responsible for Orlando Letelier's death. However, to protect the organization, it would change its name and would be subject to certain restrictions. Among them, he mentioned that the CNI's prisoners would have to appear in court within five days after being detained, or they would have to be released without being charged, within the same timeframe.

Pantoja added that we shouldn't worry because everything would continue as usual. He said the institution would sort out the problem, and that it was temporary. He said that the fact that Contreras would be the CNI's director was a sign of strong support from President Pinochet. Everything else were tirades reminding us about the almost providential nature of the institution in its cleansing of the nation. The employees were relieved. When they heard they would still be receiving their paychecks and that the change would translate, for us, into nothing more than a change of letterhead and logo, no one ascribed the matter great importance. Other than the meeting and the couple of days people talked about it in the cafeteria, nothing else happened.

However, the leadership was nervous, and it was easy to assume that more things were happening. The DINA's elite was absolutely closed-mouthed about it, except for the official version attributing responsibility for what happened to international marxism and saying that the assassination of Orlando Letelier had been a crime of passion.

During that time I was trying to find a place to live, so I didn't even read the news. I was desperate. Living with my son seemed more impossible every day.

28

COLONEL CONTRERAS

Juan Manuel Guillermo Contreras Sepúlveda was born in 1929. In 1948 he entered the corps of engineers as an officer, and he became a professor of intelligence at the War Academy in 1966. In 1971, he commanded the Engineers Regiment Number 4, "Arauco." He was named Director of the School of Engineers at Tejas Verdes in 1973, which put him in an important position of control on the day of the coup. He distinguished himself by his qualifications during his military career, and he always maintained the seniority of his rank. With the rank of colonel, he commanded the DINA from its inception.

The colonel, with his pleasant appearance, inspired doubts whenever he appeared in public. I heard someone say one day, "That's the colonel? He looks like somebody's grandfather!" It's true. He does. However, those of us who knew him know that the colonel and the DINA played an important role in exercising power in the dictatorship. The DINA advised the military regime in nearly every area of government and, with a handful of men, it raided, robbed, kidnapped, tortured, killed, and made people disappear.

The colonel knew how to motivate men and women who then built a power structure destined to break and dominate others. That power, exercised directly and brutally over victims and indirectly over society as a whole, generated denunciations, fragmentation, and terror. Today it is expressed in a code of silence that hides the truth. On September 23, 1973, the colonel, as director of the School of Engineers at Tejas Verdes, published an invitation to the general population in the newspaper *Proa* in San Antonio. It asked them to denounce those who were spreading rumors so they could be detained and tried in wartime military courts, which were already operational.

I met the colonel. The first time I saw him, I never imagined he was the DINA's director. I recognized him a year later when he told me that I was going to be a DINA employee. In spite of the fact that I felt frustrated because it wasn't freedom, I thought that at least it was a new phase. I didn't understand that the colonel couldn't give me my freedom. I didn't know then that freedom for me implied breaking away from that power, and that freedom is only reached by exercising it.

The colonel involved DINA personnel in his project. He set the groundwork for complicity. He reinforced those activities that were desirable for the DINA, and he demanded unconditional loyalty. I remember when Rolf Wenderoth said to me, "To receive something from the colonel is like signing a blank check. If he needs something, have no doubt he'll come to collect." Then, before I left for Uruguay, he warned me not to make the mistake of saying good-bye to the colonel or telling him about my trip. He told me, "Some day when all is exposed he could use that information to compromise or blackmail the CNI."

The power of the DINA turned some of its employees into victims when they failed to meet the expectation of unconditional loyalty. According to Arístides Becerra's statements, when his brother, Miguel Angel Becerra Hidalgo, suggested he wanted to distance himself from the people at Colonia Dignidad and the DINA in Parral, he was found dead. Carlos Alberto Carrasco Matus and Rodolfo Valentín González Pérez, both DINA guards, disappeared when they adopted humanitarian attitudes toward the prisoners. According to Michael Townley's statements, Manuel Leyton Robles, a DINA agent, died after receiving a dose of Sarin gas. This happened after he was arrested for robbery and confessed that it was a mission that had been ordered by his superior, Germán Jorge Barriga Muñoz, alias "Jaime."

There are other cases of former DINA agents and employees whose deaths occurred under suspicious circumstances. I'm referring to the aforementioned examples because I'm somewhat familiar with them.

The colonel took it upon himself to stoke a series of myths. One of them was the battle against international communism, a war supposedly led by Moscow. This allowed him to brutally repress the internal opposition, carry out operations to eliminate people abroad, and also to raise additional funds that filled the DINA's coffers. The colonel organized meetings each month with business leaders and gave them a speech about the domestic situation, the danger of the subversives, and international communism. The business leaders were terrified and contributed money. His advisors in the finance and business sector, among them Pedro Diet, Manuel Augusto Palacios Burgos, Lautaro Villar, and Marcos Acuña, organized these meetings. Officer Villar committed suicide.

The colonel personally kept people and dignitaries from every influential national sector informed about his views on the state of the nation.

The colonel realized that, in spite of the support from a few priests and from the most conservative sector in the Catholic Church, his supporters would be unable to make Cardinal Silva Henríquez and the bishops involved with marginalized sectors accept his position regarding a war of annihilation. This led him to support the regime's contact with the Pentecostal Methodist Church, which lent legitimacy to the goals of the dictatorship. The regime became ecumenical, and the TeDeum mass took place in 1976 in the Pentecostal Methodist Cathedral located at 3644 Alameda.

On Pinochet's recommendation, the Pro-Peace Committee closed its doors on November 27, 1975. At that time, Father Fernando Salas, Father Patricio Cariola, and Georgina Ocaranza, the committee's secretary who was several months pregnant, were all under arrest. The lawyer who headed the Judicial Department, José Zalaquett, was being held incommunicado at Cuatro Alamos. However, the colonel was unable to halt the Vicariate of Solidarity's legal actions or obtain the support of the Catholic Church. He reacted by organizing assassination attempts. One I can mention was the attack that was led by the BIM (Metropolitan Intelligence Brigade) unit against Bishop Alvear, Bishop González, and Bishop Ariztía when they returned from Río Bamba, Ecuador.

There were also attempts to plant electronic listening devices and to recruit domestic service personnel as informants at the house at Punta de Tralca, the bishops meeting place. The DINA also committed acts to intimidate employees at the Vicariate of Solidarity. The Vicariate's lawyer, Hernán Montealegre, was detained on May 16, 1976. On March 30, 1977, the DINA's unit in Valdivia, which was led by Juan Zanzani, set fire to the radio station "The Voice of the Coast" because its programming supported the rural development of farming sectors in Osorno and neighboring areas. I heard about that last event when Major Zanzani told Rolf Wenderoth about it on the day he came to report the act to the director of operations, Pedro Espinoza Bravo. Bishop Carlos Camus, Bishop Tomás González, and Bishop Jorge Hourton's movements were all under permanent surveillance. That was especially true after Monsignor Camus' statement as Secretary of the Episcopal Conference on

October 8, 1975. In brief, he stated that unemployment in Chile was over the officially recognized figure of 20 percent, that the country was living in a climate of deep hate, and that the Church would continue to be attacked because it had defended those who suffered political persecution, unemployed workers, and families with nothing to eat, in other words, the majority of Chileans.

Besides his speeches on the myth of the war with international communism, the colonel used the DINA in "acts of armed propaganda," such as creating and distributing pamphlets and "miguelitos," which were attributed to the MIR.[52] He used these to "prove" to the regime that subversion was still active, and he received authorization to intensify the repression to the point of annihilation.

Only an "enemy with an active presence" could give the colonel the arguments so that the military government would profess and adhere to a doctrine of national security. In that context of war, the DINA became necessary, and that is how it obtained the resources for its growth.

In a regime where all power was exercised by the military or civilian supporters and where the opposition is categorized as subversion at the service of international communism, the DINA grew in a disproportionate way, as did the colonel's power. He had breakfast each day with Augusto Pinochet and gave him a report on the situation, a document that was created by the DINA's Center of Operations.

The colonel used all kinds of resources to legitimize the DINA. He broadened the definition of enemies to include not only international communism and leftist organizations, but also those who were starting to defend human rights. He decided to show that the DINA was the only appropriate intelligence apparatus, which caused conflicts with other repressive organizations. He led counterintelligence measures against his colleagues in the army and other branches of the armed forces. He widened the scope of his actions outside of the country by creating Operation Condor, and he sent agents to several countries. In this war that no longer involved just the opposition, the DINA was developing its information-gathering networks throughout the entire society.

At its peak, the DINA became an enormous institution that was difficult to control. The majority of the personnel had administrative duties. There were fewer employees who were directly involved in crimi-

---

52. "Miguelito" was the name used to refer to a rubber-coated nail. When several of these were thrown into the street they could cause flat tires.

nal activities. With the information available today, it is feasible to deduce that the colonel compartmentalized the real DINA elite. The most loyal employees held different public positions from the DINA personnel who were apparently disconnected from planning operations of annihilation. They advised and helped the colonel plan actions that are public knowledge today, including assassinations and cover-ups both in Chile and in other countries. Examples include the assassination of Chile's former vice-president and former commander in chief of the army, Carlos Prats, and his wife, Sofía Cuthbert on September 30, 1974; the attempted assassination of former vice-president of Chile, Bernardo Leighton, and his wife, Anita Fresno on October 6, 1975; the assassination of the Chilean government's former vice-chancellor, Orlando Letelier del Solar, and his secretary, Ronnie Moffit on September 21, 1976; Operation Colombo and the "List of the 119," which was released on July 23, 1975.[53]

During the DINA's existence, the personnel had overestimated the colonel. They talked about his intelligence, his ability to rule, his enthusiasm to oversee all information and every situation, his absolute control over his subordinates, his management of the numerous businesses he used to obtain additional financing for the DINA, and also his "good luck." This was an image the colonel himself strove to foster.

Besides believing in his own abilities, the colonel truly believed in his "good luck," which allowed him to fulfill his mission. However, his own overestimation led him to deceive himself. His closest collaborators surrounded him like a clique that not only filled his ears with praise but also gradually started isolating him from the rest of the staff and from reality. The men who built a wall around the colonel were Vianel Valdivieso Cervantes, Alejandro Burgos de Beer, and Juan Morales Salgado, among others.

---

53. The "List of the 119" refers to the Chilean military regime's attempt to explain the deaths of 119 Chilean citizens who were believed to be disappeared. According to press releases offering the official version, these deaths had occurred outside of the country and were the result of infighting among factions of the MIR in Argentina and Brazil. Witnesses, however, including Arce, have testified that they saw members of this famous list in detention centers throughout Chile, and subsequent investigations have confirmed that the information offered by the Chilean media was fabricated with the assistance of intelligence forces in other countries. This political maneuver is known as "Operation Colombo." All 119 people are still disappeared to this day.

29

CONTRERAS'S PROMOTION TO GENERAL

As I was trying to determine where and how I was going to live, the Letelier case was increasingly the focus of press attention. The Colonel continued meeting with some of his officers to discuss it. One day, Rolf called me into the office and opened a briefcase to show me a file with documents. They were photocopies of an entire dossier that must have come from the United States where the DINA was being accused of the Orlando Letelier assassination.

Rolf was upset and annoyed as he paced around the office smoking one cigarette after another, "And now what are we going to do? That idiot! He's a complete imbecile."

He was referring to Espinoza Bravo. Seeing him like that made me sure that the DINA was responsible for those deaths. I didn't know how to act. Rolf never admitted to me that the DINA had killed people. He didn't do it that time either, but he let his anger slip at Espinoza Bravo's obvious incompetence in what I assumed had been his command of that operation and others like it.

I confess I didn't dare ask Rolf Wenderoth anything. Those were anxious days inside Headquarters. My boss was almost never at the office. After all that time, with everything I had been through, seen, and heard, it seemed highly probable to me that the DINA would have planned an operation like that one. What terrified me was supposing that Rolf Wenderoth, the only person I trusted a little bit, the one who had cared for and sheltered me, had taken part in it.

During that time, Colonel Contreras was promoted to general. All the offices received a memo communicating the promotion. Everyone at work was happy. Contreras was a man who demanded unconditional commitment, real or otherwise, from his men, and everyone at least feigned loyalty.

Contreras Sepúlveda's promotion eased the atmosphere at Headquarters. It was like a sigh that relieved the tension that had been growing in those days. The promotion made people assume that Contreras would be the director for a long time to come. Everyone assumed that the director had somehow taken care of the situation, as usual. Part of the female personnel, those who were Pinochet supporters by osmosis and who couldn't see past the ends of their noses, believed it had all been a mistake and that surely that was why it had been cleared up.

I remember that day as if it were yesterday. I had a new office that was small but functional. It was my first private office, and it was adjacent to Rolf Wenderoth's. What I liked most was the fact that they agreed to my request to cover the walls with corkboard so I could organize my work there. I took the memo announcing Contreras's promotion to the rank of general and tacked it on the wall. I looked at it for hours. . . .

I was speechless, lost in thought. I looked at Contreras's signature. He was now a general. Because of his seniority, not only had he reached the pinnacle of his career, but he could now pull rank with colonels who had more seniority. And he could also establish relationships on a par with generals who were rumored to be less skilled or at least bothered by the existence of the CNI (ex DINA) and its methods.

Apparently, Contreras Sepúlveda had gone too far in some of his counterintelligence duties directed against the armed forces and the army. But now that he was a general, he would be untouchable. As I was drifting in that sea of thoughts, my purse suddenly caught my eye. It was the purse an agent would carry, sharp, made of leather, and with space for everything. María Alicia had designed the model for that purse, and Espinoza Bravo had them made. I always complained that it was like having us wear a sign saying "I'm with the DINA." They were all alike, and they came in black, brown, or burgundy. But I ended up using it anyway. They were free, attractive, and comfortable.

I could see the contents of the purse in my mind: the handgun, emergency flares, ammunition, teargas, hidden compartments for different documents and ID cards. Then I thought about the material gains and their price. What was left of me? Contreras's memo came off the wall and grew before my eyes. I saw it floating as it grew larger and larger. Would he fall? Would he be torn to shreds someday? I had to start planning my escape, at least in my mind. All of that was ridiculous. Why have those weapons if I wouldn't use them?

I went to Rolf's office and told him I needed to talk to him. He pointed to a chair.

"Rolf, I know it may seem premature to you, but I need you to help me. But first, a question, Why did you suggest that I not take the secretarial course I was interested in a while back?"

"Because I thought it was too soon. You were recently given your freedom, so it was basically for your security."

"Would you help me get permission to study something now?"

"No!"

"Just like that? Just a no? May I ask why?"

"I don't want you to go, and I don't think the boss does either."

"Rolf, you're not going to spend the rest of your life here."

"So we'll talk then, when I go."

"Rolf, you are going to force me to ask the general for permission."

"You're a tyrant! Have you ever done anything you didn't want to?"

"Yes, Rolf, not just once, and I assure you that once was more than enough. Can't you even imagine the price I've paid? Now I have to think about the future, Rolf. I don't know if I have one, but I need to think I do. And that means not only leaving this institution that now calls itself the CNI. I must also be able to support my son, buy his clothes and his food, and pay for his tuition and a place to live."

I spoke without anger but resolutely, with passion. I had gotten the courage and I couldn't back down.

"Will you help me?"

"You know I will. I want the best for you. I can see you've already made up your mind. What do you want to study?"

"I'm not sure, maybe computers. Do you think the general would help me get into the USACH?"[54]

"I don't know. We'll have to talk about it. I'll wait for the right moment to suggest it to him."

"Thanks, Rolf. Thank you."

I left thinking about how I needed to start building some skills. But I thought, people on the outside live differently. Can I live like that? Who am I? Am I who I am? I'm almost thirty years old. Will I still be as flexible

54. USACH refers to the Universidad de Santiago de Chile, one of the Chilean capital's most well known universities.

266

as I was before? Will I be able to do without all this, like I think I can? Won't all the doors already be closed to me? I looked at the rubber-tree plant and the philodendron. We had come to the office together, and my plants had grown a lot. I thought about my son. He was safe with his father. I couldn't bring him back to the same world. I realized my son had adapted to the situation. Everybody spoiled him. For him, the DINA was just my superiors or mom's colleagues. I'm sure he doesn't remember, or maybe he does. Some day I'll ask him. . . . When I took him with me I told him, "Rafael, you were little when I didn't come home anymore, but I don't want to keep lying now that we're going to live together. It's not true that I was working outside of Santiago. I was in prison." He is my treasure, I thought, with indescribable tenderness. I said to myself, "If I'm not as strong as I used to be, I'll have to find the strength somewhere, but I have to try."

A dark past, an uncertain future. . . .

CONTRERAS IS REPLACED

I was in my office on November 3, 1977 when the commander called me in and handed me a document. It was another memo. I read it. It was also signed by General Contreras. It stated that he was retiring as of that day and that he would be replaced as director of the CNI by another army general who was in retirement, Odlanier Mena Salinas.

While the previous memo, the one about the change from the DINA to the CNI, had troubled me, this one about Manuel Contreras's removal from office threw me for a loop. Everything would be worse. How could I think about leaving? I couldn't even imagine what would happen to me, to all three of us. I reacted immediately,

"Rolf, do Alejandra and María Alicia know about this?"

"I imagine that at this very instant their superiors are going over the same memo with their staff. Espinoza probably knew about it a bit earlier."

"Rolf, even though the three of us have drifted apart quite a bit, I believe now is the time for us to get together. Do you think Pedro Espinoza knows anything else?"

Ketty, who never interrupted us when we were talking, came in to inform the commander that he had a call from what was known as the Office of Support Staff. He was supposed to have a meeting with the general.

When he returned, Rolf asked me to get all the documents on a female informant he was working with and whose contact information he had received from Pedro Espinoza. She was a female friend or a woman he knew who worked in a developmental institute, DESAL, which was located on Carmen Silva Street.[55] She regularly gave him documents with information pertaining to workers' training and nongovernmental organizations. He personally took all the DESAL documents and others from the support staff files. Then he kept them in his car and gave Ketty orders to shred the other papers.

Rolf remained in his office to meet with the heads of the internal intelligence divisions. I went with Ketty to the large shredders where I ran into María Alicia and other workers who were practically standing in line to destroy the contents of huge dossiers.

When I returned to the office and looked through the files, all I found were press reports and news clippings along with all the administrative paperwork from the Office of Support Staff. I asked Rolf to talk with Espinoza to see if he could obtain more information. The colonel wasn't in the office of the director of operations. Instead, he was at one of the apartments located at the corner of Belgrado and Vicuña Mackena. He met with him as soon as we arrived. I stayed to talk with María Alicia in the lobby. She didn't have any more information, but she said she supposed her superior was going to immediately be removed from the institution.

When he got out of the meeting, Rolf told us to call Alejandra so she could meet with us immediately. During that time, she was working with Commander Raúl Iturriaga Neumann. When the three of us were there, Rolf informed us that the general ordered them to give us fake IDs different from the ones the DINA had officially given us, in case something unexpected should happen. At the time we understood that to mean in case the CNI and the new leadership decided to eliminate us. He said a special agent would come for us soon at a meeting place in the Providencia neighborhood.

Rolf drove the three of us there in his car, and that's where I found out that the agent was Michael Vernon Townley. We had our pictures taken for the ID in a studio at a gallery in Providencia. Then we went with him to the house where he lived, the one on Vía Naranja in the neighborhood of Lo Curro.

55. DESAL refers to the Centro para el Desarrollo Económico y Social de América Latina (Center for the Economic and Social Development of Latin America).

MICHAEL TOWNLEY[56]

In a manner consistent with his political ideology, and as a militant with the rightwing group Patria y Libertad, Michael Townley immediately accepted the dictatorship's fundamental project. His qualifications, which included intellectual aptitude, experience with terrorist groups from the extreme right during the Popular Unity period, contacts in Chile and abroad, and foreign citizenship, quickly turned him into one of the DINA's most important agents.

Michael Townley's presence at DINA Headquarters was frequent. The less important employees weren't sure exactly what he did, but he came for meetings with Eduardo Iturriaga Neumann, from the Economic Department, which was a front for Foreign Operations. He also met with Pedro Espinoza Bravo, the director of operations, as well as Vianel Valdivieso Cervantes, Contreras's right-hand man who was in charge of telecommunications. In other words, Townley wasn't just a DINA agent. He also had direct access to the highest level. The general was forced to resign from the CNI because of a decision by the military junta based on the critical situation that Pinochet and Contreras were facing as a result of the U.S. State Department investigations into the assassinations of Orlando Letelier Solar and his secretary. On that day, the close relationship that existed between Michael Townley and the general became very clear to me. The agent attended the conciliatory reception for the recently deposed director of the CNI and he received from him the order to create fake IDs for us in the event that Alejandra, María Alicia, or I had problems with the CNI's new authorities.

It was shocking for personnel at Headquarters when they discovered that Michael was the "blond Chilean" involved in Orlando Letelier's assassination. It was even more unfathomable when news of his deportation was in the paper *La Segunda* on April 8, 1978. Despite the elite's

---

56. Michael Townley is perhaps the most famous U.S. citizen to be openly involved with the Chilean military regime. He worked as a DINA agent and was also affiliated with the CIA. His most famous act was involvement in the assassination of Orlando Letelier (see note 34). He worked directly with DINA commander Colonel Manuel Contreras in planning this assassination and carried it out with the help of Cuban exiles Guillermo Novo and Alvin Ross. Townley was expelled from Chile in 1978. He returned to the United States where he pled guilty to one count of conspiracy to murder a foreign official. In a plea bargain, however, and in exchange for providing testimony against the Cuban exiles he had recruited, he obtained a reduced sentence and federal protection for himself and his family.

secrecy, it was easy to see that there was more than one struggle going on. Contreras and Mena were struggling for power. The ex-DINA and the CNI fought to try to have their interests take priority, with the common denominator being to protect the military and its commander in chief from collapse. Even when Contreras was "imprisoned" at the Hosmil, he retained important powers within the CNI. That, along with the massive dismissal of people Mena labeled "Contrerists," generated a climate of confusion. The agents and employees who had been trained under Contreras, and who were sure no one would be touched because their superior wouldn't allow it, noticed, without understanding why, that the new authorities acted differently, and they didn't realize the depth of the conflict. For the CNI's personnel it was beyond comprehension that the press at the time was publishing information about the betrayals and loyalties of Michael Townley, officers René Miguel Riveros Valderrama and Manuel Rolando Mosquera Jarpa, Armando Fernández Larios, Pedro Espinoza Bravo, Raúl Eduardo Iturriaga Neumann, and Michael Townley's secretary, María Rosa Alejandra Damiani Serrano, alias "Roxana."

After Michael Townley made our IDs, he dropped the three of us off at Headquarters where Rolf was waiting for us. We went with him to General Contreras's house.

When we arrived at the house on Príncipe de Gales, we were able to observe that there were members of the general's personal guard there, that is personnel there from the CNI. I don't know if they were still employed by the institution at that time or if they had been fired and were now working for the general.

I don't share Michael's political ideology, nor do I support his actions, but I believe there is an important distinction to be made. Michael Townley was a DINA agent who was loyal to commitments he made. Michael was betrayed when he was deported and, even then, he didn't make any deals with the United States until he was given permission to do so by the military lawyer Orozco, who allowed him to provide information regarding some of the DINA's operations.

FAREWELL RECEPTION AT THE GENERAL'S HOUSE

As we passed through the security gate surrounding the property, the guards announced our arrival, and the general received us personally. We greeted him. Colonel Gerónimo Pantoja was with him and seemed happy to see us. I was quite biased when it came to Colonel Pantoja. I admit it was mostly due to Wenderoth Pozo's influence since he and the colonel apparently did not get along well.

That display of happiness bothered me. It seemed put on. Rumor already had it that he would be staying in the CNI, which, to the staff, seemed like an opportunistic attitude. People expected him to resign and support his superior. It was said that Pantoja was allying himself with Odlanier Mena Salinas and the DINE.[57]

When it was my turn to greet him, I avoided his embrace and simply said dryly, "Good evening, Colonel."

The colonel picked up on my snub and left visibly annoyed by it. The general motioned to Rolf that we should go inside the house and have something to drink. He said he was going to hold a series of short meetings in his office and that he would call us soon.

We walked through some of the rooms in his house. In one small sitting room, Rolf said hello to the general's wife and introduced us. We had just sat down with her when one of the bodyguards told Rolf his superior needed him. María Alicia and Alejandra went over to a group of officers they knew. I stayed with the general's wife a while, and we exchanged some polite remarks. It was the first time I had seen her.

The majority of the DINA's officers were there and, clustered in various groups, carrying on animated discussions. Several of them looked surprised to see us there. As I was going to the bar, I had the opportunity to see Michael Townley as he was arriving. He looked different. He had been wearing jeans and a jacket just a few hours earlier. Now he was dressed in an impeccable and elegant light gray suit. His hair was slightly wet, which meant he had just taken a shower.

When the general met with us, he asked us to be calm. He said he had been talking to Colonel Pantoja about us, that he would be sure we were all right, and that we would continue working as usual. He said he was sure he would respect us in our capacity as employees.

I mentioned I had some doubts about why Colonel Pantoja was staying with the CNI. General Contreras answered with his usual attitude of being the one running the show and said, "The colonel is staying because I ordered him to."

He was the same as always with us, attentive. We informed him of the

57. DINE (Dirección de Inteligencia del Ejército) refers to Chile's army intelligence apparatus.

steps we recently took with Michael Townley, and we showed him the new IDs. We left. Rolf drove us home. When we arrived, I told him I didn't trust Pantoja or Mena or anybody else.

"Rolf, and what if I take my vacation time?"

"That could be."

"And what if I go up north and use the occasion to see my son?"

Rolf got my vacation approved through the Human Resources Department, and I left. A few days later he suggested I return. There wasn't a choice. The CNI's director had assured us we would keep working, and he had even met with Alejandra and María Alicia.

I was in his hands, resigned to accept whatever happened. The trip home took thirty-three hours by bus back then. Each second felt like it was pulling me toward darkness. I couldn't do anything about it, but let myself be pulled by that machine.

INCIDENT WITH COLONEL PANTOJA

I arrived at my apartment. It seemed emptier without my son whose big, dark, intelligent eyes scared away my fears and forced me to struggle with myself and hold on. I left my bag on the floor and sat down looking at the fish tank. It was my son's. The fish were swimming, oblivious. At least they were all right. A cousin had agreed to feed them while I was gone.

I called Rolf who arrived at the house a few minutes later.

"They haven't thrown me out yet," he said smiling. "But it's going to happen tomorrow or the day after. There's almost no one left anymore. They're firing people left and right, every day."

"Rolf, what's going to happen to me?"

"You don't have any choice but to show up tomorrow."

"I want to resign."

"Now's not the right time, Luz. Not only that, it's the worst time. Keep working as usual. Let them get to know you."

"I won't be able to bring my son. . . ."

"They are waiting for you to give them the apartment."

"I'll do it tomorrow."

Since Espinoza Bravo was being held along with Manuel Contreras and Armando Fernández Larios at the Military Hospital, Rolf had to deal with Colonel Pantoja. He explained my housing problem to him, and he ordered me to speak with him. I went immediately.

"Your superior informed me that you don't have anywhere to live."

"That's true, sir. I haven't found anything I can afford."

"María Alicia has been given an apartment in tower 6 in the San Borja Complex. The three of you can live there. You must tell me your decision now."

I thought a minute. María Alicia had refused to live with my son in the past, and now wasn't the time to cause any friction.

"Thank you, sir, but I need a place where I can live with my son."

Pantoja got angry and yelled at me, telling me I had one hour to give them the apartment in tower 12.

"I know, sir, and everything is ready. As soon as I leave here, I will hand it over."

I returned to the office, called María Alicia, and asked her if I could store my things in her apartment for a few days. She said that wouldn't be a problem, and that I could stay in one of the rooms while I didn't have anywhere else to go.

ROLF WENDEROTH'S RESIGNATION

I continued working. I didn't have a home. Some days I went to stay with María Alicia, and other days I stayed with relatives. The tension was building at work. Every time the phone rang I felt like they were calling Rolf to tell him he was out of the CNI. It happened. Not only did they inform him that he was dismissed, but they also included him on a list at every CNI entrance and guardhouse stating that he could not enter any office or building belonging to the institution.

At least that's what he told me back then, but on July 1, 1992, during a confrontation in court, he confessed to me that he had resigned. Perhaps he didn't tell me so I wouldn't blame him for leaving me alone there. That day he hugged me tightly, and I was unable to hold back the tears. I watched him leave indignantly, and I felt orphaned.

He was temporarily assigned to the Engineers Unit, which was on Santo Domingo Street. That was where Contreras had set up his offices. Then he left for Tejas Verdes, to the School of Engineers, as the second in command and assistant governor of San Antonio. It was a good assignment for Rolf, who was happy to resume his military life.

I continued doing my work in the division and in the ENI, and they appointed me head professor of marxism in Wenderoth's absence. The course changed its name. Now it was called Subversive Movements.

273

I talked with "Max" about that one day. He was still at the ENI, but he expected them to inform him at any minute that he was returning to the army.

When Rolf left, a whole line of officers came through Internal Intelligence. The first one was Colonel Juan Jara Cornejo, who later took over as director of operations. One day I saw army Colonel Daniel Concha (retired from service), who had arrived in the office of the deputy director a few months before.

"Miss Ana María," he said, using my alias. "*Miss,* right?"

"Yes, sir."

"But you have a son, don't you? Single mother?"

"No, sir, separated," I said in a calm voice. I knew he wanted to upset me. He was a truly disgusting old man.

"Interesting. . . . Anita, I have been informed that you are an excellent collaborator. I want you to know that you are going to be even better off than before. You will be in charge of your division. You will have two secretaries, and you will have the office where Rolf Wenderoth used to be. How does that sound?"

"If it is an order, sir. . . ." I thought it sounded good since then I would be able to call Tejas Verdes and talk with Rolf on the internal phone as long as they didn't take it out. There was one in that office.

"You can move your things right away. Continue with the press report as you have done until now."

"If that is all, sir, permission to be dismissed."

"What good form, Anita. . . . I'm referring to your military form, which looks and sounds very good when you use it," he said with a smile. "But don't call me sir. Say 'my colonel.'"

"At your orders, my colonel."

"Anita, I know the general and the commander really looked out for you. Don't worry. Nothing is going to change. I know that Commander Wenderoth bought you breakfast every day. I assume you have economic troubles. I would like to buy you breakfast."

"Thank you, sir, but that isn't necessary. I can buy my own breakfast," I said dryly, thinking to myself, "If this creep thinks he's inherited me along with the job, he is very mistaken. . . ."

I left with the idea that the colonel was going to make life difficult for me. Everyone knew that he was or said he was Colonel Pantoja's friend. That already made me uneasy.

Rolf called me every day, and he came to Santiago to see me for a few hours every time he could get away. Sometimes we met at María Alicia's apartment. On other occasions it was in his car on a corner near Headquarters when I was leaving the office. We had coffee at a soda fountain or we just stayed there talking.

I continued looking for a place to rent. I kept my spending at a minimum. All I ate was the lunch they gave us at Headquarters. I had to save money to put together what was required for a security deposit. I started looking for a night school.

Around the end of January, Rolf said to me, "Why don't you bring your son to San Antonio? I can find an apartment for you. They are cheaper than in Santiago. Perhaps your mom would want to come with him. I would take care of the safety of both of them." I said I would think about it.

Colonel Concha wouldn't stop bothering me, not just me, all the women. He was the perfect caricature of the military letch. It was as if being a man to him meant that he couldn't let any woman walk by without at least trying to get himself a good grope.

INTERVAL IN SAN ANTONIO

I found a school near Headquarters. I could arrive in time for classes since they started at six-thirty in the evening. I talked with my mother, and she decided to help me so I could bring my son back. Rolf found an apartment in Barrancas, a few blocks away from the governor's office. It was pretty inexpensive, and they would be safe. It would be a summer place for my mom and my son, and I would have somewhere to go on weekends and maybe other days too.

When I rented the apartment in Barrancas, Rolf sent me a truck from the School of Engineers, and I took my things out of María Alicia's apartment. Since I only had one bed, Rolf lent me two others. They belonged to the regiment.

I feel genuine gratitude toward one of the secretaries at the Undersecretariat, Maribel. She said to me every day, "Anita, do you have somewhere to sleep? You know you can come home with me. My parents have grown fond of you."

Sometimes I went to her house with her. Rolf got me a free pass with a bus company, so I started traveling to Barrancas every day. I got there at about ten-thirty, and I was with my mom and my son. I slept there with them, and I left on the first bus to Santiago at five-thirty. I was at the office by seven-thirty.

275

On March 6, 1978, classes started at the Computer School. I couldn't go every day anymore. If the class went a little overtime, I missed the last bus.

I carried all my things in a small suitcase I kept in the office. I always carried a change of underwear, a toothbrush, and soap in my purse.

Around March 10, 1978, I still wasn't able to find a place to rent in Santiago, and mom wanted to return already. Besides that, there was the problem that all the schools had started classes already.

Around that time I realized that "Pilar," one of the secretaries who worked with me, had started dating the colonel. She knew about what I was doing because she was studying at the same institute I was. So when the colonel started creating more problems than usual, I assumed he knew about my activities. Just as I was about to leave he would call me and give me urgent work to do. I couldn't go to class, and I started escaping through the back door to the office with Maribel's help. She closed it from inside. That worked for a few days until the colonel realized I was leaving without passing by his office door.

He forced me to show I had a residence in Santiago. I gave my grandmother's address, which was even real since she rented me a room for my son and me so I could bring him to Santiago. The colonel started sending for me at my grandmother's house at night rather frequently. Sometimes he had me wait, and then would say he was sorry, that it was no longer an emergency and that I could go. On other occasions he asked me to write something.

In spite of all that, I made sure I was able to go to class, even if it was for a little while. I was able to pass the beginning courses, and I was able to get my son into a good school in Santiago, Carlton College. The only problem was that it was far away, which is why we left together every day before seven o'clock in the morning. My son came home by himself. And since there was no phone at home, I gave him some change so he could call me when he arrived. I couldn't rest until my son called me.

30

THE CNI INVESTIGATES THE DINA

I was working at the office one afternoon when Colonel Concha arrived along with Andrés Terrisse Castro, an electrical engineer who specialized in computing. He was also Italo Seccatore Gómez's advisor in L-5, which was the CNI's Computer Unit. The colonel introduced me to him and asked me to assist him in any way I could. He said he needed to understand the method we used for processing and analyzing public information.

Andrés came to my office for several days. I suggested to him that it would be better to meet in the afternoon. That way I would have already handed in my work, and I would be able to assist him. When he fully understood everything, he mentioned that it would be very useful for me to speak with his superior, Major Seccatore.

I explained to him that they should arrange the meeting since I couldn't leave the office. The major and Andrés informed me that they were making inquiries about the DINA. The questions referred to work methods. It seemed like they were interviewing other personnel at the same time since they had a lot of details, at least about internal intelligence.

There was some emphasis on having me express my personal views on certain points. I was careful not to say anything I hadn't told the DINA already.

They also asked me about the DINA's compartmentalization. I said that, in effect, Commander Wenderoth maintained a certain level of discretion regarding what were most likely secret matters.

There was a special topic for me with questions regarding the period I spent as a political militant. I answered them. I had talked about it so many times.

ANOTHER MEETING WITH PANTOJA

Around noon, Colonel Concha called me into his office to tell me he was very annoyed because he often couldn't find me when he needed me to do some work for him. I told him that surprised me since my timesheet at the guard's office clearly indicated that I arrived at least half an hour early every morning and that I had never left before five-thirty.

He mentioned that in the past I had never left right at the end of the day. Since I supposed he knew I had been taking classes, I decided to tell him. He told me I had ignored an important rule of military service by undertaking activities for which I had not received authorization.

I said to him, "Colonel, studying is something that falls within the arena of personal choice, and I believe I know the rules of military service. I would appreciate your telling me where it says I cannot study."

He got upset and ordered me to meet with Colonel Gerónimo Pantoja who had a list of complaints about my behavior. He added that from that moment on I could not continue studying without authorization from the service. Colonel Pantoja made me wait a while outside his office. Mireya, his secretary, gave me a cup of coffee. When Gerónimo Pantoja met with me, he was visibly upset and said, "I have been informed that you frequently travel to Las Rocas de Santo Domingo. That is going to end today! You must end that relationship with Commander Wenderoth immediately! That's an order!"

In those days I was a lot more impatient, intolerant, and vehement than I am now. That, along with the fact that I was scared, made me especially aggressive.

"Colonel, I haven't traveled to Las Rocas for years. I go to Barrancas because that's where my home is. You know I don't have enough money to rent a house in Santiago, and it is cheaper there. My mother and my son live in the apartment, sir. That's why I go. Regarding the commander, I suppose you won't believe it if I tell you there is nothing between us. As far as I'm concerned, Colonel, that's my personal problem, and I am not willing to make my private matters public knowledge at the service. Besides, if you have some kind of a problem, tell the commander about it. He's the military officer. I'm a civilian, sir, and I will not accept that kind of meddling."

"You listen to me, Miss Luz." He stood up and started shouting. "Don't forget who you are and that on one of those trips the MIR is going to kill you any day now. Or have you forgotten who you are?"

"No, sir. I know exactly who I am. Just like I know that if one of these days someone kills me it won't be the MIR."

"You're way out of line! You're dismissed!"

"At your orders, Colonel. I'm leaving."

As I left, I realized the colonel's shouting could be heard outside his office and that Mireya, his secretary, was giving me a frightened look. On purpose, I smiled and said to her, "See you, Mireya. Thanks for the coffee. It was delicious."

As I walked to the office I felt myself starting to cry. It wasn't sadness. It was like before: powerlessness. Where would I go? There was nowhere for me. I had to make that place. I would keep studying somehow. I looked at the time and avoided the entrance that went by Colonel Concha. It was twelve-thirty, lunchtime. In fifteen minutes I would meet Rolf a few blocks from there.

I was sure they knew about it. I thought to myself that they had probably tapped the internal phone. But I was going anyway. If they wanted to stop me they would have to tie me down. As I walked through the front door on Belgrado Street, I ran into Sergio, Rolf's brother, who was still with the CNI. He asked me how I was. I told him about the incident with the assistant director. He asked me where I was going. I told him the truth about that too. He said, "I'll go with you. I'll take you there and then I'll go." We walked together for the few blocks. Sergio asked me, "Did he really say that to you? What a bunch of assholes!"

He said hello to his brother and left. Rolf and I talked right there in the car. I only had forty-five minutes left of my lunch break. I had to go back to the office.

I told him what had happened. Rolf tried to lift my spirits. We agreed to see each other the following Saturday. He would stop by my apartment in Barrancas.

COLONEL SUAU

Colonel Juan Jara Cornejo had been working in Colonel Espinoza's position for a couple of weeks. I don't know why but one day the staff at the CNI received a memo saying that army colonel Suau would replace Jara Cornejo.

Colonel Suau took over the position. Carmen Avila Ferrada moved into what had been María Alicia's office. While the DINA existed, she had been Commander Arturo Ureta Sire's secretary in Foreign Intelligence.

According to Daniel Concha, Colonel Suau was his friend and completely trusted by Colonel Pantoja. I was called into his office on many occasions. He explained each of the mistakes in my reports with long lectures.

In previous years I had personally typed my reports and respected the format that fit the content point by point. Since I knew a secretary was going to type the report that was collated from all of the undersecretariats and the Directorate of Operations, I never worried about details like the heading or how to write the date.

With the colonel I found out that, in addition to including the date, I had to write the hour in the twenty-four hour system. He would yell at me, "Time is written with four digits!" I said all right and decided to give my work to one of the secretaries who, I supposed, knew the format well. I was surprised when he continued sending the report back to me with corrections all over in red pen. It wasn't the content. It was the format. He measured the margins with a ruler. It was exasperating. The girls kept nervously typing right up to the deadline to hand it in. One day I asked to meet with the colonel.

When I was in front of him, I told him that, besides the fact that his actions seemed absurd to me and inappropriate in a director, the only people he was harming were some very young secretaries who cried while they typed. Because the situation was becoming a serious problem for them, I asked him to give me a signed and detailed description of the format he wanted.

The colonel used the excuse that he didn't have it handy and that he would send it to me. I left. He never bothered me again about the format. He never sent me an example, but he never spoke to me again either.

Colonel Suau was the kind of person who thought a report was bad if it was short. But when you gave him enormous files, before he even looked at them, he would say, "This is good."

When Rolf Wenderoth and Iturriaga Neumann left the CNI, Alejandra returned to the Undersecretariat, to her previous position as an analyst in C-2, the section that worked with information on the Christian Democrats and the MIR. María Alicia remained for a while in the Directorate of Operations.

I was the oldest of the women who worked in Internal Intelligence. I had turned thirty. There were even girls who were really young, like Maribel, who I don't think was over twenty or twenty-one. And she looked a lot younger. Since Daniel Concha often harassed them, the girls usually got behind me when he was around, as if they were looking for protection.

That, along with my frequent conflicts with Concha, Suau, and Pantoja gave me a reputation with the female personnel as someone they could trust while the leadership saw me as difficult and hard to control.

The girls often came to me to tell me about their problems with their superiors. After all, the three colonels were the overall boss, the director of operations, and the CNI's assistant director, the complete line of command.

I knew it was a delicate situation, but I was convinced that if I let them get away with it they would make it even harder for me. I started feeling tired. I had never had trouble getting out of bed before, and despite the fact I was exhausted, I couldn't get to sleep. I started taking vitamins. It was no use. One morning I simply didn't wake up. My grandmother told my parents. I had a high fever.

THE TRIAL AND THE INCIDENT WITH COLONEL CONCHA

My mom came to see me and called the military doctor. I had a lung infection. My right lung was acting up again. The doctor told me he would take care of arranging for my leave. Even so, I asked my mom to please look for a phone and call the colonel to tell him.

My parents told me that they could take care of me better and send my son off to school if I went to their house. They took me in a taxi.

I informed Rolf I was sick. He sent me his car with a driver from Tejas Verdes so I could go to my medical appointments and also to go apartment hunting so I wouldn't have to be exposed to the cold, which was quite severe that fall.

The Vicariate of Solidarity was still looking for me, which is why I didn't dare live with my parents. My grandmother told my dad that a car from the CNI had come and that they had asked to see me. She told them I was with my parents.

I asked my mom to please call the colonel again to see what was happening. She didn't have a chance because the social worker, Sara Aguila, arrived at the house with Alejandra. They were coming to verify that I was still using my medical leave. I still had a temperature. They were giving me large quantities of antibiotics, and I had an almost constant cough. I was clearly ill.

That same day, my grandmother called again saying that the CNI had gone to her house again, and that they were looking for me because of an indictment. I was frightened, and I went with my mother and my son to an aunt's house. I called Andrés Terrisse from my relative's apartment and told him what was happening.

Andrés came to see me. He calmed me down and told me to finish my medical leave. He said he would talk with Italo Seccatore, the head of the Computer Unit.

When this happened, I went back to the office. Colonel Concha told me there was an indictment that concerned me because a classified document on the Communist Youth Movement had disappeared. I asked him to at least tell me what the document was about since I didn't remember anything classified in my files. I said that apart from my administrative work, I only dealt with publicly available information.

He took out a piece of paper where there was a reference to some of the Communist Youth's activities abroad. I had a nearly photographic memory back then, so while he did that I said, "Colonel, all we have received on that topic—at least up until the time I went home on leave—is an article from the Cuban publication *Granma*. It's in the files. Besides, not only is it not classified, but I made photocopies of it and sent them to the Caupolicán Unit. I'm sure you signed that document, Colonel. I suppose you wouldn't think I would steal a document like that. If I had wanted to hide it, I wouldn't have sent it to the unit. Excuse me."

Without waiting for his permission, I called Ketty on the phone and asked her for the file. When she brought it, I asked her, "Ketty, do you remember a document we sent to Caupolicán about Communist Youth activities abroad. It was a photocopy."

"Yes, I'll bring it right away."

"Thank goodness for Ketty's memory," I thought to myself. Concha was moving around impatiently in his chair.

"Here it is, Colonel," Ketty said. "You signed it on Wednesday, March 7th of this year."

I took a deep breath. I was sure there was something behind this dirty trick. Something told me they didn't intend to kill me at that moment, but they were going to question me. That accusation didn't hold even the slightest weight. It would take me years to find out what was happening.

The colonel came closer to me and said, "I'm glad everything has been clarified, Anita. In any case, the indictment will still run its course."

282

He put his hand on my shoulder. He started running it down my body, and it was obvious it wasn't a friendly gesture. I was overwhelmed by that violence that I had built up within me years earlier when I was sexually attacked and raped. My right hand was on the desk. Without thinking, I picked up the ruler that was there and struck the colonel's face with it. A red streak appeared followed by some drops of blood. Of course, the edge was made of metal. I turned around and ran out. I ran into Major Seccatore outside. Without thinking, and unable to control myself, I said, "Major, please get me out of here. Please!"

He gave me a surprised look, but he agreed and took me to his office. He asked Patricia, his secretary, to bring us some coffee. Andrés Terrisse came in too.

I was very nervous. I tried to explain it to him, but I couldn't stop crying. After a while I told him what had happened and said I was scared. I asked him to please help me and said I couldn't go back to Internal Intelligence.

Italo asked Patricia not to forward any phone calls to him and to say I wasn't there, if anyone asked about me. Then he called Colonel Pantoja and asked him to meet with him. He went right away. Andrés stayed with me in Italo's office.

When he returned, Italo told me everything was settled. According to him, Colonel Pantoja had understood the situation and had agreed to send me to work at L-5. I relaxed without realizing that I was being manipulated into a situation that would last for years. Italo would later admit that to me in March 1980.

However, I had to go a couple more times to Internal Intelligence. I went for my personal things and then to testify at the court proceedings. It was a farce. The officer who acted as the prosecutor was Major Bejas. He was careful and respectful as he asked me some simple questions and wrote my answers. Basically what I said was that if I had wanted to harm the organization, that was not the ideal document for it, especially since I knew that there was an original in addition to the photocopy.

The trial cleared me of any wrongdoing. I started working at L-5. I didn't say good-bye to Colonel Concha or Colonel Suau. When they sent my résumé to my new boss, they allowed themselves a little revenge by including a paragraph that said, "She inexplicably did not show up to resign from her post, which constitutes a breach in the most basic etiquette." However, in Human Resources, they considered my previous recommendations and kept me in the highest category, List 1.

283

Part 3

31

For me, leaving Internal Intelligence meant starting a new phase. I was still a CNI employee, of course, but the thought of leaving, of breaking ties with the CNI was already present in me. I didn't have the strength to do it at that time. I believe that period was crucial for me to realize that I had to differentiate myself from them, even though I was a piece of trash.

IN THE CNI'S COMPUTER UNIT

After General Contreras's removal from office and his replacement by General Odlanier Mena Salinas, there were several changes within the institution. One of them was the attempt to transform L-5 into a support center for the leadership's administration. Major Italo Seccatore was appointed to head that unit. He received extensive financial support from General Mena to purchase equipment and hire personnel.

L-5 moved to one of the apartments located on the first floor of the building at 69 Vicuña Mackena. They completely remodeled the place because the teams needed more modern equipment at that point. They created a hidden floor for the electronic network cables, and L-5 was provided with a larger support system from the company COMDAT, representatives of Basic Four.[58] This company also trained the L-5 personnel.

There was also an army lieutenant assigned to L-5, in addition to the commander and the systems analyst. They hired three programmers as well, all civilians.

While the office on the corner of Belgrado and 69 Vicuña Mackena

58. This refers to Basic Four microcomputers.

was being remodeled, the leadership and the administration moved into the CNI offices located on Pocuro Street. There were other technical units working there, such as ID production, explosives, photography, video, makeup, and the like. Andrés Terrisse Castro was one of the programmers. We set up our office in the "bird house," which was the third floor of the building that housed the leadership at Headquarters.

Terrisse Castro was an electrical engineer who had graduated from Santiago's Catholic University. The CNI hired him as a systems analyst to give the unit technical advice. Andrés Terrisse was about thirty years old, smart, and a workaholic. He designed the systems that L-5 would be implementing. He was easygoing and professionally committed. They had hired him through his personal contacts in the army and the CNI. He was Mena Salinas's godson.

I'm not sure if Terrisse Castro had strong political convictions. I can't say that I knew him very well, but it seemed difficult for him to reconcile the tasks that the service imposed on him with his personality.

I found some aspects of Terrisse Castro's personality very likeable. An exceptionally generous person, he exhibited attitudes that distinguished him from the way the personnel usually behaved. These attitudes were accepted in his case, because of his professional "brilliance."

Whatever posed a technical challenge for the engineer would leave him engrossed—as it did us all—in a dynamic that was difficult to leave once you got past a certain point. I'm not saying he didn't have any political convictions or that he lived oblivious to the CNI's world, but he did focus his attention primarily on doing his job well. And given the rudimentary nature of technology at that time, compared to what it is today, that made it necessary for him to develop software that would optimize the computer's performance and power.

As I saw it, Italo Seccatore wasn't typical of the institution's staff either. He seemed much more even-tempered and restrained than the majority of the officers. He was very respectful about the employees' work hours, days off, and vacations, which was unusual in a place where the norm was to be a "workaholic."

Italo Seccatore offered me an interesting job in L-5. I would be the unit's political analyst. Andrés Terrisse was supposed to design the systems to allow us to file and process information and pool the work the units were doing.

Seccatore Gómez and Terrisse Castro explained to me that we needed to begin a pilot plan to test the efficacy of that work method, and they asked me, "Anita, if you had to implement this pilot plan, which unit would you choose?"

I stated that the personnel had changed over the years, but that from among the unit commanders who had been my colleagues at the ENI, I would definitely choose Manuel José Provis Carrasco. When they asked me why, I told them that Caupolicán was the unit that had always focused on leftist political parties and that the captain was even-tempered, levelheaded, and honest, besides the fact that I considered him close to María Alicia, Alejandra, and myself.

The major met with Provis Carrasco, who at that time commanded the Caupolicán unit in the recently inaugurated Borgoño barracks. When the captain left, I continued talking with Seccatore and Terrisse. They were interested in finding out what I knew about Condor, about the Condor Group, and Operation Condor. I cautiously stated that it was a group composed of intelligence services from South American countries that had military regimes at the time. I also said that at the ENI, where I taught classes, I had realized that Paraguay, at least, was sending people for training at the CNI's school.

The pilot plan began, and they chose the Caupolicán unit. Not only was it a recognition of the captain's abilities, for me that choice meant that my opinion carried a certain credibility. This later became an important factor in the CNI's decision to give me the chance to remain alive.

PEACE AND INSTABILITY

I continued studying while I rented a room where I lived with my son. I had to pay for my son's food, his school, my studies, and other things. That's why I accepted Andres's proposition to create a pool of employees from L-5's data entry personnel to work nights and weekends. We would perform data entry work at banks where Terrisse offered technical support as a member of a private computer business.

That additional income increased my monthly budget, but it meant I had to leave my son alone all day and at night too when I had to work at the Banco Español or the Banco de Talca.

My budget didn't cover the cost for me to eat anything except the lunch the CNI gave its personnel, but I don't remember feeling hungry. The cafeteria workers always tried to make sure they gave me abundant servings along with something extra they brought from the officers dining hall. Andrés Terrisse often took me out to eat at the various restaurants in the Plaza Italia neighborhood.

My son Rafael was nine years old, and I tried to get him involved in activities that were normal for his age, which is why I went to the Français Stadium. The room we rented was only three blocks away. My son started working out with a group of boys who did track.

The 18th of every month was payday at both the DINA and the CNI. In the evening, my son and I divided the money for expenses and to pay the bills. He did a lot of these errands since I was at the office during the hours when places were open.

It was a seemingly peaceful time. I had overcome my problems with Internal Intelligence's leadership and with the assistant director, and I was recuperating from my lung infection. However, I did have some important concerns. When I didn't see Alejandra or María Alicia around Headquarters, I asked Major Seccatore about them. I wasn't asking for detailed information, just where they were and how they were doing. I just wanted to know if they were all right or not. The officer assured me they were perfectly fine.

I was worried because Rolf Wenderoth told me that it looked like María Alicia had given Colonel Espinoza information behind the CNI's back. This happened while he was at the Military Hospital during the trial to rule on the extradition request the United States had sent concerning the Letelier case and accusations of falsifying passports. At least this is what the officers close to Contreras were saying.

I found it irresponsible to be making comments that implicated people who were still working at the CNI and who were, therefore, subject to their measures and sanctions, which, in our case, wouldn't simply be administrative in nature. I thought it was highly probable that the CNI had knowledge of that information since I had heard about it. This was especially true since many officers, especially the lower ranked ones, kept in contact with other officers on good terms with Contreras.

It was my understanding back then that they considered the three of us to be at least a delicate matter. And the way they would decide to "resolve" the matter worried me constantly. The greater the instability, the more I thought about resigning.

In June 1978, groups of relatives of the detained and disappeared led several protests. During one of the protests, a group of women chained themselves to the bars in front of the Federal Courthouse. My name was published in the papers, which said I would have to testify in two of the lawsuits that the relatives of the detained and disappeared were filing through the Vicariate of Solidarity's legal support team. Similarly, I found out that an official legal document had arrived at the CNI's Headquarters asking them to respond to whether or not I was an employee of the organization. The CNI responded that I wasn't. The leadership suggested I change my address again, preferably using my alias and fake ID.

At that time I was using my real name since I lived with my son and I hadn't wanted to impose an even more clandestine life on him. I sent my son to live with his father again so I could go into hiding without hurting him. All of this made my situation even more unstable. I was entirely at the mercy of Andrés Terrisse and Italo Seccatore. The events seemed to indicate that the leadership had decided to remove the three of us—María Alicia, Alejandra, and myself—from the CNI, at least from Headquarters. The problem was how. Dead or alive? And I asked myself every day, where are María Alicia and Alejandra? How are they?

I took real leaps of faith regarding Italo Seccatore and Andrés Terrisse. I assumed that it was true that all they wanted was for me to be successful. I dismissed things that didn't support that view or that indicated that I was being manipulated, and I accepted each and every piece of advice they gave me.

I asked Major Seccatore for permission to seek advice regarding my legal situation. Up to then, besides not having an identity, I only did what the institution told me to do whenever I realized someone was looking for me to have me testify. I considered possibly appearing in court, and I told Seccatore Gómez about that. Italo Seccatore agreed that I should seek legal counsel before I made my decision. He put me in touch with a lawyer by the name of Víctor Gálvez Gallegos, who was the chief of the CNI's Legal Department, and he told me I could speak with him without any problem. The lawyer listened to my situation, and he promised to try to investigate the issue, which he did. Italo Seccatore and Andrés told me that the CNI maintained the same policy that the DINA had. In other words, CNI personnel could not appear in court.

I was invited to a meeting with the Legal Department a few days later. Besides Gálvez Gallegos, the lawyers Víctor Manuel Avilés Mejías, Guido Poli Garaycochea, Miguel Angel Poblete, and Miguel Angel Parra Vásquez were there. They answered all my questions. They emphasized that their recommendation was that I couldn't appear in court because if the case fell into the hands of an experienced judge, I could find myself in a difficult situation and be detained or sent to prison.

I talked it over with Italo Seccatore and Andrés Terrisse again. I told them that, before he left the CNI, I had asked Wenderoth to locate the statements on which the DINA had placed my fingerprints when I was a prisoner, if they in fact existed. With the exception of the ones I wrote at the Military Hospital, I hadn't signed any others. I said that Wenderoth told me he hadn't found them, and that I was asking them to look for them again. I said I also wanted them to erase the records from the CNI's files that had my name or the names of my family members.

They said they would, but I got the same answer: the statements were nowhere to be found. Regarding the files, I personally erased the database with that information. However, I do not know if the ones I erased were the only existing files.

My son's absence really upset me, even though his presence was also paradoxical. I didn't have the means to support him adequately, and I knew he made do without things because he loved his mom. When my son went up north to be with his father, I moved into a room near Headquarters, but pretty soon I had to look for another place again because of the typical problems of living with others. The owner of the house counted the minutes I spent in the shower and locked the front door at ten o'clock at night.

I often found the door locked after my classes were over, even when I went home as fast as I could. If I didn't have to go to work doing data entry that night, my only option was to go back to my office at Headquarters. I worked a while and slept sitting at my desk. So I moved again. The new place was in the Bustamante Park neighborhood, which was also pretty close to work. I was there until I got another lung infection and had to go home to stay at my parents' house.

Once I was back at L-5, after a long leave of absence, I started studying again, both at the institute and at COMDAT as well. There was a meeting at the end of the course where everyone who took it had to take an assessment test. We never got the results. I asked Andrés Terrisse about the exam several times. All he said was that my exam offered a conclusion that was quite different from the opinion I had of myself, and that I possessed a much greater logical ability than I thought.

One day Andrés Terrisse asked me why I carried a weapon, and I told him that it was the weapon that staff carried. I could sense he was using the influence he supposedly had over me to gradually start to suggest that it didn't make sense to carry a weapon if I wasn't prepared to use it. I sensed that the CNI would be pleased to see me without a weapon.

That worried me, and not because of the gun, but because it was clear that, one by one, they were going to take away each of the things that proved I was an employee. I decided to play along very cautiously. In any case, I was definitely not going to use the gun against anybody, and it was absurd for me to carry it. I returned it voluntarily.

This incident had two repercussions. I felt better. I would say that it was a small but important step toward trying to save what was left of myself. However, Andrés told me that María Alicia and Alejandra were upset because they were apparently asked to return their guns after I returned mine.

I remembered that before, when we were with the DINA, we thought it was important for them to give us the same kind of weapon the rest of the personnel at Headquarters carried. To the personnel who never accepted us, that was a sign that we were employees, which quelled their criticism of us a bit, at least while we were present.

I had access to some of Andrés Terrisse's work. Besides the development of the system that Caupolicán began implementing, there was another one called "LIDES." That was an acronym they used to refer to the "List of the Disappeared."

I only had access to public information stored in the "LIDES" data files. Some of that information came from the Vicariate of Solidarity, for example, the list of "the 119" and the list that the Vicariate created with 479 detained and disappeared.[59] Andrés Terrisse indicated that since the data entry personnel had been with L-5 for such a short time, that I would be responsible for entering that information.

We also began entering information from the microfiche file from the CNI's undersecretariat, a project that L-5's data entry personnel completed.

I once told Andrés Terrisse that Officer Manuel Lucero Lobos had handled the information concerning the DINA's prisoners. He said he knew nothing about that. For the sake of security, I supposed, he was not going to discuss the topic with me. I did not expect them to put that information at my disposal. I was also unable to verify if the CNI had inherited those documents or not, but I believe Manuel Contreras took that information with him when he left the helm of the CNI.

---

59. LIDES refers to the list of the detained and disappeared that was part of a file maintained by L-5, the CNI computer unit where Arce worked. The other lists were part of human rights reports compiled primarily by the Vicariate of Solidarity.

LETTER OF RESIGNATION

I am unaware of other activities in L-5. I went into hiding around September 20, 1978, and from then on I rarely went to L-5. One day, while I was talking to Andrés Terrisse and Italo Seccatore, I let slip for the first time that I planned to resign and live with my son. I remember the words I used, "I want to be a woman with her son, with a normal job, living in a neighborhood, buying bread at some corner bakery, worrying about making desserts her son likes. . . ." I didn't know what else to say. I was on the verge of tears thinking about how my son was far away and how he seemed even more distant that day.

Andrés broke in with a comment he repeated quite often. "Italo, we have to find someone for Anita to marry! If I had a brother or a friend who was single, I promise you I would grab him by the neck and make him marry you."

"And you think she isn't capable of finding a husband on her own?" Italo replied, laughing.

On impulse, I jumped up and said, "I don't want a husband. I want to have my son with me."

The conversation drifted toward that topic. "You would be a good officer's wife, Anita. Haven't you thought about it? The problem is that all those jerks are married."

I jumped and added, "Andrés, are you telling me that the only way for me to be free is to marry a man in uniform?"

"I'm telling you that you can't keep this up. You work yourself to death, and on top of that I got you a job so you can do it at night too."

Italo interrupted returning to part of my statement, "Anita, don't you consider yourself free?"

"Am I? For example, can I resign?"

"Of course."

"I'll give you my resignation then."

"Oh, Anita, don't resign now. I couldn't allow you to do that."

"Wouldn't they accept it?"

Andrés answered, "You have the right idea, Anita, but it's premature for you to go now. Don't worry, we'll find a way out."

I knew something was going on. I couldn't even map out a strategy in my mind. I was still seeing Rolf off and on. He came to Santiago every chance he could. He had become a friend who worried about my personal situation. During that period, he never asked me to talk about the

294

CNI or to give him any kind of information. Rolf didn't add to the risks in my life. I suppose they also knew we were seeing each other. The commander's trips to the capital weren't a mystery to anyone, nor were our telephone conversations.

On one occasion, Rolf told me he had to go see Manuel Contreras. I went with him and said hello to the general. He had been released and was unwell. His offices were on Ricardo Lyon Street. Nélida Gutiérrez Rivera was there. She apparently continued helping him as his secretary, which must have been after her normal workday since by then Nélida had her own boutique, "Mane," which was in the shopping center on Lyon and Providencia.

A few days later, Italo Seccatore and Andrés asked me if I had any news about Manuel Contreras. I told him I had said hello to him because I had gone with a friend who had to meet with him. They didn't ask me anything else.

During those months, a spontaneous relationship began with Andrés Terrisse. That kind of relationship confused me even more. His attitude was typical. He was attentive, down to the smallest detail, but with the obvious constraint of being a married man whose wife was about to have a baby. Andrés was an uncomplicated man in general, but he was different emotionally. I remember clearly from back then that it never occurred to me that our relationship could become something else. We spent considerable time together.

Italo Seccatore asked me if there was something going on between Andrés Terrisse and me. I told him no. I lied straight to his face knowing that it was highly probable that Andrés would have already told him, but I did it because I considered it my private business.

He pretended to believe my explanation that we had a close working relationship that was complemented by our shared interests. I mentioned it to Andrés. All he said was, "So he asked you?"

I thought maybe they had talked about it, but I respected Andrés's silence. After all those years, I knew it was useless to ask.

I had the impression they were guiding my actions, that somehow they were determining my behavior so it would meet their expectations.

I couldn't find balance in my life. The problem was that I wanted his feelings to be genuine. It hurt to realize that they were manipulating me more and more. I tried to regain my objectivity. I didn't want to suffer. I wanted to be indifferent to their actions.

I had the opportunity to take private painting classes with Matilde

Pérez. Those few hours each week became a time for me to get in touch with myself. I began to recover parts of myself that I thought were dead and buried, lost over the years. But then I felt like I was on the verge of another breakdown, like at Villa Grimaldi. I was hitting bottom again. During those months, I had learned to appreciate what Rolf had given me. Even with all the doubts and limitations, he was a true safe haven for me.

On September 11th, we were confined to the premises, and all personnel, including those of us in computer services, had to remain at the office. Italo Seccatore and his secretary went to have lunch outside the office because it was her birthday. In the afternoon, as we were leaving, Andrés Terrisse and I went to have dinner at a nearby restaurant. As we left, we passed by a candy store, and he gave me a teddy bear. He said, "No matter what happens, you won't be alone." It sounded like a good-bye. A few days later I would find out, painfully, that it was. When we were celebrating Independence Day on September 18th, Andrés Terrisse told me to go to the office. We met there, and he worked all afternoon. I worked at another computer fixing a program I had to finish for my course. He called Italo Seccatore a couple of times, but I didn't hear what they talked about.

At about six o'clock that night, Andrés stopped working and came over to me. He started getting affectionate. Pointing to the glass walls, he took me by the hand and led me to a secretary's office.

I let him lead me. Once we were there, and realizing Italo Seccatore's office was open, he said we should go in. I refused. He embraced me, and a few minutes later Italo arrived. They both went out into the hallway. I stood there thinking for a minute and left. I was still under the impression that it was a chance encounter, and I decided to take the blame for the situation to get Andrés off the hook. Officially, they took a rather prudish approach toward those kinds of relationships, despite the fact that they were quite common.

I asked the major if I could speak with him. I told him I had provoked the situation, and that Andrés had nothing to do with it. I said it was my fault, and that I accepted responsibility for it. He said we would talk the following day. He asked Andrés to leave, and he took me home. I took my letter of resignation in with me the following day. I asked the secretary to type it, and I gave it to the major. Andrés didn't go to work, and I couldn't locate him even though I tried. I never talked with him again.

Italo asked me why I was resigning. I explained quite frankly that it was not directly related to the fact he had caught Andrés and me to-gether. I said I knew I had lied to him about us, but I couldn't under-stand why I had to be an open book even in the most private aspects of my life. I admitted that I had seduced him, but that there wasn't any ul-terior motive on my part. I also said that, beyond the effects it could have on both our personal lives, which I thought were minimal, in no way did it affect the CNI as an institution.

I had the impression that they had planned that encounter, but I didn't tell him that. I underscored that I wanted my freedom.

Italo did not accept my resignation, but he did say that he understood my desire to change my situation. He asked me to give him a few days to think about it. I insisted he should accept my resignation, and that he should talk to Pantoja and Mena to ask them to accept. He asked me to relax, to take some vacation days, and rest. He said he would call me. I went to my parents' house. I slept, rested, and, in spite of the fact I was afraid they might not accept my resignation, I felt a kind of relief. I was fighting again, and this time it was to leave the CNI and stay alive too.

He told me he hadn't handed in my resignation to the leadership be-cause the general had, as it turned out, suggested an interesting mission he wanted to talk to me about before he gave them my letter.

Now I had all the pieces of the puzzle. The service needed me, and was asking me to work for three more years outside Chile. Then, if I survived, I would be free and my resignation would go into effect. That was how I accepted the mission called Operation Celeste.

FRAGMENTS OF AN IDENTITY

I never told the major I knew all my responses had been manipulated and carefully scrutinized. It wouldn't have made a difference if I had said that I had not been a part of that game. I masked the profound pain I felt knowing that Andrés had taken part in something like that, and that he and Italo had made my decision for me. However, I must admit that maybe they thought it was the best thing for me. Maybe they were also afraid I would be killed. They didn't tell me that, but they made or helped make it possible for me to show the CNI I wouldn't be-tray them.

I saw Italo years later, when they accepted my resignation. We had a drink together somewhere, and he made a remark about those days. I knowingly said, "I never understood Andrés's attitude after you caught us together. He avoided me. I just wanted to say good-bye to him, not even see him, but he never answered my calls."

That was when he said, "Anita, I have to confess that I manipulated you. . . ."

I didn't let him finish. I said, "That's okay. It's over now. I'm alive. I resigned, and perhaps it was for the best. The CNI got proof that I was outside the country for almost a year, and I didn't betray them. I suppose that was a key factor in their acceptance of my resignation now. Don't say anything else, Italo. I know. I always knew."

I didn't want to know more. I was happy. I knew there would be difficult times ahead, but I had managed to get what I wanted. I no longer belonged to the CNI.

It seems that I actually was faced with the possibility of death. Who knows anything for sure at a time like that? But in December 1989, an officer I had known from my period in the DINA called me. He told me that he had stumbled upon a report when he arrived at his new destination in the BIE (Army Intelligence Brigade), which was located at the Ministry of Defense. He told me the report was in with other documents in his new office, and that it said that the CNI would have helped me obtain an ID card a few days before.

They returned my identity fifteen years after taking it from me. During the conversation, he said he had something to give me, and he set a time for us to meet the following day in front of the Telephone Company on 1442 Agustinas Street in tower B. I went to meet him there. Then he took me to an apartment, which I knew had belonged to the CNI in 1978.

The officer gave me a file with all the documents proving I had been a DINA and CNI employee. It had my résumé and the original copy of the resignation I gave the CNI, which I presented in October 1979 and which was accepted in March 1980. There were originals and photocopies of all my ID cards I had in the DINA and the CNI, clearance passes, permission to carry a weapon, and my complete alias in an ID and passport with the name Mariana del Carmen Burgos Jiménez. That was the identity I used to travel to Uruguay and live there. There were fake ID cards with the name Ana María Vergara Rojas, which had been made by Carlos Estibil Maguida and Aníbal Rodríguez Díaz at Rolf Wenderoth's request. Another one had the name Patricia Pizarro. That was the one Manuel Contreras asked Michael Vernon Townley to make. There was a free bus pass I used to travel between Santiago and the apartment in San Antonio located in the Fifth Region, and all the certificates and diplomas that I obtained under a false name while I worked for the DINA and the CNI. There were a passport and other documents certifying I was a citizen of Uruguay. There were passes to enter General Headquarters. There were photos of my son and close relatives, along with photos of myself taken in Chile and Uruguay. There was also a collection of documents including my complete curriculum vitae listing all my activities one by one from 1972 to 1980. There were orders from Italo Seccatore as commander of L-5 requesting that my résumé be written under the name Ana María Vergara. I "smiled" when I saw how they had carried out the major's order. He thought it would be better to erase any trace of my presence in the CNI, but the employees in Human Resources kept his order in the file. Then they retyped my résumé with the name Ana María Vergara and "cleverly" put a paper clip on it to keep it with the ones that had my real name. There were also several memos in the file that had been exchanged between the Assistant Director of Foreign Intelligence and the CNI Director. These included evaluations of my personality and my work, as well as the pros and cons of killing me in Chile, outside of Chile, or letting me live and accepting my resignation.

There are a couple of lines in one of those memos that say that my resignation will be accepted under "Plan 2." I imagine "Plan 2" means something like "under observation." The colonel who gave me the file told me to destroy it after I saw it and not to mention it to anyone because he was involved. Maybe it was a way of letting me know that I had already escaped with my life once when I resigned, but that it wouldn't be so easy the next time. I don't know.

32

OPERATION CELESTE

Planning and preparing for Operation Celeste helped me realize that the organization I feared was actually mediocre and that its greatest power over those of us who felt trapped by it was the fear it inspired. That mediocrity was one of the most important factors in my ability to survive. When their only valid argument was their war and the use of brute force, it was easy to look intelligent.

While the operation was in the planning stage, I was horrified by the lack of intellectual capacity I witnessed. I didn't trust the people who would be covering my back. That's why I asked to have Italo Seccatore and Manuel Provis be my contacts and the agents in charge. They seemed more trustworthy to me, not necessarily because they were more capable, but because they acted more responsibly than the others.

They suggested that for my personal safety and to protect the operation I move to a house located on the grounds of the CNI's Borgoño barracks. They said that way I would be able to receive the training necessary for my future role. I moved there in October 1978. Provis Carrasco, who was a major at that time, was commander of that barracks.

Operation Celeste was divided into three stages. The first would take place in Montevideo, Uruguay. Its primary objective was to distance me completely from the country and the intelligence apparatus. It involved a change of identity and the implementation of an infrastructure and help networks, which were assigned. This would then allow me to obtain Uruguayan identity papers and come and go from Uruguay, which would make it possible for me to enter and "legally" reside in another neighboring country.

The final stages were never completed because I returned to Chile and resigned. For that reason, and because I could reveal issues related to national security, I won't discuss the other objectives of this mission.

I boarded a LanChile plane as planned on February 11, 1979. As I left, I tried to convince myself that the next three years would be the way for me to leave the CNI, even though my resignation hadn't been accepted yet. At least I had General Mena Salinas's word that I would be free if I survived those three years. They could keep their promise or not. I could only find that out with each passing day. Therefore, I tried not to think about it anymore, as always, and just look to the future.

I knew the first year would be the easiest. I was going to start by studying, which is how I would complete that initial phase of the operation. Besides, it was also training for me for when I would be free in the future.

Certain I would return, I left my loved ones behind. I took two suitcases with me. When I arrived at the Carrasco Airport, I took a taxi and asked the driver to take me to a hotel in the center of Montevideo. It was during carnival time, and it looked like all the hotels were full, but I found a room at the Hotel Yaguarón. It was on the corner of Yaguarón and Yi Street.

As I watched the sunset on that February 11th, I remembered my previous trip to Montevideo. Everything looked the same. I started recognizing some places along La Rambla Boulevard. I registered at the Hotel Yaguarón under my alias and with a shiny new passport identifying me as Mariana del Carmen Burgos Jiménez.

I put my things away and went to see the city center. When I returned to the room, I ordered newspapers and breakfast for the following day. The waitress told me I could go to the bar where there was a television. I took her advice. They were showing the song festival taking place in Piriápolis, a beautiful spa near Montevideo. At a nearby table there was a couple whose son was about the same age as mine. The boy came over to talk to me a few minutes later. His name was Alex. His mother called him Alito. I took him for walks several times. It was very nice pretending I was with my son. Going for a walk with him or taking him to the beach gave me mixed feelings. I was firm in my decision to do my job well so I could survive, but just thinking I would spend the next three years living under a fake name and far from my son made me shudder. And I knew that if they detained me in another country, it would be even worse than anything I had experienced up to that point.

301

I started getting up very early from my first day in Uruguay. By 7:30, I was already jogging along La Rambla, the boulevard that runs along the La Plata River. I used to jog to Pocitos, swim for a while, dry off in the sun, and jog back. I took that opportunity to memorize the names of the streets, the shops, everything. I had to know the city like the back of my hand. Someday my safety might depend on it. I was back at the hotel by 11:00. I bought newspapers from Uruguay and other South American countries. I had to familiarize myself with the reality in several countries. I made a list of projects like looking for a place to live, choosing a place to study, learning the mail, telegraph, and telephone systems and getting a post office box. I had to open a bank account in dollars before March 15th so they could deposit my monthly salary there, and so on.

As I remember, around February 13th I decided to stay a while in Pocitos. I swam a long time and did exercise. It was a really nice day. At around three o'clock, meaning to put on my clothes over my bathing suit and sandals, I left the water. I noticed a car parked nearby. It was a little white Fiat. I got nervous. I knew the man in the car was watching me. I tried to hurry up and catch the bus that was heading into the city. The guy started the car and blocked my path. He was a young guy, and he asked me if he could give me a ride.

I refused. Back then, I was terrified of all strangers. I was afraid. I wanted to run. He kept talking: "Listen. I want to buy you some juice. Look, there on the terrace. We can talk. Then I'll give you a ride or you can go, your choice. . . ."

I looked at him. He was really young, probably twenty-three or twenty-four. He had brown hair and light eyes. He was good looking. I started to relax. He was apparently just a guy who wanted to pick up a tourist at the beach. He looked like a kid in his mom's car.

"You know you're really impertinent? Now, if you'll let me go. . . ."

"You're not from Argentina. You're not Spanish. I know, you're from Paraguay."

It wasn't the first time I had heard that, and I replied, "I'm Chilean."

I realized I had opened the door to keep talking. "One drink, okay? They have a pineapple one that's delicious!"

As I looked at him, in fractions of a second I remembered all the times in previous years when I was afraid every time a man looked at me or said something to me on the street. I smiled and remembered the incident at the München restaurant.

AN INCIDENT AT THE MÜNCHEN RESTAURANT

It happened in 1978. I was working then for L-5 and living with my son on Tajamar Street. I went to have coffee and a sandwich at the München Restaurant after work one day. A little while after I arrived, a waiter came over with a drink. I said that I hadn't ordered it, that I had asked for some coffee. Courteously, he explained that some men at a nearby table had sent it. I looked over just in time to see two young men smiling at me and toasting me with their glasses. They were attractive and well dressed. One of them stood up and walked over to my table. What I felt wasn't fear; it was more like panic. I had turned pale. I brusquely asked him to leave, and I told the waiter to bring me what I had ordered. When he saw my frightened face, the waiter told me I could move to a different table. I did, and I asked to use a phone. Out of desperation, I called a friend of mine and asked her to meet me. I didn't dare leave alone. Then I called Major Seccatore right away, and he agreed to come to the restaurant. I thought those other men were surely from some other secret service, and that they had found me. The minutes that lapsed before my friend Antonella and Italo Seccatore arrived were horrific. Italo took me to his car and went to talk to the young men. When he returned, he was laughing as he told me that they were just a couple of regulars looking for a good time. He said that when they saw my terrified face and saw Antonella arrive, they thought I must have reacted that way because I was crazy or a lesbian. That was not the only incident of that type. Nothing in my life was right. I had to do something. I couldn't live in a bubble, or go around causing a scene like that every time a man approached me.

As I remembered this incident, I decided to accept. He seemed harmless. . . .

He parked his car and ran over to meet me. We sat down at one of the tables with a view of the beach. I soon found out his name was Roberto Fernández, and that he was younger than I had thought, only twenty-one. He was studying at a military prep academy. I never knew if it was a chance encounter or if it was a setup because he was connected in a number of ways to military men in his country. But I wasn't worried about it. I was totally transparent, at least at that point in my life. I had a good fake story, and whether that young man was working with the Uruguayan Intelligence Service or not, and through them, with the CNI, the only information he could give them was that I was doing my job well.

I went to the Yacht Club with him. We went to the pool, and one afternoon we went out on his father's yacht. We sailed for quite a while and stopped at the island. It was a nice way for me to realize I could meet other people. I had left behind what seemed like a heavy burden at that time: my name. I realized I didn't dare try to know or even think about who or what I was. It was impossible to ask myself what I wanted. Up until then I had been a kind of programmed machine, but for some reason an approximation of myself was beginning to emerge. I was afraid. It was a new kind of fear.

On February 18th, I went jogging as usual. Before I even got to Pocitos, I injured myself. I stepped on a stone with my bad foot and I fell and hurt the cartilage of my right leg. I sat down on the wall along La Rambla. I started getting worried because my knee was swelling and my ankle hurt more and more by the minute as my muscles started cooling down. I saw a police car in the distance. A shiver went down my spine. I tried to calm down and started saying to myself, "I've been in this country for a week. I'm a tourist here, and I have a problem. Where can I go for help? The police, of course!" So I waved them over to me. Soon the patrol car was by my side, and they took me to the hotel. It felt very strange going to the police for help.

DOLLY'S PLACE

On Tuesday the 20th, I rented a room at a pension house on Canelones Street. It was just a few steps away from the Chilean embassy, but that was coincidence.

Mrs. Dolly earned a living by renting out rooms in two big houses. At "her place," as the girls in the pension used to say, there were three or four beds in a room and only one bathroom where a few drops of water fell from a faucet that she grandiloquently presented as the shower.

Dolly said, "There will be no cooking in the rooms!" She went on with her chatter about no radios or tape players except battery operated ones, and no hairdryers. She said that clothes just fall apart if you iron them too much, so after washing them you can hang the clothes between twelve and one o'clock. That's because you have to go up a ladder through the attic to get to the roof, and the attic has three other boarders.

Despite the overcrowding, you could feel the happiness and camaraderie there. I commended myself for having chosen to stay at that pension.

304

Verónica, one of the girls in my room, had a boyfriend who sold ice cream in summer and coffee in the winter. She was a telephone operator for ANTEL. She offered to send messages to Chile for me. There were seventeen women in the pension house. I realized in just a couple of days that this group of women that had come together by chance lived in a supportive atmosphere. All of us, each in her own way, were or felt like we were outcasts.

That coexistence was a defining point in my life. The women there erased my biased upbringing that had taught me to believe since childhood that it was natural to see people from Argentina, Bolivia and Peru as potential enemies. I had been raised with an overestimation of the Chilean army's glory. . . .

They helped me learn that when you look past beliefs, nationalities, and race, we are all just people. I knew I couldn't look at anyone ever again as an enemy just because he or she had been born in another country.

Around that time I went to the embassy to verify the necessary steps to request residency, although I didn't tell them who I was. I had orders to contact the ambassador only in a life or death situation. I had to follow the bureaucratic process just like any other Chilean.

Noemí accompanied me to apply for residency, and Mara had a cousin at the Banco Pan de Azúcar who opened a checking account for me in a matter of minutes. Everything seemed to be working perfectly according to plan at that stage of Operation Celeste.

I enjoyed the company of my new friends, but I felt sad. I felt like it wasn't fair to lie to them with a made-up life, and that I would be using them if I ever let them help me at all in my assignment. I couldn't stop thinking about it.

I started writing to Rolf Wenderoth. I was taking a risk since I had been ordered not to have any direct contact with Chile. But I had my reasons. I didn't trust the CNI. I knew that that period of complete isolation was perfect if they wanted to have me eliminated. I could be detained or killed in any neighboring country. I thought it was important for someone, even if that someone was in the military, to know where I was and what I was doing. I knew Rolf wasn't part of the group of officers in the CNI, and I knew that if I needed help in the future, he would give it to me any way he could. And finally, I had told him I would write to him. At that time, Rolf was governor of Valdivia.

On Monday, February 24th, I went to the post office and took a post

305

office box for a year. They gave me number 6060. That same day I sent that information to my contact, "Francisco Valenzuela," which was Manuel Provis's alias, and also to "Alfonso González," which was the alias for Italo Seccatore, the agent in charge of Operation Celeste. I told them they could call me at the ANTEL offices. I remember that day very clearly. I walked to the post office in the historic part of town. Then I wrote the letters in a nearby café and mailed them.

The last weeks in February seemed to pass slowly for me. It was the time of Carnival and celebrations. Montevideo slept during the day. By midafternoon people would start to stretch their legs along the banks of the River Plata before the parades of confetti and the queens with their bands. It was the typical kind of crazy euphoria that saturates carnival festivities with their grape harvests and "la fiesta de las aguas."[60]

Even though I didn't consider myself a Christian back then, when I passed through the old part of town everyday, I got used to passing by the cathedral. There, in a conversation with my friend, I told Christ about my doubts, my fears, and my homesickness.

I took the necessary steps to obtain a temporary three-year resident visa, which involved having my picture taken, being fingerprinted, having interviews and consultations with the international police, and so forth. I received a Uruguayan ID card that indicated I was Chilean. It was just the first step.

In March 1979, I joined the Neptuno Club and started working out again. I began receiving letters from Rolf who told me he had opened a post office box under a false name in Valdivia.

I kept my checking account where the CNI sent me my monthly salary in dollars. The total was $350, since I left $50 for my parents in Chile every month. Then I opened an additional account in Uruguayan pesos where I could transfer funds from my account in dollars. That way I benefited from the exchange rate since I could exchange only what I needed.

The leadership in Chile sent me information sporadically. I attended classes daily. I developed a close friendship with Noemí, but I never confided in her, which was motivated more by a desire to protect her than by a lack of trust. I started meeting some of Mara's friends. She studied veterinary medicine. We started going to the "Potros Club" to

60. The water festival in Uruguay's carnival celebration is an African cultural tradition.

go horseback riding, and we went to concerts by a folk group she played in called "Banda Oriental."

VISITORS FROM CHILE

I began receiving a monthly telephone call from my superior in Chile beginning on Friday, March 28th. I was still studying, and I started having problems with my health again. I was afraid I would suffer another one of my pulmonary infections, but that wasn't it. They found a problem in my inner ear that caused me to experience dizziness and a loss of balance

The lack of privacy at the pension started to be a problem. I had to read and write my letters in a café. I would probably need my own place sometime in the future. The leadership in Chile, by phone and in letters I received, indicated that I should try to live alone, which is why they requested I make a budget to show them how much it would cost to rent an apartment and furnish it with what I needed.

On April 23rd, I found a telegram in my post office box that said, "Arriving the 23rd. Signed Francisco Valenzuela."

I thought Manuel Provis was coming. I had to wait. Soon I received a note. When I called, the man who answered told me to wait by the Heroes of the Fatherland monument. He told me he would be carrying a gift. When he arrived, the man introduced himself as Major Donoso. He gave me a package and an envelope with money to sign a lease for an apartment and pay for at least six months rent.

They thought it would be enough so that it wouldn't matter that I was foreign.

I only saw the major one more time. We sat in a café while I gave him detailed answers to all his questions about my activities and living conditions. I explained that everything was going as planned, with the only exception being the order to obtain Uruguayan identity papers. I explained to him that this would be impossible through ordinary, legal channels. Even though I had acquired a Uruguayan ID card, it would always say on it that I was from Chile. I told him I would have to live in the country for five years before I could apply for citizenship.

All they did was give orders. They just said things like, "So take your passport or your Uruguayan ID card and go to. . . ." They made it seem as simple as changing my dress or the color of my nail polish. The major kept insisting that there had to be a way. He suggested I steal someone's

307

documents and change the name and dates. I told him that would work to take a trip, but in no way would that help me establish legal residency in another country. The other way I could automatically obtain citizenship was through marriage.

He asked me if that was a possibility. I told him that I wasn't involved with anyone at the time, but that I would think about it. I said I had met a guy who was much younger than me who acted really interested in me, but that I was sure that what attracted him most was the economic independence I seemed to have with my fictitious life story. He didn't work or study. He was an only child who had been raised by his grandmother and aunts. He spent the day sleeping, playing cards at the "Potros Club," or singing and playing the guitar. He had a beautiful voice, but his only profession was dancing with a folk music group called "Banda Oriental." His family used to receive me with great kindness.

The major asked if I was willing to get married. I told him I was, but only if it was the only way and with the understanding I would get a separation as soon as I became a citizen. But I said I thought that would be very expensive since I was sure that what the guy wanted was for me to support him financially, and that he would not give me an annulment unless he got something for it. I thought a divorce would entirely justify my decision to go live in another country. The major told me to wait a while, that we would be in touch, and that he would talk it over with others in Chile. Then he left.

On May 1st, I moved into a hotel that was around the corner from Dolly's boarding house. It had a private bathroom connected to my room, and I could study and write my letters there very comfortably. It was expensive, however. On June 2nd, I moved again, this time to the Hotel France, which was across the street from the LanChile offices.

I was again able to be involved in activities I have always enjoyed, like studying and working out. Besides, it was the first time in many years I stopped feeling the pressure of the CNI personnel's constant presence in all aspects of my life. This was a decisive change for me. . . . I wasn't going to be able to fulfill the promises I had made to the CNI. Little by little, that fragile idea that had initially made me accept—that I would be fighting for my homeland—was crumbling.

It seemed unbelievable to me that people could care about me so much, and it hurt me to think that it was only because they didn't know who I was. I knew I wouldn't be able to get married just to become a citizen. With all the defects this guy had, he didn't deserve to be used like that.

I sat down facing the river one day. I had been walking for hours. It was getting dark, and there was a ferocious electric storm. Thick lightning bolts tore across the night sky. The water responded with furious waves, and I felt even tinier when it occurred to me that the only possible way out was to resign again, and this time in a way they couldn't refuse. I felt like I was defying death once more. I tried to imagine a future. . . .

On Tuesday, June 17th, I was walking down Independence Avenue after class. I thought I saw Captain Manuel Provis a block away from where I was living, and I stood there in shock. I moved closer and greeted him. I never found out when he had actually arrived, but I was sure he was checking up on me. We started walking together. I showed him the hotel where I lived, and we went to a restaurant.

He didn't know where he was staying, but he said he would pick me up the next day. He brought me a package with things my family had sent, and even though the owner of the hotel didn't want to let him come in, he insisted on seeing my room, saying that he was a relative. He didn't like the place. He found it depressing, cold, and damp, which, in fact, it was. He suggested I find something better. I told him I hadn't been able to find an apartment yet, and that something better was going to be more expensive. We saw each other everyday. I gave him details about my studies and everything that had happened since we had said good-bye at the airport in February.

We talked about Lieutenant Luis Carevic Cubillos's death. I had read in the Chilean newspaper at the Embassy that he had died while removing a bomb that had been placed at the CNI's Borgoño barracks. Provis gave me the same version, the official one.

I said good-bye to Captain Provis on Friday the 20th. He said he was leaving Uruguay that afternoon, but I don't know if he did or not. I stopped by the post office when Provis left, and I found a note in my box. It said I should go to one of the windows. When I went, they gave me a cassette tape. I listened to it when I returned to the hotel. It was from my parents and my son. I felt an immense joy as I listened to their voices, but I was also worried because they mentioned their names and called me by mine as well. I thought I shouldn't be taking that kind of risk even though it was true that nothing had happened that time. I guessed that the young man in charge of sending me my mail while

Captain Provis was away had gone to my parents' house and simply sent me whatever they gave him, without ascertaining whether or not he was breaking any rules.

TRIP TO SANTIAGO

I thought for a long time and then went to the LanChile offices. I bought a ticket for the following Monday. I called Italo Seccatore on Sunday evening and told him about my trip. I left the hotel early Monday morning. Noemí took care of my things and lent me a duffle bag. I went to Immigration Services to register my trip with them as temporary residents are supposed to do.

I had a real scare at the airport. After I was on board, and when we had already been in the air for 15 minutes, the plane returned to Carrasco. They told us a bird had damaged one of the engines. At the Carrasco airport they made us wait in the transit lounge for more than an hour. I kept trying to tell myself that they had no reason to stop this flight just because of me.

I realized that living under a false identity meant that I would be in a constant state of alert and danger. I didn't relax until I arrived in Chile. When Manuel Provis had been in Montevideo, he had confirmed my suspicion that Seccatore Gómez was no longer with the CNI, but he assured me that he continued to be the agent in charge of Operation Celeste. We got together while I was in Santiago. I told him what I thought about communications issues, and I asked that they be taken more seriously. I also told him I would take advantage of the trip to teach my family about security measures. We talked at length about what had happened while I had been away. They told me they wouldn't send any official correspondence regarding my trip. I went by the house. After lunch, I went to LanChile to reserve my ticket to return to Montevideo.

I asked the CNI to be demanding and rigorous in their compartmentalization of the operation from then on and to respect all security measures we had established regarding contact with my family, other employees, and friends.

They asked me if I had had any news from Wenderoth. I thought for a moment, and I decided to tell the truth: "Yes, we write each other often."

"And don't you think that jeopardizes your security?"

"No, I trust him."

"But surely Contreras must know then."

"If Contreras knows, he didn't find out from Wenderoth Pozo. I have no doubt about that."

"Are you sure? He's been working with Contreras for years."

"Yes, I'm sure, and of course they've worked together several times. They belong to the same military branch, and that's why they've bumped into one another more than once. And it's true he was what you would call a 'Contreras officer.' But wherever he is, he basically just does his job, and independently from Contreras. Besides," I added, "before I left, Wenderoth told me specifically, 'Don't even think about telling Contreras good-bye. If the pot boils over one of these days, "Mamo" isn't going to go down alone. He's going to take as many people with him as he can.' I asked Wenderoth why the general would want to hurt me, to which he responded, 'Maybe not you, but the CNI he would. He could say "the CNI also carried out operations internationally."' I always admitted that that had been very good advice."

"Do you plan to continue writing to Wenderoth?"

"As long as he wants me to, yes, at least at this stage. Afterwards, I don't know. I'm not sure how to write my family either in future phases of the operation."

Italo Seccatore said my reasoning seemed solid. I left there thinking that I would keep studying and think some more. Only one thing was clear: I should run my own risks, but not take on additional ones.

BACK TO MONTEVIDEO

I returned to Montevideo having made a decision. I would resign from the CNI before the operation's second phase. My visit made me realize that my time with the CNI was coming to an end. I felt very lonely and incapable of resigning right away. I gave myself some months to gather the strength I needed and to organize my thoughts.

The only new event was that it took a long time for my money to arrive in August and September. I wrote to Santiago, but I didn't receive a response. In my personal life, the most enthusiastic person was my supposed future mother-in-law who treated me like her own daughter. She wanted me to marry Marcelo.

I went to an old military fort twice with another couple, Leo and Alicia. It was the Capatacía de Santa Teresa, located near El Chuí on the border with Brazil. We went up into the solid battlements and gazed over the continent. As I saw the herds of criollo horses galloping

311

through the lush grasslands toward the deep blue Atlantic waters, I felt like I was still a prisoner of fear. I also visited the chapel. I walked through the rooms and the dungeons. I shivered with cold as I looked at the shackles hanging from heavy chains on the stone walls. I got out of there quickly, and my gaze fell on some wooden stocks in the court-yard. I was overcome by images of other prisons, of other shackles. I could almost see, almost hear the screams. I thought about the Por-tuguese and the Brazilians who were captured by the "fearless gau-chos" as Leo would call them, recounting stories of epic battles.[61] That image and remembering 38 Londres Street, the Ollagüe Detention Center, and Villa Grimaldi melded into one.

I started feeling more uneasy. I decided to travel as a way to escape, to daze my mind with landscapes, sunshine, fresh air, and beautiful sunsets by the ocean, but it was impossible. The deep, midnight blue waters of the Atlantic were full of moaning too. I felt every inch of my skin cry out, and all my fragility was beginning to surface.

I went with Mara to Pan de Azúcar. I went to Piriápolis. Unforget-table. I looked at Marcelo and thought, could I live with him? I knew I couldn't, and that wasn't all. If something happened to me, he would also be at risk, and his family, and my friends. . . . Besides, in Operation Celeste's second phase, could I see someone as an enemy just because he was born in another country? Definitely not. Traveling, rediscovering nature, and running from people and intimacy emphasized the process of my departure. I felt like I was starting to feel again, even though memories I had blocked off hadn't completely broken through yet. I thought I could make up for what I was lacking and my past by gorg-ing myself on the natural beauty of Brazil and Uruguay, and by visiting boulevards on the coast between Montevideo and Punta del Este. But I realized my personal pain was irreversible. The affection I received from people I didn't even know had awakened my longing to just be, and I had to resign.

I told myself it was good to be able to think about it, but that I had al-ready discovered I didn't know what I wanted in terms of my daily life.

---

61. This is a reference to the gauchos, horsemen and cowboys from the lands surrounding the borders between Paraguay, Argentina, Brazil, and Uruguay. Their historical identity was forever transformed through their participation in military conflicts in the region, which were often border wars such as the War of the Triple Alliance (1864–70). At the end of that conflict, Paraguay was defeated by the three neighbors that allied against it and was left as one of only two countries in South America without any coastline.

Everything, even everyday choices from toothpaste to cigarettes were made according to how they fit, or not, with my made-up story. Every choice was made to distance me from myself. I remember my clothes without name tags, my suitcases emptied of memories, and the shredded letters so I didn't put anyone at risk. That was who I was, someone who lived under a stolen name that didn't tell me anything. I wanted my own name, but without the burden it implied. I hadn't been able to bury my memories along with my name. I told myself over and over, I must break away from the CNI. I didn't know what awaited me. At times I imagined a place filled with shadows, and then my imagination came to my rescue. I pictured an arid place and told myself, "I will plant flowers even if I have to water them with my own blood. There, in the future, there will be sunshine during the day and moonlight at night."

I had to give my identity meaning, and I dreamed rocking myself in tears. I couldn't go on living my life as a role or a mission.

Major Donoso came to visit me again in September. He told me I would be receiving some news in December. I asked him directly about Manuel Provis. He was evasive, and I didn't pursue the matter. I imagined the major was no longer in the CNI, and I decided the only way to know was to go to Chile.

RETURN TO CHILE

I returned to Chile on October 12, 1979, and I got in touch with Seccatore and Provis. My suspicions were correct. They were out of the operation. They put me in touch with the man who really was my superior, Colonel Arturo Ramón Ureta Sire.

Ureta told me he was satisfied with what I had done. He took the certificates and the Uruguayan ID card to inform General Mena about it, and we set up a second meeting. That day he returned the documents to me and informed me the general had agreed to move on to the second phase of the mission. He said there would be subsequent meetings to arrange the details. I only asked him, "Colonel, how will I enter the other countries?"

"As a Uruguayan citizen," he answered.

"How will I acquire those documents?"

"You'll steal them and put your photo in them."

"Colonel, I'll be able to enter any South American country, but will I live illegally or as a legal resident?"

"As a resident, naturally."

He didn't know the steps required to apply for residency. Besides, the way to use the radio to send information not only seemed archaic, it reminded me of James Bond, agent 007.

I talked with Seccatore and told him I was going to resign. I explained I didn't trust the leadership and that I had personal problems. I told him about my conversation with Ureta word for word, to the extent possible, and I asked for his opinion. I asked him openly, "Do you think they'll accept my resignation or . . . will they kill me?"

After a while he said, "If you were my sister, I would tell you to resign."

I gave Ureta Sire my resignation. He was upset. He talked about the investment of time and money. I told him that I considered that period of separation important for me to live in Chile. He just said he would talk to General Mena, and that he would let me know. Several months went by, and I didn't hear anything from the CNI.

While I was waiting for an answer, I realized my future was at stake. I was going to find out if they would let me live out of the CNI. My parents were happy I had come home. I was going to try to reinsert myself, at least that was what I hoped.

RICARDO RUZ'S DEATH

There was an article in *El Mercurio* on November 29th about Ricardo Ruz Zañartu's death in a shootout on the previous day. Ricardo was carrying phony documents that said that I was his spouse.

The CNI used Ricardo's death to scare me and force me to withdraw my resignation because they wanted me to continue with the next phase of Operation Celeste outside the country. Provis wasn't in the DINA when they detained me, and he didn't know much about my son. He thought Ricardo might have been his father. Manuel Provis Carrasco and Carlos Estibil Maguida came to question me. Saddened by Ricardo's death and thinking about everything, I decided it would be better to face reality, so I tried to contact the CNI. I called Seccatore and informed him about the article in the paper. I told him that, no matter what, I wasn't going to withdraw my resignation. Later he told me to call the Operations Center at Headquarters, that the officer there was someone we knew.

When I called, I found out the officer was Ferrer Lima. He said he would come to my house. That day I realized we had changed. For the

314

first time I felt like there was an abyss between us. "Max" mentioned Ricardo's death and asked what I felt. I told him I felt great sadness. He got upset and basically told me that feeling sorry for that "criminal" was a betrayal. I felt doubly sad. I was hurt by Ricardo's death, and I was sad that "Max" didn't understand anything.

I thought that if Ricardo ever remembered my name, it must have been just to say "Eat shit!" And now here was "Max" accusing me of betrayal because of my pain. I was hurting, and I thought that that's what I was, nothing at all. I wasn't angry with the major, and I told him that this time I wasn't going to give up my right to cry. I said that Ricardo was the only person I had been afraid to face, and not out of fear, but out of shame. I told him I would have never done anything to harm him in spite of being the trash I am. And I said I wasn't going to hide my tears, my sadness at his death, just to obtain some dubious expression of approval.

He listened to me. He was silent for quite a while, and finally said, "Luz, it's good to see you. We've known each other such a long time, over five years. You look so sure of yourself. You're more beautiful. You get more and more interesting every time I see you." He took one of my hands.

I looked at him. Now I was furious. If he thought he was going to get me to change my mind with that kind of talk . . . he could wait the rest of his life. It bothered me that he was caressing my hand. His hand didn't seem like that of a friend anymore. His move was low, offensive, grotesque. He went on saying, "I didn't know where you were. Someone told me you were abroad, and I said she'll do the job well. She's my student." He got up laughing, and he asked me to stand up.

"Major, I called you because they said you would give me instructions."

He sat down again. His eyes didn't seem sweet anymore. They looked smaller, and his thin lips pursed together looked like a deep wound on his face. "Of course! Of course I'll tell your superior and the Foreign Operations Center. Be careful. Don't go out in public."

I thought, "You haven't reported this yet? Why did you come here?" He tried to get close to me again. He said he was glad I was able to show how I felt, that he could see what a huge step I had taken, and that he was happy for me, even though he didn't like my rejection.

The only thing that was certain that day was that Ricardo had died. I was upset, but I was finally breaking my ties to the CNI, and I was very scared.

33

MEETING JUAN MANUEL

I was glad I had been capable of giving the CNI my irrevocable resignation, even though I was afraid they wouldn't accept it. Nevertheless, I decided to stand by my decision. I tried to be with my son Rafael as much as I could, and I took up painting again. I needed to earn some money to pay the bills, so I started looking for a job.

Waiting months for an answer and knowing I was going up against the CNI gave me an allergic reaction. I went to see Doctor Roberto Lailhacar, who started treating me. During that attempt at therapy, the doctor focused on my emotions. I never managed to think of him as my doctor, and I suppose he wanted to form an opinion based on what my expectations were outside the institution. I didn't express any resentment, but I told him I wanted a normal life.

I didn't have any personal identification, so I came to the conclusion that the safest thing for me to do, in the meantime, was to teach classes as a personal trainer and give stress-reducing massages to women. I quickly filled my schedule, with the help of my cousin Elda and my friend Gloria, who recommended me to their friends.

I met Juan Manuel, who is now my husband, in early 1980. He knew about my situation. He was the first person not associated with the CNI who knew something about my past. I had to tell him I didn't have any identification and showed him the degrees I earned studying computer science under the name of Mariana Burgos. He arranged everything so I could get a job at a private business.

I was already working by the time the CNI informed me in March 1980 that they had accepted my resignation. Finding work was important to me since I needed an income, and, besides, it was proof I legally existed.

I spent my free time painting, and I wrote a couple of stories that no one read and that eventually got lost. Today I know that all of that came from an inner need to express something that was fighting to get out, if hesitantly.

I started giving classes at a computer institute in March that year. I left the other job after taking over public relations at that educational facility. Being able to work professionally in a field I enjoyed and being able to live independently reinforced the feeling I had back then that I could bury the past and that I was managing to start over. I have to confess that there were only two things that complicated my life: the fear of being recognized, and my right foot, which made it difficult for me to do anything that required walking. However, I was still afraid, and I had to force myself to travel around Santiago as much as I had to so I could live my life.

As I began studying and working, I was convinced I could erase my past. I imagined it was like opening a book with blank pages. I started a relationship with the man who is now my husband. That was when a series of issues started emerging that I hadn't realized were there. I held onto the hope of living with my son Rafael again, but I was far from having the means to offer him the stability his father and his father's new wife were able to give him at that time. They had a home, but I was still living day to day without daring to think about what would happen the following day. . . . Even so, my life was better than it had been during the previous years.

Besides our romantic relationship, I think the support and understanding Juan Manuel gave me were critical. It all came at a high price to him. I felt like Juan Manuel learned what it was like to have problems the day he met me. My first emotional need was a burning, obsessive desire to be loved and, most of all, protected. As I received the warmth he gave me, I started to feel increasingly fragile and needy. I can see that now, but I didn't realize back then that I was too demanding. Far from Juan Manuel, I felt more abandoned than ever.

Our relationship became more intimate, and we developed a profound trust. That made everything flow better, but I couldn't avoid having things from the past surface. Little things would often make me experience semiconscious flashbacks to events that happened during my captivity. It was hard for me to make out which moment I was living. Juan Manuel tenderly tried to bring me back to the present. We knew I needed help, but I never dared go to anyone because I was afraid of talking, and it was hard for me to believe I could trust anyone. All alone, Juan Manuel and I lived through those moments that were making our relationship difficult to endure. Neither one of us knew how to deal with what was happening, and our relationship deteriorated.

My job was going well. However, in addition to my fears, I started suffering from a series of somatic disorders. The symptoms were real, and I had tachycardia, nausea, and dizziness on a daily basis. I got another ulcer.

Because of this, I was able to meet a doctor I will identify only as Marcos. I realized he was treating me in a special way. My relationship with Juan Manuel was still official. People still saw us as a couple, but the situation was getting tenser everyday. I told Juan Manuel I had met someone else but that if he wanted to try and salvage what we had that I was willing. I remember we were at a table at the Plaza Italia's Burger Inn. Juan Manuel drank his coffee in silence, and then he said that it would be better for both of us if we broke up. I left there feeling a deep sense of sadness, of failure.

I knew I was mostly responsible for our breakup. Now I realize that what attracted me to Marcos, besides his intelligence, was that he was really affectionate. We had a beautiful beginning. Marcos was the kind of man who would get off the subway, run into my office just to give me a kiss and say "I love you," and then run out again on his way from one job to another. Maybe I loved the fact that he was just different. Our relationship lasted around eight months. Soon after we began seeing each other, he told me he was married, with the obvious drawbacks. Once we were over the initial attraction stage of the relationship, I realized it couldn't continue. At that time, the fact that he was married didn't bother me. I had no respect for family, and even less for marriage, but I didn't want to feel like the "other woman." It wasn't a guilty conscience. I was tired of the restrictions of always having to hide and steal time to see each other. My relationship with Marcos ended suddenly. I did things I thought I would never do, like going to see him at his house and confronting his wife. Now I really regret it.

I was hurt and more lonely than before. I was more aware of my limitations, and I found refuge in my work. The past continued not to exist.

Juan Manuel told me he was lonely. I would say we combined two solitudes and continued working together.

318

IN HIDING AGAIN

I received a message in May 1982. When I saw the phone number, I knew it was the CNI. Colonel Gustavo Rivera wanted to talk to me.

I went to Headquarters. Colonel Rivera told me that someone had warned the CNI that the Bureau of Investigation had a warrant for my arrest to force me to testify in court. They ordered me to go into hiding. I explained to the Assistant Director that I had a job. But he was very clear. I must not allow them to find me. I went to the institute where I worked, took my personal items, and left. When I was a few yards away, I saw in the rearview mirror that a Bureau of Investigation car had pulled up in front of where I worked. I looked for a phone and warned Juan Manuel.

I took some clothes, left the apartment where I had been living up to then, and got out of Santiago for a few days. When I returned, Juan Manuel helped me avoid the police by confronting each new situation. He got my things from the apartment and gave the owner back her key. Alejandra, who had also left the CNI around the same time, helped me and went with me.

PAIN AND HAPPINESS IN MY FAMILY

Juan Manuel rented an apartment early in June 1982, and we started living together. In October of that year I found out I was one month pregnant. As I look back on those days, I can only see two things clearly. First of all, I was terrified that the Bureau of Investigation, the Vicariate of Solidarity, or the courts would find me. But I was also happy feeling how my youngest child was growing inside of me. I don't remember ever feeling such tenderness. Wanting that baby made me stronger, and I felt like I was alive again. I took care of myself. I was worried about my age since I was going to have the baby when I was thirty-five years old. I turned to prayer often. I begged God to exist and for my child to be healthy. I discovered another fantasy within myself: to not be alone as I waited for the baby. Both of my children were born under similar conditions, and both times I felt the same, that I was alone. Juan Manuel and I had separated before our son was born, and I went to live near my parents in the Bellavista neighborhood.

My younger son, Juan Manuel, was born on June 16, 1983. That was when I tried to get back together with his father. I hid even more from the outside world, although I saw my parents and my older son. He was fifteen years old at the time and welcomed his younger brother with affection.

Since I was busy with the baby, the past didn't exist. However, not only did my relationship with Juan Manuel suffer ups and downs but my financial situation was also bad. Juan Manuel had to support two households, and with the birth of our son he now had five children. I tried to improve our income by starting to make stuffed animals. I sold the only valuable item I owned, a diamond and sapphire ring, and invested the money in a washing machine. Then I bought a sewing machine on credit and the material, synthetic fur, and everything else I needed. I was able to make twenty dozen Goofys, Mickeys, Smurfs, puppies, and swans. I gave twelve dozen of them to a local store to sell and sold the rest on my own.

When I started working, my son resented me for not holding him or playing with him. He refused to eat. We went to a pediatrician, and he told me to take him to daycare.

We followed the doctor's advice and enrolled him in a preschool. The teacher noticed my son was refusing to eat. That was why they made an appointment for me to speak with a psychologist. Meeting Ana María was wonderful. She had studied at a high school where I worked as one of the teachers in charge of the afternoon sports activities. I started talking to her. Anita María made an effort to supervise my son's progress, and she invited us to a parenting school. I was really scared to attend, but we did it. Ana María helped us to integrate into the group, and it was beautiful to mix with other people. I didn't mention my name back then. I hid in the shadows.

Ana María and her colleague, Verónica, gave me their theses to type and recommended me to some of their other classmates, to help me financially. I started typing papers for some of the students who were graduating from the School of Psychology.

Anita María recommended one of her professors to me so I could get into therapy. At that time Elida was a professor of behavioral psychology at the University of Chile's School of Psychology. She helped me a lot without charging me anything, and I came to understand some things. She helped me understand that I had to share my future with my family no matter what lay ahead. Even though I understood it, I couldn't put it into practice. However, I was able to leave the house again in Santiago even if it was just to go from home to the preschool and back again.

All of my attempts to be very rational came from my need to believe that I could eliminate my fear. With Elida, I came to understand that I had to accept my fear as something real.

In the beginning of 1987, with the help of my cousin Elda and my mother, I rented a store in the Bellavista neighborhood. Juan Manuel and I set up a frame shop there. I closed the shop at the end of the year since Juan Manuel had brought his four children from his previous marriage to live with us on October 19th. It was impossible for me to run the house and the frame shop all at the same time.

It was quite an experience for all of us to live together. We enrolled the children in the school run by the Dominican fathers. That was when Juan Manuel and I realized that we had to stay together no matter what, and that Father Gerardo, a Dominican priest, was a fundamental source of support.

Our lives changed radically. It's not easy to take in four children of different ages and personalities into your home. Nothing we had before seemed adequate now. We couldn't even use our pots and pans because they were too small. We went from a family of three to a family of seven, plus a babysitter.

CONVERSION AND FATHER GERARDO

I made all the mistakes a woman makes when she accepts four children all at once. We had our difficult moments, but Juan Manuel stood by me. I think we learned a lot from each crisis. I felt bad because I couldn't help but love my own son more than the others. Little by little, Father Gerardo helped me understand that my reaction was natural. I was able to explore deeply within myself with his help and to feel that I was a Christian. Conversion is one of the most beautiful things I have been given.

Exhausted and feeling sick, I started searching for God but I couldn't believe in his existence. I obtained a copy of the New Testament and started reading it. I looked desperately at Christ and the Virgin through my window, and I begged them to erase my doubts. I wanted to believe God existed. It was useless.

I was sick. I started suffering from migraines, a loss of balance, and a feeling of desperation so intense I would lose consciousness. Several doctors examined me, but nothing calmed my pain. One day I happened to pick up a book. It was the life of Saint Francis of Assisi. Reading made me feel worse, but I didn't put it down until I finished it. In the midst of the anguish caused by my physical pain, I started remembering my time in the DINA. It was crazy. My flights to the past became more frequent and longer. One day, I asked Diego, one of the older children, to please go get a priest. The boy came right away with Father Gerardo.

The father listened to that mixture of pain and shame, and I received the Holy Sacrament of the Anointing of the Sick and the Eucharist. Ana María, the psychologist at the daycare center, told Juan Manuel to call a neurologist who was a friend of hers. After examining me and consulting with one another, a psychiatrist, a neurologist, and a psychologist diagnosed me with multiple depressions, all of which were being badly handled. I began a treatment that sedated me and left me feeling spaced out. I had short moments of consciousness when I felt like my whole life had been recorded and like they had taken the cassettes from me. Due to the treatment, I started to feel better. I was very weak physically. What happened was that Juan Manuel thought the babysitter was feeding me, and she thought Juan Manuel was doing it. As a result, I went without food for several days and I didn't realize it. I started feeling better. However, it took several days for me to be able to walk on my own. One day I awoke and knew that God existed. I couldn't believe it. It was like awakening on a sunny day. I got dressed happily, and I went to the window. God was everywhere shouting out the joys of the immense wonders of his creation. I could sense His divine presence in the trees, in the cloudy sky, and everywhere I looked was like a huge book outlining a plan for life, for a full life.

Knowing God changed my life, feeling that God is love, that His word is the word of love, that, as Christians, we are called above all to obey His word. That made me think about who I was and who I am, and, of course, it also meant coming to terms not only with myself, but also with my relationships with those around me. The Luz who had been unfaithful so many times, who felt so miserable, started wanting to be able to say yes to the Lord.

Since I still couldn't walk on my own, I asked my older son, Rafael, to take me to my children's school. I looked for the priest and I told him I remembered next to nothing about what I had told him before. I asked him to please hear me again. I wanted to tell him everything, but I wanted to be conscious of it, and to take responsibility for what I said.

I started talking to the priest. I didn't understand what was happening to me. That day I awoke and knew without a doubt that God existed, but I couldn't for the life of me explain it. I wanted to search for an answer, and I asked Father Gerardo to help me study. He was full of wisdom, and, given my complete ignorance, he had me start with schoolbooks. I read everything in a couple of months, from primary school to high school, and then I returned. Deeply guided by my previous life experiences, I tried to seek God in books. But I felt humiliated when the priest told me to study schoolbooks. I couldn't grasp the lesson he was teaching me. I realized much later that I hadn't gone home to study them out of humility, but as if to start from scratch. I felt like I had been challenged to show I could do it. I studied full of empty pride, and little by little I realized that the priest, without saying so, was giving me the tools I needed to uncover my limits. There is a huge difference between recognizing knowledge and making it your own, and there was so much I didn't know about myself. I had never before faced my naked self. I had to start to open myself up to other things and to reach into my own heart to face God, that is, to face everyone else.

I felt more worthless than ever. The father tried to show me that Christ came for me too, that he came especially for us sinners. I knew there would be difficult days ahead. I told Father Gerardo several times, "It will take me two or maybe three years to face my reality. . . ." But I had the joy that comes from hope, from good news. . . .

The father never told me what to do. He helped me find the path of reflection that leads to choice. Maybe if he had suggested or told me to do this or that, maybe it would have taken less time. But one of the things I am most grateful for is that he taught me how to start taking care of myself. I felt very fragile, but the acceptance Father Gerardo gave me, along with my husband's support, were essential.

Frequently, in my ignorance, I went to Father Gerardo for a wide range of advice, even the most domestic questions regarding the children. He always displayed amazing patience.

I often didn't understand him, I got upset, and we argued. I began discovering new meanings of the words "patience" and "prudence." The clearest part of my relationship with Father Gerardo is feeling and knowing that he will be there if I need him. That was, and is, fundamental. He showed me God in this world. To him I owe learning to appreciate family, to be a mother, to keep commitments, to want to rebuild a relationship with Juan Manuel in a different way, to find out what friendship can be, and to begin to regain trust in people. Aside from my husband and children, Father Gerardo was the first person I trusted at that time in my life. He is one of the few people with whom I can just be, without barriers or being fearful. He was the first person to hear my confession and accept my shame.

FATHER JOSÉ LUIS

A member of the Dominican order does not take on responsibilities single-handedly. He has his brothers and his community. One day, when I went to speak with Father Gerardo, he told me a Spanish priest had just arrived at the Recoleta Convent. He said that besides being a scholar, he lectured at the Catholic University. He taught the novices of the order and was in charge of the library. Father Gerardo thought he was the one who should guide me in my studies. He suggested, as well, that I could begin to study at the convent's library.

I have to confess that I felt panicked. I was afraid that sooner or later I would have to tell another priest all about myself. That day I felt like Father Gerardo had betrayed me. I felt like I could never repeat everything I had said about myself, or my life, ever again. That only lasted until I started talking with Father José Luis. I don't think I have ever met anyone as wise as he is. Now I love both of them with all my heart.

José Luis is older than I am, and he has the kind of wisdom that comes from traveling. He is a great conversationalist, amusing but profound, critical and sound in his analysis. He gives off energy. I started going everyday to the library at the Dominican Recoleta Convent. In time, I also attended other places to receive instruction, such as the Catechism Institute, Ilades, and the Catholic University.[62] I started meeting more members of the Order of Preachers, and I felt a desire to be part of the Dominican family.

I started writing again, thanks to José Luis. I thought that emptying out that painful part of my life would help me face all that was festering within me, everything that continued to harm me so much.

I started several times. The pain made me cowardly and I quit. When I saw the pages accumulating, I felt great fear and thought that there

---

62. Ilades is the acronym for the Latin American Institute of Doctrine and Social Studies, which was created in 1965 in Chile to teach Catholic doctrine. It also offers graduate programs affiliated with universities in other Latin American countries, the United States, and Europe.

wasn't enough room in the world for those pages or for me. Everything seemed precarious.

My family went to southern Chile for the summer of 1988–89. I thought it would be a good time to face my writing. When I had around a hundred pages, I went to the bathroom and burned them. When I reached the point that I didn't know whether I was crying out of fear or because of the smoke that was choking me, I found an answer. Destroying my writing was analogous to my desire to hide that part of my life, not just from everyone else, but from myself as well. For a long time I thought I had managed to accept the person I was, but I realized it wasn't true, not so long as I was incapable of integrating that part of me into what was my life.

I cried as I opened the windows in my apartment and the ones to my soul. It didn't make sense for me to have survived if I couldn't manage to try to heal. Forgetting is not an option.

Becoming a member of the Dominican family and listening carefully, especially to the reflections of Father Félix, with his simple but profound insights, were an important part of my personal process.

In December 1989, Father José Luis went south to Concepción to the Order's sanctuary to replace one of his brothers who was going to visit his mother for Christmas. I wanted to give the priest a gift, but I didn't have any money. That was when I wrote the chapters "September 11, 1973" and "Lumi Videla Moya."

The father read my gift, and he urged me to resume writing. I started again. I wrote every morning. At the end of the day, I put the manuscript in a closed envelope on a bookshelf. José Luis took my writing each day. I never reread what I wrote, much less everything together.

During the time I lived so close to the Dominicans, I met others besides the priests. I met the nuns in the convent, several sisters from different Dominican congregations, and laymen from the parish and my children's school.

I thank the Lord for all the love I have received from them. Beside my Dominican family in that beautiful "Blossoming Convent" that is Recoleta, love has once again taken root in my heart and revitalized my life.

34

I am testifying before this Commission as a matter of conscience, and because I believe I have a debt and I feel I need to do it, if this contributes in any way as reparation for my actions concerning my collaboration with the DINA and having been an employee of that organization. It is important for me to also contribute to clarifying the truth and carrying out justice in the context of reconciliation. For the past several years, I have experienced a process of coming to know God, and I have lived profoundly committed to the Christian faith. Therefore, I want to be faithful to the demands of my conscience as much as I am able.

from the testimony given to the Truth and Reconciliation Commission, published in Apsi, Página Abierta, *and* Hoy[63]

DECLARATION BEFORE THE NATIONAL TRUTH AND RECONCILIATION COMMISSION

At the end of September 1990, my husband had to be admitted to a clinic to undergo a risky surgical procedure. I stayed with him night and day. I only went home to leave money for expenses, to be with the children for a while, and to coordinate their visits to see their father.

I was studying theology at the Catholic University and other educa-

---

63. *Apsi, Página Abierta,* and *Hoy* were all Chilean magazines that offered alternative, or left-of-center, political and cultural commentary. *Apsi* was the first of the three, appearing in July 1976. Along with the magazine *Hoy,* it suffered censorship during the dictatorship but ultimately survived until the return to democracy. In an ironic twist, all three journals, which received financial support from groups opposed to the military regime, went into financial crisis and disappeared during the democratic transition in the 1990s, along with other alternative news sources, such as the newspaper *La Época.* This left Chile with few alternatives after *Hoy* disappeared in 1998, although a few publications remain, such as *Punto Final.*

tional centers, and this was during my final exam period at the end of the second semester.

During one of my visits home, one of the children told me that two men had come to the house asking for me. He said they had left when they heard about my husband's state of health. I knew immediately that they were from the Truth and Reconciliation Commission. Even though I had expected them to come at any time, I was deeply moved. The time had come. . . . I went to the San Lucas chapel and thanked God that my husband had had his surgery. I felt great tranquility when I thought that the children would have their father by their side no matter what happened to me.

I asked God to help me and give me strength. The children were finishing their school year, and my husband had not yet recovered. However, despite the fact that my decision to testify was irrevocable, the immediacy of it shook me, since it would happen in just a matter of days.

On the outside, life went on as usual. I tried to keep calm because everything was coming to the surface. The fear, being torn up inside because I had to articulate my story, caused me great pain, as it still does. I would have to tell strangers what I had admitted only to myself.

In the midst of that emotional chaos, I knew I wouldn't have a future if I lost courage. I felt that everything that was my own—that is, if there is anything we can call our own in this life—such as personal relationships, children, and studies, would be plunged into uncertainty. I would lose everything. But I also knew I couldn't make them pay for my search to find myself. I didn't have the right to do that. Everything that was happening was part of my fight to survive, which came at a terrible price. But nothing would make sense if I didn't move forward to that new stage in my life.

That day, from the depths of my heart, I told God "Yes, my name is Luz, Luz Arce, the informer, the traitor, the DINA and CNI employee. . . ."

I continued trying to keep my commitment to my husband, my children, and my studies. There were difficult moments, and I turned to my people. I had an urgent need for affection. I didn't say anything to my parents or the children. I didn't want to worry them ahead of time. My friends supported me. José Luis, Gerardo, Félix, Marcela, Cecilia, Mery, and Verónica supported me with their love.

327

The tension was strong, and my health began to suffer. My insomnia returned. I took advantage of those hours to study, pray, and reflect. I asked my professor at the university, Father Luis, to minister the Sacrament of the Anointing of the Sick to me. The father agreed, and I received the Eucharist with Verónica, one of my classmates. I felt comforted by this, and I was ready to cross that new threshold that I knew would be the beginning of a long and difficult road. However, unlike that other path through the DINA and the CNI, this one was filled with a new light and, above all, great hope.

They released my husband from the hospital, and we came home. I tried to share the children's happiness at their father's return, and I was able to smile. However, I was overcome by the certainty that this would no longer be my home, and that made me truly sad.

I went to the table where I usually studied, which was in front of the window. I looked toward the top of the hill in downtown Santiago at the Virgin with her open arms, and I begged her to protect my children and their father with her benevolence. I asked that they remain as far removed as possible from what I had to do or whatever happened to me.

Someone knocked on the door. I wasn't expecting anyone. Something inside me said, "It's them, the ones from the Rettig Commission." I told my children not to open the door, and I went myself. My heart started beating faster when I saw them. There were two people in front of me, and one of them said, "Mrs. Luz Arce?"

It's so hard to describe that moment! It was as if my heart had stopped, only to continue beating until it hurt. All of my emotions welled up inside me. A great wave of absences and presences was crashing against every inch of my soul and flesh. It could either crush me forever or take me to a new port, the port of freedom. I was scared. Most of all I feared dragging my loved ones down another road of suffering.

The children milled around in the dining room. They were uneasy. They knew something was going on, even though they didn't know what. I tried to put them at ease. I asked if we could take a break. I called them over and introduced them. I told them that the two "fellows" were friends, and I asked them to let us talk alone.

My husband sat with us. That first conversation was like racing through all those years. The lawyers asked me to appear as a witness at the commission's office on Arturo Prat Street. I agreed.

328

I was still shaking when they left, and I felt the urge to hug them good-bye. I felt warmth and acceptance. They weren't cold men who looked at me with disgust.

Beyond my beloved hills, the dark fog was lifting, and I could make out the light of the sun. It was still distant. The lawyers had barely left when I started feeling very scared again, and I held my husband and asked him to go with me to see José Luis. I needed to talk with him and tell him everything that had happened. I told him that I was going to go to the commission the following day, and I felt calmer.

My testimony lasted several days. During that time, I felt human warmth, understanding, and concern for me and my loved ones. I don't dare describe the emotions that often interrupted my story. I found out that the members of the Truth and Reconciliation Commission had been involved in fighting for human rights in many ways and from dif-ferent positions. I also realized that they had developed, or perhaps "gained" would be more accurate, a special sensitivity in their difficult work. That sensitivity, in addition to their knowledge of the pain of the years of the dictatorship, made them seem like people I could trust. However, in spite of all that understanding, there were things I couldn't avoid, and I had to make decisions. There was one exceedingly painful issue, which is that from the outside it is hard for even the best of people to understand how I could develop affectionate relationships within the DINA.

A lot of what was said about Alejandra, María Alicia, and me was true, but not all of it. However, I had to answer a lot of questions since I was the first one to take that step. I think it's important to understand what it was that happened to us. I realized a lot of people wanted to understand it too. I am aware I was revealing things that are normally just between two people, but I knew that in those days I couldn't hope of being treated like a normal person. No one looked at me like that. Perhaps I didn't even see myself that way. . . .

How was I going to intrude in their private lives now?

How would it impact their families?

I often thought I didn't have the right to do that. However, in October 1990, I decided I had to tell them everything if I was going to testify.

I discovered several things when I was talking with Carlos Fresno, Gastón Gómez, and Jorge Correa. One of the realizations that had the greatest impact on me was that María Alicia, Alejandra, and I were not the only ones who had survived an experience like that.

At the Truth and Reconciliation Commission, they asked me if there had been "love affairs" in the DINA/CNI. I couldn't help remembering the time I was held at the Yucatán Detention Center, when Krassnoff Martchenko found out I had belonged to the GAP. He tried to force me to sign a statement about the supposed orgies involving President Salvador Allende and his closest collaborators. I cried and screamed until I was unconscious trying to explain that I had never seen anything like that. They didn't believe me, and they pressured me brutally to sign. That is why I told Carlos Fresno, Gastón Gómez, and Jorge Correa, "Yes, there were love affairs in the DINA, but that happens in other places as well."

I immediately realized that the lawyers' intentions were different, and I was able to articulate a response for that too. I told them that I thought the DINA was a hierarchical institution whose omnipotence, exaggerated displays of machismo, and peculiar morals, guided by and subordinate to the doctrine of national security, produced something that went beyond cases of unrestrained behavior. It was a growing and progressive combination of activities that was clearly aimed at dehumanizing and breaking militants. Something similar occurred with the DINA's female personnel, although in a different way. As soon as I started to speak, I realized that something else was motivating the lawyers from the Truth and Reconciliation Commission in their desire to know about such ins and outs, and that it was different from what had motivated the DINA in the past. Carlos, Gastón, and Jorge, the "Rettig" Commission, wanted to uncover the reasons for what happened, but not to rile or discredit anyone. They were searching for ways to know what it is that makes people treat other people that way, especially so that it would never happen again. . . .

CARLOS FRESNO

The Truth and Reconciliation Commission lawyers, Carlos Fresno, Gastón Gómez, and Jorge Correa, were the first three people involved in human rights with whom I had any contact. There is no denying that their acceptance was important in helping me accomplish what I proposed to do. In time, I met other people, and I received support from some and a lack of understanding from others, but that is a part of life. I have no doubts that, in the long run, people who tend to sign on to the search for truth and justice will come together. Only in that way, by reconstructing history collectively, can we begin to think about true reconciliation.[64]

Carlos Fresno was undoubtedly the lawyer closest to me. He gave me essential support during the time of the Rettig Commission, and he has been my lawyer since I returned from Europe. Not only has he stood by me, but many individuals have also forgiven me because of his mediation. After that, others have begun to look upon me as a person, and some beautiful encounters have taken place.

I have talked to Carlos for hours. He is one of the people who knows my story, and we have asked ourselves many questions. We have also talked about forgiveness, about asking to be forgiven, and about forgiving. Carlos Fresno is someone who knows that to really ask for forgiveness you have to go through the process of accepting what happened and then take responsibility for it individually and collectively. Carlos Fresno also knows that if someone is asked to forgive, he or she cannot forgive right away without having lived through personal experiences that predispose him or her to do so. With Carlos Fresno I learned that in order to forgive, you have to know how to put yourself in someone else's shoes, to detach yourself from your own ways of thinking, and to ask questions. And if in doubt, you have to know how to wait for the other person to show you through concrete acts, not theory, that there is genuine repentance and an attempt at reparation. Carlos Fresno is a lawyer committed to defending human rights, and he is my friend.

64. It is worth noting that Arce's book was written several years before the creation of Chile's Mesa de Diálogo, a roundtable discussion panel established in 1999. Its participants included human rights groups and their lawyers, representatives of the Chilean military, and members of the Catholic Church. The primary goal of this roundtable was to locate the whereabouts of Chile's detained and disappeared, and its timing was significant, a year following General Augusto Pinochet's detention in London in October 1998. While there was widespread support for this attempt to reconstruct history through reconciliation, as Arce is suggesting here, some from the far right criticized the dialogue because military leaders were admitting for the first time that they did indeed have knowledge of the detained and disappeared in the country. Others from the far left also criticized the roundtable since there was no legal recourse to punish those who hid behind the amnesty afforded them during the process. The results of the final report issued by the members of the roundtable have been mixed. While the report included new information regarding some prisoners and the ways they were murdered, many have criticized the report as insufficient and incomplete, citing that there have been few concrete results from its findings. While similar meetings may be possible in the future, as of yet there is still no general national consensus on important issues relevant to this dialogue, such as amnesty for the military, which remains fiercely debated in Chile today.

331

After testifying before the Truth and Reconciliation Commission, I had to make another decision. Carlos Fresno asked me if I was willing to sign the summary of my testimony that the Rettig Commission had made to send to the courts. I told him that I was. I thought the lawyers and the courts would work to uncover what happened by comparing my statement to other testimonies. I knew I couldn't hope to be a credible witness. However, the people around me, such as Carlos Fresno, Gastón Gómez, and Jorge Correa Sutil, in spite of his youth, were profoundly sensitive to what life was like for the DINA's victims. They were the first, with the exception of my Dominican friends, who considered me a victim.

Testifying for several days and trying to keep a sense of normalcy at home shook up my life. I didn't want to hurt my family, and I decided to leave the country. That gave me two sources of worry. On the one hand, there was the challenge of adapting to a different culture, integrating, working, and above all of becoming independent and caring for my younger son since my marriage had fallen apart. It was certain that this time Juan Manuel wasn't going with me. There were high risks involved, and we had a lot of children. We couldn't all embark on this adventure. We didn't officially separate, but it was obvious that it was impossible for our relationship to continue for an indefinite period of time with an ocean between us.

I fearfully and impatiently awaited the documents I needed to be able to depart. When I went to get my passport, a military lawyer had issued an order to place a hold on it. A lawyer took the necessary steps to release the hold. Each day I was afraid that that step would alert the DINA. However, that wasn't the case.

MEETING WITH ERIKA AND VIVIANA

In December 1990, I received a notice to testify before Judge Gloria Olivares in the Alfonso Chanfreau case. A subpoena came to my house to testify in the Court of Appeals, and I thought that appearing would mean that the news would soon spread about the fact that I had given the Truth and Reconciliation Commission my statement. I had finished talking with the commission lawyers, but I hadn't signed the statement yet. I have to confess that I had the urge to run away again and hide. That defense mechanism that held me prisoner for years surfaced again. I tried to set my fears aside, and I realized I felt much closer to people on the left, to those in the Concertation government, to the survivors, and to the families of the disappeared groups than to those I had met in the DINA and the CNI. I decided I would be on their side as much as I could or as much as they would let me, assuming that I would always be Luz Arce, the traitor, the informer. It never occurred to me that I could find sensitivity and affection in that setting. It is hard for me to accept that I could be known as anything other than the "ex-DINA agent."

I made another decision. I asked Carlos to put me in touch with Erika Hennings. Carlos said he would if she accepted. That was fine with me since I wasn't trying to impose my presence on her. I tried to explain what I felt to Carlos, and begged him to tell Erika that I wanted to see her and that I would go to court even if all she wanted to do was scratch my eyes out or insult me.

Time seemed to stand still while I awaited her answer. I had been detained with Erika at 38 Londres Street. I remembered Alfonso Chanfreau and that trip we took together in the DINA truck from the Villa Grimaldi Detention Center to 38 Londres Street during that frightening month of August 1974.

Erika accepted. We met at a coffee shop, just the two of us. When I arrived, I looked anxiously at every woman who walked in, trying to recover Erika's face in my memory. I had only seen her from underneath my blindfold by the Yucatán Detention Center's window in August 1974.

When Erika arrived, we recognized each other. I thought she looked thinner than I remembered her but otherwise the same, with her long, curly, black hair and her big eyes and deep, honest gaze.

We talked a while. I was very impressed. Her respectful treatment of me surprised me, as did her candor in the questions she asked me. I'll never forget her face when she said: "You know, over the years, you collect and lose hopes. We all have our fantasies too, and one of mine is that you can tell me where my husband is. . . ." Erika wasn't there attacking me or blaming me for anything. She was a woman looking for her husband, the father of her daughter.

I stopped by the church after my meeting with Erika and before going home. I had to give thanks for that day. I imagined the effort that it must have taken for Erika to speak with me because I suppose she had to overcome many things during our encounters. During that first meeting, she asked me if I would be willing to speak to her again with a friend of hers. I asked her if that person was someone she trusted. She said yes, and I accepted. That's how I met Viviana.

When I met Viviana, I realized I was very fortunate. I spent many hours with both of them until the moment I left Chile. It was wonderful to know those two women who have done so much for me since we met. Thanks to Erika, I was able to recover bits and pieces of the conversations we had, hiding from the guards, while we were detained at 38 Londres Street. Her acceptance was like a pardon granted freely. Many months later, while I was far away living in Europe, I clutched those memories. Filled with nostalgia, I realized I hadn't expressly asked them to forgive me, and I regretted it. With them, I started to feel that finding common ground was possible, at least with some people.

I feel great affection for Erika and Viviana. It's not only gratitude; it is love, admiration, and respect. Our time together was like a ticket to reflection, growth, and preparing myself for the next steps. Everything new and positive in my life began with a gesture or word I received from them.

When I decided to leave the country, they were the ones who helped me do it. They obtained the money for the tickets and made arrangements with the people who were going to meet me abroad.

Viviana also left loved ones along the way: her sister Bárbara, her brother-in-law Edwin, and "Nani," who had been her former partner and the father of her eldest daughter. I say they were "left" because I believe she hasn't lost them. They took them from her. I got to know Erika and her daughter Natalia. I also met Viviana'a current spouse, David, along with their children, Bárbara and Paulina, and I saw where she worked.

On January 9, 1991, I went to the Court of Appeals and appeared before Judge Gloria Olivares to testify in the Chanfreau case. It was the first time I had been in court, and I was worried. Erika Hennings accompanied me. Viviana also went, and she remained close by watching.

I testified for several hours before the judge, who seemed to me at that time to be someone interested in looking for the truth. I must admit that that was a surprise to me. I was asked to return the following day. While I was in the waiting area, the DINA and CNI lawyer arrived, Víctor Manuel Avilés Mejías. He said hello to me when he saw me, and he asked me what I was doing there. I told him I had been summoned to testify, but that I didn't know for which case. The lawyer told me to leave, that he would find out, and he went to see the list. I later found out that that was just a ruse to get me to leave since that kind of information doesn't appear on the list of daily court cases. I assured him all I would say was that I had been detained and that I didn't remember anything.

The lawyer left the room. He returned a short time later with another lawyer, Sergio Rodríguez Wallis, someone who also knew Manuel Contreras. I started getting nervous and entered the judge's office. I quickly informed the clerk about what was happening. I told Erika Hennings on the phone that the lawyer, Avilés, was there.

Months later, when my testimony became public, the press located the lawyer, who maintained he didn't know who I was. I am sure he didn't remember that the most recent witnesses to the fact that we did indeed know each other were an Appeals Court judge and the court clerk.

At around noon on January 15, 1991, I took a taxi to the center of Santiago with my son, Juan Manuel. I had planned on taking Juan Manuel to meet Erika and Viviana. I looked longingly at the city streets wishing I could take them with me. Once again I felt a sense of departure. Perhaps it was too late. I didn't feel like I had the same energy I had in previous years. Could I start over?

Erika and Viviana gave me the tickets. Carlos Fresno arrived to take us to the airport. On the way there in his car, I signed each page of the testimony one by one so he could send it to the courts.

We abandoned Chile in an Iberian Airlines jumbo jet. Once again my life and the lives of my two sons fit into a few suitcases. We carried the cash we had in a backpack. We had just over two hundred dollars.

35

IN EUROPE

Living in Europe was a great experience. The time I spent there helped me realize how much I need my family, my husband, and my children. Besides that, I realized that testifying before the "Rettig" Commission was not enough.

I often felt as though I was on an island where not merely the countryside, the language, and the climate were different. I had a job and support from several people who were committed to helping us, but I was the same person with all my past. I had moved from one continent to another, but retained all my conflicts and sorrows with me. An ocean separated me from my own life.

My older son learned German quickly. He found a job and got married. My younger son and I felt closer everyday. We felt like we were drifting at first, and we clung to one another as to a plank that would someday take us to dry land.

I would characterize 1991 as a year of reencounters since, from far away, the same thing was happening to Juan Manuel and to me. We were able to learn how to reassess one another as people and to discover that we wanted to keep living together. We discovered that, in the thirteen years we had lived together, we had never had the option of having a space apart from the unforeseen events that my past life constantly brought with it. The fears and the nightmares had ended up separating us.

The distance between us made all of the seeds we had sown together sprout and awakened the urgency of seeing one another again. Juan Manuel was able to travel to where I was living with our son, and we decided to get married. After so many years together, we chose to unite our lives formally. But Juan Manuel had to return. During those two weeks together, with time flying by faster than usual, we realized we

had to make some decisions. We were going to try to be a family together. However, I knew it wasn't enough for my husband, my children,
and my friends to know who I am. I knew that living with my family in
Chile came at a price, and that price was saying publicly that my name
is Luz, Luz Arce.

I started feeling again like I could leave whenever I needed to, and
that I must do it because my presence only causes problems for those I
love. I worked hard at convincing myself that I didn't need much. But
that wasn't the case. While it is true that I need and love a certain amount
of time alone to reflect or to just get away to find myself again, I also
need my children's laughter, the familiar sounds around the house, and
their complaining and whining. I need my husband with his love, his
understanding, and his support. I often thought about an instance several years before when I was feeling very ill and depressed. He said to
me, "The problem is that you don't have a project of your own." That
was true. During all those prior years, my life lacked roots and a purpose. Therefore, when I started writing this book, working on it chapter
by chapter, that was a good time to make the decision to return to Chile
and testify in court.

My husband left Europe pleading with God to help me try to understand the meaning of each hour and to find the right moment to take
each step.

ABOVE ALL A CHRISTIAN

Even though I don't say it all the time, and even though I forget to pin
my cross on my clothes, even though that may be difficult to understand, I feel I am a child of God above all else. Since the time I spent in
Europe, I believe I have learned to understand a bit more what it means
to be a Christian. My faith gave me strength as I continued writing and
revisiting the past. Giving birth to oneself can be painful, but can there
be anything more beautiful than life? . . .

Believing in God and sensing His love helped me feel in a fundamental way that all human beings must rise up against their own slavery. As I sensed that divine filiation deep inside me, I saw a new light
that would help me make a greater difference and start a new life with
the knowledge that human justice, as given by the world, is radically
different from the justice granted by God. Pain became a seedbed
within me and I started to dream the beautiful dream of reconciliation,

337

reconciliation rooted in truth. I knew that those who can look from the perspective of the marginalized, those of us who are discriminated against for various reasons, who can put themselves in the shoes of an outcast like me, all of them would be on my side.

As my awareness matured, terrified by the demands that came with it, I began to understand that God does not want injustice, does not want lies, and does not want anyone to be subject to slavery. He wants a new order. I think God questions from that standpoint, and that He listens to each one of His children.

I realized something I already knew in theory and that is so difficult to experience in life. But it is indisputable. Under no circumstances does God approve of plans that are based on death, oppression, or torture of any sort. The disappeared, the executed, the tortured, their families, and every marginalized human being are nothing but a living prophecy that invites and calls us together, based on historical experience. How could anyone hide genocide? How could anyone approve of a political order that justifies the slavery of so many human beings? How could anyone be an accomplice to hiding and covering up the truth?

ON HATRED AND REENCOUNTERS

It was winter in Austria, when at four in the afternoon light begins to flee, announcing a long and early night. When I returned home, I stood for a moment looking at the windows in the hall. Since there wasn't any heat on, they were covered in an icy lace, and through it you could make out the smoke from the chimneys as it drifted up into the blue sky. In the midst of that beauty, I was overcome by a persistent nostalgia that filled my mind with images of my homeland. I saw the profile of mountains and bits of clouds surrounding images of my loved ones, their faces and gestures.

I thought of my son doing his homework inside, and I looked at the flowerpots by the windows, the ones Juan Manuelito used to give me and that he cared for with such love. He was my beautiful gardener who managed to interrupt the pervasive whiteness that covered the city. The flowers continued to bloom, ignoring the freezing temperatures outside and breaking the monochromatic harmony with their green and red strokes of color. I was filled with joy as I remembered his face when the tiny tomato plant grew and grew until it almost filled the kitchen with its yellow flowers and its harvest of a lone tomato.

Full of Vienna's clean air and with feelings of nostalgia and tenderness, I entered the house. I kissed my son, made some coffee, and decided to read a book that had just arrived from Chile: *Los secretos del Comando Conjunto*, by Mónica González and Héctor Contreras.[65] I couldn't put it down until I finished it. I didn't sleep. I couldn't. I have felt many things since I distanced myself from the CNI, but never in such a visceral way. The question I had asked myself so many times finally seemed to have an answer. Don't I hate them? Or is my fear so great that I don't even dare hate them?

I felt myself being hurled back into the inferno. Everything started to hurt. I could smell burning flesh or blood. I perceived that stench once again, of which I had been part. I felt my own powerlessness and theirs as well. I heard that primeval scream again, the one that the tortured man makes. Father, why have you forsaken me? It is the pinnacle of humanity's pain. I was terrified. Crying, I asked "Lord, is this what hatred is?" I knew it was. It was hatred, emptiness, exile, a loss of happiness and hope. I learned that hating is another form of dying.

When hatred started to take shape, assuming the form of a monstrous presence that was swallowing me, a phrase from Saint Augustine resounded within me: "How could I hate someone who could someday be my brother." And I felt smaller, more insignificant. The mount of Nazareth and the Beatitudes seemed so far away then! I was very far away from my thought that there are no evil people, only people with a past that helps you understand them, even if it doesn't absolve them. However, the realization that hatred does indeed exist was transformed into the certainty that it is possible to vanquish hatred, just as it is possible to build love.

On January 10, 1992, I asked an Austrian friend, Elke, to go to a travel agency with me. I bought two tickets for January 15th. I had made my decision. I was going to return to Chile with my young son. As I packed our bags and made arrangements, I remembered a mental image I had

65. This book was coauthored by world-renowned Chilean journalist Mónica González and Héctor Contreras, a Chilean lawyer. It details activities of the dictatorship's "Joint Command," a clandestine military organization that existed in the mid-1970s and that focused primarily on persecuting and eliminating members of the Communist Party's Central Committee. The Joint Command was most likely created under the auspices of the SIFA (Air Force Intelligence Service). Although it is possible that the Joint Command collaborated with the DINA, evidence suggests that these organizations were involved in a power struggle with one another. Arce's references to tensions between the air force and the DINA seem to support this view.

created in the past. I saw that imaginary loft where I had hidden everything I didn't need or had forgotten, but now the light was entering the darkness and the clean air was freshening up everything. Love had helped me understand that forgetting and accepting a horrific reality can only come after recovering those pieces that have been tucked away in a corner and hidden.

GLORIA OLIVARES

In Chile, most people know about Mrs. Olivares. For several weeks during 1992, she monopolized the pages, magazine covers, and newspaper headlines. She gave the public a sense of anticipation as judicial steps were being taken in the Chanfreau case.

Gloria is an attractive, feminine, elegant, and very intelligent woman. As they say in Chile, she's "good-looking." Her abilities are undeniable. There is a reason she is one of the few women who have managed to be appointed to serve as judge in a field traditionally dominated by men.

Gloria Olivares exudes vitality in spite of the fact that she suffers terrible pain from arthritis. However, she stayed in court for long periods at a time without uttering a single complaint. She showed courage and spirit. Witnessing her integrity inspired me on more than one occasion and helped me continue testifying in spite of the late hour.

On several occasions, as I was leaving the courthouse, I saw her carrying a stack of books on human rights law as she left. She continued studying at home.

When the Chanfreau case was transferred to a military court, Mrs. Olivares left the scene. However, all of us who feel some level of commitment to defending human rights are in her debt.

It is striking to see how the officers who belonged to the DINA and who were involved in serious human rights violations arrive at different courts accompanied by their bodyguards and lawyers to tell "their version" of the story. They try to escape justice by using and abusing any opportunity or legal tool afforded them by a democratic judicial framework.

That is also part of democracy. We all have the right to defend ourselves, and they do too. And even though it may suddenly seem like injustice is prevailing, I continue appearing in court because I think that it is important to record the experience of each survivor in court.

What Gloria Olivares accomplished in 1992 did not lead to finding

340

Alfonso Chanfreau, but it was a milestone in many respects. The judge managed to force all the different officers implicated in the case to appear in court. For months, she and several magistrates sent subpoenas to which the accused did not reply. When they had no choice but to appear, they lied. But their lies were recorded in the court proceedings, in the hearts of the surviving witnesses they faced, and in public opinion by means of press reports.

Besides recognizing Gloria Olivares's efforts and achievements, I would like to state now that what I have stated here is not a simple "moral victory." What happened in 1992 in Room Six of the Court of Appeals was unprecedented. There were, however, more effective things, such as how different sectors came together and showed their support for Justice Olivares and their condemnation of judges in Room Three of the Supreme Court because of the series of outlandish rulings they made. I believe it was also important for me to realize something else at that time: even when truth could not be established through existing means, I became convinced that no extralegal solution would do. We must continue searching for the truth. If one resource runs out, then we have to create others.

During 1992, human rights were much discussed, thanks to the media. The result was that there was greater awareness about what happened.

THE CHILEAN BUREAU OF INVESTIGATION

When I returned to Chile, I was greeted not by human rights organizations but by the Bureau of Investigation. I was in the country more than twenty days before this became known. Planned or not, information began leaking to the press when I started appearing in court.

My contact with the Bureau's agents was a pleasant surprise for me. I realized in 1992 that the organization has few resources at its disposal and that they try to make up for that lack by working harder. During 1992 and so far in 1993, the Chilean Bureau of Investigation has carried out most of the human rights investigations, especially in cases where there have been results. The judges have apparently begun sending their cases to this organization.

Another encouraging sign for me was when I realized that the Bureau is an institution that functions within the institutional guidelines of a democracy. I was always under the impression that they planned their agenda on their own, but it's not like that. Every step they undertake is an order from a higher power in one of the courts. Regarding human rights, the Bureau's agents are the ones in charge of initially approaching the witnesses who must later appear in court to confirm their testimony.

Of course it's paradoxical. After years of running away from that institution, I am now able to appreciate the agents I have met. I am convinced that their contribution will be decisive someday in establishing the truth about what happened.

36

IN THE COURTS

During 1992, I participated in seventy-three court cases. It was like a marathon.

I am not going to tackle the particulars of every hearing. Nor will I reveal details that could hinder future investigations or divulge confidential information about the proceedings. However, I do want to refer to situations that occurred, especially those that may be helpful in reconstructing scenes and encounters in which I participated and that I think may be important for public knowledge.

My first face-to-face encounter in 1992 was in the case related to the kidnapping and subsequent disappearance of Alfonso René Chanfreau Oyarce. After having gone on several occasions to Room Six of the Court of Appeals to answer questions regarding my statements, I was called to appear on March 9, 1992 with Erika Hennings and Miguel Angel Rebolledo to identify police major Gerardo Ernesto Godoy García, who was in active service at that time.

I recognized Major Godoy from a distance because of how he walked. He arrived escorted by bodyguards dressed in civilian clothing and with a female lawyer from his institution.

The judge took the officer's statement before she had us confront each other. Then Mrs. Hennings arrived, who in fact identified him as the officer in charge of the group of DINA agents that kidnapped her husband, Alfonso Chanfreau, from their home on the night of July 31, 1974. Once the proceeding with Mrs. Hennings ended, it was my turn to identify Officer Godoy García. Then it was Miguel Angel Rebolledo's turn as the only survivor of a group that disappeared in its entirety along with Alfonso Chanfreau on August 13, 1974. Miguel Angel was removed from that group by Lieutenant Godoy García.

The officer admitted that he had been part of the DINA and that he was the leader of the Tucán Group. He said he remembered having detained someone called "Emilio," which was, in fact, Alfonso's alias. He also remembered Mrs. Hennings. When the identification was complete, the officer left the court and avoided the press by trying to hide behind the upturned collar of his jacket, dark sunglasses, and a cap that partially covered his face. However, he was identified in some press photos at the time.

ENCOUNTER WITH ROLF WENDEROTH POZO

I went to court. The plaintiff, Erika Hennings, and her lawyer, Nelson Caucoto, were there. Rolf Wenderoth, who had testified before the judge the previous day, arrived more than forty-five minutes late to court accompanied by his lawyer.

Before I begin, I want to clarify that I have not protected Rolf Wenderoth in court. I also confess that if someday justice is able to illuminate all that remains in the shadows and that if he is absolved of any responsibility, whether intellectual or criminal, I will be happy. However, I must admit that, as I hear other witness accounts, it is becoming increasingly clear to me everyday that his participation in the DINA was greater than I knew.

When I started writing this book, I knew I would see Rolf Wenderoth again, and I knew that, barring some chance encounter, it would be in court. I feared that moment. It happened on July 1, 1992. It was leaked to me that the day before Rolf Wenderoth had tried to deny even having known me.

The case in question concerned Alfonso Chanfreau, Erika's husband. I went to identify him knowing that it would give me the opportunity to resolve some serious doubts. I would know for sure whether or not I could stand by my statements in his presence. Then I could be certain that the bonds were broken as I thought.

The hours preceding that meeting before Judge Olivares and the court clerk, Carlos Castro, were difficult. Certain issues were making me increasingly hesitant that day. Besides my being a former DINA officer, there was the personal relationship between us during the DINA/CNI period, and I had worked with him in the Maipú School in 1989 where he was an administrator after having retired from the army.

I had tried to establish a family with my husband in 1989. It seemed

344

like Rolf was also making an effort to stabilize his personal life. There were some considerations that had not arisen in other proceedings. Perhaps I also had the desire inside me to be sure that Rolf isn't a murderer or an accomplice to murder. It wasn't so much for his sake, since everyone has to take responsibility for his or her own actions. I was thinking of his daughters. I had known them since they were children.

When Rolf Wenderoth crossed the threshold of the judge's office, any uncertainty was dispelled. I spontaneously stood up and asked Gloria Olivares for permission to greet Rolf. I went over to him, and he, though looking downcast or nervous, accepted my greeting by warmly embracing my hand. I didn't feel like it was forced. I don't know how he felt about it. There we were. In spite of everything that had happened, we could talk. Rolf formed a sad smile. I really admire his loyalty to those who, in my opinion, don't deserve it. I tried to explain to him why I had testified before the Rettig Commission. Rolf asked about my family. I would say that within a certain framework of respect, we each maintained the position that befits us at the present time.

On one of those occasions, after listening to me, Rolf asked a question about my testimony. "Luz, don't you think you said more than necessary?"

"Are you referring to our personal relationship?"

"Yes," he answered.

I gave him my reasons and explained why I had said absolutely everything. Then I added, "If I hadn't done it, all of you would have used it as an argument to discredit me."

"All of you? What do you mean 'all of you'?" he said.

"I don't know if you would have, but your superior, Contreras Sepúlveda would have."

At one point I told Rolf that all I was asking of him was that he answer the question: "Where are they?" Rolf repositioned himself in his chair and bent toward me to say, "Luz, I didn't kill anyone. . . ."

I answered him, "I believe you, Rolf. What I cannot believe is that you don't know about at least a few cases, that you don't know who made the decisions, how they murdered them, what they did later, how and where they hid them."

There was even some joking, like that we could work together and make a diagram of the DINA, to which he responded, "Ask the priests to do it." Of course everything happened within a context. He had his position, and I had mine, but we spoke respectfully to one another. We

345

said good-bye the same way, without recriminations, but I cannot say that I am still Rolf's friend.

I felt very free that day. At the same time, I realized that even though I didn't feel the least bit hostile toward Rolf, the situation was radically different from what it had been up until 1989. The abyss that separates us is final.

Rolf Wenderoth, at least from what I observed, testified just like all the army officers I have identified. That is, he tried to clear Pedro Espinoza Bravo of everything, which was very much in line with what Espinoza Bravo had testified in the Letelier case. It is worth noting that Rolf Wenderoth had no problem recognizing that the ones responsible for the MIR repression were officers Krassnoff Martchenko and Ricardo Lawrence Mires. Perhaps it's because he's sure that this is something that is impossible to deny. He only made one small attempt at pointing out the enormous contribution I made to the DINA. Rolf is smart enough to know and realize, better than others, that no one, not even the most uninformed person in these matters, will believe that I am responsible for giving the DINA all the militants from the Communist Party, the Socialist Party, and the MIR. This is, however, what other agents are saying, trying to influence the judges.

Something else Rolf's statement had in common with testimony given by other DINA/CNI officers was the attempt to place blame on high-ranking officers from other institutions, such as the navy, the air force, and the police. There he hit upon some truth: the organizational chart of the DINA/CNI, in all its many stages, is known.

One interesting fact worth stressing is that Rolf Wenderoth was the only army officer who arrived with just one lawyer, a lawyer who left at 5:30 in the afternoon, several hours before his client. He also appeared in court without bodyguards. Rolf Wenderoth left the courthouse after ten o'clock at night completely alone. Erika and I went to have some coffee. It was cold. We talked about the situation for a while. I was somewhat tired, so when my husband came to pick me up, we left. I had cleared up another unknown.

ENCOUNTERS WITH GERARDO URRICH AND MANUEL CAREVIC

On Friday, August 7, 1992, I was asked to appear before Judge Virginia Bravo in San Miguel's Third Criminal Court. I had to make two consec-

346

utive appearances to confront officers Gerardo Ernesto Urrich González and Manuel Andrés Carevic Cubillos. These proceedings were part of the case concerning the kidnapping and disappearance of Rodolfo Valentín González Pérez, the young FACH soldier who helped me while I was at the Military Hospital.

When I entered the office that Virginia Bravo had reserved for the meeting, I immediately recognized Officer Urrich González, who was sitting in a chair. My mind suddenly flashed back to July 24, 1974. Seeing him and feeling the rope being yanked when he ordered them to hang me up in the Terranova tower at Villa Grimaldi was a single sensation. I felt an enormous pressure welling up inside me, and my first reaction was rejection and disgust. But when I observed his discomfort in my presence, I realized that the situation was different now. We were in a different place, and we were in the presence of Virginia Bravo. She seemed imposing to me. In that little room, Mrs. Bravo represented the enormous difference that existed between July 24, 1974 and August 7, 1992.

I felt powerless as I listened to Urrich González say that as an analyst he had only typed reports. "I did paperwork," he said. "I wrote documents." That was a curious way, I thought, to describe those of us who had been DINA prisoners: documents, paperwork. I'm sure it goes without saying that the next officer I encountered, Carevic Cubillos, stated that he carried from one place to another the "paperwork" that Urrich González had completed.

As I listened to them lying shamelessly, and once I had overcome the extreme nervousness I initially felt, I was overcome by a new feeling of fear. But after breathing deeply, I made myself comfortable in my chair and realized that in none of those confrontations did the important thing, truth and justice, seem to exist. However, I have been able to find some answers. I know who I am, and I haven't hidden anything, even the most private part of myself. And I also knew that the way they looked at me, between surly, upset, and evasive, was just another way to prove that they also know who I am: one of their victims expressing a fragment of truth. It is the truth they hide, the truth they cannot or are unable to express. And I knew that I was finally beginning to overcome the fear that still haunted me like a ghost. I also discovered that my feelings are legitimate, like those of other survivors. All of this welled up inside of me as I listened to them saying they were just "analysts" or "letter carriers."

The officers, Urrich González and Carevic Cubillos, were the first to leave the office. They went out the back entrance to avoid the press, and they left in vehicles with very dark, tinted windows, which, like a mirror, reflect the difference between fleeing, hiding your face, and showing yourself openly. When I said good-bye to the judge, I felt at peace leaving through the front door to meet Erika Hennings and Viviana Uribe, who had accompanied me that day. I felt happy to be someone who is trying to come and go through the front door, rather than avoiding the light of day.

BASCLAY ZAPATA, ALIAS "EL TROGLO"

In the afternoon of the day I faced Urrich González and Carevic Cubillos, I had to appear before Judge Gloria Olivares in the offices of Room Six of the Court of Appeals. There were other witnesses there, and I was going to have to face "el Troglo."

I know what kind of a DINA agent this man was. I saw him for many years. He was first with Osvaldo Romo Mena. They were both assigned to the Halcón 1 Group that was led by Miguel Krassnoff Martchenko. I have also heard testimony about Basclay Zapata Reyes's brutality. For example, he once raised his gun, aimed, and killed Eulogio del Carmen Fritz Monsalve with one shot right in the middle of the street, in broad daylight, in front of several passersby. There are also accounts of the rape and sexual abuse that Basclay Zapata Reyes committed against female prisoners, some of whom survived.

Besides my statements in court, Osvaldo Romo Mena and numerous eyewitness testimonies of surviving witnesses point to Basclay Zapata Reyes as one of the agents assigned to Krassnoff Martchenko's group in the DINA. However, not only did he exhibit the same deceitful behavior in the courts that the other DINA agents had, his attitude was also crude and vulgar. It's shocking when, as in Basclay Zapata Reyes's case, ignorance is in concert with the sort of power he wielded in the DINA and that he apparently still believes he has.

As reported in the daily news, "El Troglo" left the court hiding his face behind a newspaper and with a plastic bag from a well known store on top. His bodyguards were tugging him along in his temporary and premeditated blindness. It was surely an attempt on his part to avoid being recognized by more survivors or family members or by any of the many other people who witnessed arrests or other acts and who could be added to the lists of witnesses. He hurriedly slipped out, making his way down corridors and elevators, offering a sad spectacle he repeated in all his initial appearances in Judge Olivares's court.

Since this way of leaving was both humiliating and uncomfortable, for his final appearances in the Court of Appeals as a civilian he wore a coat with a hood that covered everything but his eyes. That was the image that appeared on television and in the papers. I suppose his attitude must have seemed shameful for his institution as well, because when he had to appear in the Court of Appeals again with his superior in the DINA, Officer Krassnoff Martchenko, they both came in uniform.

Basclay Zapata participated in confrontations in Room Six of the Court of Appeals for three consecutive days. He listened to various witnesses. Then he stopped coming. The excuse he gave was that he was only passing through Santiago and that he had gone to his home in Iquique to change his clothes.

I have a vivid recollection of each time I had to face "El Troglo" to confirm my statements. The first time was in the court offices, and then I saw him again in our reconstruction of the scene to identify what had been the DINA's Yucatán Detention Center on 38 Londres Street, which is now 40 Londres Street. On both occasions, the officer denied everything the surviving witnesses had stated. But there are some things that were really ridiculous and that show what kind of person he was, like when he said that if one of us who had been arrested by the DINA had ever been taken to 38 Londres Street, it must have been to have a sandwich since, according to him, that place was a cafeteria. He stated that his official duty was to drive a truck carrying meals from the kitchen in the building the military officers called Diego Portales to the "restaurant" at 38 Londres Street. When we returned to the scene of 38 Londres Street and he was asked to point to the location of the kitchen, he said he didn't know where it was. When they asked him where he delivered the meals, he went with the clerk, Carlos Castro, to the doorway at the entrance to the building. Nor could he describe the location of the kitchen in the Diego Portales building, and he said he didn't remember where he lived during those years.

Regarding me, he said he didn't know me but that he "thought he had seen me on television a few days before." At one point I asked him if he and María Teresa Osorio, his wife, had had any children. I even pointed out to him that she herself had told me that they had gotten married. He said that they were separated and that they didn't have any children. That is also a lie. Basclay Zapata Reyes has three children. He really managed to surprise me when he said that he didn't know there were any detained and disappeared people in Chile.

In general, on the occasions I had to be present with him and the judge, Basclay Zapata Reyes acted in a rude and impertinent manner even with Mrs. Olivares. One of the things he made certain to deny was the name his own friends at the DINA had given him: "El Troglo" or troglodyte. But he won't get anywhere saying that they called him Ricardo or Roberto in the DINA. There are too many survivors who will never forget his name, his face, his long hair à la Prince Valiant—a character in children's books from my childhood—his profane language, and arrogance. Even though Basclay Zapata Reyes suffers from "total amnesia" today, there are many of us who have a better memory than he does, and our recollection isn't limited to where we lived.

FERNANDO LAURIANI

On August 25, 1992, at 2:30 in the afternoon, I had to appear in Santiago's Eighth Criminal Court. I was asked to identify Fernando Eduardo Lauriani Maturana in front of Judge Raúl Trincado and the clerk, María Eliana Parra. This event was part of Mr. Trincado's investigation of two cases related to the kidnapping and subsequent disappearance of Claudio Thauby Pacheco and Jaime Robotham Bravo.

Seeing Lauriani Maturana face-to-face was basically the same as facing the other DINA agents. They all stated they didn't know me but that they had seen me in the press or on television just a few days before. They admitted they had been in the DINA, but they were never agents. They were analysts. They said they knew about me and my collaboration, but that they didn't know anything about the DINA or its personnel, and so forth. In Lauriani Maturana's case, he stated that he had been in charge of analyzing the government's educational policies while he worked in an office at Headquarters. He said he had never been called Pablo or Pablito, which the DINA personnel used pejoratively. He said they called him Lalo and that it wasn't an alias, just the diminutive of his first name, Eduardo. He said he thought that, for who knows what personal reasons, I must have some dark, evil, and vengeful intentions and that he never set foot in the Ollagüe or Villa Grimaldi detention centers.

When I found myself alone that day with Lauriani Maturana, I couldn't hold back and said, "And what's wrong with you that you don't recognize me?"

350

Lauriani and "El Troglo" had amazed me beyond belief. As I saw him try to explain to me that he didn't have a choice, I felt real rage and asked him, "Fernando, how can you tell your children not to lie?"

He started telling me about his misfortunes. He said he lived in terror, that the sound of the phone frightened him because he was afraid they would ask him to testify, and he said that at school they tell his children that their father is a murderer. He said his wife couldn't stand it anymore, and so on.

While we were alone, Officer Lauriani Maturana was himself. He knows me. He remembers things. But when there is a third party present, he says, "I don't know this woman."

I saw him in court a second time that same year. This time we appeared in Room Six of the Court of Appeals before Judge Gloria Olivares as part of the investigation surrounding the Judicial System's attempt to establish the truth regarding what happened to Alfonso Chanfreau.

Besides testifying before the judge, the officer was identified by more than a dozen and a half witnesses in the Chanfreau case. On that occasion, he came face-to-face after eighteen years with some of the survivors of a mission that he himself had led as a DINA officer. That was the case involving Erick Zott Chuecas and Luis Enrique Peebles Skarnic. Lauriani Maturana and his Vampiro Group from the DINA's BIM Unit arrested Erick Zott in January 1975 in Valparaíso and drove him along with other prisoners to Villa Grimaldi. After that, the same Lauriani drove Zott Chuecas to the German Dignity Colony. On that trip, they stopped to "pick up" Doctor Luis Peebles where he was being detained by the navy in Talcahuano. I'm saying "pick up" in quotation marks because Lauriani Maturana practically kidnapped Peebles Skarnic and took him to the Dignity Colony with Zott. In spite of the fact that both Zott and Peebles are very convincing and thorough in their statements, Officer Lauriani Maturana didn't admit any fact that would implicate him as a DINA agent.

I also had to participate at the close of the proceedings on that occasion. Just as in the previous encounter, the officer had his pencil and notepad in hand so he could take notes and write down everything that was said in court. However, as always, things didn't seem to work out when he tried to refute something or ask for an explanation, and he never seemed to find what he was looking for in his own notes. During his appearance with me, he told only of the unusual things had happened and, of course, revealed nothing that would help explain Alfonso

Chanfreau's whereabouts since August 13, 1974. Apparently, under his lawyers' instructions, Lauriani tried to avoid letting me refer to personal things. It almost seemed like it was more painful for him to recognize his limitations than the fact that he arrested and tortured people, took prisoners to the Dignity Colony, opened up the chest of his former classmate at the Military School, Claudio Thauby, and who knows how many other things.

When I entered the court, I greeted Lauriani Maturana by his first name, with a simple "Hi, Fernando!" I knew he would deny knowing me again. When I had barely been able to say a couple of sentences, Lieutenant Colonel Lauriani asked the court to forbid me to make offensive statements in front of him.

Mrs. Olivares asked him to which offensive statements he was referring. Officer Lauriani said that I had called him an offensive name in previous proceedings that took place in Santiago's Eighth Criminal Court. The judge insisted he tell her what it was about because she hadn't heard anything offensive. The officer said that he couldn't even repeat the things I had said. Then the judge turned to me and asked, "Mrs. Arce, did you offend the officer?"

"No, Your Honor. I don't think I have offended the commander, unless it was because of a sentence I repeated word for word when Judge Raúl Trincado asked me to. It wasn't a sentence of my making, Your Honor, but the word-for-word repetition of something Krassnoff Martchenko said to Lauriani because of a series of mistakes that Lieutenant Lauriani had made. It all happened at the Terranova Detention Center, and the officer present here said that he was thinking about killing himself because of what happened. . . ."

"And what was it that you said, Mrs. Arce?" the judge asked again.

"'Dumb ass,' Your Honor. Krassnoff said that Officer Lauriani was a dumb ass."

Lauriani was visibly upset by that exchange. His face was all red, and he asked to have the exchange removed from the record. However, since the opposing party can give its version only later during these hearings and can under no circumstances interfere in the statement made by anyone else, the entire exchange appeared in the report that was sent to the Second Tribunal of the Fourth Military Court a few days later. Lauriani Maturana continued complaining to the judge about my supposed offensive treatment of him to the point that the judge eventually discovered that Officer Lauriani Maturana was also referred to by the nicknames Pink Panther and Inspector Clouseau, which is what his own subordinates called him because of all the absurd and ridiculous things that happened everyday as he carried out his duties as a DINA agent and later as leader of the Vampiro Group in the DINA's BIM Unit. He insisted that his role was that of an "education analyst," and that he did not work as an agent but as a functionary at Headquarters.

The now Lieutenant Colonel Lauriani Maturana lived up to the nicknames of days gone by when he left the judge's office. As he tried to avoid the reporters awaiting him outside, he remained trapped for quite some time in the elevator. When he managed to get out, he turned toward the side of the building where the doors were locked, and he had to turn around and walk through the entire courthouse from the door on Bandera Street to the one located on Morandé. Obviously, with all those hitches, the press not only caught up with him but completely surrounded him and followed him the whole way to the door. As usual, the guards who were with him attacked the reporters and tried to keep them from interrogating the officer who flatly refused to make any statement.

If anyone ever doubted the stories about the ridiculous situations in which that officer had found himself in the past, that day everyone was convinced that he was still the same not only with regard to the deceitfulness of his statements but also in his clumsiness and that kind of bad luck that seems to follow him. Although he puts forth in his defense that he has an unblemished record of service, which is probably true, his problems apparently arise when he has to think for himself or make decisions. As long as he doesn't have to do that, Officer Lauriani will have an "unblemished" record.

37

MIGUEL KRASSNOFF MARTCHENKO

My memory of "El Troglo" is closely tied to that of Miguel Krassnoff Martchenko, his gestures, his words, his shouting, and the torture to which he subjected me when he was a DINA officer. I confronted him in court in October 1992 along with more than a dozen other witnesses.

He is not the same as he was in 1974. Nor is he the ghost that appeared in my nightmares for more than a decade and a half.

I was able to prove that my memories are not fantasies of a deranged mind. He was there, just like I was, older. He showed a great ability to alter his personality. He was very courteous and polite to Judge Olivares and very rude to me. His gestures seemed servile at times, as he bowed before the judge as though she were his superior. He didn't inspire respect, and it didn't even help him to come wearing his institution's uniform. He showed his true self with me, by treating me badly, raising his voice, and insulting me. Krassnoff continues to think that the weapons he used during the DINA are still valid.

I must confess that, when I first saw him, my heart beat faster and my throat got dry. I picked up the glass that was on the table in front of me and took a drink of water, and when I did that I saw the judge sitting there. She looked so refined, so sure of herself, and so comfortable. That is when I noticed that I had adopted the same posture in my chair as when I was a prisoner or after I had been tortured. Without realizing it, that man's mere presence was enough to make me revert to that quasi fetal position, bent forward and looking for some warmth to alleviate the physical and psychological pain. My mind betrayed me and raced toward the past. But I was able to continue by looking at the judge, remembering my friends, knowing that I was telling the truth, and thinking of all the love, understanding,

354

and help I have received. Case after case, I continue to break those ties of terror to the past.

I must confess that after each confrontation, my inner healing process continues. I honestly think it will take me a long time to take it all in. That was why that year was exhausting, but I don't regret it because that is the only way I will be able to find Luz, by recovering myself.

FACE-TO-FACE WITH MARCELO MOREN BRITO

Other proceedings conducted by Gloria Olivares in the Chanfreau case involved encounters with retired officer Marcelo Moren Brito, in the months of September and October 1992.

More than fifteen surviving witnesses were called to testify. That hearing lasted more than twenty hours. I was scheduled to appear last on that occasion as well, and once again I was showing signs of the weighty effort that daily attendance at court entails. I even had to postpone appearances in other cases, and once again domestic responsibilities fell mostly on my husband.

I felt awful as I entered the courtroom to face Marcelo Moren Brito. In the beginning, the officer adopted the same attitude Krassnoff Martchenko had shown toward me. It was unbelievable. Everything flashed before my eyes in a fraction of a second. I felt that I didn't have the patience to put up with Moren Brito that day, nor did I feel like taking that kind of treatment from anyone. That is why I reacted and told the court that if the gentleman present there attacked me, that I would do the exact same thing, and that I would even use the same words he was using. Moren Brito raised his voice too, and I interrupted him. We were both called to order. That was when I adopted the attitude that you're supposed to have in court, but Moren Brito also had to maintain a respectful attitude.

Although those proceedings mostly required a repetition of the statements I had made in other cases, it also contributed some interesting elements. Moren Brito told me I was wrong in my statement regarding Sergio Pérez Molina's death. He said he didn't die at the Ollagüe Detention Center, that he was actually in a great deal of pain at the time when I thought he had died. He said that he had been taken from Ollagüe and driven to the DINA clinic, and that he died because it took the doctor two hours to arrive. He later told the same story in front of Lautaro Videla Moya, Lumi's brother and Sergio's brother-in-law.

355

As I sat in front of Moren Brito, I remembered the times when I could recognize him just by his booming voice, his ostentatious way of commanding by yelling, and his footsteps as he marched from office to office, usually misplacing any document that fell in his hands. As I heard him say that he never had the power to make decisions, I remembered once again the extreme conditions in which I lived for years when I was subjected to men like that one. He even claimed that I had more power in the DINA than he did. I felt more than ever that visceral need to recuperate my own identity as an individual apart from them, which is not just a legal matter. My decision to return to Chile and appear in court acquired a new sense of urgency. It was a means for me to overcome the ambiguity of a meaningless way of life, to eliminate the anguish of living without an identity.

During the years when I was incapable of confronting even my memories, it often seemed to me that the closer my words got to reality the more unintelligible they sounded. I couldn't express what I had lived through. Something inside me rebelled against accepting that all that violence was real, that I had been nothing, and that I had no rights. I wanted to believe it wasn't true, that I had gone mad at some point, and that it wasn't real. The first times I tried to articulate it, I had the impression the person listening to me couldn't understand it either. During the 1980s I asked myself why no one seemed to understand. It seemed the world that I had locked within myself was so terrifying that it could only bring about horror, rejection, and fierce condemnation. I have experienced that blemish, that stain.

That night in court, as I looked at Moren Brito and saw his attitude, I understood once again that my memories are real and that he and so many others exercised a kind of violence over the victims of the dictatorship that could only compare to the most extreme genocides that have occurred during the twentieth century. That is why I, at least, cannot remain silent.

One of the things that surprised me most during the confrontation with Moren Brito was his suggesting that the attitude of the surviving witnesses is actually normal. Word for word he said, "In every war, sooner or later, those on the losing side get their revenge, and now there are manipulative politicians who are using them to their own advantage, to start a movement that denigrates the army. . . ." It was clear to me that only those who think that people are searching for the truth just to denigrate the army are the ones who committed crimes against humanity and who are trying to shift their responsibility onto an entire institution.

It seems like Moren Brito doesn't think the DINA or his staff inflicted brutal violence upon their victims and, in an atmosphere that extended beyond those directly "violated," their victims' families. It is as though his mind were still imprisoned by the same thoughts, feelings, and motivations it was in 1974. It is clear that Moren Brito has not rebelled against that kind of enslavement to which he is still subjected. His confidence in the fact that he too will receive amnesty is another expression of impunity. I felt very sad.

ENCOUNTER WITH RICARDO LAWRENCE MIRES

Retired police officer Lawrence Mires did not receive any assistance from his institution the day he had to appear in Room Six of the Court of Appeals before Judge Gloria Olivares. He had to give a statement in the case concerning Alfonso Chanfreau's kidnapping and subsequent disappearance. According to what the officer himself said, he came with lawyers and bodyguards from the army. The witnesses there had already noticed that fact since, after attending court cases for several weeks, we managed to recognize several of the lawyers and guards who accompanied the officers. Lawrence Mires himself explained that he and all the officers who belonged to the DINA presented a problem for his institution, and he said that they didn't receive any kind of support.

The officer continued complaining as he gave a lengthy description of his career, which he characterized as brilliant, in spite of the fact that he had no alternative but to resign from active service since he didn't have the option of becoming a general. He said the fact he had been a DINA agent was a kind of stigma for him and that, on more than one occasion, when he was applying for jobs at private businesses, he was selected for an executive position only to be immediately rejected after they identified him as the DINA officer who was in charge of repressing and annihilating the MIR, along with Krassnoff Martchenko. I answered him the same way I think I answered all the officers and DINA/CNI personnel I faced in court. I said that if anyone could understand the kind of discrimination he was referring to, I could. And I said that he and other officers had once imposed on me, all of us, and our families the same discrimination more than a decade and a half ago. I said that that was one more reason for him to join us in our attempt to shed light on the truth, at least in reference to the disappeared. He reiterated his supposed ignorance on that topic and pointed to the "possible existence of an execution group under the orders of the DINA leadership," which is the same as saying "under Manuel Contreras Sepúlveda and Pedro Espinoza Bravo's direct command." He emphasized that all the prisoners "were removed during the night from the different DINA detention centers and taken in vehicles by DINA personnel, who reported to Headquarters."

That investigation didn't help either to clarify what had happened to Alfonso Chanfreau. As I left the courtroom, I saw the press running after Lawrence Mires, who used the elevator that had been especially reserved so the officers could leave the building unnoticed. I was again convinced that those officers are under orders not to say anything that could jeopardize the military elite from that period. Arrogance, lies, and slavery continue to dominate. The years of slavery the DINA imposes are lasting far too long.

OTHER COURT PROCEEDINGS

Many other DINA employees passed through the offices in Room Six of the Court of Appeals when they were subpoenaed to testify by Judge Gloria Olivares in the case regarding the kidnapping and subsequent disappearance of Alfonso Chanfreau. This was obviously before the case was transferred to the Second Tribunal of the Fourth Military Court. Among others, there was Jaime Deichler Guzmán. After retiring as an army officer, he began working at a company called Madeco, where he eventually became the staff manager. In 1974, as chief of security for the aforementioned company, he hired Osvaldo Romo Mena. According to him, it was on orders from an army colonel who led the Tacna Regiment and who is, of course, now deceased, making it difficult to verify his story. After Romo Mena "worked" at Madeco for a while, the DINA asked to borrow his services.

Retired officer Augusto Patricio Deichler Guzmán also appeared in that courtroom. He was a DINA employee and the brother of Jaime Deichler Guzmán. His other brother, who had since passed away, was Juan Deichler Guzmán, the mayor with a bad past from the time of the military regime. He was one of the ones who organized those so-called paramilitary groups or vigilantes in uniform, groups that repressed citizens in the municipalities of Pudahuel and Quinta Normal who didn't support the military government and staged public protests during the 1980s.

Besides the men I have already mentioned, Osvaldo Pincetti Gac, known as "Brujo," "Doc," or "Charla," was also subpoenaed. At the time of the investigation, he was in prison in the army's Motor Vehicles Battalion located on Beaucheff Street, accused of murdering Alegría Mundaca, a carpenter in Valparaíso. Apparently, that crime had been used as a cover-up for the murder of union leader Tucapel Jiménez. Officers Conrado Pacheco and José Manso Durán, the men who ran the Tres Alamos and Cuatro Alamos prisons, respectively, were also subpoenaed.

From press leaks or from the inevitable comments that follow the shocking experience of seeing again or hearing again the voices of those who robbed us of so much eighteen years ago, I know that valuable testimony was given. The moral importance and weight of that testimony is indisputable, as is the clarity about what happened, in short, the human and intellectual capacity of so many surviving witnesses. This was true of Erick Zott Chuecas, Luis Enrique Peebles, Lautaro Videla Moya, Pedro Matta Lemoine, Gladys Díaz Armijo, and obviously of plaintiffs such as Erika Hennings Cepeda and Viviana Uribe Tamblay. They, along with others such as Nubia Becker, her husband Osvaldo Torres, Miguel Angel Rebolledo, Cecilia Jarpa, Ofelia Nistal, Ricardo Frödden, León Gómez Araneda, Roberto Merino, and so many others who marched through the Court of Appeals exuding bravery, solidarity, and strength, contributed their testimonies. However, in November 1992, in a questionable ruling, the judges in Room Three of the Supreme Court voted in favor of transferring the Chanfreau case to the Second Tribunal of the Fourth Military Court. These Supreme Court Judges were Hernán Cereceda Bravo, Lionel Beraud Poblete, and Germán Valenzuela. In July 1993, the Military Judicial System declared amnesty in the Alfonso Chanfreau case. All of us remember how this resonated in the National Congress and how a decision was reached there that led to the removal from office of Judge Cereceda Bravo.

359

38

MARÍA ALICIA, ALIAS "CAROLA," ALEJANDRA, AND LUZ

One morning in November 1992, Alejandra told Judge Dobra Lusic Nadal that she would collaborate with the judicial system to help uncover the truth. I had the joy and pleasure of being nearby and knowing about it.

No one ever asked us if we could or wanted to live together. Given what we went through, it sounds absurd to say that, but that's how it was. The three of us arrived at the DINA at different times during 1974. Alejandra came in August, María Alicia in November, and I in March.

We had remained in contact with one another for seven or eight years under different circumstances: as prisoners, as collaborating prisoners, and as DINA/CNI employees. After my resignation, we continued to see one another for a while until our paths separated.

On a human level, there were times when we were profoundly close, but we also had our problems, just like anyone who has to live with someone else. We were forced to live together under extreme circumstances. I could even say that the circumstances pushed the limit of what a human being can withstand. I won't try to speak for them; I've had more than enough experience of others saying what I am or am not to make the same mistake myself.

They were my fellow travelers through that inferno. All of the suffering we shared, whether we expressed it or not, binds me to them. It is certain, I love them, a lot.

The three of us arrived at the DINA as prisoners under similar circumstances. We were turned in by some compañero or compañera. For a long time, we lived through situations that somehow made us feel closer, like sisters, but at the same time each of us was falling apart as individuals. The DINA didn't think of us as three human beings. For

360

them, we were "a package." It isn't a metaphor like when people used the pejorative term "Los Huevos" to refer to "Marco Antonio," "Lucas," "Nicolas," and Cristián, the MIR militants who participated in the press conference the DINA organized, where they said the MIR should disband.[66] They actually used that term when they referred to us: "The package." When anything arose that would help or hurt any one of us, all three of us suffered the consequences. We were that "package" they had to control, manage, and make efficient and functional. We didn't even have the right to live. We had to buy it.

In the midst of that madness, we obviously grew closer, most of all when we faced a conflict together. We didn't share our personal feelings with one another. It wasn't just a lack of trust. We also wanted to protect ourselves and each other in those days, when a sad thought was enough to allow cracks and fissures in the soul to give way to real avalanches of pain.

The important thing is that, in some inner corner, we managed to keep something of ourselves alive, of what we were, how we lived, and what we felt up until we were twenty-six years old.

One of my most heartfelt dreams is for Alejandra and María Alicia to be and to feel free. I'm taking a risk saying something people may not want to hear, but I can say that I will be able to accept it if one of these days María Alicia says, "I'm in the DINE. It's a decision I made of my own free will, and I'm happy here." Each of us is above all a person with her own options.

If that happens, I will understand that it is also possible to adhere to a new allegiance. Perhaps it sounds like a contradiction, but that is what life has taught me: there are no models that work for everyone. If I could be certain that María Alicia is where she wants to be, and that her soul is no longer divided, then I will be happy for her with the total conviction that no one has the right to violate anyone else's conscience.

---

66. Arce is referring here to the press conference that took place on February 19, 1975. The four MIR militants were José Carrasco, Héctor González, Cristián Mallol, and Humberto Menanteau. They had all been detained at the Terranova Detention Center prior to the meeting. Their television appearance, in which they appealed to other MIR militants and said that resisting the military regime was a useless cause that should be abandoned, was a defining moment for the MIR. The MIR officially condemned the four as traitors, but their conference was a deciding blow to the movement.

As far as I know, María Alicia is still a DINE employee. However, I must admit that it is difficult for me to accept that she chose that option of her own free will. I think that time went by and she just stayed. I'm not saying she should have done what I did or that she should feel the same way, but I was really afraid of the human rights organizations that supported the various investigations of those who were detained and disappeared, the dead, and the executed. I was so terrified that the path I had followed during those years, that inferno, was irreversible, and that every bridge had been burned and that every door was closed. But that's not the case.

Alejandra and I met at the Yucatán Detention Center in August 1974. Actually, we heard each other since our eyes were covered with tape. She also confirmed this to the press in 1991, following the publication of the summary of the testimony I gave before the Truth and Reconciliation Commission. Our proximity was totally coincidental, but, even so, it was important for me to have her there beside me. I remember her affectionately and with the feeling of companionship her presence inspired in me. It was one of the most difficult times for me, maybe not so much because of the torture, but because I had started collaborating.

I met María Alicia at the Ollagüe Detention Center in November 1974. She had been tortured a lot. When they brought her in with Alejandra and myself, I knew right away that she was collaborating. I saw her suffer and come back shattered after the torture sessions. I would say I was there almost every time the personnel from the Aguila Group, the "Strongman Group" led by Ricardo Lawrence, came for her. I remember the look on her face, her silence when they brought her back, and her desperate sobbing after they took her on the mission when DINA agents murdered "Nano de la Barra," her superior from the MIR. She came back in pieces.

When I returned to Chile on January 15, 1992, I expressed my desire to look for them, to see them and talk with them. I was told, "The Alejandra you knew died; the María Alicia you knew died." I refused to accept that. The step that Alejandra recently took confirms what my intuition told me. I know those islands that are hidden within a person, where everything is still alive and just waiting to find a place to exist. It's like bleeding to death a thousand and one times. All I can say is that that was how I started to heal.

All three of us were born in 1948, and I'm the oldest. I was born in March, María Alicia in June, and Alejandra in October. We were twenty-six years old when we met, but that point in our lives is long gone. Although this book came into being as a result of diverse motivations and has many "addressees," it is especially for them and for everyone who had similar experiences and lives. I want to give them this testimony. I have chosen to come into the light, or perhaps it would be clearer to say, to let Luz come out.

I remember one night when we were living in apartment 54 in tower 12 on 77 Marcoleta in the San Borja Complex. I was in my room, ready to go to bed, when I heard sobbing in María Alicia's room. Alejandra and I ran to her side. María Alicia was in her bed crying. Tears flowed from her eyes. She wasn't yelling, and she wasn't hysterical. I went over to her and heard her whisper. "I'm scared," she said as she held my hand. I have never forgotten that moment. It was as if her pain were surging through her hand and penetrating my skin. It was the same feeling of fear that often overwhelmed me. I couldn't resist caressing her cheeks and fixing her hair. She was a sweet child, a tender child.

I thought no one would understand us, that no one would accept the fact that cowards have tears just like heroes do. That night I felt like there would be no ships to carry us, and no doors to pass through. The ships had been burned and the doors were closed. There was only that inferno.

We didn't know how to help one another. All we could do was hold hands, cry together, be silent, or hug. It didn't happen often. It was as if we were ashamed of being weak. We had lost heart so many times!

DOBRA LUSIC NADAL

Dobra Lusic Nadal is an imposing judge. She is restrained, methodical, and intelligent. Just like Mrs. Olivares, she brings together competence and charm. I appeared in Santiago's Third Criminal Court several times, and I was impressed. She seems distant at first, but soon you realize that it's just part of the way she fulfills her duties properly. Her thorough way of working inspires trust, and you leave the courtroom convinced that she will go to any lengths in pursuit of the truth.

"I DID NOT DO THIS FOR ME ALONE"

> I went forth like a canal from a river and like a water channel into a garden. I said, "I will water my orchard and drench my garden plot"; and lo, my canal became a river, and my river became a sea.
>
> Sirach 24: 30–31[67]

I was lost, but in the inferno. In an effort to leave, I have done many things, including writing this book. However, I haven't done this for myself alone, or on my own. With those who accompany me, I share the dream that this sea will be colored by truth, justice, and reconciliation.

While it is true that *The Inferno* had goals that have been left behind, what really matters is that I have not written it for myself. It is for those who want to find elements in my truth that will help them in their search for answers. I haven't done this alone. Many people have helped me stay on my feet. Besides those I have already mentioned, there are three survivors of that inferno whose support and love gave me the strength to continue at different points during this stage of my life. They are Erick Zott Chuecas, Luis Enrique Peebles, and Pedro Matta Lemoine.

Erick met me when I arrived in Europe. He helped me find somewhere to live, a job, and everything my children and I needed. First, he found some students for me so I could tutor them in Spanish. Then he convinced me to write this book, and he contacted the foundation that gave me a contract to write it.

Luis Enrique was my doctor during the period I had to refrain from all activity in 1992, when I was exhausted and overwhelmed. He didn't just give me prescriptions. He took the time to patiently help me understand and accept what was happening.

Pedro continues to stand by me wherever I need to go. His love and support have sustained me as I have walked down the street, through the halls of justice, and into courtrooms. He is my brother through joy and tears. As we talked, we realized that we had many of the same friends back in the days of the Socialist Party. Today we are searching for new ways to try to further the cause of the defense of human rights.

Above all else, Erick, Kiko, and Pedro are my friends.

---

67. This epigraph contains two verses from the book of Sirach. The English quotation is from the Revised Standard Version. The book of Sirach belongs to the Christian Apocrypha. The term "Apocrypha" comes from the fifth-century biblical scholar St. Jerome and refers to a collection of biblical texts that include a wide range of genres written in a variety of ancient languages. They have been both included and omitted in different versions of the Bible. Arce's reference to this text is most likely the result of her ecclesiastical studies she has mentioned previously in her testimony.

FROM SLAVERY TO FREEDOM

"Who is my mother, and who are my brothers?" And stretching out his
hand toward his disciples, he said, "Here are my mother and my brothers! For whoever does the will of my Father in heaven is my brother, and
sister, and mother."

Matthew 12: 48–50

There were people in the DINA who dared to be true to themselves.
They suffered inner conflicts, and they also experienced a process full
of pain. Some of them also died, such as the guards Rodolfo Valentín
González Pérez and Carlos Carrasco Matus, who form part of the list of
those who remain disappeared to this day.

I personally knew about Rodolfo's detention and torture. I don't know
any details about Carlos Carrasco, but there are numerous testimonies
about his case. Others probably disappeared for a similar reason, because
they tried to alleviate another human being's neglect and suffering.

There are employees and agents who are alive, but at a heavy price
that they are still unable to understand, above all because they didn't
ask to work for the DINA, but were sent there by their institutions. What
they witnessed or had to do was horrifying for them, as it was for all of
us who survived that period in history. Many of them, fearing the repercussions, tried to help as much as they could with a word of support, a
little bread, a little water. . . .

There were also DINA employees who came to me to ask me to
forgive them. One of them was a noncommissioned officer I met again
while I was working at the ENI.

I didn't teach at the ENI for very long because I was on medical leave
in 1978 due to a relapse of my lung infection. However, in the second
semester of 1977, while I was Rolf Wenderoth's assistant, I had to teach
classes and correct exams in the NCOs' course. At the end of the semester, a corporal came over to me and thanked me for not being hard
on him.

At the beginning of our conversation, I didn't understand what the
young man was talking about. Then he explained to me that he had been
there when they raped me the night I was at the Yucatán Detention Center the first time. He asked me to forgive him. When I realized what he
was talking about, I felt like I didn't want to listen. I told him he didn't

365

have to explain anything to me. But he insisted, "Miss Ana María, it's that I'm going to feel awful forever if I don't ask you to forgive me. . . . That's why I wanted to talk to you, and, well, I don't know if you know. But I was there. . . . Forgive me. Please, say you forgive me."

While he was talking to me, he was wringing his hands nervously and moving his right foot back and forth against the floor. He was looking down. I felt cold. Rage. I felt centuries of humiliation. Unconsciously, I raised my hands. I realized that I wasn't tied down anymore like I was that night. "Corporal!"

"Yes, miss?"

"Corporal, if it will make you feel better if I forgive you, then go in peace. Your candor today speaks well of you."

That's what I managed to say. I was trembling. He ran off, and I would say he looked okay, as if a weight had been lifted from his shoulders. And now it was on mine. I sat down. I had to return to my job at Headquarters. I went to the restroom and looked at myself in the mirror. I tried to smile and said to myself, "Hi there! Keep your chin up. You'll be thirty in a few months. You've been doing this for four years now." Then I cleaned the mascara that had run from my eyelashes.

At that moment, "Max's" secretary, "Alicia," came in and said, "Ana María, 'Max' is looking for you."

I stopped in the hallway before I went into "Max's" office and looked outside through the window. The grass was growing wild and free. There was a cow and her calf in the middle of the field and some houses further on. There was smoke coming from a chimney. . . . Life was present everywhere, and it looked beautiful. And there I was, still behind the window. . . . I was just surviving, which is another way of dying.

HOW CAN I HATE SOMEONE WHO COULD SOMEDAY BE MY BROTHER?[68]

The Lord works in mysterious ways. The conversion of someone who has greatly offended Him, as I have, is not a personal merit. It is further

68. Arce attributes this heading to Saint Augustine of Hippo. This reference is particularly noteworthy since Saint Augustine is best known for his *Confessions*, perhaps the most influential religious autobiography ever written. Besides the obvious autobiographical parallel between Saint Augustine's *Confessions* and Arce's testimony, several other themes are also present in both texts, such as free will, forgiveness, conversion to Christianity, and the struggle between good and evil.

proof of the power and glory of the Good Father, for whom nothing is impossible.

I came face-to-face again with Gerardo Urrich in court confrontation on August 7, 1992.

Gerardo Urrich tortured me at the Terranova Detention Center. He was the one who labeled himself a fascist.

I don't hate Urrich. When he tortured me just so I would tell him that I hated him, he failed. My answer, "I don't hate you, Major," wasn't planned. I was in no condition to plan, and I guess I said it because that's how it was. I do remember feeling a deep sadness. At one point I even said to him, "I don't hate you, but I don't understand how you can treat someone, a woman, like that. Don't you have a mother? Don't you have a sister?" He laughed at me. I, the marxist whore, was trying to put myself on the same level as his relatives.

Gerardo Urrich was very hard on me at Terranova. But several months later I had the opportunity to run into him again. . . .

While I was imprisoned at Villa Grimaldi, I found out that Major Urrich had been injured in a shoot out with MIR militants toward the end of 1974. He was taken to the Military Hospital with his stomach and intestines perforated by high caliber bullets. Many thought he wouldn't survive. But he improved and returned to Villa Grimaldi about six months later.

When he arrived at the Terranova Detention Center, he found out that I was alive in the "little house" near the tower. I felt the door suddenly fly open, and there was Gerardo Urrich.

I was paralyzed by fear. He came in and started shouting, without taking his eyes off me.

"I'm back. Here I am again. I survived, just to kill all of you."

He repeated this several times. He started telling me that when he was suffering in the Military Hospital the only thing that kept him alive was the desire to get even with "the marxist dogs."

Then he left. It took me several minutes to stop trembling. I was afraid he would run toward me and start kicking me again.

Then there was an emergency a couple of months later. Major Wenderoth asked me if I was willing to go along on a mission. General Pinochet had ordered the DINA to take over the investigation of a criminal situation. We had to locate a vehicle. I told him yes, that I didn't mind going, thinking that I would go with him. Some months before, Rolf secretly gave me a small pistol since he knew I was afraid of the guards. (I couldn't erase from my mind the recent New Year's experience.) I always carried it in the right pocket of the leather jacket that Lumi gave me.

I knew that if I used the weapon in Rolf's absence, even if it was only to defend myself or intimidate someone by shooting into the air, I would immediately be riddled with bullets. It would give those who didn't accept me the argument they needed to justify my death, but I preferred that to being raped again.

That day the leadership decided that all available personnel would participate in the search for the stolen vehicle. When it was time to get into the cars, Rolf received orders to stay at Terranova to coordinate the search mission. Marcelo Moren Brito would tell me what car to get in. Rolf said good-bye and told me, "It doesn't matter if they see the pistol. I'll take responsibility."

I left through the entrance of Villa Grimaldi's main house. The noncommissioned officer who was organizing the departure of the vehicles was surprised, "You're going too, Lucecita?"

"Yes. . . . Which car do I get in?"

"The next one, Lucecita . . . "

At that moment, a white Fiat 125 appeared.

The young man told me, "Get in, Lucecita, and may God protect you!"

I ran and jumped into the car, which took off right away. I got out my weapon without before looking at the driver. Pointing the barrel toward the floor, I loaded it and put the safety on. The vehicle started traveling very fast, at breakneck speed. When the driver heard the gun being cocked, he slammed on the brakes, and I almost hit the windshield.

I looked at the driver and saw he was pale, with thick beads of sweat running down his face from his temples, and I saw the terror on Major Urrich González's face.

He kept looking at me with his eyes wide open, unable to start driving again. Someone shouted to the car behind us and told them to leave before us. The other driver blew his horn, accelerated, and went roaring by us, turning left. The corporal banged on the door of the car and yelled, "Are you going or not? Turn on the radio!"

I realized that Major Urrich thought I was going to kill him. I was calm. I pretended not to notice his confusion, and I showed him the weapon in the open palm of my hand. Being careful that the barrel was

pointed at me and not at him, I said, "Good afternoon, major. They gave
me an order to go in this car. I know the weapon is small, but if it's necessary, I know how to use it. I am at your command. Will you give me
permission to turn on the radio? I think it's one of the duties I'm supposed to fulfill here."

I turned on the radio without waiting for an answer. The Command
Center at Headquarters immediately assigned us the number we would
use during that mission. Since they used the international communications code, that wasn't a problem for me. I changed the radio to the channel the operator indicated. We started listening to all the communications between different mobile units and the Command Center. They
ordered us to go toward Santiago's northern sector.

I had taken out the map from the glove compartment, but I folded
it and put it away when I heard the order. And when it was our car's
turn to transmit our route, I did it without any problem at all. I grew
up in those neighborhoods. The major just looked at me, and he hesitated a few more minutes before starting the car. When we got moving, he started asking . . . "Since when have you been carrying a
weapon?"

"For a couple of months, major."

"Where did you learn to use the radio?"

"I didn't know how, sir, but I have seen them use it a couple of times
when they've taken me out, and it's easy."

"And the code?"

"It's international code, sir, and I learned it in a militants school when
I was in the GAP."

He asked me for the route I had given Central Command, and then he
kept quiet. I did too, and I only responded to Central Command when
they asked for confirmation of our exact location.

I remembered the corporal's sudden God-fearing expression when he
saw the car that I was going to have to get in. Pretty soon we had caught
up with the other vehicles. The major was driving as fast as he could.
I put on my safety belt, and I asked him if he wanted me to help him put
his on. He let me do it.

The major was calming down. He took out his cigarettes and passed
me the pack. "Did you meet Salvador Allende?" he asked.

"Yes, sir."

"And was he like they say?"

"Like who says, sir?"

369

"Well, everybody says he was a drunk and that he lived from orgy to orgy. . . ."

"I never saw him drunk, sir, nor did I see any orgies."

"But you wouldn't have had any reason to know about his messy life. . . ."

"Although it was only for a short time, I lived at Tomás Moro and also at Cañaveral."

"But Cañaveral was his lover's house."

"His secretary's, sir."

When we arrived at the sector indicated by Central Command, another officer had already located the vehicle. They thought there might be a bomb.

We got out, and the major said, "Will you cover me?"

"Yes, sir."

We moved forward along the side of a brick wall. As we looked toward the rooftops, we could see the lights being turned off in the houses, and there were people peeking out from behind their curtains and blinds when they heard the sirens and realized what was happening. Someone with a megaphone started ordering people away from their windows in case there was an exchange of gunfire.

There was no bomb and no shoot out. The car had only been stolen in order to escape. They abandoned it there after robbing a tobacco store, and they must have fled in another vehicle. Other groups that had climbed up on the nearby rooftops started coming down and gathering there.

When we returned to Villa Grimaldi, Urrich went with me to Major Wenderoth's office. He laughed and told him he was more frightened when he saw me get in the car and load my gun than he was the day they shot him. When he left, Rolf put his hand on my shoulder and said, "I believe you've made another friend." He was never a friend, of course, but he was no longer my enemy.

39

THE IRON FIST

It was the DINA's symbol. I imagine that this design encapsulated Colonel Manuel Contreras Sepúlveda's idea of what the DINA should be. That fist didn't move all by itself. It had arms. Each of the DINA's units carried out its movements, which were themselves controlled by an elite group that gave the orders to set that fist in motion.

I remember how, in 1977, the personnel at Headquarters were happily commenting on the development of the amnesty law. I'm referring to the legal monstrosity that was born as a glorification of impunity. The DINA celebrated it as another of Contreras's strokes of genius. Very few understood what the law said or how it worked. They were satisfied with the knowledge that the amnesty law was a law of impunity.

It's strange how all that pain makes sense to me now from a distance. By allowing the memories to return and by working slowly through the bitterness, the resentment, and the hate, I am now able to understand how the violent history of an epoch became a part of my life, and how my actions affected the lives of others.

Today, twenty years after September 11, 1973, when I hear that the state violence was a necessary and measured response to the violence exercised by those who opposed the dictatorship, I feel that the effects of the two don't allow for comparison. For me, the dictatorship means prison, torture, the disappearance of people, and exile. Perhaps for someone outside the situation, who places what happened in the context of violence in general, the situation might seem of little significance. What is terrible is that the repressive system seems to have succeeded in carrying out the horror so nonchalantly.

The torture, the swift executions, and the disappearance of people were all tools of authoritarian power. It was all part of the government's dirty logic that led to submission, rebellion, or escape. And this doesn't only affect the families of the victims, but the entire community, because our plural society was replaced by one divided into opposing extremes. It was determined what was "good" and what was "evil," and society was divided into "the clean" and "the dirty."

That idea of eliminating the opposition distorted a lot of things. To be an opponent, whether you were a sympathizer or a marxist militant, took on a different meaning. It became synonymous with threat and fright.

This omnipotence led victims to a choice between saving themselves, surviving, or risking death. Furthermore, the use of torture that shatters bodies and silences voices is an attack on human beings, and it tore the whole society apart.

The gray years tried to leave us with a legacy whereby the majority of the population would have no memory and be deaf and indifferent to the years of terror while the wounded minority could not and would not want to forget. These are the days of "save yourself if you can" and "charity begins at home," where zones of modernity are created within certain boundaries, and safety measures are reinforced that assure the efficacy of marginalization. All this is reflected in institutions and guides all social bonds.

Similar collective and individual experiences show that the effects of terror do not end because the cause has ceased to exist. It is important to determine how these effects are expressed, since it seems, at times, that they are disconnected from their cause and origin.

Experience from other genocides shows that articulating the horror requires decades and involves several generations. From experience, I know that the illusion of erasing everything and starting over isn't feasible, and that the pact of silence to abolish and exorcise the lived horror feeds conflicts and resentment. The only way to exorcise that inferno and set the stage for a genuine reconciliation is by recovering memory, as sad as it may be.

The country needs to reclaim itself and face its truth to be able to leave the past where it belongs and to plan and build a future free from oblivion and lies. I realize that I needed to do it. It was important, indispensable to tell myself once more: my name is Luz, Luz Arce.

Index

374

Comité Pro-Paz. *See* Pro-Peace Committee
Concertation government, 23, 332
Concha, Daniel, 274–83
Condor Group, 289
Confessions (Saint Augustine), 366n
Contreras, Héctor: *Los secretos del Com-
mando Conjunto*, 339
Contreras, Walter, 126
Contreras Bell, Mirya, 6, 370. *See also*
"Payita"
Contreras Sepúlveda, Juan Manuel, 197,
269n, 270–71, 276, 298, 355; authority of,
214, 247–49, 290, 371; career of, 85,
259–63, 273; CNI replacement of, 267–68,
287, 293; conviction of, 149n; as DINA di-
rector, 125, 219–21, 225–27, 231–32, 255,
358; friendship with Hasbún, 234; held at
Hosmil, 270, 272; legal action against,
159; Letelier assassination and, 269n;
"Max" and, 171, 245–46; in possession of
Enríquez Espinoza's weapon, 167–68;
promotes LA in DINA, 143; promotion
of, 264–65; Wenderoth and, 254, 310–11
Contreras Valdebenito, Manuel, 168. *See
also* "Mamo"
Contreras Valdebenito, María, 254, 271
Correa Sutil, Jorge, 329–30, 332
Cortázar, Julio: *Historias de cronopios y de
famas*, 46
"Cristián," 203
CUP (Popular Unity Committee), 20
Cuthbert, Sofía, 263

Damiani Serrano, María Rosa Alejandra,
270. *See also* "Roxana"
Daniel, 120
"David," 10, 18, 21–22
Deichler Guzmán, Augusto Patricio, 358
Deichler Guzmán, Jaime, 358
Deichler Guzmán, Juan, 358
Delgado (nurse at Hosmil), 66
"Delia" (Fidelia Herrera), 208–10
"Diana/Dianita" (nickname of LA). *See*
Arce, Luz
Díaz Armijo, Gladys, 203, 208, 359
Diet, Pedro, 261
Dignity Colony (Colonia Dignidad), 130n,
200, 260, 351–52
DINA (Directorate of National Intelli-
gence), xx, 31, 61, 208, 259–60; agents

of, 149–50, 200, 343–44, 346, 357–59;
change to CNI, 255–58; collaboration
with "Joint Command," 339n; criticism
of, 138; Enríquez Espinosa and, 167–68;
fear of, 26; goals of, 111, 125; growth of,
133, 241; LA and, 63, 134–35, 140,
143–44; Letelier case and, 264; structure
of, 50, 117–18, 128–29, 371
Directorate of National Intelligence. *See*
DINA
Dockendorf Navarrete, Muriel, 126, 130n
Dolly (proprietor), 304
"Don Gonzalo" (Rolf Wenderoth Pozo),
187–88
"Don Jaime" (Germán Jorge Barriga
Muñoz), 210, 260
Donoso (major), 307, 313
"Don Rodrigo" (Pedro Espinoza Bravo),
176, 178–79
Dragicevic, Cecilia, 49
Dragicevic (doctor), 49–50
Droully Yurick, Jacqueline, 147

Eagleson, John, 237n
Elda (cousin of LA), 316, 321
Elgueta (doctor), 51, 55, 63–64, 68–69
Elida (professor of psychology), 320
Elke (Austrian friend of LA), 339
Elmo Catalán Brigade. *See* BEC
Emiliano (cousin of LA), 74
"Emilio" (Alfonso Chanfreau Oyarce),
112, 344
Enríquez Espinosa, Miguel, 94, 169; death
of, 157, 163–64, 166–67; DINA pursuit
of, 167–68; as MIR general secretary, 7,
40, 49
Enríquez Espinoza, Edgardo, 238–39
Época, La (newspaper), 159, 326n
Escobar Fuentes, Jorge Marcelo, 252
Espejo Gómez, Rodolfo, 103, 223
Espinoza Bravo, Pedro, 125, 146n, 202, 226,
244, 279; in Directorate of Operations,
236; as head of Terranova, 146, 173,
175–76, 180, 183, 187–88; held at Hosmil,
272; LA's custody battle and, 185; leaves
for Brazil, 210–11; legal action and, 238,
290, 346, 358; replacement of Contreras
and, 267–68; sentence of, 238n; Townley
and, 269–70; Wenderoth and, 254, 261,
264–65. *See also* "Don Rodrigo"

375

MacLeod Trever, John, 117–18
Mallol, Christian, 49, 203, 361
"Mamo" (Manuel Contreras Valdebenito), 254
Mancilla Ramírez, Ariel Adolfo, 210
"Mano Negra" (Gerardo Ernesto Godoy García), 152
"Manque, El," 21
Manso Durán, Orlando José, 128, 359
MAPU (Movimiento de Acción Popular Unitaria), 11, 29
Mara (Uruguyan friend of LA), 305–7, 312
Marambio, Max Joel, 7, 222, 257. *See also* "Fontanarosa, Ariel"
Marcela (friend of LA), 327
Marcelo (Urugyan friend of LA), 311
"Marco Antonio" (José Carrasco), 203, 242, 361
Marcos (doctor/boyfriend of LA), 318
"Marcos" (Gerardo Ernesto Godoy García), 124, 152
"Marcos-PS" (Sergio Iván Zamora Torres), 220
María Teresa (compañera), 122, 124
Maribel (secretary at Undersecretariat), 275–76, 280
"Marisol" (María Teresa Osorio), 155
"Marta" (Purén agent), 212
"Martín" (Raúl Juvenal Navarrete Hancke), 5
Martínez González, Hugo Ramón, 33, 197; death of, 199. *See also* "Tano"
Matta Lemoine, Pedro, 359, 364
Matthew: book of, 365
"Mauro" (Gustavo Ruz Zañartu), 101–2
"Max" (Francisco Maximiliano Ferrer Lima), 139, 366; at ENI, 244–46, 274; LA's perceptions of, 169–71; relationship with LA, 187–89, 205, 251–53, 315. *See also* "Lenou, Max"
Melo Pradenas, Mario Ramiro, 7
Mena Alvarado, Nalvia Rosa, 147
Menanteau, Humberto, 361n
Mena Salinas, Odlanier, 301, 313–14; godson of, 288; Pantoja and, 271–72, 297; replaces Contreras at CNI, 267, 287
Mercurio, El (newspaper), 25, 314
Merino, Roberto, 359
Merino Vega, Marcia Alejandra. *See* Alejandra

Mery (friend of LA), 327
Mesa de Diálogo, 331n
Miguel Fernandez de, José Luis, xix, 324–25, 328–29
MIR (Movimiento de Izquierda Revolucionaria), 7, 11, 25, 34, 104, 262; Central Committee of, 32, 203; Political Commission of, 164; press conference of, 202, 361; survivors of, 153; tactics of, 156–57, 161; use of name "Camp 26th of July," 201; Valparaíso region and, 194, 199, 224, 351
Mireya (secretary of Pantoja), 278–79
Mirtha (secretary), 242
Moffit, Ronnie, 146n, 238, 263, 269
Molina, Joaquín, 168
Monsalve Ortiz, María Olivia, 129–30
Monsalve Ortiz, Silvia, 129–30
Montealegre, Hernán, 261
Montiglio Murúa, Juan José, 8
Montti Cordero, Iván, 146
Morales Salgado, Juan, 124, 245, 263; as captain, 225–26; crimes of, 118; as major, 239
Moreaux, Leonardo, 157
Moren Brito, Marcelo, 125–27, 166–67, 368; collaboration of LA and, 110–11; in court, 355–57; creation of Vampiro Group and, 186–87; as head of Caupolicán unit, 175; nephew of, 202; perception of LA, 141; promotion of, 199, 211. *See also* "Jefe Ronco"
Mosquera Jarpa, Manuel Rolando, 270
Movimiento de Acción Popular Unitaria. *See* MAPU
Movimiento de Izquierda Revolucionaria. *See* MIR
Muñoz, Sergio, 24. *See also* "Cochín"

National Information Center. *See* CNI
National Truth and Reconciliation Commission. *See* Truth and Reconciliation Commission
Navarrete Hancke, Raúl Juvenal, 98, 252; arrest of, 100; collaboration of, 95–96; 102, 104. *See also* "Martín"
"negro Paz," 103–4, 112, 125
Nelson (prisoner at Hosmil), 53
"Nicolás" (Héctor González), 203, 361
Nistal, Ofelia, 359

Noemí (Urugyan friend of LA), 305–7, 310
Novo, Guillermo, 269n

Ocaranza, Georgina, 261
Olivares, Gloria: compared to Dobra Lusic Nadal, 363; as judge in Chanfreau case, 332, 334, 344–45, 348–52, 355, 357–58; legacy of, 340–41
Operation Celeste, 297, 310; stages of, 300–301, 305, 312
Ordenes, María Gabriela, 155. *See also* "Soledad"
Organization of American States, 239n
Orozco, Hector, 99
Orquesta Rosa (Perrault), 136, 156
Osorio, María Teresa, 155, 349. *See also* "Marisol"

"Pablo" (Fernando Ernesto Lauriani Maturana), 139, 350
Pacheco, Conrado, 128, 359
Página Abierta (magazine), 326
Palacios Burgos, Manuel Augusto, 261
Palestro, Julio, 52–55, 65–66
Pallini González, Rosseta, 128–29
Pantoja, Gerónimo, 258, 274 , 283, 297; Daniel Concha and, 280–81; encounters with LA, 270–73, 278–79
Parada, Alejandro, 115, 124. *See also* "Cano," "Jano"
Parra, María Eliana, 350
Parra Vásquez, Miguel Angel, 291
Pascal Allende, Andrés, 156n, 197, 226
Patria y Libertad, 10, 120, 269
"Patricia," 42–44, 46
Patricio, 230–34, 251
"Payita" (Mirya Contreras Bell), 6–7, 19
"Pedro," 181
Peebles Skarnic, Luis Enrique, 351, 359, 364. *See also* "Kiko"
Peña, Luis, 124
Peña Herreros, Michelle, 147, 248n
"Pepa" (Palmira Isabel Almuna Guzmán), 139, 145–46
Pereira Plaza, Reinalda del Carmen, 147
"Pérez, Chico" (Sergio Pérez Molina), 33–34, 160, 164
Pérez, Matilde, 295–96
Pérez Molina, Sergio, 7, 33, 159–60, 162, 355; death of, 163; torture of, 164–65.

See also "Pérez, Chico," "Chicope"
Pérez Vargas, Dagoberto, 226–27
Pérez Videla, Dago, 158–59
Perrault, Gilles: *Red Orchestra, The,* 136n
"Pilar," 276
Pincetti Gac, Osvaldo, 359
"Pink Panther" (Fernando Eduardo Lauriani Maturana), 149, 353
Pinochet, Augusto, 130n, 239n, 258, 265, 367; Colonel Contreras and, 261–62; detention in London of, 331n
"Pizarro, Patricia" (alias of LA). *See* Arce, Luz
Poblete, Miguel Angel, 257, 291
Poli Garaycochea, Guido, 291
Ponce Vicencio, Exequiel, 29, 221–22
Portales, Diego, 349
Prats, Carlos, 17, 263
Proa (newspaper), 259
Pro-Peace Committee (Comité Pro-Paz), 220, 237, 261; DINA and, 228; description of, 71n; father of LA and, 185
Provis Carrasco, Manuel José, 170, 314; command of Caupolicán unit and, 289; as contact in Operation Celeste, 300, 306, 307, 313; encounter with LA, 309–10. *See also* "Valenzuela, Francisco"
Puccio, Osvaldo, 52–54, 55, 65–66
Punto Final (newspaper), 15, 326n

"Quila," 42

Rafael (son of LA), 258, 276; birth of, 4; father and, 242, 267, 291–92, 317; living with LA, 241–43, 289–90, 322; used against LA, 120, 123; visits with LA and, 155, 177
Ramírez, María Julieta: disappearance of, 117–18
Rammsy Villablanca, Carlos, 104
Ramos Hernández, Rosa Humilde, 155, 177
"Raúl" (Manuel Andrés Carevic Cubillos), 85
Rebolledo, Miguel Angel, 343, 359
Rekas Urra, Elizabeth de las Mercedes, 147
Rettig Commission, 328, 330–32, 336, 345; testimony of LA before, 115, 345
Rettig Report, xxn, 130n

mony before, 17, 53, 62, 115, 174, 183, 199, 329–30; report of, 200

Tschaikowsky, Peter Ilich, 194

Ulloa, Ariel, 18–19

Ureta Sire, Arturo Ramón, 255, 279, 313–14

Uribe Gómez, María Alicia, 204, 280; at CNI, 267–69, 272, 291; death of Pérez Vargas and, 226–27; designs agent purse, 265; at ENI, 244–45, 253; LA's memories of, 249, 361–63; as MIR leader, 201–2; moves with LA and Alejandra, 140, 219; opinion of LA's son, 229, 273; as "package," 144, 244, 293, 329, 360–61; receives gift from Espinoza Bravo, 211; relationship with LA, 187–88, 194–95, 289–90; at Terranova, 173, 176–78, 236; torture of, 171, 175. *See also* "Carola"

Uribe Tamblay, Bárbara, 334

Uribe Tamblay, Viviana, 174, 332–35, 348, 359

Urrich González, Gerardo Ernesto, 61, 152, 367–70; acts of torture by, 80–85; in court, 346–48

Urrutia, Adriana, 127n

Valedivieso Cervantes, Vianel, 254, 263, 269

"Valenzuela, Francisco" (Manuel José Provis Carrasco), 306, 307

Valenzuela, Germán, 359

Vallavela (prisoner at Hosmil), 53

Vampiro Group, 199, 351, 353; creation of, 186–87

Van Yurick, Christian, 115

Van Yurick, Edwin, 334

Vásquez Chahuán, Manuel Abraham, 176, 211

Vergara, Roque, 256

"Vergara Rojas, Ana María" (alias of LA). *See* Arce, Luz

Verónica (friend of LA), 327

Verónica (psychologist), 320

Verónica (Uruguayan friend of LA), 305

Vicaría de la Solidaridad. *See* Vicariate of Solidarity

Vicariate of Solidarity (Vicaría de la Solidaridad), 71n, 239, 255, 281, 319; creation of, 237; DINA and, 261; legal team of, 291

Videla Moya, Lautaro, 159, 199, 355; arrest of, 201–2. *See also* "Santiago, Chico"

Videla Moya, Lumi, 33, 142, 169, 201, 325, 368; death of, 34, 163–64, 170; relationship with LA, 158–62

Vilches Figueroa, Abel Alfredo, 200

Villar Quijón, Elías Ricardo, 200

"Wally" (Roberto Fuentes Morrison), 224

War of the Triple Alliance, 312n

Wenderoth, Sergio, 279

Wenderoth Pozo, Rolf Gonzalo, 202, 219–20, 261, 271–72, 370; allows LA to visit prisoners, 197–99, 207, 221; Contreras and, 254; DINA and, 125, 264; encounters LA in court, 344–46; gives LA information, 146, 168, 203, 221–22, 227–28, 290, 292; gives LA weapon, 367–68; in Internal Intelligence, 236–37; LA writes to, 305, 306, 310–11; relationship with LA, 187–94, 211–17, 229–34, 243, 294–95; resignation of, 273–75, 280; role in LA's move to Uruguay, 255–57; role in United Nations hearing, 200, 234–35; as superior of LA, 210, 225, 252, 264–68, 277–78; at Terranova, 176, 178, 184–85, 204, 206

Willike Flöel, Christoph George Paul, 255–56

Yepes, Narciso, 73

Zalaquett, José, 261

Zamora Torres, Sergio Iván, 220–21. *See also* "Marcos–PS"

Zanzani, Juan, 261

Zapata Reyes, Basclay, 207, 241; in court, 348–50; LA and, 125–27, 133–34; role in arrests, 103–4. *See also* "Troglo"

Zerega, Víctor, 29

"Zorro, El," 226–27

Zott Chuecas, Erick, 200, 351, 359, 364